Vicki H

vickiruth...............@gmail.com

MINDFULNESS & ACCEPTANCE IN BEHAVIORAL MEDICINE

Current Theory & Practice

Edited by
LANCE M. McCRACKEN, PH.D.

CONTEXT PRESS
An Imprint of New Harbinger Publications, Inc.

Publisher's Note

Distributed in Canada by Raincoast Books

Copyright © 2011 by Lance M. McCracken
New Harbinger Publications, Inc.
5674 Shattuck Avenue
Oakland, CA 94609
www.newharbinger.com

FSC
Mixed Sources
Product group from well-managed
forests and other controlled sources

Cert no. SW-COC-002283
www.fsc.org
© 1996 Forest Stewardship Council

Cover design by Amy Shoup; Acquired by Catharine Sutker; Text design by Tracy Marie Carlson; Edited by Karen Stein

Library of Congress Cataloging in Publication Data
Mindfulness and acceptance in behavioral medicine : current theory and practice / edited by Lance M. McCracken.
    p. ; cm.
  Includes bibliographical references and index.
  ISBN 978-1-57224-731-4 (pbk.) -- ISBN 978-1-57224-732-1 (pdf ebook)
  1. Acceptance and commitment therapy. 2. Mindfulness-based cognitive therapy. I. McCracken, Lance M., 1962-
  [DNLM: 1. Cognitive Therapy. 2. Adaptation, Psychological. 3. Awareness. 4. Health Behavior. 5. Mind-Body Therapies--methods. 6. Patient Acceptance of Health Care--psychology. WM 425.5.C6]
  RC489.A32M56 2011
  616.89'1425--dc22

               2010046098

13   12   11

10   9   8   7   6   5   4   3   2   1

First printing

To my parents, Patricia and Terrence McCracken, and to Sherry

Contents

PART 1

INTRODUCTION

1

HISTORY, CONTEXT, AND NEW DEVELOPMENTS IN BEHAVIORAL MEDICINE 3

Lance M. McCracken

■ A Brief Early History of Behavioral Medicine ■ Process and Outcome in Behavioral Medicine ■ Behavioral Medicine and Empirically Supported Treatment ■ The Development of Mindfulness-Based Approaches in Health Care ■ ACT Model and Process ■ Meta-Analyses of Mindfulness-Based Treatments ■ Summary ■ References

PART 2

APPLICATIONS OF ACT AND MINDFULNESS TO SPECIFIC CONDITIONS AND POPULATIONS

2

ACCEPTANCE AND COMMITMENT THERAPY FOR CHRONIC PAIN 31

Kevin E. Vowles & Miles Thompson

- The Development of Psychological Models of Chronic Pain
- Critique of Cognitive Behavioral Approaches for Chronic Pain
- ACT and Mindfulness-Based Approaches for Chronic Pain
- Measures ■ Treatment Outcome ■ Clinical Issues
- Summary ■ References

13

FOREWORD

Healthy Flexibility: Applying Acceptance, Mindfulness, and Values to Behavioral Medicine

Psychological flexibility helps human beings rise to the health challenges they face. It is hard to avoid that conclusion after reading this volume. In all of the major areas of behavioral medicine examined, acceptance, mindfulness, and values provide new ways forward in the management of health and chronic illness. When we remember how recently the behavioral sciences and helping professions have turned to these methods, the breadth of applications described is impressive: cancer, chronic pain, diabetes, epilepsy, obesity, smoking, insomnia, end-of-life issues, and the stigma of health conditions have all received attention. Other applications are on the horizon, with projects and early reports in an even wider range of areas, including everything from multiple sclerosis to exercise programs.

Lance McCracken has edited this volume in a way that addresses a range of key purposes. It provides practical information that should encourage practitioners to pick up the tools of acceptance and commitment therapy, mindfulness-based interventions, and other contextual methods in the behavioral and cognitive therapies and to begin to explore how they might be applied in practical settings across the full range of medical populations needing help.

In some areas, such as chronic pain, there has been enough work that these practical efforts can use turnkey protocols and modify them from there. In this volume, practitioners will learn what these protocols contain and how they can be expected to work.

In most areas, early adopters will need to modify programs to fit their specific needs. This is a greater challenge, but the work reported in this groundbreaking volume enormously simplifies the task, and for a critical reason. Instead of focusing exclusively on specific techniques, the research and development work in acceptance, mindfulness, and values has attended to critically important processes of change that lead to behavioral progress. These processes can be measured, as a key chapter in the present volume describes, so that practitioners and treatment developers can use their creativity to alter processes of known importance and use changes in these processes as a proximal guide to long-term success.

The book is also designed to encourage further empirical research and evaluation. Researchers, students, and program evaluators will find many hints for possible ways to move forward in a manner that is strategically sensible, empirically sound, and clinically meaningful. If the progress in this volume is an indication, we are at the threshold of what promises to be a rapid expansion of new programs.

Psychological flexibility—the ability to face challenges in a manner that is open, aware, and active—is gradually becoming a model shared by acceptance- and mindfulness-based methods across the board. As chapters in this volume point out, that model can readily encompass existing methods of empirical importance, such as exposure, skills training, and motivational interviewing. Indeed, it does not appear that any component or method needs to be left behind that is known empirically to be key to the success of existing methods; what is left behind are components that were not critical to the effectiveness of the existing methods. Beyond just changing terminology or adding a few new techniques, however, what psychological flexibility does as a model is to recast the purpose of our methods, alter their form, orient us to the set needed to establish change, and integrate treatment components into a coherent whole. That is an enormous step forward, not just theoretically and strategically but practically.

The present volume ends with a section on the implications of these developments for health care providers themselves. Research in ACT and mindfulness has shown that acceptance, mindfulness, and values apply to practitioners themselves, not just to clients. These methods have implications for bias and health disparities, and for the stress faced by providers. There are also challenges that need to be addressed in integrating acceptance, mindfulness, and values into health care settings that may customarily have a "repair and discharge" orientation. Fortunately, psychological flexibility applies even to those very social and educational challenges within health care delivery. We need to learn how to create teams, organizations, and systems that are themselves open, aware, and values based. The processes described in this volume can be a guide to that very project.

Every theory and every model in science is ultimately shown to be incorrect. In areas that are progressive, innovation occurs in a way that expands our vision, empowers rapid development, systematizes what we know now, and leaves behind a solid base of information and progress that serves as a launching pad for future departures in new directions. ACT, mindfulness-based treatments, and the other contextual forms of the behavioral and cognitive therapies are creating progress in behavioral medicine. They have indeed expanded our vision, leading to a phase of rapid development and systematization. This volume will help the field of behavioral medicine engage in this phase in a way that is both vigorous and rigorous, so that real progress can be created in the interests of those we serve.

—Steven C. Hayes, Ph.D.
University of Nevada
October 2010

PART 1

Introduction

1

History, Context, and New Developments in Behavioral Medicine

Lance M. McCracken
Centre for Pain Services, Royal National Hospital for
Rheumatic Diseases and Centre for Pain Research, University
of Bath, Bath, United Kingdom

There are influences on our behavior that can and do affect our experiences of our physical health or disease. Behavioral medicine is the field that studies these influences, derives principles and treatment methods, and then applies these to improve health and disease outcomes. The "behavioral" in behavioral medicine is not meant in a narrow sense, as in "overt behavioral," but in a broad sense, as in all of the activity of the whole individual in a context of cognitive, emotional, physical, and social influences. Applications within behavioral medicine include disease prevention, health promotion, symptom management, and disease management, particularly where medical methods provide incomplete solutions, such as with chronic medical conditions. There is a strong emphasis here on helping patients to participate more fully in their daily lives in cases where health problems have restricted or may restrict this participation. The field of behavioral medicine has had remarkable success over the past thirty years. Even so, its principles and methods continue to expand and evolve.

Treatments within behavioral medicine have always drawn heavily from developments in the cognitive and behavioral therapies, and this trend continues. The most recent developments here include applications of acceptance and commitment therapy (ACT; Hayes, Strosahl, & Wilson, 1999). These applications blend with another trend that was already in place to a certain extent, that being the use of mindfulness-based methods (e.g., Kabat-Zinn, 1982). Together, mindfulness and ACT, and other approaches like them, are making substantial contributions to the promotion of health and the treatment of disease, and this trend seems likely to both continue and accelerate.

Development in the field of behavioral medicine may seem like a process of addition and subtraction, with possibly more addition than subtraction. New variables or methods come into favor and older ones are discredited or fall out of favor. At times it may seem as if there is a growing and increasingly thinly sliced list of behavioral, cognitive, and emotional variables and methods. Mindfulness and ACT-based approaches may offer something different from that. They may offer integration, both in theory and in practice. ACT in particular includes a broad and coherent theoretical stance, one that seems to illuminate both the successes and possibly some of the shortcomings of current methods. In practice, the general applicability of these approaches is virtually established, cutting across medical diagnoses, psychiatric syndromes, levels of problem severity, and even categories of health care provider and service user.

The purpose of this first chapter is to present a brief history of behavioral medicine and lay out the theory and general background of mindfulness and ACT as extensions of this history. Subsequent chapters will develop further the theme of integration and will present evidence for specific applications.

A Brief Early History of Behavioral Medicine

The notion that experiences, emotions, and behavior can somehow influence the functioning of the body is so old that its origins may be untraceable. The earliest formal developments in behavioral medicine as we understand it today, however, are said to have begun in the 1970s with the Laboratory for the Study of Behavioral Medicine at Stanford University, under the direction of Stewart Agras, and at the Center for Behavioral Medicine at the University of Pennsylvania, under Paul Brady and Ovide Pomerleau (Agras, 1982; Pattishall, 1989). An early appearance of the term *behavioral medicine* appeared in the title of a book, *Biofeedback: Behavioral Medicine* by Lee Birk, published in 1973. The earliest journal in the field, *Journal of Behavioral Medicine*, was first published in 1977, following a recommendation from the Yale Conference on Behavioral Medicine held that same year (Schwartz & Weiss, 1977). This conference is given credit for producing the first formal definition of the field. The Society of Behavioral Medicine was founded the following year, in 1978.

Behavioral medicine has been variously defined during its nearly forty-year history. It was the Yale Conference in 1977 that was commissioned with the task of establishing the scope and aims of the field. The group of attendees at the conference from the fields of psychology, sociology, anthropology, epidemiology, public health, psychiatry, cardiology, and internal medicine produced the following definition (Schwartz & Weiss, 1977, p. 379):

> "Behavioral medicine" is the field concerned with the development of behavioral-science knowledge and techniques relevant to the understanding of physical health and illness and the application of this knowledge and these techniques to diagnosis, prevention, treatment and rehabilitation. Psychosis, neurosis and substance abuse are included only insofar as they contribute to physical disorders as an end point.

Shortly thereafter, Pomerleau and Brady (1979) chose to emphasize the contribution of behavior therapy and behavior modification, seeing these as having provided the greater impetus to the field, and offered the following:

> *Behavioral medicine* can be defined as (a) the clinical use of techniques derived from the experimental analysis of behavior—behavior therapy and behavior modification—for the evaluation, prevention, management, or treatment of disease or physiological dysfunction; and (b) the conduct of research contributing to the functional analysis and understanding of behavior associated with medical disorders and problems in health care. (p. xii)

They left the door open, however, for later changes in their definition, stating, "ultimately, a field is defined by what it does; if conditions change, then the definition of behavioral medicine should be modified accordingly" (p. xii). Even where there were disagreements in boundaries, scope, or aims, there has been consensus that behavioral medicine includes both research and practical applications in relation to assessment, prevention, treatment, and management.

The emergence of behavioral medicine is attributed to the confluence of a number of overlapping events (Agras, 1982), including the development of an effective technology for producing behavior change in the form of early behavior therapy; developments in epidemiology that were able to identify specific risk factors for illness, including behavioral risk factors; and growing interest in health efficiencies obtainable through prevention rather than treatment. This latter influence was brought on, somewhat ironically, by successes in medicine. Antibiotics were first mass-produced in the 1940s, and by the 1960s infectious diseases were much better controlled. This gave way to a greater focus on cancer and cardiovascular disease, including identified behavioral risk factors for these conditions, and on chronic diseases that required management rather than cure (Blanchard, 1982).

Process and Outcome in Behavioral Medicine

From the beginning, there has been a mixed focus in behavioral medicine in relation to its independent and dependent variables, or what might be called "process and outcome." Some researchers and clinicians, such as proponents of biofeedback and those primarily interested in psychophysiology, those interested in what might be called "psychosomatic medicine," have pursued a focus on psychological methods to get "inside" the individual in order to alter the pathophysiology of disease and reduce symptoms. Psychosomatic medicine itself evolved from a biomedical model and therefore carries an emphasis on physical disease and on etiology, pathology, and diagnosis, albeit one that is more "holistic," including psychological factors as causes (Alexander, 1950). This type of focus—where physiology is centrally important—is reflected in psychoneuroimmunology, in approaches to headache that emphasize muscle tension and vascular responses, in approaches to chronic low back pain that emphasize muscle tension or muscular reactivity, in work in diabetes focused on glycemic control as a primary outcome, and in research that includes the use of physiological assessment technologies, such as functional magnetic resonance imaging (fMRI), as a means to understand patient experiences or behavior. These approaches tend to work from a disease model to some extent and apply psychological methods primarily for the purpose of reducing signs and symptoms as primary outcomes, while improved aspects of daily functioning may be secondary outcomes. From this perspective, behavioral medicine justifies its existence on the basis that psychological processes affect physiological processes.

Alongside the psychosomatic approach is another approach within behavioral medicine that takes behavior—not disease or symptoms—as the primary focus. More than twenty years ago Robert Kaplan presented the argument that behavior ought to be regarded as the central outcome in health care (Kaplan, 1990). In his words, "behavioral outcomes are the most important consequences

7

in studies of health care and medicine. These outcomes include longevity, health-related quality of life, and symptomatic complaints" (p. 1211). He suggested that a focus on biological rather than behavioral outcomes has led many researchers down the wrong path: to a primary focus on what affects biology instead of a primary focus on what affects behavior. He further questioned what he saw as a trend at the time toward the "biologicalization" of both behavioral and biomedical science. He noted that measures of blood chemistry and disease categories were increasingly seen as critically important to research, and that biological processes are more seen as pure, reliable, and valid than behavioral indicators, and he questioned that. While behavioral measures may have limitations, biological measures do, too. Reviewing all of this literature is beyond the scope of this chapter (see Kaplan, 1990). Suffice it to say, there are many examples in health care where mortality and morbidity track more closely with behavioral processes than with biological processes, and some of these are reviewed in later chapters.

It is suggested here that there are contrasting approaches within behavioral medicine. Sometimes these are not explicit in the work of researchers or clinicians. Sometimes they blur unintentionally or are blended, and in some ways the contrast between the two is being exaggerated here. Nonetheless, in one approach behavior is important because it has an impact on disease processes or can be used to reduce symptoms. In this approach, the reduction of disease processes and symptoms is seen as the route to full health and functioning. In the other approach, behavior is important because full health and functioning are fundamentally behavioral outcomes and to some degree independent of symptoms or disease. Another way to describe the distinction is to say that these approaches differ in their relative emphasis on mediators. In what we will call the "psychosomatic" approach, physiological processes and the experience of symptoms mediate defined health outcomes. In what we will call the "behavioral" approach, there is more a wholehearted focus on direct manipulable influences on behavior, without an emphasis on intervening variables that are not directly manipulable by psychological means.

It seems fair to say that the impacts of today's biggest health problems are not entirely explained by medical diagnosis or disease categories. Inside cancer, diabetes, heart disease, and chronic pain are many varied outcomes. The same is true of exposure to carcinogens or the presence of a tumor, hypertension, high cholesterol, and nerve injury or nociception. The labels we apply to conditions or even their pathophysiological processes do not indicate who is living well and who is not. And yet diagnoses are not irrelevant. So, this must mean that it is not just the having of a disease or getting a particular result on a biochemical assay that is critical to health and functioning. It is these things combined with other influences.

We all have our implicit biases. More than that, our minds will tend to stick to ideas, views, and strategies they have stuck to in the past even when another way could be more successful. We judge and categorize experience and then are guided in our actions not by direct experience but by these judgments and categories. The main point here is that even though the existence of two approaches looks like an either-or situation, like one way must be correct and the other incorrect, it is entirely possible to reconcile and integrate the psychosomatic and the behavioral approaches. It is possible for those who do research and provide services in behavioral medicine to be at once interested in processes of physical disease and symptom control and interested in behavioral outcomes, and it is possible for them to be interested in these behavioral outcomes whether or not physical disease processes are regarded as mediating between behavior and healthy functioning. If the main goal is to improve and extend patient health and functioning, then there seems to be no contradiction in consciously adopting one perspective and then another depending on which best achieves the desired result.

Behavioral Medicine and Empirically Supported Treatment

In order to promote the dissemination of therapy methods with known efficacy, the American Psychological Association appointed a Task Force in 1993. This Task Force eventually produced a list of criteria for empirically supported treatments, also called ESTs. These criteria were initially presented in a number of published reports in 1995 and 1998, and a useful review was published shortly thereafter (Chambless & Ollendick, 2001). The assumptions behind this work were that (a) patient care could be enhanced if psychological treatments were based more firmly on research evidence, and (b) clinicians require guidance for keeping their practice in accord with the latest findings. The promotion of ESTs is as important to behavioral medicine as it is to any other area of psychological practice, and it is important for the development of mindfulness and ACT-based treatment approaches.

The promotion of ESTs is not without controversy. Arguments against this approach include the belief that quantitative analyses in general are inappropriate as a method of guiding psychology practice; the belief that the use of treatment manuals, a part of the criteria within this approach, will lead to reduced quality of treatments; the belief that all therapies are essentially equivalent and that empirical comparison is unnecessary; and the belief that evidence based on research trials will not generalize to actual clinical practice (Chambless & Ollendick, 2001). There are also concerns raised that the identification of ESTs will be used as a basis for denial of coverage by insurers or managed care organizations for some therapies or as a basis for malpractice suits, or that this process will stifle flexibility and innovation in practice. Where possible, many of these arguments and concerns have been addressed (Chambless & Ollendick, 2001). ESTs continue to attract considerable attention and appear to be gaining momentum.

The criteria for well-established ESTs based on group comparison designs include the following: (a) at least two high-quality experiments must demonstrate either superiority to a pill or psychotherapy placebo condition or to an alternate treatment or equivalence to an established treatment; (b) clear descriptions of treatment, such as manuals, must be used; (d) sample characteristics must be carefully specified; and (e) results must be demonstrated by at least two different research groups (Chambless & Ollendick, 2001).

A review of the current list of ESTs reveals that there are efficacious treatments for nine separate conditions typically considered as broadly within the range of behavioral medicine. These include chronic low back pain, obesity, insomnia, anorexia nervosa, binge-eating disorder, bulimia nervosa, chronic headache, fibromyalgia, and rheumatologic pain (Society of Clinical Psychology, 2010). The efficacious treatments for these conditions generally include forms of cognitive and behavioral therapy. As of August 2010, ACT is established as having moderate support as a treatment for general chronic pain, including a range of different pain conditions. ACT or mindfulness-based treatments are not yet established as ESTs for any of the other conditions listed here, owing particularly to their relatively early stage of development and the time required for multiple high-quality published studies to emerge from more than one group. On the other hand, ACT was also recently recognized as an EST for depression.

The Development of Mindfulness-Based Approaches in Health Care

Mindfulness is now pervasive in psychological research and in health care applications. Much of the momentum behind this work began in the early 1980s with the work of Jon Kabat-Zinn at the University of Massachusetts Medical School in Worcester, Massachusetts. At that time the project was called the Stress Reduction and Relaxation Program (SR&RP), an outpatient service designed to explore the "clinical effectiveness of meditation as a self-regulatory coping strategy for long-term chronic patients for whom the traditional medical treatments have been less than successful" (Kabat-Zinn, 1982, p. 33). There had been studies of mindfulness before this time, but this particular program of treatment and research is significant because it has become the prototype from which most current treatments have emerged, including applications inside (Kabat-Zinn, 2004) and outside of behavioral medicine (e.g., Teasdale et al., 2000). What began as the ten-week SR&RP course eventually became known as the eight-week Mindfulness-Based Stress Reduction course (MBSR). As a testament to growth in this area, it was estimated in June 2004 that there were more than one hundred scientific papers on clinical applications of mindfulness (Kabat-Zinn, 2004), and this number has certainly grown at an increasing rate since that time.

Mindfulness can be defined in a number of different ways. One working definition that includes some of the most common features is "the awareness that emerges through paying attention on purpose, in the present moment, and nonjudgementally, to the unfolding of experience moment by moment" (Kabat-Zinn, 2003, p. 145). Despite decades of interest, there had been an absence of attempts to provide what might be regarded as a more technical or "operational definition" of mindfulness. To remedy this, a group of eleven experts in mindfulness held a series of meetings and produced such a definition (Bishop et al., 2004). Their proposal was a two-component model of mindfulness involving, first, "the self-regulation of attention so that it is maintained on immediate experience, thereby allowing for increased recognition of mental events in the present moment" and, second, "adopting a particular orientation toward one's experience in the present moment, an orientation that is characterized by curiosity, openness, and acceptance" (Bishop et al., 2004, p. 232).

It is often noted that mindfulness did not enter into health care and psychological treatments via a route of scientific development. It was developed outside of science, and only later was it scrutinized scientifically. It has been challenging, then, for definitions of mindfulness to be true to their tradition and to serve needs within a science of clinical psychology. Although the definition by Bishop et al. (2004) was meant to serve further study and development, it has been observed that it includes potentially unrecognized "philosophical attachments" that might limit its ability to do so (Hayes & Shenk, 2004). The concept of "attention" included in the definition, for example, is a case in point. For some, "attention" is a mental capacity or instrument for locating and examining sources of information, a capacity directed at will by the individual doing the attending. For those from the more behavioral wings of cognitive behavioral therapy (CBT), attention is a manner of speaking about elements of a situation that are exerting influence over behavior. Here, "I pay attention to X" is like saying that "I bring my behavior under the influence of X" or "X is influencing my behavior." In this view, no tangible or "thing-like" quality of attention is assumed; it is a hypothetical construct, and there is no central requirement of an initiating and attention-directing agent.

ACT Model and Process

The first sentence of the first book on ACT states, "The single most remarkable fact of human existence is how hard it is for humans to be happy" (Hayes et al., 1999, p. 1). The authors briefly review the relevant data on human suffering and quickly conclude that suffering is a basic element of human life. It is ubiquitous, and this is a fundamental assumption underlying ACT.

To truly understand ACT requires understanding, to some extent, some of its philosophical roots. A complete philosophical examination is beyond the scope of this chapter; however, a few key notions can be presented, and a more detailed analysis is available elsewhere (e.g., Hayes et al., 1999; Hayes, Luoma, Bond, Masuda, & Lillis, 2006). Some of these notions are repeated or expanded on in later chapters. Briefly, the philosophy underlying ACT is called "functional contextualism." As applied to psychology, it defines its goals as the prediction and influence of behavior. Its "truth criterion" is pragmatic—"true" is what successfully achieves the goals of the analysis. This is in contrast to the correspondence truth criterion, which assumes a knowable external reality and defines "true" as that which accurately reflects this reality. In its analysis of causality, the ACT approach excludes any events as causes if they are not directly manipulable, and this is the basis for its contextual focus. Those who provide treatment are regarded as residing in the context around the actions of patients or clients, and thus their only means for creating behavior change is by manipulating elements of this context. From this particular focus, thoughts and feelings alone do not cause other actions but do so as determined by context. For example, feelings of anxiety alone do not cause avoidance, but feelings of anxiety in a context where one is unwilling to experience anxiety do. Hence, the work of ACT is based on certain assumptions. These assumptions differ from those of other approaches. They guide the methods used and interpretations made, and when they are not understood it can lead to confusion.

ACT is based in part on a basic theory of human language and cognition called relational frame theory (RFT; Hayes, Barnes-Holmes, & Roche, 2001). Once again, it is not possible to do justice to all of the complexities and nuances of RFT in the space of this chapter, yet a few of its features and implications are important to note. Some of the features of RFT are technically daunting and practically inaccessible from a brief exposure. Even when readers do not entirely understand some details of RFT, however, most will appreciate its originality and depth and may understand its potentially broad applicability.

For RFT, the core of human language and cognition is the learned and contextually regulated ability to arbitrarily relate events in ways that are mutual, include combinations of events, and allow changes in the functions specific to these events through their relations with other events. The processes underlying this relating involve words, thoughts, or images as central events. The relations applied in acts of relating can include, for instance, equivalence, opposite, greater than, less than, and before and after. Words, thoughts, and images can become psychologically equivalent to the events they describe, can coordinate or influence behavior as the events themselves would do, can transfer these influences to other events, and can participate in processes that alter, amplify, diminish, or otherwise transform the psychological meanings or behavioral influences of the events to which they have been related. This is learning unconstrained from contact with contingencies in the natural world. Almost any event can come to mean, for example, catastrophe, danger, harm, or pain and coordinate behavior accordingly. These processes are entirely dependent on verbal ability and do not appear to happen without it.

The critical notions within RFT are that human cognition is learned behavior, it can alter the influences of other behavioral processes, and these influences are regulated or determined by contextual features of the situation where they occur. In turn, these features lead to direct implications for behavior and behavior change:

- Because suffering and behavior problems arise largely in verbally based processes, verbally based problem-solving and reasoning may be inadequate to fully undermine them.

- Because cognition is learned behavior, and it is known that learning can be inhibited but not eliminated, it is contradictory to seek to eliminate or logically reduce cognitive networks.

- Direct attempts at cognitive change may increase and not decrease the functional importance of the elements targeted.

- Since the content and influences of cognitive networks are controlled by different contextual elements, it is possible to reduce the influence of cognition without necessarily changing its form or frequency of occurrence.

Taken together, these implications mean, in essence, that it may be both unnecessary and imprudent to focus mainly on change in the *content* of cognitive processes. Instead, treatment may focus on what is referred to as their "functions," or the psychological processes around them from which they derive their impact (Hayes et al., 2006).

RFT helps to explain how, for example, visiting a hospital or seeing a doctor can be a frightening experience and can be completely avoided following an experience of another person dying in a hospital or being harmed while having treatment from a doctor, even if this was not observed directly and even if the situations avoided bear only the most superficial similarity to the original "learning" events. It helps to explain how a heavy smoker might continue to smoke related to the fact that his or her grandmother was a similarly heavy smoker and lived to be 105 years old. It helps to explain how a doctor's description of some grisly back injury can lead a person to adhere to an instruction, "Never lift more than ten pounds," basically forever. In each case an experience never directly contacted, but only related to other experiences with words and thinking, takes a role in determining an extremely durable behavior pattern that in some way either risks health or is extremely limiting.

According to the model underlying ACT, people suffer psychological problems largely from *psychological inflexibility*. This is typically described as a process based in the interaction of language and cognition with the direct experience of environmental contingencies in ways that either block certain behaviors or drive certain behaviors forward unceasingly, in both cases contrary to one's goals and values. The notion is that people often experience the world from inside verbal constructions of the world, including constructions of the past, the future, or the self. Behavior patterns that emerge from these verbally based experiences are simply less flexible and often less effective than behavior patterns that contact and track with direct moment-to-moment experience outside of verbal processes. When behavior is dominated by verbally based experience, and under the influences of processes we might call "inside the head," it can be inconsistent with what the environment affords in relation to values or goals.

Processes of psychological inflexibility are sustained and elaborated on by what is called the *context of literality*, a psychological situation where descriptions and evaluations become confused as if they are the same thing. Within this context, evaluations, such as the thought "I am worthless," are treated as if they are descriptions, in this case meaning "I have no value as a person." Inflexibility is also sustained by the social context where cognitive and emotional "reasons" for actions are promoted into de facto "causes," and by what is called the *context of control* that promotes wrestling with cognitive and emotional experiences as a means for better living. ACT questions on some occasions the utility of the well-worn human tendencies to analyze, to explain, to defend that we are right, to defend stories about who we are, and to try to regulate our behavior by focusing inward. It aims to bring positive and desired qualities of life to bear on behavioral choices and to loosen up influences based on negative qualities, such as experiences one is attempting to avoid, and influences that give actions a "must do" quality, with the emphasis on the "must."

Psychological inflexibility emerges from six interrelated component processes: experiential avoidance, cognitive fusion, dominance of the conceptualized past or future, attachment to a conceptualized self, lack of values clarity or values-based action, and lack of a committed quality in action (Hayes et al., 1999). Each of these is essentially the opposite of one of the ACT therapeutic processes.

The six core therapeutic processes of ACT are depicted in figure 1.1, with those that are addressed in mindfulness methods set inside a box. These six interrelated processes are addressed in ACT for the overall purpose of promoting psychological flexibility. Each of the core processes of ACT expresses a kind of quality of action. None of them is a belief, a cognitive structure, a coping strategy, or primarily a way to reduce symptoms. The quality in each process arises contextually in the nature of the controlling influences on the behavior pattern.

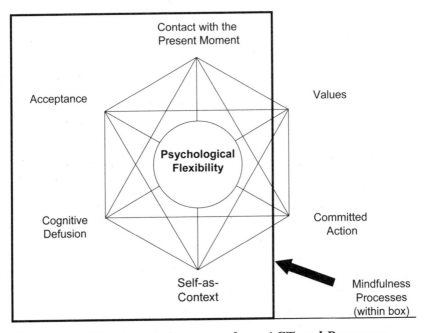

Figure 1.1 Therapeutic Processes from ACT and Processes Encompassed Within Mindfulness

Acceptance involves openly contacting negatively evaluated experiences when doing so serves one's goals and values and when not doing so leads to psychological problems or unnecessary restrictions in functioning. It is a quality of taking action toward what one desires while permitting the presence of experiences that are unwanted, such as feelings, physical sensations, memories, and urges. It is a quality of taking action that permits these experiences to be present and does not give them a controlling role over behavior, in a way that is without defense, without engaging in attempts at controlling them. Acceptance is sometimes mistakenly treated like a decision, belief, or mental act, such as a mental acknowledgement that control does not work or that a problem is unchangeable, or like a clever symptom-control strategy. In ACT, acceptance is not these things and does not depend on these things.

Cognitive defusion involves altering the way that thoughts and other cognitive content are experienced so that some of the functions of this content are changed. ACT researchers and therapists seem to monotonously harp on about the difference between form and function, and it is here again with cognitive defusion. Defusion is about altering functions. It is sometimes referred to as an awareness of the process of thinking and not just the content of thinking. This core ACT process involves realizing the distinction between our actual selves and actual events and the *thoughts* we have about ourselves and events. Defusion is said to decrease the "believability" of thoughts or their dominating influence over other potentially present experiences. Defusion is not just the knowledge that one is thinking or of what one is thinking; it is the experience of a reduction in the dominating impacts otherwise included in this thinking.

Contact with the present moment is a part of what is done in mindfulness exercises. It is the ability to track fluidly with the ongoing moment-to-moment experience of our environment. In a sense, when one is fused with verbal constructions of events, particularly events that occurred in the past or that may or may not occur in the future, there is automatically an insensitivity to the moment-to-moment experiences of the present. It is like one is living in another time. As in mindfulness, contact with the present moment is not a rigid attachment to the present, and it does not fail when events at another point in time are contacted. It is fluid. It is a repeated process of catching occasions of being elsewhere and returning to the present when this is useful.

Self-as-context is the ability to recognize the distinction between experiences and who is having the experiences. Alternatively it is the ability to have the experience that we are the context or location where situations and our history coordinate our psychological experiences and our behavior. It is the ability to not become overly attached to our experiences, our beliefs, or our stories about ourselves as a matter of personal identity. Thus, I am not defined by verbal descriptions or evaluations about myself: a perfectionist, a person who never quits, a victim, worthless, hopeless, or repulsive. As a matter of experience and not belief, I am the observer who notices that these are thoughts or beliefs that I have. Self-as-context as viewed here is not an issue of ontology or referential truth but rather an issue of workability, as with other principles and methods from ACT.

Values are qualities of action or life directions that are in accord with what a person holds as important and desirable. Unlike goals, values are never completely reached. Where *goals* typically have a future-focused and reachable quality, *values* have a moment-to-moment and ongoing quality. When being a loving partner is the germ of a value, values-based actions may include communicating openly, showing affection, and making sacrifices when needed to help a partner live a better life. Values are how ACT coordinates behavior to the longer term yet keeps it present focused. Values provide a present guide for action where symptoms, pain, or "negative" emotional experiences have provided a dominating guide in the past. At the same time they legitimize contact with pain and other unwanted experiences during acts of acceptance and provide a measure of the workability of choices.

Committed action is sometimes called the active choosing and rechoosing of particular directions in life. In treatment, building committed action usually starts within a values domain and first includes setting of goals and taking the steps to achieve them. Other processes, such as acceptance, defusion, and contact with the present moment, are included when steps toward goals touch on psychological barriers. Once behavior change is initiated, the work of committed action includes the step-by-step building of larger patterns of behavior and integrating them into daily life. Committed action is the quality of meeting difficulties, failure experiences, or pain and changing how one proceeds if needed, letting go of a particular goal in a particular situation if needed, and keeping the action going in the chosen direction nonetheless.

There is one final part of ACT that is not always explicitly explained in short descriptions. This is the ACT therapeutic stance. It is often said that ACT is an approach to psychological treatment based on particular theoretical processes, and that although it includes behavior change technology it is itself not merely a technology—it is bigger. Part of the breadth of ACT emerges in its explicit approach to the therapeutic relationship. In fact, in ACT what is called the "therapeutic stance" is not simply the nonspecific factors, nor is it another module of treatment technique. It is a fully integrated part of the process of creating psychological flexibility in patient behavior. Elements of the therapeutic stance are listed in table 1.1. The first "core competency" is said to most encompass the stance. The elements are entailed by approach to language in ACT where evaluative concepts like "sick" and "well" or "whole" and "broken" do not refer to inherent qualities in any person but are ways of speaking that emerge in our culture, sometimes useful and sometimes not. For ACT it is differences in history, sometimes small differences, that lead a person to one situation or another, whether that is a life filled with success and honest pain or dominated by despair and struggling with that despair. The main point, however, is that, regardless of what a person's history has set in place, it appears that contextual change around psychological problems can provide a potent means for creating deep and lasting changes in his or her life.

TABLE 1.1
Core Competencies of the ACT Therapeutic Stance

1	Speaks to the client from an equal, vulnerable, compassionate, and genuine point of view and respects the client's inherent ability to make change.
2	Willing to self-disclose when in the interest of the client.
3	Fits methods to the needs of the client and situation, and changes course when needed.
4	Tailors methods and exercises to client's experience, culture, and language habits.
5	Models acceptance of challenging content, including the client's difficult feelings, without needing to fix it.

6   Uses experiential exercises, paradox, and metaphor as appropriate and deemphasizes literal sense-making of these.

7   Brings emphasis back to client's experience, not his or her opinions.

8   Does not argue, lecture, coerce, or attempt to convince.

9   Recognizes processes of flexibility in the moment and supports them within the therapeutic relationship.

Based on Luoma, Hayes, & Walser (2007).

Meta-Analyses of Mindfulness-Based Treatments

In 2002 a review was done of the current literature on MBSR for a range of conditions, and the most frequently included condition was chronic pain (Bishop, 2002). In the review, the author noted the "growing use of the approach within medical settings in the last twenty years" (p. 71) and he proposed to evaluate the effectiveness of MBSR and its mechanisms of action. Thirteen uncontrolled and controlled studies published between 1985 and 2000 were identified, and the author conducted a narrative summary. In the end, the author noted methodological problems and concluded that "the available evidence does not support a strong endorsement of this approach at present. However, serious investigation is warranted" (Bishop, 2002, p. 71).

Baer (2003) presented a subsequent review that was both "conceptual" and for the first time also quantitative. She included both pre-post and group comparison designs and she included studies of patients with chronic pain, patients with Axis I psychiatric disorder, patients with other medical conditions, patients with mixed clinical conditions, and people from nonclinical groups. The review included twenty-two studies, published between 1982 and 2001, yielding fifteen independent post-treatment effect sizes. The mean effect size (d) here was .74 and when weighted by sample size was .59. It appeared that ten of the effects included in this mean were from between group designs and seven of these ten included random assignment to conditions. The mean post-treatment effect size for those studies that utilized random assignment to conditions was .75. Comparison conditions here typically included waiting list or treatment as usual. Baer (2003) concluded that, "in spite of significant methodological flaws, the current literature suggests that mindfulness-based interventions may help alleviate a variety of mental health problems and improve psychological functioning" (p. 139).

A very similar meta-analysis was published shortly thereafter by Grossman, Neimann, Schmidt, and Walach (2004). These researchers similarly identified twenty studies of MBSR meeting their criteria for a summary quantitative review. Again the studies covered a wide range of disorders: chronic pain, cancer, heart disease, anxiety, and depression, as well as nonclinical groups. They calculated similar effect sizes (d) around .54 for both uncontrolled and controlled studies. In five studies involving control groups and assessing physical health variables as outcomes, the mean effect size was .53. The authors concluded that "our findings suggest the usefulness of MBSR as an intervention for a broad range of chronic disorders and problems" (Grossman et al., 2004, p. 39). They further noted that "the consistent and relatively strong level of effect sizes across very different types of sample[s] indicates that mindfulness training might enhance general features of coping with distress and disability in everyday life, as well as under more extraordinary conditions of serious disorder or stress" (p. 39).

The current standard form of MBSR includes twenty-six hours of session time, including eight sessions of two and one half hours each and one additional day including six hours. There are, however, much shorter, modified versions of MBSR treatments of twelve, ten and one half, and even six hours, for example. In a study of thirty trials of MBSR, correlations were calculated between mean effect sizes with total number of in-session hours and with assigned practice time (Carmody & Baer, 2009). No significant correlations were found in either case. Essentially these researchers found no evidence that shortened versions of MBSR are less effective than the standard format, although they recommended that the standard format remain the format of choice, as it has accrued the most empirical support.

Meta-analyses of ACT

Öst (2008) recently conducted a review and meta-analysis focusing on "third wave" therapies, including ACT, dialectical behavior therapy, cognitive behavioral analysis system of psychotherapy, functional analytic psychotherapy, and integrative behavioral couples therapy. This review included thirteen trials of ACT. Among these trials were five studies of stress, stress and pain, smoking, opiate dependence, and diabetes. The estimated controlled effect sizes (d) from the ACT studies were .96 in comparison to wait list, .79 in comparison to treatment as usual, and .53 in comparison with active comparison conditions. The overall effect size was medium, .68. In this review Öst criticized the quality of the research methods in the ACT trials and concluded that none of the ACT treatments nor any of the other approaches reviewed met criteria for ESTs. This criticism was based on a comparison in which he paired ACT studies with CBT studies from similar journals and publication dates and then submitted them all to a rating scale of methodological stringency.

In a subsequent commentary on the review by Öst, Gaudiano (2009) welcomed the feedback provided by the earlier review but criticized some of the methods used in it. He noted that apparent differences in design quality between trials of ACT with CBT could be accounted for by differences in amount of grant support, the particular stage of treatment development, and differences in specific populations being studied. His analyses indicated that the average ACT study was funded at a rate of about 23 percent of that secured by the average CBT study, which is not surprising given the preliminary and pilot nature of the ACT studies now published.

A second review and meta-analysis was recently published by Powers and colleagues (Powers, Zum Vörde Sive Vörding, & Emmelkamp, 2009). In this review of eighteen randomized controlled trials they found significant effect sizes (Hedges's g) for ACT of .68 in comparison to waiting list conditions and .42 in comparison to treatment as usual. They found that ACT was not superior to currently established treatments, effect size .18, $p = .13$. They also found that there was no significant relationship within the ACT studies between design quality and effect size, $\beta = -.06, p = .50$. Half of the eighteen studies reviewed addressed problems areas considered as more or less related to behavioral medicine, including work stress, stress and pain, smoking, diabetes, substance abuse, weight control, epilepsy, and low back pain.

Summary

In many ways, behavioral medicine is what the term says. It is a field that focuses on behavior, both as process and as outcome. This is "behavior" taken in a broad sense. It also focuses on medicine, not so much in the sense of substances used for treating disease, but in the alternate sense of this word, the science and practice of maintaining health and preventing and treating disease (Merriam-Webster, 2010). The relatively new field of behavioral medicine has had many successes, and it is ever developing. Part of this development is a thirty-year history of work in mindfulness and a ten- or fifteen-year history of work in ACT.

Mindfulness and ACT have different roots, the former in ancient Asian religious traditions and the latter in science, specifically the behavior analytic wing of current cognitive and behavioral approaches. In some ways mindfulness is a well-developed method, but the psychological processes it contains remain somewhat obscure from a scientific point of view. Those who "know it" may recognize it when they see it and may be able to duplicate the experience reliably, but science has not been able to define it with precision. Mindfulness has been practiced for centuries. On the other hand, ACT is very much a developing approach, with theory and principles abstracted from less than twenty years of empirical study. Treatments based on ACT have been designed and tested in earnest only in the early 2000s.

Even with their histories and differences in their methods of delivery, mindfulness and ACT have a similar psychological sensibility. For both, language, thoughts, judgments, and evaluations can present traps and impose limitations on human behavior and daily functioning. Both approaches include methods to dispel what is called "the illusion of literal language," this mistaken sense that we are seeing the world in our thoughts when in actuality we are constructing the world with our thoughts. Both include methods of acceptance, methods to help us contact and make room for our psychological experiences without being pulled into a struggle with these experiences.

There are already different approaches within behavioral medicine. There are, after all, professionals in what we call the "psychosomatic" and the "behavioral" camps already working side by side possibly without even knowing it. It is perhaps too soon to know with certainty whether what mindfulness and ACT offer is new or more of the same and whether these approaches offer something radical and progressive. Evidence for this will be seen in how well they (a) yield some integration of current observations around a finite number of precise and broadly applicable core principles, (b) promote a productive program of research, (c) identify specific manipulable and testable treatment processes, and (d) guide the design of efficient and highly impactful treatment methods. The data up to this point appear promising.

Of course, mindfulness and ACT are just approaches or directions. Progress in behavioral medicine will be based on how well these approaches coordinate the behavior of those who work in this field. Without trying to oversimplify the task, part of this process then is in understanding and managing this behavior.

References

Agras, W. S. (1982). Behavioral medicine in the 1980's: Nonrandom connections. *Journal of Consulting and Clinical Psychology, 50*, 797–803.

Alexander, F. (1950). *Psychosomatic medicine: Its principles and applications.* New York: Norton and Company.

Baer, R. A. (2003). Mindfulness training as a clinical intervention: A conceptual and empirical review. *Clinical Psychology: Science and Practice, 10*, 125–143.

Bishop, S. R. (2002). What do we really know about mindfulness-based stress reduction? *Psychosomatic Medicine, 64*, 71–84.

Bishop, S. R., Lau, M., Shapiro, S., Carlson, L., Anderson, N. D., Carmody, J., et al. (2004). Mindfulness: A proposed operational definition. *Clinical Psychology: Science and Practice, 11*, 230–241.

Blanchard, E. B. (1982). Behavioral medicine: Past, present, and future. *Journal of Consulting and Clinical Psychology, 50*, 795–796.

Carmody, J., & Baer, R. A. (2009). How long does a mindfulness-based stress reduction program need to be? A review of class contact hours and effect sizes for psychological distress. *Journal of Clinical Psychology, 65*, 627–638.

Chambless, D. L., & Ollendick, T. H. (2001). Empirically supported psychological interventions: Controversies and evidence. *Annual Review of Psychology, 52*, 685–716.

Gaudiano, B. A. (2009). Öst's (2008) methodological comparison of clinical trials of acceptance and commitment therapy versus cognitive behavior therapy: Matching apples with oranges? *Behaviour Research and Therapy, 47*, 1066–1070.

Grossman, P., Niemann, L., Schmidt, S., & Walach, H. (2004). Mindfulness-based stress reduction and health benefits: A meta-analysis. *Journal of Psychosomatic Research, 57*, 35–43.

Hayes, S. C., Barnes-Holmes, D., & Roche, B. (Eds.). (2001). *Relational frame theory: A post-Skinnerian account of human language and cognition.* New York: Kluwer Academic/Plenum Publishers.

Hayes, S. C., Luoma, J., Bond, F., Masuda, A., & Lillis, J. (2006). Acceptance and commitment therapy: Model, processes and outcomes. *Behaviour Research and Therapy, 44*, 1–25.

Hayes, S. C., & Shenk, C. (2004). Operationalizing mindfulness without unnecessary attachments. *Clinical Psychology: Science and Practice, 11*, 249–254.

Hayes, S. C., Strosahl, K. D., & Wilson, K. G. (1999). *Acceptance and commitment therapy: An experiential approach to behavior change.* New York: Guilford Press.

Kabat-Zinn, J. (1982). An outpatient program in behavioral medicine for chronic pain patients based on the practice of mindfulness meditation: Theoretical considerations and preliminary results. *General Hospital Psychiatry, 4*, 33–57.

Kabat-Zinn, J. (2003). Mindfulness-based interventions in context: Past, present, and future. *Clinical Psychology: Science and Practice, 10*, 144–156.

Kabat-Zinn, J. (2004). Introduction to the 15th anniversary edition. In J. Kabat-Zinn. *Full catastrophe living: How to cope with stress, pain and illness using mindfulness meditation* (15th Anniversary Edition, pp. 5–11). Chippenham, UK: Anthony Rowe, Ltd.

Kaplan, R. M. (1990). Behavior as the central outcome in health care. *American Psychologist, 45*, 1211–1220.

Luoma, J. B, Hayes, S. C., & Walser, R. D. (2007). *Learning ACT: An acceptance & commitment therapy skills-training manual for therapists.* Oakland, CA: New Harbinger Publications.

Merriam-Webster. (2010). Online Dictionary. Retrieved March 11, 2010, from http://www.merriam-webster.com/dictionary/medicine

Öst, L. (2008). Efficacy of the third wave of behavioral therapies: A systematic review and meta-analysis. *Behaviour Research and Therapy, 46*, 296–321.

Pattishall, E. G. (1989). The development of behavioral medicine: Historical models. *Annals of Behavioral Medicine, 11*, 43–48.

Pomerleau, O. F., & Brady, J. P. (1979). *Behavioral medicine: Theory and practice.* Baltimore: Williams & Wilkins Company.

Powers, M. B., Zum Vörde Sive Vörding, M. B., & Emmelkamp, P. M. G. (2009). Acceptance and commitment therapy: A meta-analytic review. *Psychotherapy and Psychosomatics, 78*, 73–80.

Schwartz, G. E., & Weiss, S. M. (1977). Editorial: What is behavioral medicine. *Psychosomatic Medicine, 39*, 377–381.

Society of Clinical Psychology, American Psychological Association, Division 12. (2010). Retrieved February 13, 2010, from http://www.psychology.sunysb.edu/eklonsky-/division12/disorders.html

Teasdale, J. D., Segal, Z. V., Williams, J. M. G., Ridgeway, V. A., Soulsby, J. M., & Lau, M. A. (2000). Prevention of relapse in major depression by mindfulness-based cognitive therapy. *Journal of Consulting and Clinical Psychology, 68*, 615–623.

PART 2

APPLICATIONS OF ACT AND MINDFULNESS TO SPECIFIC CONDITIONS AND POPULATIONS

2 ACCEPTANCE AND COMMITMENT THERAPY FOR CHRONIC PAIN

Kevin E. Vowles
Musculoskeletal Pain Assessment and Community Treatment
Service Haywood Hospital, Stoke-on-Trent PCT & Primary
Care Sciences Research Centre, Keele University

Miles Thompson
Bath Centre for Pain Services, Royal National Hospital
for Rheumatic Diseases NHS Foundation Trust

Chronic pain is a frequent human experience. Prevalence estimates typically indicate that between 15 and 21 percent of adults experience chronic pain, although some prevalence estimates are substantially higher than this, at 46.5 percent (Breivik, Collett, Ventafridda, Cohen, & Gallacher, 2006; Elliott, Smith, Penny, Smith, & Chambers, 1999). For many individuals, chronic pain has significant adverse impacts on daily activity, employment, relationships, and emotional functioning (Breivik et al., 2006). It also leads to significant health care use and expenditures (Haetzman, Elliott, Smith, Hannaford, &

Chambers, 2003). A key element in the problem of chronic pain is the way it leads to a wide range of persistent and inflexible efforts to avoid pain exacerbation and to an incessant cycle of escalating distress and disability when these efforts fail (Crombez, Eccleston, Van Hamme, & De Vlieger, 2008).

Unfortunately, the modern medical armamentarium does not appear adequate for solving the problem of chronic pain. For example, opioid medications often fail to provide sustained relief and can contribute to additional problems in the form of opioid dependence, misuse, or other adverse effects, such as constipation, sedation, nausea, and the like (Ballantyne & Fleisher, 2010; Martell et al., 2007). Pain relief achieved with devices or interventional procedures, such as injections, transcutaneous electrical nerve stimulation, implantable devices, and surgery, are often transient, and these procedures rarely produce beneficial impacts on functioning or health care costs (e.g., Armon, Argoff, Samuels, & Backonja, 2007; Chou et al., 2009; Nnoaham & Kumbang, 2010). It could be argued that pain per se is essentially untreatable for at least a proportion of chronic pain sufferers. In other words, for at least some with chronic pain, there will not be a treatment that reliably leads to durable and clinically significant pain relief. Furthermore, although additional interventions aimed at pain relief can be and often are done with the laudable intention of decreasing pain and suffering, the unending pursuit of new treatments can reinforce a message that pain must be reduced in order for meaningful functioning to be restored, which is not necessarily true (McCracken, 2005). Additionally, the cumulative effect of recurrent failures of treatment to achieve pain relief often include feelings of defeat, confusion, and dismay, and these experiences may further exacerbate pain-related difficulties (e.g., Benner, 2007).

Historically, psychologically oriented treatment approaches have pursued an agenda alternative to the more mainstream one of pain reduction. In essence, these approaches have aimed at the restoration of effective and adaptive functioning within a context of continuing pain (e.g., Mayer & Gatchel, 1988). The development of acceptance and commitment therapy (ACT; Hayes, Strosahl, & Wilson, 1999) offers a number of refinements that are directly relevant to this aim.

The present chapter provides a review of the history of psychological interventions for chronic pain and how developments within clinical psychology more broadly have been specifically integrated into chronic pain settings up to the more recently developed "third wave approaches" (Hayes, 2004), of which ACT and mindfulness-based approaches are prominent examples. It is hoped that a review of this history will allow for a better understanding of how these approaches were developed and may clarify their specific applicability to chronic pain. While mindfulness and ACT have developed from separate roots, there are similarities between them that deserve discussion. Among these, both ACT and mindfulness-based approaches have substantially overlapping clinical goals, including a general loosening of verbally based influences on behavior, the strengthening of present-focused, moment-to-moment awareness, and the increasing of flexibility in responding to aversive experiences, so that this responding is more congruent with vital and meaningful living (Hayes & Wilson, 2003).

In addition to an overview of how the history of psychologically based interventions has contributed to ACT and related approaches, the chapter has a number of other purposes. First, key treatment processes targeted for change within ACT will be reviewed, as will methods for measuring a subset of these processes. Evidence with regard to the effectiveness of ACT for chronic pain will be reviewed. The chapter concludes with a brief discussion of two specific clinical issues.

The Development of Psychological Models of Chronic Pain

While psychological models of chronic pain have been in existence since early human history, it is possible to argue that the advent of more modern approaches began after the publication of Melzack and Wall's 1965 paper outlining their Gate Control Theory of pain. The essence of the theory was that pain perception is a dynamic affair, one that is modified by both physiological and psychological variables. Furthermore, although not directly specified in the original paper, a second key implication of the theory was that situational and historical variables may play a role in pain perception, as they provide additional influences on ongoing physiological and psychological experiences (Fordyce, 1976; Skinner, 1953).

From Gate Control Theory to Cognitive Behavioral Approaches

The theoretical assumptions posited within the Gate Control Theory were of topical relevance to clinical psychology. At that point in time, clinical psychology was developing alternate conceptualizations with regard to the cause, consequences, and treatment of problematic human behavior, unlike those posited within the psychodynamic theories of Freud and colleagues. In particular, operant approaches were becoming increasingly dominant and were demonstrating success across a wide variety of personal and societal problems (e.g., Baum, 2003; Franks & Wilson, 1974). Within chronic pain settings, Wilbert Fordyce and colleagues (e.g., Fordyce, 1976) recognized the relevance of operant theory to chronic pain, as well as the potential utility of treatment techniques such as exposure, skills training, shaping, modeling, and use of specific schedules of reinforcement.

For example, Fordyce, Fowler, Lehmann, and DeLateur (1968) introduced the idea of "pain behavior" as a unit available for clinical analysis. Pain behavior referred to the combination of verbal and observable behavior used to communicate that someone was experiencing pain. For instance, the verbalization "Ouch!" followed by rubbing of the area where pain is occurring is an instance of pain behavior. It was theorized that the occurrence of pain behavior, like any other behavior, is influenced by situation, context, and history. Taking the above example one step further, if the rubbing leads to pain reduction, then rubbing has been reinforced and is therefore more likely to occur again in the future.

The approach developed by Fordyce and colleagues was quite sophisticated and is detailed in Fordyce (1976). Patients with pain were brought into the clinic where pain behavior and functional status were assessed in an in-depth fashion. Following assessment, functional analysis, and formulation of the patient's presenting behavior patterns, operant methods were used to gradually extinguish problematic behaviors, such as unhelpful or excessive analgesic consumption; shape and reinforce more adaptive behaviors, such as sustained improvements in activity; and train in skills where deficiencies were identified. There is persuasive evidence for operant approaches in terms of the achievement of marked reductions in pain behavior and analgesic consumption, as well as improvements in overall levels of functioning in those suffering from chronic pain (e.g., see the meta-analysis of Flor, Fydrich, & Turk, 1992). These successes are consistent with those observed in other clinical arenas, where interventions based on operant behavioral theory have good evidence of effect (Baum, 2003; Skinner, 1981).

Even early on, however, there were concerns that operant approaches were not able to adequately account for human cognition and language (e.g., Bandura, 1969). In particular, concerns were raised that verbal behavior, including inaudible behavior in the form of self-talk or cognitions, was somehow unique and that the tried-and-true behavioral principles that came from the laboratory were not applicable (cf. Chomsky, 1959; Hayes, Luoma, Bond, Masuda, & Lillis, 2006). At the same time, commonsense models of cognition were being postulated within the wider area of clinical psychology—a prominent example is the cognitive therapy of Beck, Rush, Shaw, and Emery (1979), where a principle of treatment is the logical analysis, alteration, and testing of cognitions that are deemed to be dysfunctional or maladaptive (Clark, 1995). Cognitive techniques were combined with the operant approaches that had proven utility, and cognitive behavioral therapy, or CBT, emerged.

As with the previous work including operant behavioral methods, wider developments in clinical psychology were adapted for use within chronic pain settings. In particular, the idea that a core problem within chronic pain had to do with problematic beliefs *about* pain seemed plausible, and treatment approaches were outlined (e.g., Turk, Meichenbaum, & Genest, 1983). Over the ensuing decades, evidence emerged that provided support for the role of thoughts and beliefs in the functioning of those with chronic pain. In fact, many concepts related to chronic pain that are now widely known have emerged from this commonsense cognitive tradition and have been shown to be related to functioning. These include constructs such as catastrophizing, anxiety sensitivity, self-efficacy, control beliefs, illness perceptions, and motivation for change, among many others (Gatchel, Peng, Peters, Fuchs, & Turk, 2007).

Consistent with CBT more generally, treatment methods integrating cognitive change approaches, as well as operant techniques, also emerged. To date, there is good evidence that a CBT approach to chronic pain works reasonably well. For example, there are at least three meta-analyses that indicate relatively good outcomes of operant and cognitive behavioral approaches to chronic pain (Hoffman, Papas, Chatkoff, & Kerns, 2007; Morley, Eccleston, & Williams, 1999; Ostelo et al., 2005). On the other hand, the most recently performed meta-analysis pointed out several shortcomings of the extant literature and, using a more stringent and conservative meta-analytic approach in comparison to previous work, indicated that outcomes are not as good as previously suggested (Eccleston, Williams, & Morley, 2009).

Critique of Cognitive Behavioral Approaches for Chronic Pain

Although studies of CBT approaches for chronic pain provide generally supportive evidence, there are a number of areas where there is a lack of clarity or where the extant data do not provide specific support for the principles derived from the model. These limitations do not undermine CBT as a whole; however, they do highlight areas in need of focused work to improve clarity or areas where adjustments to the model may be considered.

First, CBT has become a catch-all term for a broad combination of techniques that are often applied in the absence of a clear and well-integrated theoretical framework (Eccleston et al., 2009). Particular packages of CBT can include specific components that differ substantially from one treatment to another (Morley et al., 1999). Given this lack of coherence across CBT packages, it is not possible to discern individual contributions of specific techniques to specific outcomes, nor can one identify the inert components of treatment from those that are active. In short, the processes by which CBT works are not clear.

Second, one of the key specific hypotheses of cognitive approaches, which is that specific cognitive change techniques are fundamental to the achievement of adaptive behavior change (Clark, 1995; Beck et al., 1979), hasn't held up under empirical scrutiny. It is not necessary, for example, to include methods directed at achieving cognitive change in order to achieve positive treatment outcomes in chronic pain (Vowles, McCracken, & Eccleston, 2007). Furthermore, the inclusion of cognitive change methods does not appear to reliably increase the effectiveness of interventions for chronic pain (Smeets, Vlaeyen, Kester, & Knottnerus, 2006). Such findings are present in treatment trials for depression and anxiety as well, where specific cognitive change techniques are not required ingredients for positive outcomes, nor does their inclusion lead to greater improvement (Hayes et al., 2006; Longmore & Worrell, 2007).

Third, the lack of a coherent theoretical model within CBT has meant that there is significant ambiguity and confusion within the model itself. It is not clear how the significant number of thoughts, beliefs, and perceptions previously identified as relevant within chronic pain settings are distinct from or serve to influence one another (Vowles, Wetherell, & Sorrell, 2009). There is, in fact, evidence of significant shared variance among relevant constructs (e.g., Foster, Thomas, Bishop, Dunn, & Main, 2010).

Fourth, in contrast to operant behavioral techniques, which were based on established experimental paradigms from the behavioral laboratories (Franks & Wilson, 1974; Hayes et al., 2006), the link between applied cognitive therapy interventions and basic cognitive science is weak. For example, while cognitive neuroscience has increasingly gone in the direction of imaging studies examining cortical functioning to understand cognitive processes, such as pain perception (e.g., Borsook & Becerra, 2006; Guedj, 2009), it is not clear how these studies are relevant to clinical situations or helpful in deriving interventions that will contribute to adaptive changes in behavior in those suffering from pain.

Finally, from a practical standpoint, many of the behaviors targeted for change within cognitive and behavioral treatments for chronic pain may have little relevance to current or future functioning. These behaviors include use of relaxation or distraction strategies, activity pacing, exercise, and positive thinking. At present, there is persuasive evidence from a variety of studies that indicates that these traditionally conceived "coping strategies" are only weakly related to emotional and physical functioning (see Curran, Williams, & Potts, 2009, and Vowles & McCracken, 2010, for brief reviews). These results are striking, particularly when one considers that interventions such as training in relaxation or distraction, activity pacing, exercise, and the challenging of maladaptive cognitions are recommended and often regarded as crucial components of interdisciplinary treatment programs for chronic pain (e.g., chapters 9 through 11 of Main, Sullivan, & Watson, 2008). At the very least, it would seem reasonable to reevaluate the role of these specific components within treatments for chronic pain.

In sum, there is a degree of incongruity within the literature on CBT for chronic pain. On one hand, it offers the possibility of a more sophisticated model with regard to human cognition, and there is reasonable data indicating that CBT is efficacious. On the other, there is a lack of clarity within the model with regard to ingredients and key processes, and the extant data do not support some of the specific hypotheses posited, particularly with regard to the core assumption that cognitive techniques and cognitive change are necessary for improvement.

ACT and Mindfulness-Based Approaches for Chronic Pain

The recent "third wave" approaches can be viewed as adjustments and further developments of previous operant and cognitive models. In many ways, these emerging methods are more consistently aligned to operant behavior theory in that they emphasize functional analysis over description of behavior and work to identify basic processes that are common across settings and syndromal definitions (Hayes et al., 2006). In addition, they also emulate the early goals of cognitive approaches by providing a more accurate and sophisticated understanding of human language and cognition, particularly with regard to the arbitrary nature of language-based processes and the deleterious effects these processes can have on people's lives. At their core, these approaches are about deriving a more adequate understanding of human suffering and using this understanding to directly inform treatment technologies so that treatments are ultimately more effective at decreasing suffering, as well as augmenting effective and meaningful functioning.

With regard to chronic pain, there is an inherent appeal to the idea that "acceptance" is likely to be of assistance. This idea is actually not all that new and has been around since the time of Fordyce (1976) and perhaps even longer (e.g., Rogers, 1946). In reality, the ACT model as applied to the problem of chronic pain is much broader and more complex than the idea that treatment is simply about acceptance of chronic pain. The term "acceptance" itself carries with it some unhelpful connotations, and patients with pain may see it as the equivalent of "giving up hope" (Viane et al., 2003). What has been discussed as acceptance within early work in this area (e.g., McCracken, 1998) can now be more precisely and broadly defined as psychological flexibility, the promotion of which is the primary goal of ACT (Hayes et al., 2006). "Psychological flexibility" is defined as direct and open contact with present experiences on a moment-to-moment basis in a way that allows behavior to continue or change according to opportunities present and one's goals and values (Hayes et al., 2006). It is also worth noting that "psychological" is used within ACT so that it not only includes private psychological experiences such as thoughts and feelings but also explicitly includes flexibility in action regardless of whether it is private or public behavior (Hayes et al., 2006).

In essence, ACT-based treatment aims to enable pain sufferers to flexibly respond to pain, distress, and related experiences in a particular way, such that needless and ineffective struggling with these experiences decreases in frequency, options for living well with them increase, and behavior follows one's goals and values. For example, if a person with pain was fully willing to have pain, without reservation or condition, in the service of living a fuller and more meaningful life, then that pattern of behavior would likely be an instance of psychological flexibility. Further, if one were more sensitive to moment-to-moment, and sometimes arbitrary, variations in urges, thoughts, feelings, and sensations, as well as the consistent presence of one's values, then options for behavior in these experiences can be broad rather than narrow and less restricted by the influence of pain or other aversive experiences. These processes are the primary focus of treatment within ACT.

Within the ACT model, psychological flexibility is an overarching process that is, in itself, composed of six interrelated processes, which are examined in detail in chapter 1 of this volume (see also Hayes et al., 2006). These six processes are briefly detailed in table 2.1 as they specifically relate to chronic pain. It is important to note that each of these processes is assumed to relate to and overlap with the others. An analysis of any one, therefore, by definition includes at least a peripheral analysis of the others.

Measures

To date, several measures have been developed from the ACT model for use in chronic pain settings, which are reviewed in the following few sections. Further, there are a number of additional measures, not reviewed here, that tap into ACT processes, such as those assessing mindfulness (e.g., the Mindful Attention and Awareness Scale in Brown & Ryan, 2003) and those that are not specific to chronic pain (e.g., the Acceptance and Action Questionnaire in Bond et al., in press). Chapter 8 includes a review of the wider range of measures related to acceptance and mindfulness. We examine two of these measures, as these are pertinent to treatment process results we will subsequently present.

TABLE 2.1 ACT Processes as Applied to the Experience of Chronic Pain

ACT Process	Psychological Inflexibility	Psychological Flexibility
Experiential avoidance/ Acceptance	Pain, fatigue, other challenging body sensations, difficult thoughts, traumatic memories and aversive emotions	Pain, fatigue, other challenging body sensations, difficult thoughts, traumatic memories and aversive emotions
(Unwillingness/ Willingness)	Are met with avoidance and struggling for control not by their mere presence but by an unwillingness to experience them, or by unworkable attempts to control, escape, or avoid them.	Are still present and the person is willing to experience them, in this moment, and in the next, and so on, in the pursuit of their values and goals.
Fusion/Defusion	Experience is dominated by thoughts, images, memories and other responses that might include: Predictions, evaluations, reasons, rules, "have-to's, "musts," and "can't"s	Predictions, evaluations, reasons, rules, "have-to's, "must"s and "can't"s "I am a failure," "I am sick," "I am a patient," "I must struggle on," "I am a perfectionist," "I always push through."

Self as content/self as context	Actions are determined by stories, evaluations, and judgments referring to the self such as: "I am a failure," "I am sick," "I am a patient," "I am a perfectionist," "I must struggle on," "I always push through."	Still occur, but the powerful linkage between these thoughts and specific actions are loosened and now there is the possibility of choices and options.
Dominance of past or future/Present moment awareness	Actions and choices are determined by memories of the past and fears of the future.	The mind still wanders to the past and future, and the individual has the ability to notice this, to track fluidly with thoughts in different times, and to bring awareness back to behavior in the present moment.
Lack of values/ Clear values	There is a lack of clarity of what is most important personally. Behavior is instead dominated by urges to reduce or remove pain, or the experience of other painful psychological experiences.	The individual has clear contact with what gives meaning to their life (their values) engages in behaviors that serve this meaning.
Inaction or "stubborn" persistence/ Committed action	Actions have an impulsive or non-persistent quality or persistently failing quality.	Actions include flexible persistence, choosing and rechoosing a course of action for positive non-avoidant purposes, and changing course is possible when a particular course is not working.

Chronic Pain Acceptance Questionnaire

Arguably the most widely used measure of ACT processes in chronic pain has been the Chronic Pain Acceptance Questionnaire (CPAQ). The original version of the CPAQ was used within an unpublished doctoral dissertation (Geiser, 1992). Work using this early version of the measure indicated that the CPAQ total score accounted for significant variance in functioning in those with chronic pain above and beyond that accounted for by pain intensity (Esteve, Ramírez-Maestre, & López-Martínez, 2007; Mason, Mathias, & Skevington, 2008; McCracken, 1998). Further research (McCracken, 1999; McCracken, Vowles, & Eccleston, 2004) examined the content, internal consistency, and factor structure of the instrument. Ultimately, upon further analysis, a revised twenty-item scale was developed, including two subscales: Activity Engagement and Pain Willingness. The former scale reflects the extent of participation in activities explicitly with continuing pain (e.g., "I lead a full life even though I have chronic pain") and the latter willingness scale reflects the capacity to experience pain fully and without attempts to avoid or control it (e.g., "Before I make any serious plans, I have to get some control over my pain"—reverse scored). Numerous studies provide support for the revised version of the CPAQ and indicate good convergent and divergent validity (see Reneman, Dijkstra, Geertzen, & Dijkstra, in press, for a review).

More recent work (Vowles, McCracken, McLeod, & Eccleston, 2008) carried out both exploratory and confirmatory analyses on two large samples and provided further support for the twenty-item, two-factor version described above. In a recent systematic review of the psychometric properties of a number of pain acceptance questionnaires, which judged the measures against strict psychometric criteria, the CPAQ was found to have the best overall results, with positive ratings for internal consistency, construct validity, and reliability (Reneman et al., in press). The CPAQ has been translated into German (Nilges, Koster, & Schmidt, 2007), Spanish (Esteve et al., 2007), Swedish (Wicksell, Olsson, & Melin, 2009), and Cantonese (Cheung, Wong, Yap, & Chen, 2008) and also adapted for adolescent populations (McCracken, Gauntlett-Gilbert, & Eccleston, 2010).

Chronic Pain Values Inventory

For those working within the ACT model, the importance of values is self-evident; however, attempts at its careful measurement are in still in their infancy. The Chronic Pain Values Inventory (CPVI) measures self-reports of importance, success, and the discrepancy between them across six valued life areas including family, intimate relations, friends, work, and growth or learning. Primary scores include mean success and the discrepancy scores between success and importance (McCracken & Yang, 2006). To date, the values success score has most often been used in research. Results indicate that greater success at valued activities is associated with better concurrent and future functioning (McCracken & Yang, 2006; McCracken & Vowles, 2008) and that greater improvement in values success is associated with greater improvements in functioning over the course of treatment, particularly through a three-month follow-up appointment (Vowles & McCracken, 2008).

Treatment Outcome

At present, to our knowledge, there are nine ACT-specific treatment outcome studies published in the area of chronic pain, plus a tenth examining the results of a brief experimental manipulation. There are an additional nine studies that examine primarily mindfulness-based treatment methods.

The first ACT-specific study was a small randomized controlled trial (RCT) published by Dahl, Wilson, and Nilsson (2004). In this study, nineteen public health service employees suffering from pain and stress were enrolled in either medical treatment as usual, or four 60-minute individual ACT sessions in addition to their usual medical treatment. At a six-month follow-up appointment, participants who had received ACT had taken substantially fewer sick days, averaging 0.5 days (SD = 1.8 days), in comparison to the medical treatment as usual group, who averaged 56.1 sick days (SD = 78.9 days). Interestingly, there were no significant differences found in pain or stress levels between the groups, suggesting that these factors were not responsible for the differences between the groups or improvements within the group receiving ACT.

The United Kingdom–based Bath Centre for Pain Services (BCPS) has published several treatment outcome studies involving ACT and chronic pain. Treatments offered within the BCPS are group based and interdisciplinary, with input from clinical psychology, physical therapy, occupational therapy, and nursing/medicine. The active phase of treatment is three to four weeks, with patients attending treatment five days per week for approximately 6.5 hours each day. The typical treatment day includes approximately 2.25 hours of physical conditioning, 1 hour of psychological methods, 30 minutes of mindfulness training, and 1 hour of activity management; the balance of the time is devoted to skills training and health/medical education. See McCracken (2005) for an overview of treatment methods and philosophy.

The studies from this group evaluate outcomes across a range of domains. Although there has been some variation in specific measures across studies, outcome evaluation has typically included measures of physical and psychosocial disability, depression, pain-related fear, daily rest due to pain, pain-related health care visits, and pain intensity, as well as two measures of physical functioning, including a two-minute walking-speed test and one-minute repeated sit-to-stand test.

The first outcome study published by the BCPS involved 108 consecutive completers of a three- or four-week program of residential treatment who were followed through a three-month follow-up appointment (McCracken, Vowles, & Eccleston, 2005). Changes over the course of treatment and follow-up were evaluated relative to change observed in the same group of patients while they were waiting for treatment. Results indicated an almost uniform absence of change during the waiting phase, with the sole exception of work status, which inexplicably improved. Significant improvements in all other measures of outcome were indicated at the end of treatment, and these improvements were generally maintained through follow-up. A later study using an expanded sample of 252 replicated these outcomes. It also found that increases in CPAQ scores during treatment accounted for significant unique variance in improvements across measures of functioning above and beyond that accounted for by changes in pain intensity or catastrophizing (Vowles, McCracken, & Eccleston, 2007).

A second study examined outcomes in a group of 53 highly disabled individuals requiring treatment as inpatients, meaning that these patients required assistance with self-care or mobility in order to participate in treatment (McCracken, MacKichan, & Eccleston, 2007). Results indicated statistically significant improvements across outcome measures during the post-treatment and follow-up stages. In addition, there was good evidence of clinical significance, with medium to large effect sizes observed across measures of outcome and indications of reliable change, similar in magnitude to change achieved by a separate group of patients who completed the standard residential course of treatment.

The most recent outcome study from the BCPS involved 171 treatment completers, entirely independent from the previous trials, two-thirds of whom also completed a three-month follow-up (Vowles & McCracken, 2008). The significant improvements through follow-up in outcome measures found in previous studies were replicated. Treatment effect sizes were medium or large. In addition, at follow-up, 75.4 percent of patients demonstrated reliable change in at least one of the following key domains: disability, pain-related anxiety, and depression. Further, 61.4 percent showed reliable change in at least two of these domains. Process analyses suggested that improvements in acceptance of pain (CPAQ) and values-based action (CPVI) were related to improvements in functioning, accounting for an average of 17 percent of the variance in the outcomes measured.

A Swedish group, based at the Karolinska Hospital in Stockholm, has also published several outcome studies. Two of these examine ACT for use with adolescents experiencing chronic pain. The first was a case series of fourteen adolescents with chronic idiopathic pain (Wicksell, Melin, & Olsson, 2007). Treatment duration averaged 14.4 weekly sessions ($SD = 6.6$) with the adolescents alone and an average of 2.4 ($SD = 2.9$) additional meetings with adolescents and parents. At the conclusion of treatment and at follow-up at three and six months, significant improvements were found in functional ability, school attendance, pain intensity, pain interference, and catastrophizing. The second study was an RCT involving thirty-two adolescents with chronic pain (Wicksell, Melin, Lekander, & Olsson, 2009). Patients were randomized to receive either ten 60-minute sessions of ACT or a non-ACT multidisciplinary treatment. Results at post-treatment and at follow-up at three and six months indicated significant improvements as a result of both interventions. Adolescents receiving the ACT intervention, however, had greater reductions in disability, pain interference, and pain-related discomfort, with the differences in favor of ACT achieving a medium to large effect size.

This group has also examined ACT within an RCT for adults with whiplash-associated disorders (Wicksell, Ahlqvist, Bring, Melin, & Olsson, 2008). Outcomes in twenty-one adults were compared to a waiting list. Those in the ACT group received ten 60-minute individual sessions. In comparison to the wait-list controls, those receiving ACT showed greater improvements in disability, life satisfaction, fear of pain, depression, and psychological flexibility through follow-ups at four and seven months following treatment conclusion.

In addition to the above, Vowles et al. (2009) published the results of two pilot studies, one conducted at a university-based outpatient pain-management clinic and another based at a Veterans Administration hospital in the United States. The outpatient study involved eight 90-minute group sessions, and results indicated that nine of eleven patients made at least moderate improvements in measures of emotional and physical functioning. The second study involved group sessions of either ACT or CBT. Results indicated that five of six patients in the ACT group and three of five in the CBT group showed at least moderate improvement in measures of emotional and physical functioning.

Finally, a randomized and controlled experimental study evaluated the effects of a brief instructional set on physical test performance in a sample of seventy-four individuals with low back pain (Vowles, McNeil, et al., 2007). Participants were asked to complete a series of seven physical tasks on two occasions. In between the two sets of tasks, participants were randomized to listen to one of three brief audiotaped instructional sets on how to improve performance on the tasks. The first set instructed them to control pain (Pain Control), the second instructed them to willingly have pain and discontinue attempts to control it (Pain Acceptance), and the third set, which was intended as an inactive control, instructed them to simply repeat their previous performance (Continued Practice). Primary analyses indicated that participants receiving the Pain Acceptance instructions demonstrated greater overall improvements in functioning in comparison to the group receiving the Pain Control instructions. The Pain Acceptance group exhibited a 16.3 percent improvement in performance, the Pain Control group exhibited an 8.3 percent worsening in performance, and the Continued Practice group improved by 2.5 percent.

Parallel to the ACT literature, mindfulness outcome research has also been conducted in the area of chronic pain. The early work was pioneered by Kabat-Zinn and colleagues (Kabat-Zinn, 1982; Kabat-Zinn, Lipworth, & Burney, 1985; Kabat-Zinn, Lipworth, Burney, & Sellers, 1986). The first outcome research, published in 1982, studied fifty-one subjects who completed ten 2-hour sessions of what later became known as mindfulness-based stress reduction (MBSR). At the end of treatment, nearly two-thirds showed 33 percent or more reduction in pain; three-quarters showed 33 percent or more reduction in mood disturbance, while over half showed 33 percent or more reduction in psychiatric symptoms (Kabat-Zinn, 1982). In 1985, ninety subjects followed the same program and reported significant improvements in pain, negative body image, interference with activity, anxiety, depression, medication use, and self-esteem. Interestingly, more than 70 percent of respondents were still practicing mindfulness up to fifteen months after the initial training period (Kabat-Zinn et al., 1985).

More recent mindfulness research has been undertaken in different areas of chronic pain, with separate studies examining MBSR in rheumatoid arthritis (Pradhan et al., 2007), back pain in older adults (Morone, Greco, & Weiner, 2008), women with fibromyalgia (Grossman, Tiefenthaler-Gilmer, Raysz, & Kesper, 2007; Sephton et al., 2007), and the loss associated with chronic pain (Sagula & Rice, 2004). Each of these studies has indicated positive treatment outcomes, even up through long-term follow-ups of three or four years (Kabat-Zinn et al., 1986; Grossman et al., 2007).

The evidence presented above suggests that pain sufferers can achieve significant reductions across many areas from treatment based on ACT or mindfulness approaches. Those studies that employ control conditions tend to show that ACT or mindfulness is at least equal, and often superior, to control conditions. Follow-up data are generally promising, although results from longer follow-up intervals are needed, particularly from the ACT-based treatments. Of course, the studies above are also notable in the ways they differ. The length of treatment varies (from just four to over ninety hours), as do characteristics of the sample (for example, adolescent and older adult), the setting (for example, individual, group, outpatient, residential, and inpatient), sample sizes, and the measures used. This widespread applicability is perhaps not surprising, since the processes targeted in ACT and mindfulness appear relevant not just in pain sufferers but in human beings generally. There is clearly a need for more work, including more adequately powered and controlled trials, and assessment of outcomes over a longer term, in the case of ACT trials particularly.

Clinical Issues

Thus far, this chapter has discussed subject matter fairly common within reviews and book chapters. It has reviewed the history contributing to contemporary practices and developments, discussed process and measurement issues, and reviewed treatment outcome literature. Within this chapter, however, we also want to highlight some key clinical issues of relevance to the practice of ACT. First is a section on clinical stance, or the way that one conducts oneself within the clinical interaction. Second, we discuss the history that pain patients often bring with them to treatment, since that may allow for a better understanding of the often problematic patterns of behavior that they exhibit.

Therapeutic Stance

There is a risk that therapists coming to ACT for the first time may focus on metaphors and experiential exercises, with the assumption that a faithful replication of these is all that is required to "do" ACT. While it is understandable that novice therapists might begin their ACT careers following rigid protocols, it should be remembered this is only a starting point, and practice can be improved over the longer term. Doing ACT is not about delivering material in a rote fashion but about acting with flexibility and an ability to adapt material, moment to moment, as best suits the situations we and our patients find ourselves in.

In a nutshell, ACT is primarily concerned with increasing psychological flexibility, and naturally the therapist's role is to support and encourage this both inside and outside of the therapeutic encounter. ACT tends not to find terms like "psychopathology" useful, nor does it demarcate hard boundaries between "normal" and "abnormal" behavior. Instead, the model suggests that psychological inflexibility stems from ordinary language processes that are present in all of us—both therapist and client. The ACT therapist thinks about behavior along a continuum from "adaptive" to "not adaptive," "functional" to "dysfunctional," or "workable" to "unworkable." ACT invites the therapist not to simply apply the model, and its processes, to the behavior of the client, but to apply it to his or her own behavior. Indeed, a challenging job for the ACT therapist is to keep track of the client's processes, and his or her own, and the dynamic interaction between them. A key task for the therapist is identical to the key objective of treatment for the client: to be aware of the unfolding influences on his or her own behavior and to have the flexibility within this to allow for action toward values and goals.

There are many ways therapists' own psychological inflexibility might unhelpfully emerge in their behavior and influence client behavior. For example, in trying to help clients solve difficulties they are recounting, predicting, or experiencing in the session, we might provide information, impart advice, or try to aid understanding. In doing so, we may comfort our clients or reassure them. We may do something to lessen our clients' suffering—we may even do it to lessen our own discomfort at witnessing the suffering of another human being. Although these reactions may be normal, natural, and automatic—they may seem caring and kind for clients and therapist alike—it is possible that sometimes a better way to encourage psychological flexibility in these moments is to allow our clients to stay with this discomfort and provide a space to allow them a fuller, more willing experience of the situations with which they struggle and suffer. This possibility may be particularly applicable when the presenting problems are severe or complex; in such cases, simple advice may not be particularly useful. Much of the reflective listening techniques that are so key in a number of approaches are consistent with this purpose in that the therapist's primary job is to attempt to understand, communicate the desire to understand, and show understanding of what the client is going through (e.g., Rogers, 1946; Miller & Rollnick, 2002; Tsai et al., 2008).

In addition, the therapist might notice his or her need to be "right," and the behavior pattern this can contribute to—maybe the tendency to defend one's position, lecture about what is the correct thing to do, or convince or coerce the patient into a certain course of action. It may be helpful for the therapist to determine what purpose is being served by this behavior and whether it directly contributes to freer, more functional and effective living in the patient. At times it may; many times it may not.

The Pain Patient's History

It is worth taking a moment to review some of the different scenarios that may have played out for our patients before they presented for treatment, because this may allow for a better understanding of how current patterns of behavior, both helpful and unhelpful, have emerged. These scenarios seem rather common across different patients in our experience, although not all patients will have had all, or any, of these experiences.

When pain began, perhaps the patient's mind told the patient that his or her general practitioner or family physician had the answer or could make a quick referral to a colleague who would. Perhaps friends told the patient their stories of similar problems and how they were resolved swiftly. Maybe professionals at this time spoke confidently that they had seen lots of people in similar situations for whom one particular procedure or another had removed the pain and solved the problem.

Perhaps time moved on and the pain remained the same or didn't lessen for as long as had been promised, or perhaps relief came only at a price that was paid in the form of lost work, relationships, independence, or concentration; mood disruptions; later increases in pain; or dependence on medication or other substances. Despite these costs, perhaps the patient's mind maintained that the answer was out there and the patient needed to work harder, demand more, see another professional, or invest in some additional intervention to find the answer. Perhaps these too failed, and then perhaps desperation to save a life that was falling apart really set in.

Maybe a medical test showed something abnormal but the patient was told by the professional interpreting the test that nothing could be done. Maybe, as is more often the case, all tests were negative and the patient was told that there was "nothing wrong." Even when a patient is given a diagnosis, or an explanation for a condition, he or she might be told in the next breath that there is nothing to be done. What if the patient heard, was told, or feared that the pain was believed to be psychological, a mental problem, as in "it's all in your head"? What patterns of behavior might these experiences lead to?

People suffering with pain often have many years of experience where they have been not heard, not believed, and not helped. When we become caught up in our own frustration about our clients' inability to move forward and we act from the stance of frustration, perhaps we further impede progress. Perhaps instead we can notice our own feelings of inadequacy about how we don't know what to do and may be feeling desperate ourselves, about how we worry we may be poor therapists. Perhaps we can use this opportunity to model psychological flexibility and demonstrate acceptance, willingness, and values in our own behavior.

Summary

Chronic pain occurs frequently and can tax the lives of sufferers and their families along with the resources of those professionals who care for them. Despite significant attention and investment from health care professionals, interventions and medications are often not adequate for meeting the challenge of pain.

The psychological therapies have historically promoted functional improvement as an alternative to that of symptom reduction.

While ACT builds on the history of both behavioral and cognitive traditions, it encompasses a number of changes in theory and technique, some obvious and some more subtle. At its core, ACT promotes the notion of psychological flexibility—an openness to private experiences and commitment to maintaining or changing behavior depending on what successfully moves one in the direction of values and goals. At present, a number of well-developed assessment measures have been developed, and at least nine treatment trials have examined the effectiveness of treatment, with positive results. The ideas and advances offered within the ACT model suggest ways of reorienting ourselves to chronic pain generally and, perhaps more importantly, toward the therapeutic work that we do alongside our patients.

References

Armon, C., Argoff, C. E., Samuels, J., & Backonja, M. (2007). Assessment: Use of epidural steroid injections to treat radicular lumbosacral pain: Report of the Therapeutics and Technology Assessment Subcommittee of the American Academy of Neurology. *Neurology, 68*, 723–729.

Ballantyne, J. C., & Fleisher, L. A. (2010). Ethical issues in opioids prescribing for chronic pain. *Pain, 148*, 365–367.

Bandura, A. (1969). *Principles of behavior modification.* New York: Holt, Rinehart, & Winston.

Baum, W. M. (2003). *Understanding behaviorism: Science, behavior, and culture.* Oxford: Wiley-Blackwell.

Beck, A. T., Rush, A. J., Shaw, B. F., & Emery, G. (1979). *Cognitive therapy of depression.* New York: Guilford Press.

Benner, D. E. (2007). Who can help me? A chronic pain patient's view of multidisciplinary treatment. In M. Schatman & A. Campbell (Eds.), *Chronic pain management: Guidelines for multidisciplinary program development* (pp. 117–128). New York: Informa.

Bond, F., Hayes, S. C., Baer, R. A., Carpenter, K. M., Orcutt, H. K., Waltz, T., et al. (submitted for publication). Preliminary psychometric properties of the Acceptance Action Questionnaire-II: A revised measure of psychological flexibility and acceptance.

Borsook, D., & Becerra, L. R. (2006). Breaking down the barriers: fMRI applications in pain, analgesia, and analgesics. *Molecular Pain, 2*, 30. DOI: 10.1186/1744-8069-2-30.

Breivik, H., Collett, B., Ventafridda, V., Cohen, R., & Gallacher, D. (2006). Survey of pain in Europe: Prevalence, impact on daily life, and treatment. *European Journal of Pain, 10*, 287–333.

Brown, K. W., & Ryan, R. M. (2003). The benefits of being present: mindfulness and its role in psychological well-being. *Journal of Personality and Social Psychology, 84*, 822–848.

Cheung, M. N., Wong, T. C., Yap, J. C., & Chen, P. P. (2008). Validation of the Chronic Pain Acceptance Questionnaire (CPAQ) in Cantonese-speaking Chinese patients. *Journal of Pain, 9*(9), 823–832.

Chomsky, N. (1959). A review of *Verbal Behavior* by B. F. Skinner. *Language, 35*, 26–58.

Chou, R., Baisden, J., Carragee, E. J., Resnick, D. K., Shaffer, W. O., & Loeser, J. D. (2009). Surgery for low back pain: a review of the evidence for an American Pain Society Clinical Practice Guideline. *Spine, 34*, 1094–1109.

Clark, D. A. (1995). Perceived limitations of standard cognitive therapy: A consideration of efforts to revise Beck's theory and therapy. *Journal of Cognitive Psychotherapy, 9*, 153–172.

Crombez, G., Eccleston, C., Van Hamme, G., & De Vlieger, P. (2008). Attempting to solve the problem of pain: A questionnaire study in acute and chronic pain patients. *Pain, 137*, 556–563.

Curran, C., Williams, A. C. de C., & Potts, H. W. (2009). Cognitive-behavioral therapy for persistent pain: Does adherence after treatment affect outcome? *European Journal of Pain, 13*, 178–188.

Dahl, J., Wilson, K. G., & Nilsson, A. (2004). Acceptance and commitment therapy and the treatment of persons at risk for long-term disability resulting from stress and pain symptoms: A preliminary randomized trial. *Behavior Therapy, 35*, 785–801.

Eccleston, C., Williams, A. C. de. C., & Morley, S. (2009). Psychological therapies for the management of chronic pain (excluding headache) in adults. *Cochrane Database of Systematic Reviews, 2*. Art. No.: CD007407. DOI: 10.1002/14651858.CD007407.pub2.

Elliott, A. M., Smith, B. H., Penny, K. I., Smith, W. C., & Chambers, W. A. (1999). The epidemiology of chronic pain in the community. *Lancet, 354,* 1248–1252.

Esteve, R., Ramírez-Maestre, C., & López-Martínez, A. E. (2007). Adjustment to chronic pain: The role of pain acceptance, coping strategies, and pain-related cognitions. *Annals of Behavioral Medicine, 33,* 1–10.

Flor, H., Fydrich, T., & Turk, D. C. (1992). Efficacy of multidisciplinary pain treatment centers: A meta-analytic review. *Pain, 49,* 221–230.

Fordyce, W. E. (1976). *Behavioral methods for chronic pain and illness.* St. Louis, MO: Mosby.

Fordyce, W. E., Fowler, R. S., Lehmann, J. F., & DeLateur, B. J. (1968). Some implications of learning in problems of chronic pain. *Journal of Chronic Diseases, 21,* 179–190.

Foster, N. E., Thomas, E., Bishop, A., Dunn, K. M., & Main, C. J. (2010). Distinctiveness of psychological obstacles to recovery in low back pain patients in primary care. *Pain, 148,* 398–406.

Franks, C. M., & Wilson, G. T. (1974). *Annual review of behaviour therapy: Theory and practice.* New York: Brunner/Mazel.

Gatchel, R. J., Peng, Y. B., Peters, M. L., Fuchs, P. N., & Turk, D. C. (2007). The biopsychosocial approach to chronic pain: Scientific advances and future directions. *Psychological Bulletin, 133,* 581–624.

Geiser, D. S. (1992). *A comparison of acceptance-focused and control-focused psychological treatments in a chronic pain treatment center.* Unpublished doctoral dissertation, University of Nevada, Reno.

Grossman, P., Tiefenthaler-Gilmer, U., Raysz, A., & Kesper, U. (2007). Mindfulness training as an intervention for fibromyalgia: Evidence of postintervention and three-year follow-up benefits in well-being. *Psychotherapy and Psychosomatics, 76,* 226–233.

Guedj, E. (2009). Neuroimaging findings in fibromyalgia: What clinical impact? *Joint, Bone, Spine, 76,* 224–226.

Haetzman, M., Elliott, A. M., Smith, B. H., Hannaford, P., & Chambers, W. A. (2003). Chronic pain and the use of conventional and alternative therapy. *Family Practice, 20,* 147–154.

Hayes, S. C. (2004). Acceptance and commitment therapy, Relational frame theory, and the third wave of behavior therapy. *Behavior Therapy, 35,* 639–665.

Hayes, S. C., Luoma, J. B., Bond, F. W., Masuda, A., & Lillis, J. (2006). Acceptance and commitment therapy: Model, processes and outcomes. *Behaviour Research and Therapy, 44,* 1–25.

Hayes, S. C., Strosahl, K., & Wilson, K. G. (1999). *Acceptance and commitment therapy: An experiential approach to behavior change.* New York: Guilford Press.

Hayes, S. C., & Wilson, K. G. (2003). Mindfulness: Method and process. *Clinical Psychology: Science and Practice, 10,* 161–165.

Hoffman, B. M., Papas, R. K., Chatkoff, D. K., & Kerns, R. D. (2007). Meta-analysis of psychological interventions for chronic low back pain. *Health Psychology, 26,* 1–9.

Kabat-Zinn, J. (1982). An outpatient program in behavioral medicine for chronic pain patients based on the practice of mindfulness meditation: Theoretical considerations and preliminary results. *General Hospital Psychiatry, 4,* 33–47.

Kabat-Zinn, J., Lipworth, L., & Burney, R. (1985). The clinical use of mindfulness meditation for the self-regulation of chronic pain. *Journal of Behavioral Medicine, 8,* 163–190.

Kabat-Zinn, H., Lipworth, L., Burney, R., & Sellers, W. (1986). Four-year follow-up of a meditation-based program for the self-regulation of chronic pain: Treatment outcomes and compliance. *Clinical Journal of Pain, 2,* 159–173.

Longmore, R. J., & Worrell, M. (2007). Do we need to challenge thoughts in cognitive behavior therapy? *Clinical Psychology Review, 27,* 173–187.

Main, C. J., Sullivan, M. J. L., & Watson, P. J. (2008). *Pain management: Practical applications of the biopsychosocial perspective in clinical and occupational settings.* Edinburgh, Scotland: Elsevier.

Martell, B. A., O'Connor, P. G., Kerns, R. D., Becker, W. C., Morales, K. H., Kosten, T. R., et al. (2007). Systematic review: Opioid treatment for chronic back pain: Prevalence, efficacy, and association with addiction. *Annals of Internal Medicine, 146,* 116–127.

Mason, V. L., Mathias, B., & Skevington, S. M. (2008). Accepting low back pain: Is it related to a good quality of life? *Clinical Journal of Pain, 24,* 22–29.

Mayer, T. G., & Gatchel, R. J. (1988). *Functional restoration for spinal disorders: The sports medicine approach.* Philadelphia: Lea & Febiger.

McCracken, L. M. (1998). Learning to live with the pain: Acceptance of pain predicts adjustment in persons with chronic pain. *Pain, 74*(1), 21–27.

McCracken, L. M. (1999). Behavioral constituents of chronic pain acceptance: Results from factor analysis of the Chronic Pain Acceptance Questionnaire. *Journal of Back and Musculoskeletal Rehabilitation, 13,* 93–100.

McCracken, L. M. (2005). *Contextual cognitive-behavioral therapy for chronic pain.* Seattle, WA: IASP Press.

McCracken, L. M., Gauntlett-Gilbert, J., & Eccleston, C. (2010). Acceptance of pain in adolescents with chronic pain: Validation of an adapted assessment instrument and preliminary correlation analyses. *European Journal of Pain, 14,* 316–320.

McCracken, L. M., MacKichan, F., & Eccleston, C. (2007). Contextual cognitive-behavioral therapy for severely disabled chronic pain sufferers: Effectiveness and clinically significant change. *European Journal of Pain, 11,* 314–322.

McCracken, L. M., & Vowles, K. E. (2008). A prospective analysis of acceptance and values in patients with chronic pain. *Health Psychology, 27,* 215–220.

McCracken, L. M., Vowles, K. E., and Eccleston, C. (2004). Acceptance of chronic pain: component analysis and a revised assessment method. *Pain, 107*(1-2),159–166.

McCracken, L. M., Vowles, K. E., & Eccleston, C. (2005). Acceptance-based treatment for persons with complex, long standing chronic pain: A preliminary analysis of treatment outcome in comparison to a waiting phase. *Behaviour Research and Therapy, 43,* 1335–1346.

McCracken, L. M., & Yang, S. (2006). The role of values in a contextual cognitive-behavioral approach to chronic pain. *Pain, 123,* 137–145.

Melzack, R., & Wall, P. D. (1965). Pain mechanisms: A new theory. *Science, 19,* 971–979.

Miller, W. R., & Rollnick, S. (2002). *Motivational interviewing: Preparing people to change* (2nd ed.). New York: Guilford Press.

Morley, S., Eccleston, C., & Williams, A. C. de. C. (1999). Systematic review and meta-analysis of randomized controlled trials of cognitive behaviour therapy and behaviour therapy for chronic pain in adults, excluding headache. *Pain, 80,* 1–13.

Morone, N. E., Greco, C. M., & Weiner, D. K. (2008). Mindfulness meditation for the treatment of chronic low back pain in older adults: A randomized controlled pilot study. *Pain, 134,* 310–319.

Nilges, P., Koster, B., & Schmidt, C. O. (2007). Pain acceptance—concept and validation of a German version of the chronic pain acceptance questionnaire. *Schmerz, 21*(1), 57–58, 60–67.

Nnoaham, K. E., & Kumbang, J. (2010). Transcutaneous electrical nerve stimulation (TENS) for chronic pain. *Cochrane Database of Systematic Reviews* 2008, Issue 3. Art. No.: CD003222. DOI: 10.1002/14651858. CD003222.pub2.

Ostelo, R. W. J. G., van Tulder, M. W., Vlaeyen, J. W. S., Linton, S. J., Morley, S. J., & Assendelft, W. J. J. (2005). Behavioural treatment of chronic low-back pain. *Cochrane Database of Systematic Reviews,* Issue 1. Art. No.: CD002014. DOI: 10.1002/14651858.CD002014.pub2.

Pradhan, E. K., Baumgarten, M., Langenberg, P., Handwerger, B., Gilpin, A. D., Magyari, T., et al. (2007). Effect of mindfulness-based stress reduction in rheumatoid arthritis patients. *Arthritis and Rheumatism, 15,* 1134–1142.

Reneman, M. F., Dijkstra, A., Geertzen, J. H., & Dijkstra, P. U. (in press). Psychometric properties of chronic pain acceptance questionnaires: A systematic review. *European Journal of Pain.*

Rogers, C. R. (1946). Significant aspects of client-centered therapy. *American Psychologist, 1,* 415–422.

Sagula, D., & Rice, K. G. (2004). The effectiveness of mindfulness training on the grieving process and emotional well-being of chronic pain patients. *Journal of Clinical Psychology in Medical Settings, 11,* 333–342.

Sephton, S. E., Salmon, P., Weissbecker, I., Ulmer, C., Floyd, A., Hoover, K., et al. (2007). Mindfulness meditation alleviates depressive symptoms in women with fibromyalgia: Results of a randomized clinical trial. *Arthritis & Rheumatism, 57,* 77–85.

Skinner, B. F. (1953). *Science and human behavior.* New York: Macmillan.

Skinner, B. F. (1981). Selection by consequences. *Science, 213,* 501–504.

Smeets, R. J. E. M., Vlaeyen, J. W. S., Kester, A. D. M., & Knottnerus, J. A. (2006). Reduction of pain catastrophizing mediates the outcomes of both physical and cognitive-behavioral treatment in chronic low back pain. *Journal of Pain, 7,* 261–271.

Tsai, M., Kohlenberg, R. J., Kanter, J. W., Kohlenberg, B., Follette, W. C., & Callaghan, G. M. (2008). *A guide to functional analytic psychotherapy: Awareness, courage, love, and behaviorism.* New York: Springer.

Turk, D. C., Meichenbaum, D., & Genest, M. (1983). *Pain and behavioural medicine: A cognitive-behavioral perspective.* New York: Guilford Press.

Viane, I., Crombez, G., Eccleston, C., Poppe, C., Devulder, J., Van Houdenhove, B., et al. (2003). Acceptance of pain is an independent predictor of mental well-being in patients with chronic pain: Empirical evidence and reappraisal. *Pain, 106,* 65–72.

Vowles, K. E., & McCracken, L. M. (2008). Acceptance and values-based action in chronic pain: A study of effectiveness and treatment process. *Journal of Consulting and Clinical Psychology, 76,* 397–407.

Vowles, K. E., & McCracken, L. M. (2010). Comparing the influence of psychological flexibility and traditional pain management coping strategies on chronic pain treatment outcomes. *Behaviour Research & Therapy, 48,* 141–146.

Vowles, K. E., McCracken, L. M., & Eccleston, C. (2007). Processes of behavior change in interdisciplinary treatment of chronic pain: Contributions of pain intensity, catastrophizing, and acceptance. *European Journal of Pain, 11,* 779–787.

Vowles, K. E., McCracken, L. M., McLeod, C., & Eccleston, C. (2008). The Chronic Pain Acceptance Questionnaire: Confirmatory factor analysis and identification of patient subgroups. *Pain, 140*(2), 284–291.

Vowles, K. E., McNeil, D. W., Gross, R. T., McDaniel, M., Mouse, A., Bates, M., et al. (2007). Effects of pain acceptance and pain control strategies on physical impairment in individuals with chronic low back pain. *Behavior Therapy, 38,* 412–425.

Vowles, K. E., Wetherell, J. L., & Sorrell, J. T. (2009). Targeting acceptance, mindfulness, and values-based action in chronic pain: Findings of two preliminary trials of an outpatient group-based intervention. *Cognitive and Behavioral Practice, 16,* 49–58.

Wicksell, R. K., Ahlqvist, J., Bring, A., Melin, L., & Olsson, G. L. (2008). Can exposure and acceptance strategies improve functioning and life satisfaction in people with chronic pain and whiplash-associated disorders (WAD)? A randomized controlled trial. *Cognitive Behaviour Therapy, 37,* 169–182.

Wicksell, R. K., Melin, L., Lekander, M., & Olsson, G. L. (2009). Evaluating the effectivenss of exposure and acceptance strategies to improve functioning and quality of life in longstanding pediatric pain—a randomized controlled trial. *Pain, 141,* 248–257.

Wicksell, R. K., Melin, L., & Olsson, G. L. (2007). Exposure and acceptance in the rehabilitation of adolescents with idiopathic chronic pain—a pilot study. *European Journal of Pain, 11,* 267–274.

Wicksell, R. K., Olsson, G. L., & Melin, L. (2009). The Chronic Pain Acceptance Questionnaire (CPAQ)—further validation including a confirmatory factor analysis and a comparison with the Tampa Scale of Kinesiophobia. *European Journal of Pain, 13,* 760–768.

3

ANALYSIS AND TREATMENT OF EPILEPSY USING MINDFULNESS, ACCEPTANCE, VALUES, AND COUNTERMEASURES

JoAnne Dahl & Tobias Lundgren
Department of Psychology, University of Uppsala, Sweden

In this chapter you will be introduced to behavioral treatment of epilepsy and related problems. You will learn about the history of behavioral treatment for epilepsy and how respondent and operant principles can provide a psychological understanding of epileptic seizures and related problems. You will also learn about outcome and process research into behavioral treatments for epilepsy and a model for the treatment of epilepsy based on acceptance and commitment therapy (ACT).

The word "epilepsy" is derived from the Greek word meaning "to seize" and refers to an individual being seized by an epileptic attack. From the traditional perspective of a pathological or mechanistic model, the epileptic seizure is seen as the symptom of damaged brain cells producing dysfunctional activity, or what is called "paroxysmal" activity. In the medical model, seizure occurrence is seen to be random, and no consideration is given to internal or external factors. Epilepsy is generally classified into categories of partial and generalized seizures, referring to how much of the brain is affected. Medical treatment of choice is generally antiepileptic drugs. The general principle of these drugs is to reduce nerve cell reactivity. Side effects including impaired cognitive function and emotional disturbances are common, and a significant number of individuals with epilepsy continue to experience seizures despite optimal medication.

In contrast, the behavioral medical model views epilepsy as a predisposition or seizure tendency arising from intrinsic and extrinsic factors that can facilitate or inhibit seizure occurrence.

Nonspecific facilitating factors include sleep (Wolf, 2005), high fever, and excessive alcohol intake or other toxins. More specific known eliciting factors are sensory (flashing lights, sudden sounds, smells) and cognitive inputs (stress-related tasks) that directly activate certain cortical areas that, due to some functional instability (genetic or caused by damage), elicit an epileptic discharge. The behavioral medical model entails both the underlying pathophysiology along with principles of conditioning.

Conditioning mechanisms related to the epileptic seizure have been under study for more than century. As early as 1881, Gowers published a series of studies illustrating that the epileptic seizure was actually a chain of behaviors, which could be interrupted by manipulating parts of the body (Gowers, 1881). Gowers identified the actual chain of seizure behavior and proceeded to change the context by both specific and general stimulation. Specific stimulation could be a manipulation of that body part that is first influenced by the epileptogenic activity, for example by rubbing the affected hand or smelling an arousing aroma. Around the same time, Brown-Sequard (1857) presented a series of case studies also showing successful control of seizures using sensory stimulation contingent on the seizure start. Somewhat later, Jackson (1931) demonstrated how a motor seizure could be stopped by rubbing the parts of the body affected by the seizure activity. These studies provide a sense of our early understanding of conditioning of the epileptic seizure as well as evidence of the effectiveness of behavioral techniques in the control of the seizure event. The general principle provided by these authors is that of *competitive recruitment*. Epileptic seizures are elicited by groups of hyperexcitable neurons in the brain. In some seizures, these groups have specific and predictable behavioral correlates, for example a sensation in the limbs. By stimulating these behavioral correlates, normal brain cell activity can be recruited and the progress of hyperexcitability can be blocked. By increasing normal activity, the hypersynchronization of the seizure focus is reduced or stopped altogether. Using this principle of competitive recruitment, many more studies from the 1950s showed that seizures in animals could be elicited and interrupted (Efron, 1956; Gelhorn, 1947).

Efron (1956) was the first to demonstrate how *second order conditioning* could be used to control seizures of a jazz singer who tended to seize while performing onstage. Efron first conditioned the smell of jasmine to the high-seizure-risk situation of performing onstage as well as to the first links of seizure behavior. This appeared to lower cortical activity, and seizures subsided. Efron subsequently paired the jasmine smell to a bracelet and finally to the thought of the bracelet. This study showed how seizures could be controlled by counteracting the seizure start with a decrease in the cortical activity, similar to those reports of the previous century.

When electroencephalographic (EEG) technology became available, conditioning mechanisms for epilepsy became further understood. Using a video EEG, Forster, Ptacek, Peterson, Chun, and Bengzon (1964) showed in a series of studies over a thirty-year period how seizures could be manipulated using operant conditioning methods. Studying children with reflex epilepsy, Forster was able to identify seizure-triggering stimuli and specific thresholds for these stimuli. Children were exposed to seizure-triggering stimuli and at the same time taught to perform a distracting ritual. Forster demonstrated nearly complete seizure control using these methods along with significant reductions in epileptoform abnormalities for more than thirty children who had drug refractory seizures.

Conditioning and the Epileptic Seizure

Fenwick (1994) theorized the conditioning mechanism underlying seizure and suggested that this may be used as the basis for the behavioral treatment of epilepsy. Fenwick proposes that seizures occur when populations of neurons surrounding the epileptic focus become sufficiently excited and subsequently spread. He suggests that these epileptogenic activities in the brain act in a predictable manner and can at any point be influenced by the behavior of the individual. Fenwick refers to the monkey model of Lockard and Ward (1980) conceptualizing the conditioning mechanism in terms of what they call "group one" and "group two" neurons. These authors define group one neurons as the "pacemaker" collection, which is consistently firing epileptogenic activity. Group two, on the other hand, are those neurons surrounding the group one neurons, and these are only partially affected. Group two neurons mostly behave normally but occasionally get recruited by group one neurons and, when this happens, spread epileptogenic activity out and away from the focus, resulting in the epileptic seizure. Typically, the individual may be aware of this movement from the first sign of the seizure onset to the full-blown seizure, as the activity moves out throughout the brain. Lockard and Ward (1980) showed that not all animals with damaged brains develop seizures. The authors concluded that brain damage creates a predisposition to epilepsy but the behavior response to the dysfunction is critical to whether epilepsy actually develops. This was based on the observation of monkeys who increased activity contingent on seizure start but never developed seizures, whereas those who decreased activity developed seizures.

Based on a functional analysis of the particular conditioning or learning history for each individual, treatment strategies include the principles of prediction, prevention, interruption of seizure behavior, and reinforcement of seizure control. Individuals with epilepsy are taught to discriminate between intrinsic and extrinsic factors associated with seizure onset (high risk) as well as occasions of few or no seizures (low risk). High and low risk factors include situations, activities, and emotions, as well as physical states. Prediction involves a mindful awareness and data collection of constellations of events and reactions correlated to seizure occurrence. Ability to predict a seizure aids the individual in increasing antiepileptic behaviors and thus preventing seizure occurrence.

Interruption

The seizure process can be interrupted at different stages. At the initial signs of the seizure (often called the "aura"), when the discharge is locally restricted, the behavioral correlate can be used as the discriminative stimuli to initiate nonspecific or specific techniques that target sensory or cognitive stimulation, either increasing or decreasing cortical activity. The specific techniques activate the epileptogenic circumscribed cortical areas involved in the seizure process. Most individuals with epilepsy have attempted to interrupt their own seizures, with varying results. Most commonly, individuals either increase or decrease cortical activity, depending on the upward or downward shift in cortical activity induced by the seizure trigger. Based on the functional analysis, the countermeasure would be determined by the baseline state and direction of the seizure trigger (Dahl, 1992). If the trigger is characterized by high cortical excitation, the countermeasure would constitute a transition toward reduced excitation. If the trigger is a drowsy state, the countermeasure requires an increase in cortical activity. Examples of techniques used to increase cortical activity include stimulation of different senses such as chewing ginger, smelling strong aromas, use of vibrators, and blowing whistles (Dahl, Brorson, & Melin, 1992). Decreasing cortical activities has been achieved by, for example, applying relaxation, yoga, meditation, and breathing techniques, all aiming at stimulating the parasympathetic nerve system. In general, individuals are taught the underlying principles of how seizures have been conditioned and subsequently learn to apply appropriate countermeasures contingent on the start of the seizure.

Function

The functional analysis aims at identifying the "function" of the seizure, as with any recurring behavior. Perhaps due to the traditional view of epilepsy, it may even be provocative to assume that seizures serve a "function." Actually, the term "functional seizures" in the medical sphere refers to psychogenic or nonepileptic seizures. In the behavioral medicine model, we refer to function as in the operant conceptualization, as operating on the environment. The seizures have certain effects on both the individual experiencing them, as well as others in the immediate environment, and these effects may be categorized as positive or negative reinforcement or punishment. In a long-term study it was shown that the majority of children with refractory seizures reported a wish to retain at least some seizures, in contrast to the wishes of parents, teachers, and physicians that they become seizure free (Dahl et al., 1992). Children in this study reported enjoying positive reinforcement contingent on seizure occurrence in the form of special privileges, attention, feeling special, and physical contact, as well as self-stimulation and feeling of euphoria.

Negative reinforcement is when seizures are "used" to get out of what might be perceived as a difficult or demanding situation. In this same long-term study, children and young persons reported desired effects of seizures in that they got relief from anxiety and demands at school and at home, and even got away from abuse (Dahl et al., 1992).

In sum, the understanding of the seizure's function is critical as the underpinning to designing a treatment strategy. If an individual's seizures function in a desirable direction by effectively reducing something undesirable, conventional treatment is not likely to work.

Reviews of Psychological Treatment of Epilepsy

The literature on psychological treatments for epilepsy has been reviewed a number of times since the mid-1970s. Mostofsky and

Balaschak (1977) reviewed sixty published treatment studies, Goldstein (1990) added eleven subsequent treatment studies, and there is a more recent review (Ramaratnam, Baker, & Goldstein, 2004). In general, studies of psychological treatments for epilepsy are seen to be too small and methodology too inadequate to support the use of these treatments for epilepsy. However, new studies have been conducted since 2004, with interesting results (Lundgren, Dahl, Melin, & Kies, 2006; Lundgren, Dahl, Yardi, & Melin, 2008).

Acceptance and Commitment Therapy and Epilepsy

Acceptance and commitment therapy (ACT) consists of six core components: acceptance, defusion, values, contact with the present moment, self-as-context, and committed action. The general aim of ACT treatment is to create psychological flexibility around stuck behavior patterns and establish contact with direct and natural contingencies of valued directions.

With regard to epilepsy, acceptance entails embracing aspects of the illness that cannot be changed. An individual with epilepsy can learn to accept his predisposition to seize, along with his learning history or previous conditioning of thoughts, feelings, fears, and functions of the seizure. Rather than regard epilepsy as the enemy and going to war to fight seizures, the individual can learn to accept the risk of seizing while mobilizing himself toward living a vital life. Acceptance is routinely observed as "antiepileptic" in EEG laboratory examinations. It is commonly reported that when patients are hooked up to the EEG video monitoring in order to document seizures, no seizures occur. In this situation, patients "try" to show the seizure and this "trying" or accepting seizure occurrence more often than not dramatically lowers the probability of seizure occurrence (Dahl, 1992).

Defusion entails training the ability to view a thought as a thought rather than as a reality or a truth. It is helpful for the individual to be aware of verbal constructions associated with epilepsy and seizures. There is a significant amount of stigmatization associated with having the diagnosis of epilepsy, and defusing from thoughts surrounding this stigmatization can be beneficial.

Contact with the present moment is the ACT component that helps the individual to get into contact with natural contingencies of real life rather than live in a fantasized past or future. Individuals with epilepsy are often seen to engage in problems of the past or worries about the future. Learning how to make contact with the here and now provides the means to be able to let go of the struggle with epilepsy and everything associated with it and start taking steps in a valued direction.

Self-as-context helps the individual to create a place or perspective from which to observe the changing content of life. From this observer position, all forms of life can be seen to be impermanent. "Thoughts, feelings, and the physical body are constantly changing and therefore in some sense I cannot 'be' that content. I can be the observer of the ever-changing topography of my life." With regard to epilepsy, this could mean that the individual learns that "I have epilepsy" but "I am not epilepsy." Being able to distinguish "self" from life experiences allows the individual to put epilepsy in perspective. Epilepsy and seizures become simply one of many changing experiences in life and do not define one's identity.

Values in ACT function as the motivation for the behavior changes needed in order to get back on a vital life track. "Values illness" is a term used to describe the problem of giving up important valued life directions in the service of controlling symptoms. Symptom or seizure control can become a main occupation, while activities connected to natural positive reinforcement become neglected. The more the individual struggles and organizes her life around prevention, avoidance, and control of her seizures, the less time she has to be involved in meaningful life activities. As the avoidance agenda grows, quality of life dissipates. In the ACT treatment, identifying valued directions provides a compass for finding a path toward a meaningful, vital life. This compass also illustrates the discrepancy of behavior that has veered off course because of its focus on avoiding seizures. An example of finding valued directions is deciding how one wants to act in loving social relationships. Getting in contact with this value helps the individual to see that behavior such as staying at home to avoid having seizures can significantly reduce a social life.

The final ACT component is committed action. This component entails a commitment regarding actual steps the individual with epilepsy is willing to take here and now in order to reclaim a valued life together with any obstacles that present themselves. With regard to epilepsy, this component would be seen as asking the individual to commit to steps in identified valued directions together with his tendency to seize and his learning history.

Acceptance and Change

Early treatment protocols for epilepsy focused primarily on interrupting or aborting seizures. An ACT protocol for epilepsy combines acceptance and change to increase valued living and interrupt ongoing seizures (Lundgren et al., 2006). The combination of acceptance and change in treatment protocols is common in developed behavior therapies (Linehan, Armstrong, Suarez, Allmon, & Heard, 1991; Jacobson, 1992; Hayes, Strosahl, & Wilson, 1999). Acceptance is an action that involves change, and the effectiveness of actions is measured in reference to the client's values and goals. For example, in integrated behavioral couples therapy (IBCT), acceptance is used to change unworkable communication patterns (Jacobson, 1992). In the epilepsy work, accepting the tendency to seize or accepting private events (thoughts, memories, emotions, and sensations) associated with seizures is not the same as accepting the actual seizure occurrence. Acceptance is not a passive process but an active choice of experiencing private events associated with epilepsy that function as barriers to valued living. Acceptance of private events has proven to be a crucial part of the work to stimulate valued living (Lundgren, Dahl, & Hayes, 2008). Furthermore, perhaps paradoxically, acceptance may alter the response to previous seizure triggers and actually function as a countermeasure. An example of how acceptance might serve these two functions can be seen in the case of Carlos. This young man had learned to associate seizure occurrence with accidents and getting himself hurt. These fears had successively driven Carlos into avoiding many of the activities he valued, and his quality of life diminished. Carlos learned in ACT treatment to make room for and accept his conditioned fears, and this served as a base for him to take steps and reclaim valued directions. The fact that Carlos then became more active had the direct effect of reducing paroxysmal activity, making seizures less likely. In this way, acceptance of fears correlated with seizures facilitated behavior change, which subsequently acted as antiepileptic behavior. During ACT for epilepsy, a client and a therapist need to learn as much about seizure triggers and consequences of seizures as possible in order to build an individual treatment plan. Research suggests that both acceptance and values interventions decrease the probability of seizure occurrence and increase quality of life (Lundgren, Dahl, et al., 2008). In the next section, a treatment protocol for epilepsy is described.

A Short-Term ACT Treatment Protocol for Severe Epilepsy

A short, four-session treatment protocol was developed for participants from an institution for epilepsy in South Africa and an epilepsy clinic in India. The general aim of this ACT treatment was to create psychological flexibility and space for valued living. Furthermore, the protocol was designed to integrate previous work on behavior modification of epilepsy into a model based on acceptance, values, and mindfulness processes. Following is an outline of the main objectives for the protocol.

Session one is conducted in an individual setting and focuses on establishing the "life compass," a metaphor used to identify and get into contact with valued life directions. These valued directions are used as a calibrating instrument for staying on the "right" valued path. The participant learns to discriminate this valued direction as well as recognize the discrepancy when wandering off the valued direction path. Discrepancies between what the participants say they want to be and how they actually behave come to light. For example, one man said he valued being a present, active father with his children, and at the same time he saw that he was avoiding contact with his children, embarrassed that he might have a seizure while with them. This father was able to discriminate between what behaviors were on track and which were in the service of avoidance. Valued directions are identified in ten life dimensions: working, leisure time activities, education and personal development, social relationships, intimate relationships, spirituality, caretaking, health, family, and community involvement. Participants are asked to (a) identify constant, deep valued directions in each dimension in terms of quality or striving, (b) rate (from 0 to 10) the general importance of each dimension, (c) rate (from 0 to 10) their own behavior invested in creating this identified quality in the past two weeks, (d) calculate the discrepancy between the ratings of importance and the rating of current behavior, and (e) identify or name the obstacles believed to stand between current and desired actions. In other words, what is the "excuse" for not fully living according to the description of how one wants to live? All rules of contingencies are mapped out, such as "I would like to have an intimate relationship, but first I need to get rid of my seizures." All experiential avoidance during the session is noted. Identifying valued directions is often painful, since it becomes obvious when doing the life compass that one's behavior is perhaps largely steered by wanting to avoid seizures rather than by living in one's valued directions. The subsequent sadness regarding this discrepancy appears, and the participant relates to this discomfort, here and now in the session. In this way, this first session provides a sample of behavior, showing potential influences on behavior, contact with valued directions, experiential avoidance, fusion with rules and life stories, willingness to feel discomfort, and degree of commitment to valued directions. A functional analysis of the behavior chain leading up to a seizure is also conducted.

Sessions two and three consist of group sessions with six to eight participants, lasting three hours. The aim of these group sessions is to put ACT core components into practice, building on the functional analyses created in session one. Members of the group can be used as instruments in the dramatization of ACT metaphors. Experiential metaphors are developed in order to provide the experience of these core processes. During our experience delivering treatment both in South Africa and in India, there was no common language readily available, and so dramatization of metaphors facilitated the experience of core components. Valued directions could be symbolized by using pictures or music or by activities such as dance or sports. Defusion could be experienced by first identifying words that were charged with feelings and then playfully sounding these words while dancing or singing. Learning to relate in a more accepting, flexible manner to words and thoughts is easily done in a group, for example by acting out the bus metaphor (Hayes et al., 1999). This same metaphor may be used for practicing taking steps in valued directions together with verbal obstacles.

The final session, like the first session, is done individually. This final session aims at supporting the participant in taking steps in his home environment together with the conditioned verbal obstacles. New commitments to taking steps in valued directions are made. Clients are also helped to develop countermeasures as possible alternative responses to early triggers for seizures.

For both of these studies, in South Africa (Lundgren et al., 2006) and in India (Lundgren, Dahl, et al., 2008), dependent measures used to evaluate the effects of this treatment model were the following: seizure frequency and duration, quality of life, vitality, and experiential avoidance with regard to epilepsy. Standardized measures such as the WHO Quality of Life (WHOQOL-BREF; World Health Organization, 1996; Amir et al., 2000) and Satisfaction with Life Scale (SWLS) (Diener, Emmons, Larsen, & Griffin, 1985) were used along with an instrument developed for this study: the Bull's-Eye and Acceptance and Action Epilepsy Questionnaire (AAEpQ) (Lundgren, 2006; Lundgren, Dahl, & Hayes, 2008). The Bull's-Eye measures participants' functioning level along with persistency and vitality in actions. It consists of four diagrammed dartboards. Each of the first three dartboards asks the participant to choose a life domain or valued direction that he would like to improve in or move toward. The participant is asked to rate, by placing an X on the board, how close he has come to living in this direction of vitality and meaningfulness in the past two weeks. An X close to the bull's-eye means that the client is living consistent with chosen values in that life domain. An X far from the middle of the dartboard suggests that the client is living in a way that is inconsistent with his values. The final dartboard asks the participant to rate how often he attempts to follow (or is persistent in following) his direction in the face of difficulties or obstacles.

Results

As far as we are aware, there are only two studies evaluating ACT and epilepsy that have been done in recent years (Lundgren et al., 2006; Lundgren, Dahl, et al., 2008). The results show that a brief intervention for persons suffering from epilepsy significantly increases quality of like and significantly decreases the frequency and duration (combined into a seizure index) of epileptic seizures as compared to active control groups at post-treatment, at six months, and at one year follow-up. Both studies (Lundgren et al., 2006; Lundgren, Dahl, et al., 2008) were randomized controlled design studies. Participants in Lundgren et al. (2006) ($N = 27$) were randomized into one of the two groups, ACT or supportive treatment (ST). In Lundgren, Dahl, et al. (2008) ($N = 18$), participants were randomized into either an ACT condition or a Yoga condition. Inclusion criteria in both studies were the following: EEG-verified epilepsy diagnosis, able and willing to participate, no other ongoing progressive illnesses, and between 18 and 55 years of age. Changes in medication during the project period were an exclusion criterion. Clients who were excluded from the study were allowed to continue treatment for ethical reasons but excluded from measurement. Figure 3.1 shows a graph of the results of the seizure index from the Lundgren et al. (2006) study. Table 3.1 displays results of the quality of life results from Lundgren et al. (2006).

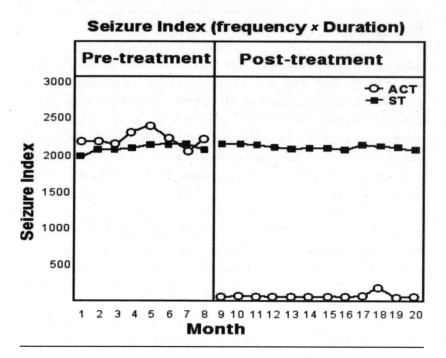

Figure 3.1 Participants in the ACT group have reduced their seizure index significantly following the intervention as compared to the support treatment (ST) group. There are no significant changes in the ST group. Intervention takes place during the eighth and ninth month.

TABLE 3.1

Description of the quality of life measures SWLS and WHOQOL-BREF as to mean, standard deviation, and effect size.

Cohen's d, interaction effect, and Tukey post-hoc test at pre, post, six months and one year.

Dependent variable	Group	Pre M (SD)	Post M (SD)	6 mo M (SD)	1 yr M (SD)	Interaction effect Cohen's d	Tukey
SWLS	ACT	16.29 (5.82)	23.28 (4.58)	27.07 (4.56)	27.07 (3.94)	$F_{(3,75)} =$ 18.497**	Post*
	ST	17.23 (5.99)	13.85 (5.98)	14.46 (6.28)	15.77 (5.17)	Post 1.72	6 mo*
						6 mo 2.29	1 yr*
						1 yr 2.47	
WHOQOL-BREF	ACT	52.36 (9.62)	58.36 (9.66)	61.21 (8.13)	66.07 (6.04)	$F_{(3,75)} =$ 9.739**	Post Ns
	ST	54.69 (6.50)	55.31 (6.59)	56.08 (8.58)	51.85 (9.51)	Post 0.37	6 mo Ns
						6 mo 0.61	1 yr *
						1 yr 1.78	

** $p < 0.001$.   * $p < 0.05$.   Ns: not significant.

The results of Lundgren, Dahl, et al. (2008) show that there was a significant decrease of the seizure index in both groups, ACT= $t(9)=3.3$ and ST= $t(7)=3.8$ $p<0.01$. However, the decrease in the ACT group is significantly larger, $t(16)=2.4$. $p<0.05$. The results of the quality of life instruments show that the ACT group increased their quality of life significantly on the WHOQOL-BREF ($F(3,21)=4.49$ $p<0.05$.) and that the Yoga group increased their life quality significantly measured by the SWLS ($F(3,27)=5.50$ $p<0.01$.). Lundgren, Dahl, and Hayes (2008) published a mediation analysis of the results in Lundgren et al. (2006). A series of bootstrapped nonparametric multiple mediator tests showed that pre to follow-up changes in seizures, quality of life, and well-being outcomes were mediated to a degree by ACT process measures of epilepsy-related acceptance or defusion, values attainment, persistence in the face of barriers, or their combination.

Summary

A broadly behavioral approach to epilepsy includes specific control techniques that can cheaply and simply help stop seizure behavior and contextual methods that help the individual to relate to her epilepsy in ways that allow for living fully in valued directions. Integrating countermeasures in an ACT model based on acceptance, mindfulness, and values work seems to increase quality of life and decrease seizure frequency. However, future research is needed to evaluate correlations between our behavioral interventions and physiological measures. At the very least, behavioral treatments using the principles of conditioning that have been documented for more than a century should be made available as a complement to conventional drug therapies. For those who prefer a nondrug approach or for those in developing countries without access to modern antiepileptic drugs, behavioral treatment, which has the most evidence-based support of any of the available alternatives, should be considered.

References

Amir, M., Fleck, M., Herrman, H., Lomachenkov, A., Lucas, R., & Patrick, D. (2000). Reliability, validity and reproducibility of the WHOQOL-BREF in six countries. http://www.hrainc.net/pdf/ISOQOL_2000_Vancouver_BREF.pdf

Brown-Sequard, C. (1857). *Researches on epilepsy: Its artificial production in animals, and its etiology, nature and treatment in man*, Boston: Clapp.

Dahl, J. (1992). *Epilepsy: A behavior medicine approach to assessment and treatment in children.* Göttingen, Germany: Hogrefe & Huber.

Dahl, J. Brorson, L-O., & Melin, L. (1992). Effects of a broad-spectrum behavioral medicine treatment program on children with refractory epileptic seizures: An eight-year follow-up. *Epilepsia, 33*(1), 98–102.

Diener, E., Emmons, R. A., Larsen, R. J., & Griffin, S. (1985). The Satisfaction with Life Scale. *Journal of Personality and Social Psychology, 49,* 71–75.

Efron, R. (1956). Effect of olfactory stimuli in uncinate fits. *Brain, 79,* 267–281.

Fenwick, P. (1994). The behavioral treatment of epilepsy generation and inhibition of seizures. *Neurologic Clinics, 12,* 175–202.

Forster, F., Ptacek, L., Peterson, W., Chun, R., & Bengzon, A. (1964). Stroboscopic-induced seizures altered by extinction techniques. *Transactions of the American Neurological Association, 89,* 136.

Gelhorn, E. (1947). Effects of afferent impulses on cortical suppression areas. *Journal of Neurophysiology, 10,* 125–138.

Goldstein, L. (1990). Behavioral and cognitive behavioral treatments for epilepsy: A progress review. *British Journal of Clinical Psychology, 29,* 257–269.

Gowers, W. (1881). *Epilepsy and other chronic convulsive diseases.* London: Churchill.

Hayes, S. C., Strosahl, K., & Wilson, K. G. (1999). *Acceptance and commitment therapy: An experiential approach to behavior change.* New York: Guilford Press.

Jackson, J. H. (1931). On epilepsy and epileptiform convulsions. In J. Taylor (Ed.), *Selected writings of John Hughlings Jackson* (Vol. 1). London: Hodder and Stoughton.

Jacobson, N. (1992). Behavioral couple therapy: A new beginning. *Behavior Therapy, 23,* 493–506.

Linehan, M. M., Armstrong, H. E., Suarez, A., Allmon, D., & Heard, H. L. (1991). Cognitive-behavioral treatment of chronically parasuicidal borderline patients. *Archives of General Psychiatry, 48,* 1060–1064.

Lockard, J. S., & Ward, A. (1980). *Epilepsy: A window to brain mechanism*s. New York: Raven Press, 51–68.

Lundgren, T. (2006, July). *Validation and reliability data of the Bull's-Eye.* Presentation at the Second World Conference on ACT/RFT, London.

Lundgren, T., Dahl, J., & Hayes, S. C. (2008). Evaluation of mediators of change in the treatment of epilepsy with acceptance and commitment therapy. *Journal of Behavioral Medicine, 31,* 225–235.

Lundgren, T., Dahl, J., Melin, L., & Kies, B. (2006). Evaluation of acceptance and commitment therapy for drug refractory epilepsy: A randomized controlled trial in South Africa—a pilot study. *Epilepsia, 47*(12), 2173–2179.

Lundgren, T., Dahl, J., Yardi, N., & Melin, L. (2008). Evaluation of acceptance and commitment therapy and yoga for epilepsy: A randomized controlled trial in India. *Epilepsy and Behavio*r, *13*(1), 102–108.

Mostofsky, D. I., & Balaschak, B. A. (1977). Psychobiological control of seizures. *Psychological Bulletin, 84,* 723–750.

Ramaratnam, S., Baker, G.A., & Goldstein, L.H. (2008). Psychological treatments for epilepsy. Cochrane Database of Systematic Reviews 2008, Issue 3. Art. No.: CD002029. DOI: 10.1002/14651858.CD002029.pub3

Wolf, P. (2005). From precipitation to inhibition of seizures: Rationale of a therapeutic paradigm. *Epilepsia, 46*(Suppl. 1), 15–16.

World Health Organization. (1996). *WHOQOL-BREF: Introduction, administration and generic version of the assessment.* Geneva, Switzerland: WHO-Programme on Mental Health.

4 Health Behavior Problems in Diabetes, Obesity, and Secondary Prevention

Jennifer A. Gregg, Priscilla Almada,
& Eric Schmidt

San Jose State University

The increasing rates of obesity and diabetes in many of the world's developed and developing nations represent a significant health problem. These problems are devastating to individuals and nations alike in their degree of illness, disability, psychological and social overlay, and economic costs. In the present chapter, we will explore the realized and potential contributions of acceptance and commitment therapy (ACT) and other mindfulness-based approaches to these problems and discuss how interventions such as these may help turn the tide at the level of disease processes, particularly where these disease processes intersect with larger social contexts and with key health-related behaviors.

Obesity

With 400 million people meeting the diagnostic criteria for obesity and another 1.6 billion categorized as overweight, obesity is considered a global epidemic (Haslam & James, 2005). The rapid growth in obesity rates poses a significant threat when paired with the difficulty of weight-loss maintenance, making it one of the most critical public health challenges of the century (National Institutes of Health, 1998).

The consequences of being obese are complex and proliferate physical, psychological, and social health problems, making the overall risk associated with obesity greater than that of smoking, drinking, or poverty (Sturm, 2002; Sturm & Wells, 2001). People who are obese are at increased risk for developing several comorbid health complications, including hypertension, high blood pressure, diabetes, gallbladder disease, cardiovascular disease, kidney disease, heart failure, stroke, some types of cancer, and pregnancy complications (Centers for Disease Control, 2005; Kenchaiah et al., 2002).

Traditional Conceptualization and Approaches

In obesity, the primary goal is often the reduction of overall body mass index (BMI) and maintenance of lost weight. There have been three main types of medical interventions that have received at least some support in the literature toward the goal of the reduction of weight. First, there are lifestyle interventions that include low-fat/low-calorie diets, modification of eating patterns and portions, reduced sodium intake, physical exercise, and education about the causes of obesity and means for maintaining weight loss. These interventions have demonstrated efficacy in reducing weight (Multiple Risk Factor Intervention Trial Research Group, 1990; Tuomilehto et al., 2001). For example, in one study, participants randomly assigned to lifestyle intervention lost an average 4.2 kg at the end of one year and had maintained a loss of 3.5 kg at the end of two years, versus a consistent 0.8 kg loss for control participants after both one and two years (Tuomilehto et al., 2001).

A second form of intervention that has demonstrated efficacy in assisting with weight loss is pharmaceutical—drugs that have been approved to treat obesity, such as orlistat, rimonabant, and sibutramine. These medications have been shown to produce an average of 3 kg (orlistat) to 4 to 5 kg (rimonabant and sibutramine) weight loss after one year in double-blind trials (see Padwal & Majumdar, 2007, for review).

The third form of intervention with support is gastric surgery, which has been shown to be effective for obese and morbidly obese individuals when less invasive treatments have not been effective (Andersen, Backer, Stokholm, & Quaade, 1984; Schauer, Ikramuddin, Gourash, Ramanathan, & Luketich, 2000). Specifically, two-year weight loss rates after gastric surgery for patients in one study were as high as 23.4 percent of body weight, compared to a 0.1 percent weight gain for control patients (Sjostrom et al., 2004).

The use of a weight-loss program involving diet, exercise, and behavior modification can produce an initial weight loss of approximately 10 percent (Wing et al., 2004). This type of weight loss can produce clear health benefits for patients. One study exploring this issue randomly assigned 3,234 obese individuals without diabetes to a lifestyle-modification program, metformin, or a placebo condition. At follow-up (average 2.8 years later), the incidence of diabetes was 4.8 percent, 7.8 percent, and 11.0 percent for lifestyle modification, metformin, and placebo groups respectively. Both lifestyle intervention and metformin significantly reduced the likelihood of developing diabetes, and the lifestyle-intervention program significantly reduced the chances compared to metformin (Knowler et al., 2002).

Even when weight loss is achieved, however, the maintenance of losses is difficult to sustain. Studies have consistently demonstrated poor maintenance rates, and most patients regain weight lost within three to five years of treatment (Perri, 1998; Wadden, Sternberg, Letizia, Stunkard, & Foster, 1989; Wing, 1998).

Psychological Features

Considerable research and literature has been devoted to developing effective weight control interventions, but the problem of unsuccessful weight management may be partly due to a lack of attention to the wider psychological context of being overweight. The psychological features of obesity not only impact an individual's ability to lose weight but are also key factors in weight maintenance (Elfhag & Rossner, 2005).

STIGMA

Obesity is considered one of the last accepted and unchallenged sources of stigmatization and prejudice, in that cultural norms continue to largely condone discrimination, stigma, and maltreatment of obese individuals (Puhl & Heuer, 2009). In addition to being widespread within the general public, discrimination against and stigmatization of obese people is also pervasive among health professions specializing in weight-loss treatment programs (Davis-Coelho, Waltz, & Davis-Coelho, 2000; Maroney & Golub, 1992; Price, Desmond, Krol, Snyder, & O'Connell, 1987; Teachman & Brownell, 2001; Wiese, Wilson, Jones, & Neises, 1992).

SHAME

Related to stigma is the experience of shame related to one's body or weight. Shame is conceptualized as a negative emotional state that typically includes some element of feeling exposed or worthless (Lewis, 1993). A primary source of shame in obesity is social discrimination or stigma (Puhl & Brownell, 2003), and stigmatizing experiences are thought to serve as a potential trigger for body shame experiences (Friedman et al., 2005). In a study examining the effect of shame on weight-loss maintenance, Burk-Braxton (1996) reported that at eight months post–successful weight loss, individuals who had not maintained their weight loss had significantly higher rates of guilt and shame than maintainers.

Emotional Eating

Another psychological factor related to obesity is the concept of "emotional eating." Emotional eating is the use of food consumption as a coping mechanism used to regulate mood (Byrne, Cooper, & Fairburn, 2003; Ganley, 1989). A comprehensive literature review found that 75 percent of obese participants receiving weight-loss treatment were characterized as being emotional eaters (Ganley, 1989).

Mindfulness/Acceptance Conceptualization

Given the psychological factors deeply integrated within the process of weight loss and weight-loss maintenance, there has been an increased interest in using psychobehavioral interventions, specifically acceptance and mindfulness-based treatments, to target the specific behaviors affecting weight loss and maintenance.

When one is considering the acceptance and mindfulness approach to sustained weight loss, it is important to examine the factors that contribute to weight gain and regain. For example, rigid control of eating behavior has been significantly related to weight regain (Westenhoefer, 1991; Westenhoefer, Stunkard, & Pudel, 1999). Rigid attempts at control of eating are likely to emerge within inflexible dichotomous "all or nothing" thinking patterns and "alternating periods of severe restriction and no weight control efforts" (Lillis, 2007, p. 20). From this point of view, any behavioral outcomes that fall short of individually specified weight-loss goals are considered failures.

This type of dichotomous thinking is similar to problematic thought patterns seen in more psychologically conceptualized problems and may be considered as reflecting cognitive fusion. Cognitive fusion is the process by which the literal meaning of words or beliefs become "attached" to the objects, events, or people they describe, increasing the behavior influence of verbal rules about the environment or private events and decreasing the influence available from direct experience. Private events, such as the thoughts an individual has regarding his or her weight-loss performance, are therefore experienced as "truth" and not as events that can be noticed without being believed. As a result, dichotomous thinking and cognitive fusion serve as catalysts for experiential avoidance, resulting in decreased behavioral and psychological flexibility. By continuing to engage in cognitive fusion and wage war with their private events, these individuals are unable to commit to behaviors that better reflect their health-related values.

Emotional eating can also be characterized as an example of experiential avoidance. Emotional eating reduces aversive private events, and as a result the behavior is maintained by negative reinforcement (Agras & Telch, 1998; Telch & Agras, 1996). Within this process, stimulation from eating has a blocking effect on other negatively evaluated experiences, such as experiences of sadness, anxiety, or shame. This process can be detrimental to an individual's ability to cope with discomfort in the future and engage in successful long-term weight management, because the person can become more and more reliant on eating as a coping response.

People who are obese are cognizant of the stigma and negative attributions associated with their weight. Self-stigma is common and is often coupled with the obese person avoiding making contact with others, including health professionals, who could potentially reject or discriminate against them (Rudman, Feinberg, & Fairchild, 2002). Stigma plays an important role in reinforcing experiential avoidance (Hayes, Niccolls, Masuda, & Rye, 2002), which creates a negative feedback loop, with both self-stigma and stigma from others contributing to difficult emotions. With the emotional eating that can occur in response to those emotions, weight loss is difficult and lost weight is frequently regained before final weight-loss goals are met.

Mindfulness Interventions

There are several studies examining the effect of mindfulness and acceptance interventions on weight maintenance and weight loss (Kristeller, Baer, & Quillian-Wolever, 2006; Kristeller & Hallett, 1999; Baer, Fischer, & Huss, 2005a; Baer, Fischer, & Huss, 2005b; Lillis, Hayes, Bunting, & Masuda, 2009).

In one intervention of this kind, Kristeller and Hallett (1999) integrated components of cognitive behavior therapy with mindfulness-based stress reduction (MBSR) and guided eating meditations. This Mindfulness-Based Eating Awareness Training (MB-EAT) addresses issues related to shape, weight, and eating-related self-regulatory processes, including appetite and satiation, to "wisely" utilize awareness to inform behavior and experience (Kristeller, 2003). Like MBSR, the intervention focuses on mindful meditation, in this case focused on food, cues, mind, and body (Kristeller et al., 2006). In a nonrandomized, extended baseline study with binge eaters, Kristeller and Hallett (1999) found significant decreases in binge frequency, as well as Beck Depression Inventory, Beck Anxiety Inventory, and Binge Eating Scale scores, in a nonrandomized, extended baseline study. Additionally, in this study, amount of time spent meditating predicted decreases in scores on the Binge Eating Scale.

In a series of case studies, Singh and colleagues (2008a; 2008b) developed an alternative mindfulness-based intervention to bring about improved health in two obese individuals. The first individual had been diagnosed with Prader-Willi syndrome, a disorder that is characterized by inability to resist urges to eat both nutritive and nonnutritive substances, and the second individual was an otherwise-healthy obese man. Both subjects demonstrated significant weight loss (20 percent and 36 percent of body weight, respectively) with the administration of the multicomponent intervention, which included a focus on mindfulness and mindful eating.

Acceptance and commitment therapy (ACT) has been applied to obesity and weight problems. Lillis and colleagues (2009) developed an intervention targeting weight-loss maintenance in individuals who had previously lost weight. The ACT intervention was designed to enhance acceptance and mindfulness of private events related to eating and exercise behaviors, including experiences of stigma, and connect participants with their health-related values. Participants in the ACT group achieved significantly better outcomes for weight loss and maintenance, psychological distress, obesity-related stigma, and self-reported health behaviors. Specifics of this study are discussed below.

TREATMENT OUTCOME AND PROCESS

ACT may be more effective than traditional approaches in the maintenance of behavioral changes (Gifford et al., 2004, Hayes, Masuda, Bissett, Luoma, & Guerrero, 2004) and this is particularly relevant to the problem of weight loss. In a randomized controlled trial evaluating the efficacy of ACT with sixty-two women with a BMI of greater than 20 who were attempting to lose weight, Tapper and colleagues (2009) found that, at six-month follow-up, those who had received ACT had significantly greater increases in physical activity compared to control participants. When participants who reported that they had "never" implemented workshop strategies were excluded ($n = 7$), a significant difference in both exercise frequency increase and BMI reduction was found, relative to control participants. Qualitative data from this study indicated that the cognitive defusion component of the ACT intervention was particularly useful for exercise adherence (Tapper et al., 2009).

The study by Lillis and colleagues (2009) included an ACT intervention utilizing mindfulness and health-related values particularly focused on weight maintenance. Participants were randomly assigned to either the ACT group ($n = 40$) or a wait list control ($n = 44$). Both groups participated in at least six months of a nutrition and exercise weight-loss program prior to participation in this study. Participants in the ACT condition received a one-day mindfulness and acceptance-based workshop, which focused on obesity-related stigma and psychological distress. All participants were assessed for obesity-related stigma, obesity-related quality of life, psychological distress, weight (BMI), and distress tolerance, and both general and weight-specific acceptance and psychological flexibility pre-treatment and at three-month follow-up. General acceptance and psychological flexibility were measured via the Acceptance and Action Questionnaire (AAQ; Hayes, Strosahl, et al., 2004) and weight-related psychological flexibility was measured via the Acceptance and Action Questionnaire for Weight (AAQW; Lillis & Hayes, 2008), which measures specifically weight-related thoughts and feelings and their interference with values-based action.

Individuals in the ACT condition demonstrated significantly improved obesity-related stigma, quality of life, distress, weight, distress tolerance, and both general and obesity-related acceptance at three-month follow-up. The resulting outcomes for the ACT group were all mediated by increased weight-related acceptance. The relationship between treatment group and BMI, weight change, stigma, psychological distress, QOL, binge eating, and physical activity were significantly mediated by scores on a measure of acceptance of obesity-related thoughts and feelings. The relationship between treatment group and stigma, psychological distress, QOL, and binge eating were also significantly mediated by general acceptance scores. These results strongly imply that acceptance and mindfulness-based interventions may be a step forward in the development of more successful long-term weight-control programs.

Diabetes

Diabetes is another disorder reaching epidemic levels worldwide. Although often related to obesity, diabetes is a unique, complex medical condition characterized by problems with glucose production or utilization in the body. Complications from diabetes result in high levels of morbidity and mortality, and they include vision loss, neuropathy, kidney, heart, and liver disease, and circulation problems, among others. Diabetes is currently a leading cause of death across industrialized nations and is projected to continue to dramatically increase in prevalence in developing nations between now and 2030 (Wild, Roglic, Green, Sicree, & King, 2004).

There are two distinct types of diabetes: type 1 and type 2. Type 1 diabetes is estimated to represent 5 to 10 percent of the diabetes population and is caused by a genetically predisposed autoimmune response (Gale, 2001; Nerup et al., 1997). This response is characterized by immune-system T cells inducing the death of beta cells in the pancreas. In other words, a basic immune system mechanism malfunctions so that the cells responsible for producing and releasing insulin into the blood are destroyed. Although it is agreed that a genetic component is heavily involved, factors such as prenatal exposure to viruses or toxins, birth weight, maternal vitamin D levels, and seasonality are being investigated in the risk for type 1 diabetes (Harder et al., 2009; Moltchanova, Schreier, Lammi, & Karvonen, 2009).

Individuals with type 1 diabetes are generally left without the ability to produce adequate amounts of insulin, hence their dependence on an external source of the hormone. This source is self-administered through various routes such as insulin injections or an insulin pump. Onset of type 1 diabetes generally occurs in childhood, although adults who suffer damage to their pancreas can be susceptible as well.

In contrast to type 1 diabetes, where endogenous insulin is insufficiently produced, type 2 diabetes is normally characterized by a resistance to the action of insulin on skeletal muscles, adipose tissue, and the liver (DeFronzo, 2004; Scheen & Lefebvre, 1996). A host of problems may be present in those with type 2 diabetes, such as chronic hyperglycemia, decreased pancreatic beta-cell function in response to dietary sugar intake, and decreased glycogen storage in the liver and muscles. The etiology of type 2 diabetes is complicated, as not all people with insulin resistance develop diabetes (Campbell, 2009; Gerich, 1999). As with type 1 diabetes, the risk for continually elevated blood glucose is of concern for people with type 2 diabetes. A diagnosis is usually made using a fasting glucose or glucose tolerance test, where a person who maintains high levels of blood sugar is indicated as having insulin resistance and/or diabetes. The prevalence of type 2 diabetes as well as rates of obesity are increasing worldwide, with increasingly younger populations receiving diagnoses of type 2 diabetes (Hjartaker, Langseth, & Weiderpass, 2008; Seidell, 2000; Wild et al., 2004). Furthermore, a general metabolic syndrome and cardiovascular disease have been considered important components of the disease burden expected with increased rates of obesity and type 2 diabetes (Ginsberg & Maccallum, 2009).

Paramount to a discussion of obesity is the association between increased body fat and the risk for developing insulin resistance and type 2 diabetes. Evidence for the relationship between obesity and insulin resistance is often cited through studies showing weight reduction and increased sensitivity to the effects of insulin

(Beck-Nielsen, Pedersen, & Lindskov, 1979; Freidenberg, Reichart, Olefsky, & Henry, 1988; Jimenez, Zuniga-Guajardo, Zinman, & Angel, 1987; Olefsky, Reaven, & Farquhar, 1974). In fact, insulin activity may be close to normalized in some obese individuals with weight reduction (Gerich, 1999). Specifically, increased ability to clear insulin from the body has been described as beginning at around 10 percent loss of body weight, but a higher percentage of weight loss may be required for substantially increased sensitivity to the action of insulin (Valera Mora, Scarfone, Calvani, Greco, & Mingrone, 2003).

Traditional Conceptualization and Approach

Diabetes is a distinctive disease in a number of respects. First, it is overall blood glucose concentrations, rather than the disease characteristics or presentation, that affect morbidity and mortality. Specifically, large-scale demonstration projects utilizing individuals with either type of diabetes have demonstrated that if an individual maintains appropriate blood glucose concentrations, long-term health problems and complications can largely be avoided in both type 1 and type 2 diabetes (DCCT Research Group, 1993; UKPDS Group, 1998), and overall health levels similar to those of an individual without diabetes can be achieved.

Another feature of diabetes that makes it unique from a behavioral standpoint is that management of the disorder is nearly completely carried out by the patient, rather than by health care professionals. This entails a high level of self-management behavior, including eating healthfully in a manner that is unlikely to produce highs and lows in glucose, regular exercise to manage glucose levels, self-testing of blood glucose, regular medication adherence and/or insulin injections tied to observed blood glucose levels, and consistent checks for eye, foot, and other circulation-related problems.

As noted above, recent large-scale trials have demonstrated that, with individuals with either type 1 or type 2 diabetes, a significant reduction of risk in the development of microvascular and macrovascular complications can be achieved through consistent management of blood glucose levels (DCCT Group, 1993; UKPDS

Group, 1998). However, only an estimated 55.7 percent of adults in the United States with type 2 diabetes achieve the glucose levels in the appropriate range (Hoerger, Segel, Gregg, & Saaddine, 2008). This is largely attributable to psychological factors such as stress and motivation problems, as well as other behavioral factors.

Psychological Features

Living with diabetes is distressing. Fisher and colleagues (2007) reported that 22 percent of individuals with diabetes report elevated distress levels, a number that was clinically and statistically distinct from the distress found in depressed individuals with diabetes. Psychosocial stressors appear to be related to glycemic control through both biological and psychological pathways.

Biological pathway. In the first pathway, stress experienced by individuals with diabetes is thought to physiologically influence glucose levels through the increased output of counter-regulatory hormones, such as cortisol. Multiple studies have demonstrated this effect (e.g., Surwit & Schneider, 1993), and there is clearly a relationship between neuroadrenal activation in response to stress and glucose production in the body. Stress activates the sympathoadrenal system and the hypothalamic-pituitary-adrenocorticoal (HPA) axis that involves a number of systems, including vagal tone, cortisol secretion, and catecholamine release, among others (McEwen, 1998).

Psychological/behavioral pathway. The second way distress is thought to influence diabetes is through its impact on self-management behaviors, including adherence to a healthful diet, regular exercise, consistent blood glucose self-monitoring, and administration of exogenous insulin or oral hypoglycemic agents. Peyrot, McMurry, and Kruger (1999) found that regimen adherence mediates the relationship between stress and glycemic control. This pathway has received considerable support (Peyrot & McMurry, 1985; Norris, Engelgau, & Narayan, 2001) and has produced many interventions designed to increase coping, with the goal of improved self-management.

Traditional cognitive behavioral interventions in diabetes focus on the management of difficult thoughts and feelings, including stress, through the increased use of logical thinking strategies and the suppression of maladaptive or irrational beliefs and assumptions (Surwit et al., 2002; Henry, Wilson, Bruce, Chisolm, & Rawling, 1997). This reduction in maladaptive thinking patterns affects both biological reduction of the stress response and an increased ability to carry out self-management behaviors once stress is reduced. What these interventions sometimes fail to consider, however, is the high rate of distress inherent in both the presence of the disease and the experiences that arise in managing it, and the fact that this distress is often not based in distorted thought patterns.

Acceptance and Mindfulness Conceptualization

Traditional interventions seek predominantly or partly to reduce aversive private events and stressors in order to facilitate behavior change. Alternatives to these approaches include acceptance and mindfulness approaches seeking to produce behavior change in the presence of these difficult experiences.

Throughout a given day, individuals with diabetes are faced with multiple reminders of the fact that they have diabetes and of the fragility of their health. Testing blood glucose, taking or injecting prescribed oral medications or insulin, carefully monitoring and managing diet, engaging in regular physical exercise, and consistently monitoring for diabetes-related complications all must be executed day in and day out. These activities, along with the underlying threat present when living with a potentially life-threatening illness, cause marked distress in individuals with diabetes. Rather than regarding this distress as part of the problem to be fixed or eliminated, mindfulness or acceptance models understand this distress as a naturally occurring part of the disease to be observed and noticed as one maintains a focus on healthy functioning at the same time.

Although similar in these goals, the proposed mechanism of action differs slightly among mindfulness and acceptance approaches to diabetes, related to the biological and psychological/behavioral stress pathways. ACT proposes a behavioral, solution-focused element possible with mindful noticing of difficult thoughts and feelings (Gregg, Callaghan, Hayes, & Glenn-Lawson, 2007). MBSR, on the other hand, proposes a mind-body mechanism related to the reduction of stress (Rosenzweig et al., 2007). From both perspectives, the purpose of mindfulness training is to bring a patient's attention to his or her current experience, objectively observed, and to reduce the patient's automatic responses. Both emphasize the awareness of thoughts, the ability to notice or observe one's experience and "sit with" it. The purpose of this, from an MBSR perspective, is the overall reduction of stress and autonomic activity. This reduction in stress, then, is thought to be related to a reduction in activation of the HPA axis and other neuroadrenal mechanisms through which stress affects physical functioning (Fisher et al., 2007).

ACT, on the other hand, does not consider the mechanism an overall reduction of the deleterious effects of stress, but rather considers it the activation of behavior. Mindful noticing or awareness of one's experiences is hypothesized to allow for more skillful engagement of effective health-related behavior brought about by increased psychological flexibility. For example, if one values healthful eating but continuously snacks on high-fat, high-sugar snacks when the urge arises, an ACT intervention would target mindfully noticing the urge in order to respond behaviorally in a values-consistent manner rather than in a manner designed to reduce or eliminate the urge.

Mindfulness Interventions

MBSR is a general, relatively consistently applied approach, delivered similarly regardless of the particular patient group involved, and it is based on the protocol developed by Kabat-Zinn (1990). Generally, MBSR utilizes various informal and formal meditation training techniques in order to increase mindfulness. Programs include eight to ten weekly group training sessions, typically with one session structured as a full-day retreat. The training is typically skills based and involves information about the psychophysiology of stress and emotions. Sitting meditation is practiced in session, and daily practice is encouraged outside of session as homework.

ACT interventions for diabetes involve multiple core processes with the overall goal of increasing health behaviors. More specifically, ACT for diabetes includes the following components.

Making Contact with the Results of Previous Ineffective Methods of Coping

As noted above, many individuals with type 2 diabetes have utilized methods of coping with difficult thoughts and feelings that have led to the exacerbation of their health problems. For example, emotional eating (Byrne et al., 2003; Ganley, 1989), sedentary distractions such as computer games and watching television (Dunstan et al., 2007), smoking (Gifford et al., 2004), and other potentially problematic behavior patterns, can all function as attempts to avoid unpleasant thoughts, feelings, or bodily sensations. Further, an individual with the belief that the presence of diabetes means certain death may avoid thinking about, monitoring, taking care of, or getting support for the illness in order to avoid experiencing unpleasant feelings associated with this thought. Within the ACT intervention for diabetes, treatment focuses on first having individuals contact the experience that the strategy they have used to try to solve their problem has not worked well for them. In fact, in many cases, the solution is part of the problem. That is, attempts to control distress often lead to more distress, as is the case when an individual "soothes" his or her distress by eating high-fat or high-carbohydrate food or engages in other avoidance behavior rather than the behaviors required to actively manage the diabetes. In this phase of ACT, patients are asked to examine whether that is true in their own lives.

Cognitive Defusion

ACT teaches the individual to "deliteralize" the content of thoughts—that is, to focus more on the process of thinking and the workability of behavior tied to particular thoughts than on their content per se. For example, the person who believes that "even though my doctor says that my diabetes is manageable, I still feel as though my life is over" would be encouraged to see that thought as a thought to be noticed, not necessarily to be believed or disbelieved.

TEACHING EXPERIENTIAL WILLINGNESS/PSYCHOLOGICAL ACCEPTANCE

Individuals with diabetes often experience many difficult and uncomfortable feelings in response to their illness. For instance, in the course of a day, a person with diabetes may experience sadness at the loss of certain kinds of foods and activities, shame about his weight and the fact that he developed diabetes due to it, fear for his life or longevity, and anger and frustration at the limits placed on his eating. Willingness or acceptance, from an ACT perspective, allows individuals with diabetes to experience these feelings without defense, in order to increase flexibility and options in terms of response. For individuals with diabetes, as in other conditions treated by ACT, the flexibility is especially focused on personal values.

VALUES AND COMMITMENT/VALUES ASSESSMENT

Health values are key to diabetes self-management from an ACT perspective. First, many patients receiving the treatment may not view their difficulties as psychological in nature. Values allow for a less pathologizing approach, which may be more appropriate for medical settings and medical patients. Values work within ACT treatment for diabetes involves clarifying the directions in life patients desire to take and helping to elucidate which behaviors are moving the individual toward values versus away from negative thoughts and feelings.

EXTENDING EMOTIONAL WILLINGNESS AND COGNITIVE DEFUSION INTO REAL-LIFE BEHAVIOR CHANGE

Patients experiencing difficult diabetes-related thoughts and feelings may disconnect from important people in their lives, may stop engaging in healthy behaviors, and may avoid dealing with any feelings in order to not have to feel these difficult emotions. Again, it is not the negative feelings themselves that are problematic, but the individual's behavior in relation to them.

Treatment Outcome and Process

There have been few randomized studies directly examining the impact of mindfulness or acceptance interventions with individuals with diabetes. In one observational study, Rosenzweig and colleagues (2007) explored the effectiveness of MBSR in an eight-week group intervention centered on mindfulness training and practice in fourteen individuals with diabetes. Researchers reported a downward trend in glycosylated hemoglobin (a measure of average blood glucose levels), a significant reduction in blood pressure, and reductions in anxiety, depression, and distress. It is important to note that researchers reported no changes in self-care behavior, weight, or other lifestyle factors that could explain the reductions in blood glucose, and they hypothesized that outcomes were mediated by a down regulation of stress reactivity and its subsequent effect on physiological processes involved in the production of cortisol, norepinephrine, beta endorphin, glucagons, and growth hormone.

Consistent with this finding, in a recent examination of archival program data on MBSR with twenty-five patients with diabetes, Young, Cappola, and Baime (2009) reported that at pre-treatment, individuals with diabetes demonstrated significantly higher Profile of Mood States (PMS) scores compared to population norms and that following treatment levels matched population norms. This reduction of distress appears important within an MBSR treatment context and again may address outcomes at the level of cortisol changes. However, more directed studies are clearly required in order to fully evaluate this pathway.

In a randomized study examining the effectiveness of ACT for individuals with type 2 diabetes, Gregg, Callaghan, Hayes, and Glenn-Lawson (2007) assigned individuals to receive either a one-day ACT workshop intervention or a one-day diabetes education intervention. At three-month follow-up, individuals in the ACT condition were more likely to have blood glucose levels in the desired range and reported higher levels of self-care behaviors and diabetes-related acceptance. This diabetes-related acceptance and self-care behavior change was then found to mediate the relationship between group membership and blood glucose.

Beyond Obesity and Diabetes: Metabolic Syndrome and the Future of Secondary Prevention

When one is discussing diabetes and obesity and their respective causes, it is important to also consider the complex relationship between them. Clearly there is a commonality between obesity and diabetes, with the former a causal agent in the latter for many patients (Lazar, 2005). However, the two are also both thought to be related to a condition called "metabolic syndrome." Metabolic syndrome, also known as Syndrome X, insulin resistance syndrome, or dysmetabolic syndrome, is an amalgam of obesity-related risk factors that dramatically increase an individual's coronary artery disease–related risk, along with increasing incidence of the development of both diabetes and stroke. This syndrome is generally thought to be tightly tied to relevant health behavior, and thus treatments are thought to require a lifestyle modification component (Wyatt, Winters, & Dubbert, 2006).

Metabolic syndrome is characterized by a number of health risk factors, including hypertension, dyslipidemia, insulin resistance, and visceral obesity. This constellation is highly related to cardiovascular problems and is considered a primary marker for early detection of coronary heart disease risk.

Although metabolic syndrome is composed of multiple factors, insulin resistance appears to be a key element. In fact, some form of insulin dysregulation must be present for the diagnosis. Obesity, hypertension, and dyslipidemia entail complex relationships with insulin resistance, and researchers have hypothesized a link to the sympathoadrenal system (Reaven, Lithell, & Landsberg, 1996; Brook & Julius, 2000) and a proinflammatory state (Das, 2002). However, the combination clearly appears to be related to physical inactivity and unhealthy eating patterns as well (Wyatt et al., 2006). Metabolic syndrome is quickly becoming the number one cause of morbidity and mortality in the industrialized world (Wilkin & Voss, 2004).

One advantage to considering diabetes, obesity, and cardiovascular problems in relation to a metabolic syndrome that collates risk factors is that the specific secondary preventive health behaviors associated with the collective can be considered together. For example, rather than helping patients reduce only carbohydrate or glucose levels in food in order to address diabetes-related complications and problems with one intervention, and then teaching fat reduction to reduce cardiovascular risk, and sodium reduction for hypertension, we can target eating behaviors as a whole, with a reduction in microvascular and macrovascular complications achieved simultaneously.

Summary

Psychological factors are an important consideration when attempting to effect secondary prevention across diseases. Unlike in other psychological problems treated with ACT or other mindfulness approaches, in problems such as diabetes and obesity the focus of treatment is generally not on psychopathology, but rather on health-related values, processes underlying the physical health conditions, as well as quality of life. For example, if a depressed individual comes in to treatment for assistance in reducing his or her depressed thoughts and feelings, a mindfulness- or acceptance-focused therapist may first need to untangle this goal from others. This is the case because moving one in the direction of one's values is sometimes distressing, and thus the elimination of distress at all costs is an untenable agenda if one wants to live a meaningful life.

Individuals with medical problems such as diabetes and obesity may often assume that there will be an amount of uncomfortable lifestyle change associated with improving their health—that diet modifications, increased exercise, and medication adherence will all go along with reaching one's goals. This is important because they are not typically experiencing acute symptoms or pain related to their disease; they may, however, experience a lack of "motivation" for making lifestyle changes. Alternatively, patients may not fully anticipate the distress-management role many of the unhealthy behaviors are playing. In other words, lifestyle modification interventions utilizing a values-based or awareness-focused (rather than distress-reduction) framework are often easier for patients to understand, but the approach involves discussing values rather than relief from sadness and pain as motivating factors.

References

Agras, W. S., & Telch, C. F. (1998). The effects of caloric deprivation and negative affect on binge eating in obese binge-eating disordered women. *Behaviour Therapy, 29,* 491–503.

Andersen, T., Backer, O. G., Stokholm, K. H., & Quaade, F. (1984). Randomized trial of diet and gastroplasty compared with diet alone in morbid obesity. *New England Journal of Medicine, 310*(6), 352–356.

Baer, R., Fischer, S., & Huss, D. (2005a). Mindfulness and acceptance in the treatment of disordered eating. *Journal of Rational-Emotive & Cognitive-Behavior Therapy, 24*(4), 281–300.

Baer, R., Fischer, S., & Huss, D. (2005b). Mindfulness-based cognitive therapy applied to binge eating: A case study. *Cognitive and Behavioral Practice, 12,* 351–358.

Beck-Nielsen, H., Pedersen, O., & Lindskov, H. O. (1979). Normalization of the insulin sensitivity and the cellular insulin binding during treatment of obese diabetics for one year. *Acta Endocrinology (Copenh), 90*(1), 103–112.

Brook, R., & Julius, S. (2000). Autonomic imbalance, hypertension, and cardiovascular risk. *American Journal of Hypertension, 13*(6), 112–122.

Burk-Braxton, C. L. (1996). *Is shame a factor in overweight relapse?* Unpublished dissertation. University of Texas, Austin.

Byrne, S., Cooper, Z., & Fairburn, C. (2003). Weight maintenance and relapse in obesity: A qualitative study. *International Journal of Obesity, 27*(8), 955–962.

Campbell, R. K. (2009). Type 2 diabetes: where we are today: An overview of disease burden, current treatments, and treatment strategies. *Journal of the American Pharmacists Association, 49*(Suppl. 1), S3–9.

Centers for Disease Control (2005). Obesity and overweight. Retrieved October 15, 2009, from http://www.cdc.gov/needphp/dnpa/obesity

Das, U. N. (2002). Obesity, metabolic syndrome X, and inflammation. *Nutrition, 18*(5), 430–432.

Davis-Coelho, K., Waltz, J., & Davis-Coelho, B. (2000). Awareness and prevention of bias against fat clients in psychotherapy. *Professional Psychology: Research and Practice, 31*(6), 682–684.

DCCT Research Group. (1993). The effect of intensive treatment of diabetes on the development and progression of long-term complications of insulin-dependent diabetes mellitus. *New England Journal of Medicine, 329*, 977–986.

DeFronzo, R. A. (2004). Pathogenesis of type 2 diabetes mellitus. *Medical Clinics of North America, 88*(4), 787–835, ix.

Dunstan, D. W., Salmon, J., Healy, G. N., Shaw, J. E., Jolley, D., Zimmet, P. Z., et al. (2007). Association of television viewing with fasting and 2-h postchallenge plasma glucose levels in adults without diagnosed diabetes. *Diabetes Care, 30*(3), 516.

Elfhag, K., & Rossner, S. (2005). Who succeeds in maintaining weight loss? A conceptual review of factors associated with weight loss maintenance and weight regain. *Obesity Reviews, 6*(1), 67–85.

Fisher, L., Skaff, M. M., Mullan, J. T., Arean, P., Mohr, D., Masharani, U., et al. (2007). Clinical depression versus distress among patients with type 2 diabetes. *Diabetes Care, 30*(3), 542.

Freidenberg, G. R., Reichart, D., Olefsky, J. M., & Henry, R. R. (1988). Reversibility of defective adipocyte insulin receptor kinase activity in non-insulin-dependent diabetes mellitus. Effect of weight loss. *Journal of Clinical Investigation, 82*(4), 1398–1406.

Friedman, K. E., Reichmann, S. K., Costanzo, P. R., Zelli, A., Ashmore, J. A., & Musante, G. J. (2005). Weight stigmatization and ideological beliefs: Relation to psychological functioning in obese adults. *Obesity Research, 13*(5), 907–916.

Gale, E. A. (2001). The discovery of type 1 diabetes. *Diabetes, 50*(2), 217–226.

Ganley, R. M. (1989). Emotion and eating in obesity—a review of the literature. *International Journal of Eating Disorders, 8*(3), 343–361.

Gerich, J. E. (1999). Is insulin resistance the principal cause of type 2 diabetes? *Diabetes Obesity Metabolism, 1*(5), 257–263.

Gifford, E. V., Kohlenberg, B. S., Hayes, S. C., Antonuccio, D. O., Piasecki, M. M., Rasmussen-Hall, M. L., et al. (2004). Acceptance-based treatment for smoking cessation. *Behavior Therapy, 35*(4), 689–705.

Ginsberg, H. N., & Maccallum, P. R. (2009). The obesity, metabolic syndrome, and type 2 diabetes mellitus pandemic: II. Therapeutic management of atherogenic dyslipidemia. *Journal of Clinical Hypertension (Greenwich), 11*(9), 520–527.

Gregg, J. A., Callaghan, G. M., Hayes, S. C., & Glenn-Lawson, J. L. (2007). Improving diabetes self-management through acceptance, mindfulness, and values: A randomized controlled trial. *Journal of Consulting and Clinical Psychology, 75*(2), 336.

Harder, T., Roepke, K., Diller, N., Stechling, Y., Dudenhausen, J. W., & Plagemann, A. (2009). Birth weight, early weight gain, and subsequent risk of type 1 diabetes: systematic review and meta-analysis. *American Journal of Epidemiology, 169*(12), 1428–1436.

Haslam, D. W., & James, W. P. T. (2005). Obesity. *Lancet, 366*(9492), 1197–1209.

Hayes, S. C., Masuda, A., Bissett, R., Luoma, J., & Guerrero, L. F. (2004). DBT, FAP, and ACT: How empirically oriented are the new behavior therapy technologies? *Behavior Therapy, 35*(1), 35–54.

Hayes, S. C., Niccolls, R., Masuda, A., & Rye, A. K. (2002). Prejudice, terrorism, and behavior therapy. *Cognitive and Behavioral Practice, 9*(4), 296–301.

Hayes, S. C., Strosahl, K. D., Wilson, K. G., Bissett, R. T., Pistorello, J., Toarmino, D., et al. (2004). Measuring experiential avoidance: A preliminary test of a working model. *Psychological Record, 54*, 553–578.

Henry, J. L., Wilson, P. H., Bruce, D. G., Chisholm, D. J., & Rawling, P. J. (1997). Cognitive-behavioural stress management for patients with non-insulin dependent diabetes mellitus. *Psychology, Health & Medicine, 2*(2), 109–118.

Hjartaker, A., Langseth, H., & Weiderpass, E. (2008). Obesity and diabetes epidemics: Cancer repercussions. *Advances in Experimental Medicine and Biology, 630,* 72–93.

Hoerger, T. J., Segel, J. E., Gregg, E. W., & Saaddine, J. B. (2008). Is glycemic control improving in U.S. adults? *Diabetes Care, 31,* 81–86.

Jimenez, J., Zuniga-Guajardo, S., Zinman, B., & Angel, A. (1987). Effects of weight loss in massive obesity on insulin and C-peptide dynamics: Sequential changes in insulin production, clearance, and sensitivity. *Journal of Clinical Endocrinology and Metabolism, 64*(4), 661–668.

Kabat-Zinn, J. (1990). *Full catastrophe living: Using the wisdom of your body and mind to face stress, pain, and illness.* New York: Dell Publishing.

Kenchaiah, S., Evans, J. C., Levy, D., Wilson, P. W. F., Benjamin, E. J., Larson, M. G., et al. (2002). Obesity and the risk of heart failure. *New England Journal of Medicine, 347*(5), 305.

Knowler, W. C., Barrett-Connor, E., Fowler, S. E., Hamman, R. F., Lachin, J. M., Walker, E. A., et al. (2002). Reduction in the incidence of type 2 diabetes with lifestyle intervention or metformin. *New England Journal of Medicine, 346*(6), 393–403.

Kristeller, J. L. (2003). Mindfulness, wisdom and eating: Applying a multidomain model of meditation effects. *Journal of Constructivism in the Human Sciences, 8*(2), 107–118.

Kristeller, J. L., Baer, R. A., & Quillian-Wolever, R. (2006). Mindfulness-based approaches to eating disorders. In R. A. Baer, (Ed.), *Mindfulness and acceptance-based interventions: Conceptualization, application, and empirical support* (pp. 75–91). San Diego, CA: Elsevier.

Kristeller, J. L., & Hallett, C. B. (1999). An exploratory study of a meditation-based intervention for binge eating disorder. *Journal of Health Psychology, 4,* 357–363.

Lazar, M. A. (2005). How obesity causes diabetes: Not a tall tale. *Science, 307*(5708), 373.

Lewis, M. (1993). Self-conscious emotions: Embarrassment, pride, shame, and guilt. *Handbook of Emotions, 563,* 573.

Lillis, J. (2007). *Acceptance and commitment therapy for the treatment of obesity-related stigma and sustained weight loss.* Unpublished doctoral dissertation, University of Nevada, Reno.

Lillis, J., & Hayes, S. C. (2008). Measuring avoidance and inflexibility in weight related problems. *International Journal of Behavioral Consultation and Therapy, 4,* 30–40.

Lillis, J., Hayes, S. C., Bunting, K., & Masuda, A. (2009). Teaching acceptance and mindfulness to improve the lives of the obese: A preliminary test of a theoretical model. *Annals of Behavioral Medicine, 37*(1), 58–69.

Maroney, D., & Golub, S. (1992). Nurses' attitudes toward obese persons and certain ethnic groups. *Perceptual and Motor Skills, 75*(2), 387–391.

McEwen, B. S. (1998). Protective and damaging effects of stress mediators. *New England Journal of Medicine, 338*(3), 171.

Moltchanova, E. V., Schreier, N., Lammi, N., & Karvonen, M. (2009). Seasonal variation of diagnosis of Type 1 diabetes mellitus in children worldwide. *Diabetic Medicine, 26*(7), 673–678.

Multiple Risk Factor Intervention Trial Research Group. (1990). Mortality rates after 10.5 years for participants in the multiple risk factor intervention trial: Findings related to a priori hypotheses of the trial. *Journal of the American Medical Association, 263*(13), 1, 795–801.

National Institutes of Health (1998). *Clinical guidelines on the identification, evaluation, and treatment of overweight and obesity in adults: The evidence report.* National Institutes of Health.

Nerup, J., Mandrup-Poulsen, T., Pociot, F., Karlsen, A. E., Andersen, H. U., Christensen, U. B., et al. (1997). On the pathogenesis of insulin-dependent diabetes mellitus in man: A paradigm in transition. In G. R. Zahnd & C. B. Wollheim (Eds.), *Contributions of physiology to the understanding of diabetes: ten essays in memory of Albert E. Renold* (pp. 148–159). Berlin, New York: Springer.

Norris, S. L., Engelgau, M. M., & Narayan, K. M. V. (2001). Effectiveness of self-management training in type 2 diabetes: A systematic review of randomized controlled trials. *Diabetes Care, 24*(3), 561–587.

Olefsky, J., Reaven, G. M., & Farquhar, J. W. (1974). Effects of weight reduction on obesity. Studies of lipid and carbohydrate metabolism in normal and hyperlipoproteinemic subjects. *Journal of Clinical Investigation, 53*(1), 64–76.

Padwal, R. S., & Majumdar, S. R. (2007). Drug treatments for obesity: Orlistat, sibutramine, and rimonabant. *Lancet, 369*(9555), 71–77.

Perri, M. G. (1998). The maintenance of treatment effects in the long-term management of obesity. *Clinical Psychology: Science and Practice, 5*(4), 526–543.

Peyrot, M., & McMurry Jr, J. (1985). Psychosocial factors in diabetes control: Adjustment of insulin-treated adults. *Psychosomatic Medicine, 47*(6), 542.

Peyrot, M., McMurry Jr, J. F., & Kruger, D. F. (1999). A biopsychosocial model of glycemic control in diabetes: Stress, coping and regimen adherence. *Journal of Health and Social Behavior, 40*(2), 141–158.

Price, J. H., Desmond, S. M., Krol, R. A., Snyder, F. F., & O'Connell, J. K. (1987). Family-practice physicians' beliefs, attitudes, and practices regarding obesity. *American Journal of Preventive Medicine, 3*(6), 339–345.

Puhl, R. M., & Brownell, K. D. (2003). Psychosocial origins of obesity stigma: Toward changing a powerful and pervasive bias. *Obesity Reviews, 4*(4), 213–227.

Puhl, R. M., & Heuer, C. A. (2009). The stigma of obesity: A review and update. *Obesity, 17,* 941–964.

Reaven, G. M., Lithell, H., & Landsberg, L. (1996). Hypertension and associated metabolic abnormalities—the role of insulin resistance and the sympathoadrenal system. *New England Journal of Medicine, 334*(6), 374.

Rosenzweig, S., Reibel, D. K., Greeson, J. M., Edman, J. S., Jasser, S. A., McMearty, K. D., et al. (2007). Mindfulness-based stress reduction is associated with improved glycemic control in type 2 diabetes mellitus: A pilot study. *Alternative Therapies in Health and Medicine, 13*(5), 36.

Rudman, L. A., Feinberg, J., & Fairchild, K. (2002). Minority members' implicit attitudes: Automatic ingroup bias as a function of group status. *Social Cognition, 20*(4), 294–320.

Schauer, P. R., Ikramuddin, S., Gourash, W., Ramanathan, R., & Luketich, J. (2000). Outcomes after laparoscopic roux-en-Y gastric bypass for morbid obesity. *Annals of Surgery, 232*(4), 515.

Scheen, A. J., & Lefebvre, P. J. (1996). Insulin action in man. *Diabetes Metabolism, 22*(2), 105–110.

Seidell, J. C. (2000). Obesity, insulin resistance and diabetes—a worldwide epidemic. *British Journal of Nutrition, 83*(Suppl. 1), S5–8.

Singh, N. N., Lancioni, G. E., Singh, A. N., Winton, A. S. W., Singh, J., McAleavey, K. M., et al. (2008a). A mindfulness-based health wellness program for an adolescent with Prader-Willi syndrome. *Behavior Modification, 32*(2), 167.

Singh, N. N., Lancioni, G. E., Singh, A. N., Winton, A. S. W., Singh, J., McAleavey, K. M., et al. (2008b). A mindfulness-based health wellness program for managing morbid obesity. *Clinical Case Studies, 7*(4), 327.

Sjostrom, L., Lindroos, A. K., Peltonen, M., Torgerson, J., Bouchard, C., Carlsson, C., et al. (2004). Lifestyle, diabetes, and cardiovascular risk factors ten years after bariatric surgery. *New England Journal of Medicine, 351*, 2683–2693.

Sturm, R. (2002). The effects of obesity, smoking, and drinking on medical problems and costs. *Health Affairs, 21*(2), 245.

Sturm, R., & Wells, K. B. (2001). Does obesity contribute as much to morbidity as poverty or smoking? *Public Health, 115*(3), 229–235.

Surwit, R. S., & Schneider, M. S. (1993). Role of stress in the etiology and treatment of diabetes mellitus. *Psychosomatic Medicine, 55*(4), 380.

Surwit, R. S., van Tilburg, M. A. L., Zucker, N., McCaskill, C. C., Parekh, P., Feinglos, M. N., et al. (2002). Stress management improves long-term glycemic control in type 2 diabetes. *Diabetes Care, 25*(1), 30.

Tapper, K., Shaw, C., Ilsley, J., Hill, A. J., Bond, F. W., & Moore, L. (2009). Exploratory randomised controlled trial of a mindfulness-based weight loss intervention for women. *Appetite, 52*(2), 396–404.

Teachman, B. A., & Brownell, K. D. (2001). Implicit anti-fat bias among health professionals: is anyone immune? *International Journal of Obesity, 25*(10), 1525–1531.-

Telch, C. F., & Agras, W. S. (1996). Do emotional states influence binge eating in the obese? *International Journal of Eating Disorders, 20,* 271–279.

Tuomilehto, J., Lindstrom, J., Eriksson, J. G., Valle, T. T., Hamalainen, H., Ilanne-Parikka, P., et al. (2001). Prevention of type 2 diabetes mellitus by changes in lifestyle among subjects with impaired glucose tolerance. *New England Journal of Medicine, 344*(18), 1343.

UKPDS Group. (1998). Intensive blood-glucose control with sulphonylureas or insulin compared with conventional treatment and risk of complications in patients with type 2 diabetes. *Lancet, 352,* 836–853.

Valera Mora, M. E., Scarfone, A., Calvani, M., Greco, A. V., & Mingrone, G. (2003). Insulin clearance in obesity. *Journal of the American College of Nutrition, 22*(6), 487–493.

Wadden, T. A., Sternberg, J. A., Letizia, K. A., Stunkard, A. J., & Foster, G. D. (1989). Treatment of obesity by very low calorie diet, behavior-therapy, and their combination: A five-year perspective. *International Journal of Obesity, 13,* 39–46.

Westenhoefer, J. (1991). Dietary restraint and disinhibition: Is restraint a homogeneous construct? *Appetite, 16*(1), 45–55.

Westenhoefer, J., Stunkard, A. J., & Pudel, V. (1999). Validation of the flexible and rigid control dimensions of dietary restraint. *International Journal of Eating Disorders, 26*(1), 53–64.

Wiese, H. J. C., Wilson, J. F., Jones, R. A., & Neises, M. (1992). Obesity stigma reduction in medical students. *International Journal of Obesity, 16*(11), 859–868.

Wild, S. H., Roglic, G., Green, A., Sicree, R., & King, H. (2004). Global prevalence of diabetes: Estimates for the year 2000 and projections for 2030. *Diabetes Care, 27*(10), 2569.

Wilkin, T. J., & Voss, L. D. (2004). The metabolic syndrome: Origins and implications. *Journal of the Royal Society of Medicine, 97,* 1–10.

Wing, R. R. (1998). Behavioral approaches to the treatment of obesity. In G. A. Bray, C. Bourchard, & P. T. James (Eds.), *Handbook of obesity* (pp. 855–873). New York: Marcel Dekker.

Wing, R. R., Hamman, R. F., Bray, G. A., Delahanty, L., Edelstein, S. L., Hill, J. O., et al. (2004). Achieving weight and activity goals among diabetes prevention program lifestyle participants. *Obesity Research,* *12*(9), 1426–1434.

Wyatt, S. B., Winters, K. P., & Dubbert, P. M. (2006). Overweight and obesity: Prevalence, consequences, and causes of a growing public health problem. *American Journal of the Medical Sciences, 331*(4), 166.

Young, L. A., Cappola, A. R., & Baime, M. J. (2009). Mindfulness based stress reduction: Effect on emotional distress in diabetes. *Practical Diabetes International, 26*(6), 222–224.

5 ACCEPTANCE AND COMMITMENT THERAPY: A PROMISING APPROACH TO SMOKING CESSATION

Jonathan B. Bricker
Fred Hutchinson Cancer Research Center
& the University of Washington

Smoking is a huge problem in the United States and worldwide. Despite great progress in the reduction of the U.S. smoking prevalence (Fiore et al., 2008), this decline has recently stalled (Centers for Disease Control and Prevention, 2006). Currently, 21 percent of American adults smoke, far above the Healthy People 2010 national goal of 12 percent (Centers for Disease Control and Prevention, 2006). Cigarette smoking remains the leading cause of preventable death in the United States, accounting for over 400,000 deaths annually

(Centers for Disease Control and Prevention, 2006). Worldwide, there are now about 1.2 billion smokers (Mackay, Ericksen, & Shafey, 2006). Smoking causes 5 million deaths per year, and, if the present trends continue, 10 million smokers per year are projected to die by 2025. The prevalence of smoking tends to be highest in Eastern Europe and in Asia, with men smoking more than women (Hatsukami, Stead, & Gupta, 2008).

Smoking causes a large number of cancers. The first cancer known to be caused by smoking was lung cancer. Since then, the types of cancers found to be caused by smoking have increased dramatically and now include cancer of the oral cavity, oropharynx and hypopharynx, esophagus, stomach, liver, pancreas, larynx, nasopharynx, nasal cavity and nasal sinuses, urinary bladder, kidney, and uterine cervix. More than 1.3 million new lung cancer cases and 644,000 cancers of the oral cavity, nasopharynx, other pharynx, or larynx are diagnosed annually (Parkin, Bray, Ferlay, & Pisani, 2005). Most of these cancers are attributable to smoking. Nearly 1.2 million lung cancer patients and 352,000 patients with cancer of the oral cavity, nasopharynx, other pharynx, or larynx die each year. Most of these deaths are caused by cancer (Parkin et al., 2005). The International Agency for Research on Cancer, the U.S. Surgeon General, the National Academy of Sciences, the U.S. Environmental Protection Agency, and many other authorities have determined that exposure to secondhand smoke (SHS) causes lung cancer in humans (International Agency for Research on Cancer, 2004; National Research Council, 1986; U.S. Department of Health and Human Services, 2006). This chapter shows how the problem of smoking is now being addressed in the current standard smoking cessation interventions and presents the promise of acceptance and commitment therapy (Hayes, Strosahl, & Wilson, 1999) for improving the quit rates of behavioral interventions.

Current Smoking Cessation Intervention Approaches

In addition to effective government policy and media interventions to control tobacco use and exposure (Bala, Strzeszynski, & Cahill,

2008; National Cancer Institute, 2008; World Health Organization, 2005) a key strategy for reducing the U.S. and worldwide morbidity and mortality attributed to smoking is to directly help individuals to quit (Fiore et al., 2008). The current standard in smoking cessation interventions is the combination of some form of psychological therapy and pharmacotherapy (for reviews see Fiore et al., 2008; Ranney, Melvin, Lux, McClain, & Lohr, 2006). This combination results in higher smoking cessation rates than psychological therapy alone (Fiore et al., 2000, 2008). Regarding pharmacotherapies, there are a number of effective drugs for smoking cessation (Fiore et al., 2008). One of the most common is the nicotine patch (a form of nicotine replacement therapy, or NRT) that is designed to reduce nicotine cravings and withdrawal symptoms (Fiore et al., 2008). The most recently introduced pharmacotherapies are the innovative nicotine partial agonists (e.g., Varenicline) that partially block the binding of nicotine to neurotransmitter receptors in the brain that stimulate smoking-induced feelings of pleasure (for a recent review, see Cahill, Stead, & Lancaster, 2008). Through this mechanism, these innovative pharmacotherapies are designed to undermine the positively reinforcing (i.e., rewarding) functions of smoking.

Regarding psychological approaches, most of the methods used focus on enhancing motivation and social support for quitting, providing basic health information about smoking and quitting, teaching coping skills, and helping smokers set a quit date (Fiore et al., 2000, 2008). One commonly used approach is cognitive behavioral therapy (CBT), which, in addition to focusing on managing external events (e.g., seeing other smokers), includes methods directed toward internal events associated with smoking (e.g., cravings, sadness; Fiore et al., 2000, 2008). The reason for the focus on internal cues is that both theory (Balfour & Ridley, 2000) and research (Shiffman et al., 2002; Shiffman & Waters, 2004) support the notions that emotions, thoughts, and physical sensations are potent internal events associated with smoking. Cravings, for example, can be very powerful: every one-point increase in smoking craving (on a zero to ten scale) predicts a 33 percent increase in the odds of subsequent smoking (Shiffman et al., 2002). Moreover, theory (Otto, Powers, & Fischmann, 2005; Perkins, Conklin, & Levine, 2008) and research (e.g., Baer & Lichtenstein, 1988) suggest that external events (e.g., elements of social settings) lead to smoking by inducing internal events such as cravings and expectancies. CBT addresses internal cues to smoke by teaching smokers skills designed to *reduce* or *avoid* these internal events. The U.S. Public Health Service's Clinical Practice Guideline recommends that CBT interventions aimed at smoking cessation include advice for smokers to (a) avoid situations associated with smoking, (b) try to reduce or control sensations, thoughts, and emotions associated with smoking, and (c) engage in distracting activities (Fiore et al., 2000, 2008). A recently published guide to the most effective CBT interventions recommends very similar strategies (Perkins et al., 2008).

The weighted average standard CBT plus pharmacotherapy counseling thirty-day quit rate at twelve-month follow-up, primarily from studies of smokers motivated to quit, ranges from 14 to 19 percent, with highly similar success rates across all the major modes of intervention delivery (i.e., group, individual, and telephone-based intervention; Fiore et al., 2008; Lancaster & Stead, 2005; Silagy, Lancaster, Stead, Mant, & Fowler, 2004; Stead & Lancaster, 2005; Stead, Perera, & Lancaster, 2006). While the success rate of psychological therapy is considerably higher than the 4 percent success rate of those who try quitting on their own (Fiore et al., 2008), the fact that these therapies are not successful at helping 81 to 86 percent of smokers trying to quit is sobering. These low cessation rates partly reflect the serious lack of progress that has been made in behavioral interventions for smoking cessation (Brandon, 2001; Hajek, 1996; Niaura & Abrams, 2002; Shiffman, 1993). Indeed, there are no new, proven-effective approaches to improve the success rates of current standard therapies described here. However, there are developing and not yet fully investigated approaches that appear to offer substantial potential in this area of pressing clinical and public health need.

Acceptance and Commitment Therapy

As discussed in previous chapters of this book, acceptance-focused interventions are an emerging psychological treatment approach focusing on enhancing individuals' willingness to experience their physical sensations, emotions, and thoughts (Hayes, Luoma, Bond, Masuda, & Lillis, 2006). In particular, acceptance and commitment therapy (ACT, pronounced like the word "act") has special prominence among the various acceptance-focused therapies (Hayes et al., 1999). ACT's psychological methods, as the name suggests, are designed to change two fundamental processes underlying behavior change: acceptance and commitment. In accordance with its Latin root, *capere*, meaning "take," *acceptance* in ACT is the act of receiving or "taking what is offered." In ACT, acceptance means making room for intense physical sensations (e.g., urges associated with smoking), emotions (e.g., sadness associated with smoking), and thoughts (e.g., thoughts associated with smoking) while allowing them to come and go without a struggle. *Commitment* in ACT, paired with a focus on values, means articulating what is deeply important and meaningful to individuals and using that knowledge to motivate and guide specific plans of action (e.g., stopping smoking).

Overall, ACT is designed to help people fundamentally change their relationship to intense sensations, emotions, and thoughts while making committed behavioral changes guided by their values. Over thirty-five randomized treatment outcome studies of ACT have been published for interventions in a wide variety of problem areas, including depression and drug addiction (Hayes et al., 2006; Gregg, Callaghan, Hayes, & Glenn-Lawson, 2007; Lappalainen et al., 2007). Across these studies, ACT has demonstrated medium to large effect sizes (Cohen's d ranging from .57 to .95; Hayes et al., 2006), but since ACT is an emerging therapy, a recent meta-analysis recommended more trials of ACT in comparison with active treatments (Powers, Zum Vörde Sive Vörding, & Emmelkamp, 2009). Overall, ACT is especially promising, particularly given that this intervention is relatively new (Powers et al., 2009).

How ACT Differs from CBT

ACT and CBT share a focus on enhancing motivation and social support for quitting, providing basic health information about smoking and quitting, and helping smokers set a quit date (Fiore et al., 2000, 2008; Gifford et al., 2004; Hernandez-Lopez, Luciano, Bricker, Roales-Nieto, & Montesinos, 2009). Beyond these important similarities, ACT and CBT have fundamental distinctions.

Regarding theory, ACT is based on contemporary operant conditioning theory (Hayes, Barnes-Holmes, & Roche, 2001) while CBT is consistent with information-processing theories (Newell, 1990). To intervene on internal events associated with smoking (e.g., urges), ACT focuses mostly on acceptance and willingness to experience internal distress (Gifford et al., 2004, in press; Hernandez-Lopez et al., 2009), whereas CBT focuses mostly on the reduction or control of internal distress (Fiore et al., 2008; Perkins et al., 2008).

With regard to processes of change, ACT predominantly aims to alter the function of internal events associated with smoking (e.g., urges) whereas CBT aims predominantly to alter the form or content of internal events associated with smoking. Moreover, ACT promotes predominantly value-driven behavior change (Hayes et al., 1999; Luoma, Hayes, & Walser, 2007; Gifford et al., 2004, in review; Hernandez-Lopez et al., 2009) whereas CBT promotes *predominantly goal*-driven behavior change (Fiore et al., 2008; Perkins et al., 2008).

The methods for promoting skillful action are, in ACT, primarily through metaphors and experiential exercises that operate outside of literal language (Hayes et al., 1999; Luoma et al., 2007; Gifford et al., 2004, in press; Hernandez-Lopez et al., 2009), whereas in CBT teaching of skills is primarily done through logical and literal explanation and other methods that work inside literal language (Fiore et al., 2008; Perkins et al., 2008).

Finally, empirical support for these distinctions comes from randomized trials showing that outcomes from ACT, but not CBT, are mediated by increases in acceptance of internal psychological experiences (Lappalainen et al., 2007; Bond & Bunce, 2000; Forman, Herbert, Moitra, Yeomans, & Geller, 2007), present awareness (Forman et al., 2007), and distancing from thoughts (Hayes et al., 2006; Zettle, Raines, & Hayes, in press).

ACT for Smoking Cessation: A Brief Clinical Overview

Since ACT for smoking cessation is in a relatively early stage of empirical testing—and is thus not widely disseminated in the clinical community—this section will provide just a brief clinical overview of this intervention. The overriding goals of ACT for smoking cessation are to (a) develop *acceptance*-related skills for dealing with internal smoking cues while (b) enhancing an enduring *commitment* to quitting smoking (Hayes et al., 1999; Hernandez-Lopez et al., 2009). Clients are encouraged to make behavioral choices on the basis of commitment to goals linked to life values, and not on the basis of seeking to modify or alleviate certain sensations, emotions, and thoughts.

To help the client achieve these goals, intervention focuses on ACT's core interdependent processes: *acceptance and commitment*. In ACT for smoking cessation, *acceptance* refers to allowing one's self to have, without defense, the sensations, emotions, and thoughts that cue smoking (Hayes et al., 1999). The process of *commitment* in ACT means choosing and rechoosing actions to quit smoking while consciously in the presence of sensations, emotions, and thoughts that cue smoking. Overall, ACT is designed to help people fundamentally change their relationship to intense sensations, emotions, and thoughts while making committed behavioral changes guided by their values. A number of acceptance strategies (cognitive defusion, being present, observing self) and commitment strategies (values and committed action), as they are presented in the author's research on ACT for smoking cessation, are shown in table 5.1.

TABLE 5.1   Acceptance and Commitment Processes and
Their Application to Smoking Cessation

Acceptance Processes

Process	Definition	Function
1. Cognitive Defusion ("Unhooking from Thoughts")	Recognizing thoughts, self-judgments, images, and memories as just words and pictures. Allowing them to come and go without trying to alter, control, or avoid them.	To see what thoughts refer to without needing to act on them; to not take thoughts literally; to reduce the believability of thoughts.
An example for smoking cessation	*To reduce the believability of a thought that often cues smoking (e.g., "I want to smoke"), reduce it to one key word (e.g. "smoke") and then say the word out loud repeatedly for 30 seconds, while not smoking.*	
2. Being Present ("The Here and Now")	Being fully aware of the present moment with openness, interest, and receptiveness. Observation and non-judgmental description of experiences in the present moment. Focusing on engaging fully in what you are doing.	To experience the world around a person more directly, rather than as constructed by sensations, emotions, and thoughts. Practice with the observing self facilitates being present.

An example for smoking cessation	While holding an unlit cigarette, take one minute to describe out loud its color, length, texture, and smell. Next, describe in the present tense what thoughts, feelings, emotions, and sensations come up. For example, "I am now having a strong craving to smoke this cigarette."	
3. Observing Self ("Pure Awareness")	Unchanging part of a person that witnesses everything that a person experiences. Internal cues (e.g., sensations) are like scenes playing (changing) on a movie screen. A person is the movie screen (unchanging) on which they play.	To see that sensations, emotions, and thoughts are things a person has some of the time. They are not permanent identifying characteristics.
An example for smoking cessation	Stare at an object in front of you for 45 seconds. Observe it as if you have just seen it for the first time. As you are observing it, notice who's doing the observing.	

Commitment Processes

Process	Definition	Function
1. Values ("What Matters to You")	Chosen life directions. Values are the purposely chosen and deeply important things to a person. Valuing is a process, not a life goal achieved or an outcome.	To motivate change. Values remind people of what changing is about for them when they are facing challenges. Values make acceptance worth experiencing.

An example for smoking cessation	Therapist may ask: "Imagine that today is your 90th birthday. You are gathered with the people who love you. And you are looking back on your life as it is today. What would be the things that you would most want your loved ones to say about you? Why would those things be important?"	
2. Committed Action ("Taking Action")	Committing to repeated behavior changes guided by a person's values. Acting on value-guided goals while accepting all the challenges that may come up.	To move a person to act in ways that are consistent with the life they value. Once actions are taken, person sees that more effective behaviors become possible.
An example for smoking cessation	Quit Plan: a step-by-step smoking cessation plan. In this plan, (1) values guide the goals (e.g., quitting on March 10), (2) goals guide the actions to be taken (e.g., start by not smoking in the car), (3) actions might bring up barriers (e.g., cravings), and (4) barriers lead to strategies for facing barriers (e.g., practicing a Being Present exercise).	

ACT's Promise as a Smoking Cessation Intervention: Evidence from Three Trials

Overall, the three trials of ACT for smoking cessation conducted to date have been promising, with the ACT intervention groups obtaining 30 to 35 percent quit rates at twelve months post-intervention (Gifford et al., 2004, in press; Hernandez-Lopez et al., 2009)—about double the 14 to 19 percent (Fiore et al., 2008; Stead & Lancaster, 2005) quit rates at twelve months post-intervention for CBT plus nicotine replacement therapy (NRT). Recruitment appears feasible, the ACT intervention appears well attended, and participants appear receptive to ACT.

In the first trial, group plus individual-based ACT (with no NRT) was compared to physician-delivered NRT in a randomized controlled trial of adult smokers (Gifford et al., 2004). Smokers were recruited from the community (e.g., via newspaper ads, flyers, physician referrals) and 76 out of 124 screened were eligible and randomized. The ACT treatment was well attended: 64 percent completed all of the ACT treatment. The majority of participants rated themselves as being highly receptive to the ACT intervention. In analyses of the survey respondent-only twelve-month post-treatment follow-up data (72 percent data retention), ACT participants showed a twenty-four-hour biochemically supported abstinence rate of 35 percent versus 15 percent for the NRT control arm (OR = 4.20; 95% CI: 1.04 to 16.73). In addition, in intent-to-treat analyses of the twelve-month post-treatment data (where all missing data is coded as smoking), ACT participants showed a twenty-four-hour biochemically supported abstinence rate of 21 percent versus 9 percent for the NRT control arm (OR = 2.62; 95% CI: .70 to 9.88).

The second randomized trial of 302 smokers was group-based ACT plus bupropion intervention that was compared to physician-delivered bupropion (Gifford et al., in review). A sample was successfully recruited from the community (e.g., via newspaper ads, flyers, physician referrals); 303 (of 717 total screened) participants were entered and randomized. The ACT treatment was well attended: 70 percent completed all of the ACT treatment. Participants were receptive to ACT: ACT participants reported being more receptive to the intervention than the control group participants ($p < .001$; Cohen's $d = .73$). The twelve-month post-treatment outcome data retention rate was low (44 percent) but was not different between the ACT and control groups ($p = .99$). In intent-to-treat analyses at twelve months post-intervention, the ACT intervention group had a seven-day biochemically supported point prevalence quit rate of 35 percent versus 18 percent in the comparison group ($p < .05$). While results were encouraging and suggest the effectiveness of ACT, the control groups in both trials did not include active psychological methods.

The third trial explored a key question: is ACT for smoking cessation an advance over the current standard CBT? The author collaborated on this recent study, which compared ACT to CBT (both with no pharmacotherapy) for smoking cessation in a sample of 81 adult smokers (Hernandez-Lopez et al., 2009). To create a shorter, lower-cost, and more convenient treatment that could be readily compared with a standard CBT intervention, in this trial, the ACT intervention protocol was a five-session (ninety minutes per session) group therapy ACT for smoking cessation intervention. This study did not include any pharmacotherapy. Eighty-one participants (of 103 screened) were enrolled. Unfortunately, however, random assignment to treatment was not possible because one of the two recruitment sites (a community-based cancer prevention clinic) required that CBT be offered to participants recruited from their location. To strengthen the study's quasi-experimental design, the authors (a) used similar recruitment procedures in both conditions, (b) matched the two treatments on intervention length and structure (i.e., five-session, ninety minutes per session group therapy), (c) had the two conditions compared on important baseline characteristics empirically known to predict smoking cessation relapse, and (d) statistically controlled for any observed baseline differences between conditions. The authors found that each treatment was well attended: 69 percent completed all of the treatment, with no differences between the ACT and CBT groups ($p = .19$). Participants were receptive to ACT: in the ACT condition, (a) 92 percent of participants reported that the treatment was useful, as compared to 79 percent for CBT ($p = .22$), and (b) 88 percent regularly practiced treatment techniques, as compared to 65 percent for CBT ($p = .07$). The twelve-month post-treatment outcome data retention rate was low (53 percent) but was not different between the ACT and CBT groups ($p = .45$). In intent-to-treat analyses at twelve months post-treatment, participants in the ACT condition had a biochemically supported thirty-day point prevalence quit rate of 30 percent, versus 13 percent in the CBT group (OR = 2.86; $p = .05$).

Finally, a primary influence on early relapse after initial cessation (Abrantes et al., 2008) is difficulty tolerating internal cues to smoke (Brown et al., 2008). Fortunately, ACT showed promise for improving distress tolerance in a one-arm study of early-lapse nicotine-dependent smokers (Brown et al., 2008). The majority ($n =$ 13, 81 percent) were able to remain quit for longer than seventy-two hours, and seven (43 percent) for longer than one month. Given that participants had not achieved abstinence for longer than seventy-two hours in the preceding ten years, these results are encouraging.

ACT as a Telephone-Delivered Intervention for Smoking Cessation: A Feasibility Study

A commonly used intervention modality for smoking cessation is telephone counseling (Fiore et al., 2008). Advantages include the following:

- Accessibility: 95 percent of U.S. households have a telephone (U.S. Census Bureau, 2005) and 92 percent of individuals in the United States have cell phones (Cellular Telecommunications & Internet Association, 2009).

- Reach: All fifty U.S. states, all provinces in Canada, and many countries in the European Union have established quit lines (Fiore et al., 2004).

- Cost-effectiveness: Quit lines save millions of dollars in medical costs and worker productivity losses (Fiore et al., 2004).

- Relatively brief duration: Telephone counseling can be delivered in three to seven calls, with an average total intervention length of ninety minutes (Stead et al., 2006). This average total length is consistent with research showing no evidence of smoking cessation efficacy enhancement beyond a total of ninety minutes of intervention contact time (Perkins et al., 2008).

Unfortunately, in randomized trials of telephone counseling, the percentages of participants not smoking in the past thirty days at the twelve-month follow-up, among smokers motivated to quit, are well established as 12 percent and 14 percent, for counseling and for counseling combined with the option of NRT, respectively (Stead et al., 2006). These low quit rates are remarkably consistent with those obtained through other modes of intervention delivery (e.g., face-to-face group therapy).

To build on ACT research to date and address the great public health need for more-effective telephone-delivered smoking cessation interventions, the author and his colleagues conducted a study to determine the feasibility of the first telephone-delivered ACT intervention for smoking cessation (Bricker, Mann, Marek, Liu, & Peterson, 2010). Specifically, the study was a telephone-delivered five-session (ninety minutes of total intervention contact time) ACT adult smoking cessation one-arm pilot study of fifteen smokers. No pharmacotherapy was provided. Of the sample of fifteen smokers, 64.3 percent were at or below the U.S. federal poverty level (U.S. Census Bureau, 2005), 40 percent were female, 53.3 percent belonged to racial/ethnic minority groups (eight were African American); median age was forty-nine years (range twenty-seven to sixty-two), 33.3 percent were currently married, and 26.7 percent had no more than a high school education (or GED). As measured by a validated clinical screening tool (Means-Christensen, Sherbourne, Roy-Byrne, Craske, & Stein, 2006), a significant fraction screened positive for depression (40 percent) and anxiety (60 percent). At baseline, the median level of cigarettes per day was eleven to twenty, and 64 percent reported smoking more than half a pack per day.

The mean (SD) of the number of counseling calls per participant was 3.5 (1.3), with 33.3 percent of participants completing all five calls, and the mean (SD) duration of all telephone counseling contacts was 81.9 (33.1) minutes. At twenty days post-treatment, (a) 100 percent of participants reported that they had felt respected by the counselor, (b) 86 percent said the intervention was a good fit for them, and (c) 93 percent said the intervention had helped them in their quit attempt. Participants rated 79 to 93 percent ($M = 86\%$) of the ACT telephone intervention exercises as useful during the quitting process.

The twenty-day post-treatment and twelve-month post-treatment smoking outcome data retention rates were both 93 percent (fourteen out of fifteen). In the conservative intent-to-treat analysis (where all with missing data are coded as smokers) of the twenty-days post-treatment survey, (a) 43 percent of participants had not smoked the day of the post-treatment survey, (b) 29 percent had not smoked in the past seven days or more, (c) 71 percent had quit smoking for at least twenty-four hours one or more times since the start of counseling, and (d) 62 percent reduced from daily to less-than-daily (including quitting) smoking. In the intent-to-treat analysis of the twelve-month post-treatment survey, the twelve-month and thirty-day abstinence rates were each 29 percent (13/14). Using the respondent-only data (n = 13), the twelve-month and thirty-day abstinence rates were each 31 percent.

The smoking cessation/progress outcomes are encouraging. First, the twenty-day post-treatment cessation outcomes *and* twelve-month post-treatment outcomes are nearly equivalent to the end-of-treatment twenty-four-hour abstinence and twelve-month post-treatment outcomes observed in both prior studies of face-to-face ACT offered without pharmacotherapy (Gifford et al., 2004: 35 percent abstinence at post-treatment, 35 percent abstinence at twelve months post-treatment; Hernandez-Lopez et al., 2009: 42 percent abstinence at post-treatment, 30 percent abstinence at twelve months post-treatment). Second, this study's twelve-month prolonged abstinence outcomes of 29 percent are over double the twelve-month post-treatment cessation outcomes of 12 percent observed in trials of telephone-based counseling offered without pharmacotherapy (Stead et al., 2006). Third, these outcomes were obtained from individuals primarily from low-income and racial/ethnic minority groups. These individuals, especially African Americans, are under-represented in smoking research (Dickerson, Leeman, Mazure, & O'Malley, 2009) and have lower smoking cessation rates than those who are not low income or racial/ethnic minority (Centers for Disease Control, 2008). Fourth, these promising cessation rates were observed without the offer of pharmacotherapy (e.g., NRT).

Overall, telephone-delivered ACT shows promise for smoking cessation and changing processes of smoking cessation, was well accepted by participants, and warrants future testing in an adequately powered randomized trial.

Is ACT for Smoking Cessation Mediated by Acceptance and Commitment?

Little is known about the mechanisms through which psychologically based smoking cessation interventions exert their effects. Research into this area has been strongly recommended by the PHS Clinical Practice Guideline (Fiore et al., 2000, 2008). The main processes hypothesized to mediate the effectiveness of ACT are (1) *acceptance* and (2) *commitment* (Hayes et al., 1999). In smoking cessation, this means acceptance of internal smoking cues and commitment to quitting (Gifford et al., 2004; Hernandez et al., 2009). Regarding acceptance, the ACT treatment was effective, compared to the pharmacotherapy control groups, at increasing acceptance of internal smoking cues by the end of treatment (Gifford et al., 2004, in review). Moreover, acceptance of internal smoking cues was associated with an increased likelihood of smoking cessation at twelve months post-randomization (Wald c^2 = .11, p = .01, Gifford et al., 2004; β = .17, p < .001, Gifford et al., in review). In a statistical model, the cessation effects of both of these ACT interventions were significantly mediated by overall increases in acceptance of internal smoking cues (p < .05 in both trials) (Gifford et al., 2004, in review). And in the study of telephone-delivered ACT, acceptance of physical cravings, emotions, and thoughts that cue smoking increased from baseline to end of treatment (p = .001, p = .038, p = .085, respectively; Bricker et al., 2010). At this point, no trials have examined whether this mediation effect involving acceptance of internal cues is exclusive to ACT and absent in CBT. The cessation trial comparing ACT with CBT did not examine mediators of ACT's effectiveness (Hernandez-Lopez et al., 2009). Regarding *commitment*, greater commitment to quitting predicted a 2.32 (p = .003) higher chance of smoking abstinence (Kahler et al., 2007). In the telephone-delivered intervention, commitment to quitting increased from baseline to end of treatment (p = .01; Bricker et al., 2010). Further mediation analyses of commitment have not yet been done.

Future Directions

Overall, the three trials of ACT for smoking cessation conducted to date have been promising, with the ACT intervention groups obtaining about 30 to 35 percent quit rates at twelve months post-intervention (Bricker et al., 2010; Gifford et al., 2004, in review; Hernandez-Lopez et al., 2009)—about double the 14 to 19 percent (Fiore et al., 2008; Stead & Lancaster, 2005; Stead et al., 2006; Lancaster & Stead, 2005; Silagy et al., 2004) quit rates at twelve months post-intervention for CBT plus NRT. Recruitment was feasible, the ACT intervention was well attended, and participants were receptive to ACT. Telephone-delivered ACT for smoking cessation also appears promising (Bricker et al., 2010).

While promising, all three ACT trials to date had key methodological limitations, making it difficult to determine whether ACT is indeed more effective than CBT—the current standard in behavioral intervention. The first comparison of ACT with CBT for smoking cessation was limited by a small sample size, lack of random assignment, and low follow-up data retention (Hernandez-Lopez et al., 2009).

An adequately powered randomized trial, designed to ensure higher follow-up data retention, that compares ACT with CBT for smoking would thus provide an innovative and rigorous test of the effectiveness of ACT for smoking cessation. Moreover, all ACT smoking cessation interventions to date have been recruited through and conducted within university laboratory settings, which, while valuable, do not provide a real-world and generalizable test of ACT's effectiveness for smoking cessation. If ACT were shown to be equally effective or more effective than CBT in a real-world setting, it would demonstrate the viability of this intervention as an alternative to CBT.

Ideal trials would compare ACT with the current standard care CBT programs already offered in real-world clinical settings. These trials need to be tested for a variety of common intervention modalities, including group therapy, individual therapy, and telephone therapy.

Regarding ACT's impact on underlying processes of smoking cessation, no trials have examined whether ACT, but not CBT, is mediated specifcally by acceptance of internal smoking cues and commitment to quitting. An important next step of research would be to determine to what extent ACT, but not CBT, is mediated by higher levels of acceptance and commitment. Such mediational analyses would (a) provide an innovative test of the mechanisms underlying ACT for smoking cessation, (b) provide empirical support for the idea that ACT for smoking cessation works through processes that are distinct from CBT for smoking cessation, and (c) potentially refine methods within ACT for smoking cessation by clarifying processes that may need to be targeted further in future interventions.

Summary

ACT shows great promise for improving the quit rates of smoking cessation interventions. The exciting challenge ahead is to conduct adequately powered and methodologically sound randomized trials testing ACT in comparison with the current standard in behavioral interventions, with the aim of demonstrating quit success rates and changes in theory-based underlying processes of smoking cessation. If proven effective, ACT stands to make a strong impact. Not only could it increase abstinence rates over current best-practice treatment, but the option of this new therapy could also encourage smokers to enroll in treatment who otherwise might not because they have already tried and failed with existing therapies.

References

Abrantes, A. M., Strong, D. R., Lejuez, C. W., Kahler, C. W., Carpenter, L. L., Price, L. H., et al. (2008). The role of negative affect in risk for early lapse among low distress tolerance smokers. *Addictive Behaviors*, *33*(11), 1394–1401.

Baer, J. S., & Lichtenstein, E. (1988). Classification and prediction of smoking relapse episodes: An exploration of individual differences. *Journal of Consulting and Clinical Psychology, 56*(1), 104–110.

Bala, M., Strzeszynski, L., & Cahill, K. (2008). Mass media interventions for smoking cessation in adults (review). *Cochrane Database of Systematic Reviews,* 1. CD004704. Retrieved February 10, 2010, from PubMed.

Balfour, D. J., & Ridley, D. L. (2000). The effects of nicotine on neural pathways implicated in depression: A factor in nicotine addiction? *Pharmacology Biochemistry & Behavior, 66*(1), 79–85.

Bond, F. W., & Bunce, D. (2000). Mediators of change in emotion-focused and problem-focused worksite stress management interventions. *Journal of Occupational Health Psychology, 5*(1), 156–163.

Brandon, T. H. (2001). Behavioral tobacco cessation treatments: Yesterday's news or tomorrow's headlines? *Journal of Clinical Oncology, 19*(18 Suppl.), 64S–68S.

Bricker, J. B., Mann, S. M., Marek, P. M., Liu, J. L., & Peterson, A. V. (2010). Telephone-delivered acceptance & commitment therapy (ACT) for smoking cessation: A feasibility study. *Nicotine & Tobacco Research, 12,* 454–458.

Brown, R. A., Palm, K. M., Strong, D. R., Lejuez, C. W., Kahler, C. W., Zvolensky, M. J., et al. (2008). Distress tolerance treatment for early-lapse smokers: rationale, program description, and preliminary findings. *Behavior Modification, 32*(3), 302–332.

Cahill, K., Stead, L. F., & Lancaster, T. (2008). Nicotine receptor partial agonists for smoking cessation: *Cochrane Database of Systematic Reviews,* 3. CD006103 review.

Cellular Telecommunications & Internet Association. (2009). *CTIA's semi-annual wireless industry survey, 2009.* Retrieved September 17, 2010, from http://files.ctia.org/pdf/CTIA_Survey_Year_End_2009_Graphics.pdf

Centers for Disease Control and Prevention. (2006). Tobacco use among adults—United States, 2005. *Morbidity and Mortality Weekly Report, 55*(42), 1145–1148.

Centers for Disease Control and Prevention. (2008). Cigarette smoking among adults—United States, 2007. *Morbidity and Mortality Weekly Report, 57,* 1221–1228.

Dickerson, D. L., Leeman, R. F., Mazure, C. M., & O'Malley, S. S. (2009). The inclusion of women and minorities in smoking cessation clinical trials: A systematic review. *American Journal of Addiction, 18,* 21–28.

Fiore, M. C., Bailey, W. C., Cohen, S. J., Dorfman, S. F., Goldstein, M. G., Gritz, E. R., et al. (2000). *Treating tobacco use and dependence. Clinical practice guideline.* Rockville, MD: U.S. Department of Health and Human Services, Public Health Service.

Fiore, M. C., Croyle, R. T., Curry, S. J., Cutler, C. M., Davis, R. M., Gordon, C., et al. (2004). Preventing 3 million premature deaths and helping 5 million smokers quit: A national action plan for tobacco cessation. *American Journal of Public Health, 94,* 205–210.

Fiore, M. C., Jaén, C. R., Baker, T. B., Bailey, W. C., Benowitz, N. L., Curry, S. J., et al. (2008). *Treating tobacco use and dependence: 2008 update—clinical practice guideline.* Rockville, MD: U.S. Department of Health and Human Services, Public Health Service.

Forman, E. M., Herbert, J. D., Moitra, E., Yeomans, P. D., & Geller, P. A. (2007). A randomized controlled effectiveness trial of acceptance and commitment therapy and cognitive therapy for anxiety and depression. *Behavior Modification, 31*(6), 772–799.

Gifford, E. V., Kohlenberg, B. S., Hayes, S. C., Antonuccio, D. O., Piasecki, M. M., Rasmussen-Hall, M. L., et al. (2004). Acceptance-based treatment for smoking cessation. *Behavior Therapy, 35,* 689–705.

Gifford, E. V., Kohlenberg, B. S., Hayes, S. C., Pierson, H. M., Piasecki, M. M., Antonuccio, D. O., et al. (in review). Applying the acceptance and relationship context model to smoking cessation: A randomized controlled trial integrating acceptance and commitment therapy and bupropion for adult nicotine dependent smokers.

Gregg, J. A., Callaghan, G. M., Hayes, S. C., & Glenn-Lawson, J. L. (2007). Improving diabetes self-management through acceptance, mindfulness, and values: A randomized controlled trial. *Journal of Consulting and Clinical Psychology, 75*(2), 336–343.

Hajek, P. (1996). Current issues in behavioral and pharmacological approaches to smoking cessation. *Addictive Behaviors, 21*(6), 699–707.

Hatsukami, D. K., Stead, L. F., & Gupta, P. C. (2008). Tobacco addiction. *Lancet, 371*(9629), 2027–2038.

Hayes, S. C., Barnes-Holmes, D., & Roche, B. (Eds.). (2001). *Relational frame theory: A post-Skinnerian account of human language and cognition.* New York: Kluwer Academic Plenum Press.

Hayes, S. C., Luoma, J. B., Bond, F. W., Masuda, A., & Lillis, J. (2006). Acceptance and commitment therapy: Model, processes and outcomes. *Behavior Research & Therapy, 44*(1), 1–25.

Hayes, S. C., Strosahl, K., & Wilson, K. G. (1999). *Acceptance and commitment therapy: An experiential approach to behavior change.* New York: Guilford Press.

Hernandez-Lopez, M. C., Luciano, C., Bricker, J. B., Roales-Nieto, J. G., & Montesinos, F. (2009). Acceptance & commitment therapy for smoking cessation: A preliminary study of its effectiveness in comparison with cognitive behavioral therapy. *Psychology of Addictive Behaviors, 23,* 723-730.

International Agency for Research on Cancer. (2004). *Monographs on the evaluation of carcinogenic risks to humans. Tobacco smoke and involuntary smoking* (Vol. 83). Lyon, France: IARC Press.

Kahler, C. W., Lachance, H. R., Strong, D. R., Ramsey, S. E., Monti, P. M., & Brown, R. A. (2007). The commitment to quitting smoking scale: Initial validation in a smoking cessation trial for heavy social drinkers. *Addictive Behaviors, 32*(10), 2420–2424.

Lancaster, T., & Stead, L. F. (2005). Individual behavioural counselling for smoking cessation [review]. *Cochrane Database of Systematic Reviews, 2.* CD001292 online.

Lappalainen, R., Lehtonen, T., Skarp, E., Taubert, E., Ojanen, M., & Hayes, S. C. (2007). The impact of CBT and ACT models using psychology trainee therapists: A preliminary controlled effectiveness trial. *Behavior Modification, 31*(4), 488–511.

Luoma, J. B., Hayes, S. C., & Walser, R. D. (2007). *Learning ACT: An acceptance & commitment therapy skills-training manual for therapists.* Oakland, CA: New Harbinger Publications.

Mackay, J., Ericksen, M., & Shafey, O. (2006). *The tobacco atlas* (2nd ed.). Atlanta, GA: American Cancer Society.

Means-Christensen, A. J., Sherbourne, C. D., Roy-Byrne, P. P., Craske, M. G., & Stein, M. B. (2006). Using five questions to screen for five common mental disorders in primary care: Diagnostic accuracy of the Anxiety and Depression Detector. *General Hospital Psychiatry, 28*(2), 108–118.

National Cancer Institute. (2008). *The role of the media in promoting and reducing tobacco use. Tobacco control monograph no. 19* (NIH Publication No. 07-6242). Bethesda, MD: U.S. Department of Health and Human Services, National Institutes of Health, National Cancer Institute.

National Research Council. (1986). *Environmental tobacco smoke. Measuring exposures and assessing health effects.* Washington, DC: National Academies Press.

Newell, A. (1990). *Unified theories of cognition.* Cambridge, MA: Harvard University Press.

Niaura, R., & Abrams, D. B. (2002). Smoking cessation: Progress, priorities, and prospectus. *Journal of Consulting and Clinical Psychology, 70*(3), 494–509.

Otto, M. W., Powers, M. B., & Fischmann, D. (2005). Emotional exposure in the treatment of substance use disorders: Conceptual model, evidence, and future directions. *Clinical Psychology Review, 25*(6), 824–839.

Parkin, D. M., Bray, F., Ferlay, J., & Pisani, P. (2005). Global cancer statistics, 2002. *CA: A Cancer Journal for Clinicians, 55*(2), 74–108.

Perkins, K. A., Conklin, C. A., & Levine, M. D. (2008). *Cognitive-behavioral therapy for smoking cessation: A practical guide to the most effective treatments.* New York: Routledge.

Powers, M. B., Zum Vörde Sive Vörding, M. B., & Emmelkamp, P. M. (2009). Acceptance and commitment therapy: A meta-analytic review. *Psychotherapy & Psychosomatics, 78*(2), 73–80.

Ranney, L., Melvin, C., Lux, L., McClain, E., & Lohr, K. N. (2006). Systematic review: Smoking cessation intervention strategies for adults and adults in special populations. *Annals of Internal Medicine, 145*(11), 845–856.

Shiffman, S. (1993). Smoking cessation treatment: Any progress? *Journal of Consulting and Clinical Psychology, 61*(5), 718–722.

Shiffman, S., Gwaltney, C. J., Balabanis, M. H., Liu, K. S., Paty, J. A., Kassel, J.D., et al. (2002). Immediate antecedents of cigarette smoking: An analysis from ecological momentary assessment. *Journal of Abnormal Psychology, 111*(4), 531–545.

Shiffman, S., Hickcox, M., Paty, J. A., Gnys, M., Kassel, J. D., & Richards, T. J. (1996). Progression from a smoking lapse to relapse: Prediction from abstinence violation effects, nicotine dependence, and lapse characteristics. *Journal of Consulting and Clinical Psychology, 64*(5), 993–1002.

Shiffman, S., & Waters, A. J. (2004). Negative affect and smoking lapses: A prospective analysis. *Journal of Consulting and Clinical Psychology, 72*(2), 192–201.

Silagy, C., Lancaster, T., Stead, L., Mant, D., & Fowler, G. (2004). Nicotine replacement therapy for smoking cessation [review]. *Cochrane Database of Systematic Reviews, 3*. CD000146 online.

Stead, L. F., & Lancaster, T. (2005). Group behaviour therapy programmes for smoking cessation [review]. *Cochrane Database of Systematic Reviews, 2*. CD001007 online.

Stead, L. F., Perera, R., & Lancaster, T. (2006). Telephone counseling for smoking cessation [review]. *Cochrane Database of Systematic Reviews, 3*. CD002850 online.

U.S. Census Bureau. (2005). *American community survey, 2005*: Detailed tables. Generated April 2, 2009, by Jingmin Liu, using American FactFinder, from http://factfinder.census.gov

U.S. Department of Health and Human Services. (2006). *The health consequences of involuntary exposure to tobacco smoke. A report of the surgeon general.* Atlanta, GA: USDHHS., Public Health Service, Centers for Disease Control, Office on Smoking and Health.

World Health Organization. (2005). *WHO framework convention on tobacco control.* Retrieved August 25, 2008, from http://www.fctc.org

Zettle, R. D., Raines, J. C., & Hayes, S. C. (in press). Processes of change in acceptance and commitment therapy and cognitive therapy for depression: A mediational reanalysis of Zettle and Raines (1989). *Behavior Modification.*

6 INSOMNIA

Lars-Gunnar Lundh
Department of Psychology, Lund University, Sweden

Insomnia is a frequent complaint. In a recent study with a representative sample of more than 25,000 individuals from seven European countries (Ohayon & Reynolds, 2009), more than 30 percent of the population reported at least one symptom of insomnia (difficulty either initiating or maintaining sleep, or a complaint of nonrestorative sleep, at least three nights per week). Nearly 10 percent of the sample suffered from negative daytime consequences of their insomnia symptoms; 6.6 percent satisfied the *DSM-IV* criteria for an insomnia diagnosis (American Psychiatric Association, 1994).

Not only is the experience of insufficient or nonrestorative sleep common, but it may also have important repercussions in daytime functioning. Insomnia has been found to be significantly associated with poor quality of life, work productivity loss, and activity impairment (Bolge, Doan, Kannan, & Baran, 2009). Further, experimental evidence shows that sleep deprivation can have strong adverse effects on mood (e.g., Dinges et al., 1997; Drake et al., 2001) and on cognitive functioning and learning (e.g., Ratcliff & Van Dongen, 2009; Stickgold & Walker, 2007). This suggests that insomnia may be causally involved in a number of other problems, including the ability to cope with adverse experiences and the development of mood disorders. Although insomnia has traditionally been seen as a secondary symptom of other psychiatric disorders, new evidence (e.g., Harvey, 2008) suggests that insomnia may be an important but underrecognized mechanism in the multifactorial cause and maintenance of psychiatric disorders. This would mean that successful treatment of insomnia might also lead to improvements in mood and other aspects of psychological functioning.

In terms of treatment, there is evidence for cognitive behavioral methods like stimulus control and sleep restriction (for a brief summary of the basic principles of these treatments, see table 6.1). One common element to these treatments is the restriction of the time spent lying awake in bed, which may serve to strengthen the association of the bed with sleep. The documented effects of these approaches, however, are far from optimal (Harvey & Tang, 2003), and there is a need for the development of more effective treatments. One possible candidate for such a development is the application of acceptance and mindfulness techniques to the treatment of insomnia. The purpose of the present chapter is to explore possible reasons why such techniques may be beneficial in the treatment of insomnia, and to develop a rationale for such a treatment. This is done in two steps. First, it is argued that there are two broad categories of psychological processes involved in insomnia: processes that interfere with sleep (e.g., cognitive and emotional arousal), and processes whereby the individual interprets sleep and sleeplessness in a dysfunctional manner. Second, it is argued that both of these factors may be addressed by acceptance and mindfulness techniques. Finally, a review is made of the so-far rather limited empirical evidence that exists regarding applying this approach to the treatment of insomnia, and a call is made for further research on these matters.

TABLE 6.1 Brief Summary of the Basic Principles of Stimulus Control and Sleep Restriction Treatments of Insomnia

Stimulus control instructions (Bootzin, 1972)

Rule 1. Lie down intending to go to sleep only when you feel sleepy.

Rule 2. Do not use your bed or bedroom for anything except sleep. Sexual activity is the only exception to this rule.

Rule 3. If you do not fall asleep quickly, get up and go into another room. Do something relaxing while there, and go back to bed only when you feel sleepy again.

Rule 4. If you still cannot fall asleep, see rule 3. Also, if you wake out of your sleep and do not fall asleep quickly, you should go out of bed as in rule 3. (You may have to get up many times in the same night.)

Rule 5. Set an alarm for the same time each morning and get up when the alarm goes off, regardless of how much sleep you have had.

Rule 6. Do not nap during the daytime, even for short periods.

Sleep restriction (Restriction of time in bed; Spielman, Saskin, & Thorpy, 1987)

1. Patients complete two weeks of sleep diaries, and the therapist uses these to calculate average total subjective sleep time (TST).

2. The amount of time patients are allowed to spend in bed is initially restricted to this average TST. However, no patient is asked to limit time in bed (TIB) to less than 4.5 hours, regardless of baseline TST. Napping or lying down during periods outside of the prescribed time limits is prohibited throughout treatment.

3. Patients choose fixed times to enter and leave bed. Thus a patient prescribed 6 hours in bed may choose an 11:00 p.m. to 5:00 a.m. schedule.

4. Based upon daily telephone reports, when the mean TST exceeds 90 percent of TIB over a period of five days, the patient's TIB is increased by allowing the patient to enter bed fifteen minutes earlier. Five days of unaltered sleep schedule always follow a TIB increase.

5. If the patient's TST drops below 85 percent of TIB for a period of five days, TIB is reduced to the mean TST for those five days. No curtailment of TIB occurs during the first ten days of treatment or for ten days following a sleep schedule change.

Sleep-Interfering and Sleep-Interpreting Processes

On the basis of a review of theories and empirical research on psychological factors in insomnia, Lundh and Broman (2000) argued that the psychological processes involved in insomnia may be grouped into two broad categories: (1) Sleep-interfering processes, including cognitive, emotional, and physiological arousal due, for example, to stressful life events, emotional conflicts, or other disturbing stimuli and moderated by individual differences in arousability, neuroticism, and so on. (2) Sleep-interpreting processes, which make the person perceive or interpret his or her sleep patterns in a distorted or dysfunctional manner, as seen, for example, in misperceptions of sleep, rigid beliefs about sleep requirements and about the consequences of not meeting these requirements, intolerance of natural variations in sleep, misattribution of negative aspects of daily functioning to poor sleep, attentional biases, and the like.

The central tenet of this meta-model is that various forms of insomnia may be differentiated according to various combinations, and interactions, of sleep-interfering and sleep-interpreting processes. These two categories of processes may also be assumed to have a bidirectional causal relationship. For example, sleep-interfering arousal might lead the person to develop increasingly negative interpretations of his or her sleep difficulties. Similarly, negative sleep-interpreting processes (dysfunctional beliefs about need to sleep, worries about sleep, rumination about causes and effects of poor sleep, and so on) can contribute to an increased arousal that interferes with sleep. It also follows that this form of reciprocal causality can result in various kinds of "vicious cycles of sleeplessness" (e.g., Lundh, Lundqvist, Broman, & Hetta, 1991), whereby sleep-interfering and sleep-interpreting processes mutually reinforce each other. For example, if a person has certain kinds of beliefs (e.g., catastrophic beliefs about the disastrous consequences of insufficient sleep), he or she is more likely to respond with negative emotional arousal to temporary sleep difficulties—and this emotional arousal may then interfere further with sleep, which will in turn reinforce negative beliefs about one's self-efficacy with regard to sleep.

The analysis and treatment of insomnia would probably benefit from a much more detailed elaboration of the various kinds of combinations and interactions that may take place between different varieties of sleep-interfering and sleep-interpreting processes in different cases of insomnia. The purpose of the present chapter, however, is more specific: to analyze and discuss the role of acceptance and mindfulness techniques in the treatment of insomnia, with a special focus on their potential for addressing sleep-interfering and sleep-interpreting processes (Lundh, 2005). With regard to sleep-interfering processes, it is argued (a) that sleep is facilitated by cognitive, emotional, and behavioral deactivation, with less verbal, purposive, effortful psychological processes than are used during daytime functioning, and correspondingly more acceptance of spontaneously occurring physiological and mental processes, and (b) that mindfulness practice, in the form of nonjudgmental observation of physical and psychological processes, may be an effective way of training the skills of cognitive deactivation. With regard to sleep-interpreting processes, it is argued that techniques derived from acceptance and commitment therapy (ACT) and mindfulness may serve the development of more functional ways of valuing and interpreting sleep and wakefulness.

Sleep-Interfering Processes

To understand the nature of sleep-interfering processes, and how to counteract these, we need to know what kinds of processes are conducive *to* sleep. In other words: what psychological processes promote sleep, and how is it possible to strengthen these by psychological treatment? In this section, it will be argued (a) that cognitive and emotional deactivation is important for the transition from wakefulness to sleep and (b) that acceptance and mindfulness techniques may be used to strengthen a person's deactivation skills.

THE IMPORTANCE OF COGNITIVE AND EMOTIONAL DEACTIVATION

Normal sleep is regulated according to homeostatic principles (Borbély, 1982). The need for sleep, as experienced in the form of sleepiness, increases as a function of how long the individual has stayed awake, and decreases as a function of the duration and quality of sleep. Like other homeostatic mechanisms, normal sleep is characterized by a certain degree of *automaticity* (Espie, 2002)—that is, a well-adjusted sleep schedule is basically involuntary, involving a rather passive individual who responds to internal and external cues that work as automated setting conditions for sleep. In terms of psychological processes, this automaticity involves a cognitive, emotional, and behavioral deactivation. In other words, the individual goes to rest, both overtly and covertly.

The degree of overt behavioral activation or deactivation can be measured by actigraphy. By means of a small actigraph, which is worn like a watch on the wrist of the nondominant arm, data on the individual's gross motor activity is recorded and later read to a computer where it can be analyzed. Sleep actigraphs produce valid data and are increasingly being employed both in research and in sleep clinics as a replacement for full polysomnography (Ancoli-Israel et al., 2003; Tryon, 2004).

There are still no similar measures of the degree of cognitive activation. A general measure of this kind would have to capture the degree of cognitive activity that takes place at a certain moment in time, independently of whether it involves functional, productive

136

forms of thinking (e.g., problem solving) or dysfunctional and unproductive forms (e.g., worry and rumination). A number of researchers have formulated concepts that are highly relevant in this context, such as "controlled vs. automatic information processing" (Shiffrin & Schneider, 1977) and degree of "effortful control" (Posner & Rothbart, 2000). Common to these conceptualizations is that they are contrasting two opposite poles along a dimension of cognitive activation/deactivation: toward the cognitive *activation* pole, the psychological processes are characterized by selective attention, conscious purpose and control, mental effort and tension, problem solving, reality testing, and decision making, whereas toward the cognitive *deactivation* pole they are characterized by automaticity, spontaneity, effortlessness, associative thinking, imagery, and intuition.

People's level of cognitive activation shows considerable diurnal fluctuations. While awake, the individual engages with more or less effort in conscious, purposive thinking and problem solving, to handle various challenges in living and in adjusting to a changing environment—although the degree of tension, effort, and control may recede during relatively more restful moments of the day (e.g., when the person is traveling to or from work on the bus or subway, during coffee breaks, or when taking a nap). In normal sleepers, there typically occurs a clear cognitive deactivation at the end of the day, as part of the natural transition from wakefulness to sleep. However, to the extent that this cognitive deactivation does not occur but the individual's psychological processes remain dominated by verbal thinking, effort, and purpose, this will interfere with sleep. In view of the fact that insomnia is one of the symptoms of generalized anxiety disorder (GAD), it is highly relevant in the present context that the chronic worries that are typical of GAD patients seem to represent an overreliance on verbal thinking, and a suppression of imagery, affect, and emotional processing (Borkovec, 1994). Another example that strongly points in the same direction is Nolen-Hoeksema's (2000) research on the role of verbal rumination for the development and maintenance of depression and of mixed depression/anxiety states.

Among sleep researchers, Espie (2002) has emphasized the role of cognitive as well as physiological dearousal for sleep. In terms of cognitive processes, this means a disengagement from daily concerns, where the person lets go of goal-directed activities and allows sleep to take over—that is, a process characterized by automaticity. Consistent with this, Harvey (2001) found that people with insomnia generally report more of meta-cognitive thought-control strategies, in particular thought suppression, reappraisal, and worrying, than good sleepers. In a further experimental study, Harvey (2003) showed that the use of thought suppression during the pre-sleep period led to longer sleep latencies and poorer sleep quality both among insomniacs and among normal sleepers; she therefore concluded that active control strategies in the pre-sleep situation may be maladaptive and that the process of falling asleep should involve minimal effort. There is also evidence that (a) higher degrees of rumination are associated with longer sleep latencies and poorer sleep quality, even when controlling for negative mood (Thomsen, Mehlsen, Christensen, & Zachariae, 2003); (b) people with insomnia are involved in excessive verbal thinking that is counterproductive with regard to both sleep and daytime functioning (Nelson & Harvey, 2002, 2003); (c) verbal thinking about stressful matters during the pre-sleep period is associated with longer sleep latencies and more anxiety and discomfort the next morning, as compared with thinking about the same stressful matters in terms of mental images (Nelson & Harvey, 2002); and (d) patients with insomnia show less pre-sleep imagery than good sleepers (Nelson & Harvey, 2003).

Focusing specifically on psychophysiological insomnia, Espie, Broomfield, MacMahon, Macphee, and Taylor (2006) have proposed an explanatory model that they refer to as "the attention-intention-effort pathway," which gives a central role to *sleep*-focused thinking. That is, as a way of handling experiences of sleep disruption, sleep loss, and perceived sleep inadequacy, a person with this variety of insomnia becomes inordinately preoccupied with sleep. As a result, he or she develops (a) selective attention to sleep-related internal and external stimuli, (b) an explicit intention to sleep, and (c) a destructive combination of direct and indirect sleep effort. Because sleep is beyond voluntary control, this sleep preoccupation, with its goal-directed use of various strategies designed to deliver sleep and to avoid sleeplessness, is doomed to perpetuate the person's sleeping problem.

The role of this "sleep effort syndrome" in the causation of insomnia needs to be more thoroughly studied empirically. It is reasonable to assume, however, that an insufficient ability for cognitive deactivation may interfere with sleep even when the cognitive activation is not due to sleep-related concerns. We may also ask to what extent individuals who are unable to deactivate cognitively and emotionally at sleep time suffer from this inability even at other times during the day. In other words, are there individuals who suffer from a generalized deficit in deactivation skills, and is this deficit overrepresented among sufferers from insomnia?

The hypothesis that individuals who suffer from insomnia are also less able to deactivate in other situations of rest is consistent with results from the Multiple Sleep Latency Test (MSLT). During the MSLT, which is used in sleep disorder clinics to test for the patient's degree of sleepiness, patients are offered five 20-minute naps at two-hour intervals throughout the day, and the speed with which they fall asleep provides an objective measure of sleepiness. Patients with insomnia are typically not very sleepy at the MSLT, and they even show evidence of longer MSLT latencies than normal sleepers (e.g., Bonnet & Arand, 1995). That is, the difficulties falling asleep that characterize many insomniacs at night are quite likely to characterize them also during the day—which is what should be expected if deficits in the capacity for cognitive and emotional deactivation represent a core mechanism in insomnia. An alternative explanation, as pointed out by Espie et al. (2006), is that the typical task instruction in the MSLT, by explicitly asking the patient to "try to fall asleep," activates the attention-intention-effort pathway in patients with psychophysiological insomnia and thereby prevents them from falling asleep.

With the purpose of studying people's cognitive and emotional activity both at bedtime and at other times of rest during the day, Lundh and Hindmarsh (2002) developed a Cognitive-Emotional Self-Observation Task (CEST), which was partly modeled after the MSLT. In the daytime version of this task (CEST-d) the participants were asked to lie down in a dark room and observe their own thoughts, feelings, and body sensations, without trying to change these in any way. After five minutes they were asked to sit up and respond to a questionnaire, where they were instructed (1) to name in a few words the kinds of thoughts that had occurred to them during the past five minutes and (2) to make a number of ratings on a zero to three scale of (a) how easy or difficult it was to remember these thoughts ("meta-cognitive awareness"), (b) the degree to which they had tried to control these thoughts ("meta-cognitive control"), and (c) their actual emotional state (seven ratings: degree of alertness/arousal, happiness, tension/worry, anger/annoyance, sadness/depression, tiredness/sleepiness, and pleasant/relaxed bodily feelings). Lundh and Hindmarsh (2002) found that the CEST-d showed criterion validity by predicting the corresponding cognitive and emotional measures at nighttime before sleep onset, as measured by a nighttime version of the same task (CEST-n). This relative stability in levels of cognitive and emotional activation from daytime rest situations to the nighttime pre-sleep situation is consistent with the hypothesis that people differ in their generalized capacity for cognitive and emotional deactivation.

To the extent that Espie et al.'s (2006) "sleep effort syndrome" hypothesis is correct, psychophysiological insomnia should be treatable by methods like paradoxical intention, in which the patient is instructed to "try to stay awake" or something similar (e.g., "keep your eyes open, and try to keep them open, just for a little while longer"). To the extent that the hypothesis of *deficient deactivation skills* is correct, however, there is no reason to assume that the substitution of one purposive activity ("try to stay awake") for another ("try to fall asleep") should facilitate sleep—that is, the cognitive content of the activity should, in principle, not matter. The fact that paradoxical intention has demonstrated a certain degree of efficacy as a single therapy in controlled trials (Turner & Ascher, 1979; Espie, Lindsay, Brooks, Hood, & Turvey, 1989), therefore, speaks for Espie's "sleep effort syndrome" hypothesis—as does the finding that paradoxical intention has been found to reduce sleep effort and sleep anxiety in another experimental study (Broomfield & Espie, 2003). But it is also highly relevant that paradoxical intention is not recommended as the treatment of choice for insomnia, and that it has even led to opposite effects (i.e., prolonged sleep latency) in some cases (Espie & Lindsay, 1985); one possible interpretation is that these patients suffered more from deficient deactivation skills than from a sleep effort syndrome.

If the hypothesis of deficient deactivation skills is correct, then insomnia should be possible to treat by programs that *teach deactivation skills* in an efficient way. Three examples of methods that have been used for this purpose are progressive relaxation (Jacobson, 1938), meditation (e.g., Woolfolk, Carr-Kaffashan, McNulty, & Lehrer, 1976), and imagery training (Woolfolk & McNulty, 1983). It is important to note, however, that all of these methods risk being misapplied, in a manner that is analogous to the use of other methods for the purpose of falling asleep, as part of what Espie et al. (2006) refer to as the "sleep effort syndrome." That is, if deactivation (like falling asleep) is an involuntary process, then relaxation and meditation methods risk being drawn into a counterproductive "relaxation effort syndrome" or "meditation effort syndrome," in the form of futile, effortful strivings to deactivate.

How, then, is it at all possible to use some kind of deactivation technique to promote sleep, if all techniques involve attention, intention, and effort as necessary ingredients? The answer that is suggested here is twofold: (1) If relaxation training or meditation is done in a mindfulness context, the risk of getting drawn into some kind of "effort syndrome" is considerably decreased. (2) Even though the training of skills (including deactivation skills) necessarily involves attention, intention, and effort, all fully developed skills involve automaticity rather than effortful strivings.

MINDFULNESS TRAINING AS A
WAY OF PROMOTING PEOPLE'S DEACTIVATION SKILLS

The concept of "mindfulness" refers to a specific way of disengaging from daily concerns and strivings, namely by "paying attention in a particular way: on purpose, in the present moment, and nonjudgmentally" (Kabat-Zinn, 1994, p. 4), thereby fostering "a decentered relationship to mental contents" (Segal, Williams, & Teasdale, 2002, p. 41), or what Hayes, Strosahl, and Wilson (1999) refer to as "cognitive defusion." The very similarity among the terms "deactivation," "disengagement," "decentering," and "defusing" suggests that they refer to related phenomena. Most important in the present context, although mindful observation involves its own kind of attention, intention, and effort, these are very different from typical forms of cognitive activation in at least two ways: (1) the only intended result is to observe what occurs in one's sensations, feelings, and thoughts; (2) the only possible way in which this process may fail is when the individual gets distracted by thoughts—as soon as the person *observes* these thoughts, however, he or she is in fact back into observing again. That is, even failures of being mindful are "food" for the mindful observing process. In a certain sense, therefore, this is a process that cannot fail—because, as soon as one observes a failure to stay mindful, one is, in fact, being mindful again.

The increased interest in research on mindfulness during the first decade of the twenty-first century has led to attempts to formulate theoretical models of mindfulness. According to the two-component model of mindfulness proposed by Bishop et al. (2004), for example, one component involves the self-regulation of attention so that it is maintained on immediate experience, and the other component involves adopting a particular orientation toward these experiences, characterized by curiosity, openness, and acceptance. These two components are seen in the instructions that are common to most mindfulness exercises. For example, participants are asked to focus their attention on their sense impressions (sounds, sights, body sensations) or on some ordinary activity (e.g., breathing, walking, or eating) and to observe their experiences carefully. They are also instructed to notice that their attention will eventually wander off into thoughts, memories, or fantasies—and, when this occurs, they are to simply observe in a nonevaluative way that this has happened and to resume attending to their experiences in the present moment. Similarly, if urges, desires, or emotions arise, participants are instructed to observe them carefully, without trying to eliminate or change these experiences, but also without necessarily acting on them—and if they are acting on them, to act with awareness, again observing their experiences in a nonjudgmental way.

Although not so often mentioned, it should be noted that this process requires the participants to keep these instructions "in mind," that is, to store them as self-instructions easily available in working memory. To expand on Bishop et al.'s (2004) model, this means that mindfulness basically involves at least three components: (1) an intentional activity of attending to, and observing, the experiences that unfold in the present moment; (2) doing this in a nonevaluative stance, with open, friendly curiosity, accepting the experiences without trying to change them; and (3) keeping the mindfulness instructions easily activated in working memory, so that the individual is "kept on track." A pivotal point in this process is when the intended process fails, either because (a) the person's attention is drawn away from present experience (e.g., by preoccupation with memories, fantasies, plans, or worries) or because (b) the person loses the nonevaluative stance and thinks self-critical thoughts about his or her inability to stay mindful. In both cases, the state of mindfulness is reinstated by the activation of the mindfulness instructions in working memory, leading to continued nonjudgmental observing of what is occurring.

Does mindfulness represent one complex skill, or a multidimensional combination of separate skills? On the basis of factor analyses of the combined pool of items from five questionnaires intended to measure degree of mindfulness, Baer, Smith, Hopkins, Krietemeyer, and Toney (2006) identified five factors—(1) observing, (2) describing, (3) acting with awareness, (4) nonjudging of inner experience, and (5) nonreactivity to inner experience—all of them considered to be *skills*. Of these, *observing* refers to the skill of being attentive to experiences, *describing* to the skill of labeling internal experiences with words, *acting with awareness* to the skill of attending to one's activities of the moment, *nonjudging of inner experience* to the skill of taking a nonevaluative stance toward thoughts and feelings, and *nonreactivity to inner experience* to the skill of allowing thoughts and feelings to come and go, without getting caught up in or carried away by them. Although the skills may be divided in this way for analytical purposes, it is the *combination* of skills that represents mindfulness. A high level of observing, for example, would not count as an example of mindfulness, if it were combined with low levels of nonjudging or nonreactivity (i.e., high levels of judging and reacting) to what was observed.

Why, then, should we expect increased mindfulness skills to be associated with better sleep? First, if one of the causal factors of insomnia is a cognitive overactivation in the pre-sleep situation, in the form of an excess of purposive, effortful thinking (e.g., problem solving, worrying, or ruminating) and a deficit in the ability to accept spontaneously occurring physical and psychological processes (e.g., imagery, sensations of sleepiness, and so on), then it follows that increased skills in cognitive deactivation (i.e., the ability to let go of conscious control and effort and allow more spontaneous physiological processes to take place) should be of help. Second, if mindfulness training can help people develop these cognitive deactivation skills, mindfulness training should be one way to improve sleep. It is important to remember, however, that it is when these cognitive deactivation skills reach a stage of automaticity, in the sense that they are (a) well developed in the individual and (b) automatically associated with the pre-sleep situation, that they may be expected to facilitate the transition from wakefulness to sleep. The latter suggests that the training of mindfulness skills should be carried out not only during the day, but in the pre-sleep situation—with the explicit instruction, however, that this is a time-limited training session in bed and is not to be used as a method to fall asleep. This means that, if mindfulness training is combined with traditional stimulus-control treatment, then rule 2 (see table 6.1) should be modified to include mindfulness exercises as allowed in bed.

Applied to the pre-sleep situation, mindfulness training exercises include the nonjudgmental observation and acceptance of body sensations, thoughts, images, feelings, and memories that appear in the pre-sleep situation—just noticing them and letting them go. The instructions should prepare the individual for distracting thoughts that lead to a temporary loss of the mindful stance, encouraging the person to simply observe and label these distracting thoughts and then continue observing. These bedtime mindfulness exercises should be time limited, to prevent their being misused as a purposive method for falling asleep—which would risk drawing the individual into what Espie et al. (2006) refer to as "the sleep effort syndrome."

Generally, it is important to note that all methods for the treatment of insomnia, including mindfulness exercises, may be drawn into potentially self-defeating attempts to fall asleep by means of controlled efforts—that is, they may all be misused as methods for the explicit purpose of falling asleep more or less instantly. One way of preventing counterproductive efforts of this kind in the treatment of insomnia is to use "counter-demand instructions" (Steinmark & Borkovec, 1974) as part of the rationale—that is, to instruct the patient that no improvement is to be expected during the first weeks of treatment. Most important, however, the patient may be instructed that treatment is a matter of learning new skills—which is a process that takes time—and not a matter of finding methods that can be used to instantly fall asleep.

Sleep-Interpreting Processes

The way a person with insomnia thinks about sleep and interprets his or her sleeping problems is, of course, highly relevant in the treatment of insomnia. Of general importance is both how the person values the role of sleep (and rest) in his or her life, in relation to more activity-related strivings and accomplishments, and what he or she believes about, for example, (a) the need for sleep and the consequences of insufficient sleep, (b) what constitutes "natural" variations in sleep and how one compensates for poor sleep, and (c) what causes good or poor sleep and what can be done to improve one's sleep. Some of these values and beliefs are dysfunctional, in the sense that they may contribute to an imbalanced, stressful lifestyle or lead to exaggerated worries and emotional concerns about sleep that produce a sleep-interfering cognitive and emotional activation at sleep time. The category of dysfunctional beliefs also includes exaggerated beliefs about the role of willful strivings and effortful behavior in producing outcomes that are not under voluntary control, including falling asleep. In this field, Morin (1993) and Harvey (2002) have contributed important new knowledge concerning the role of distorted perceptions of sleep, unrealistic sleep expectations, misattributions or amplifications of the consequences of insomnia, and faulty beliefs about sleep-promoting practices.

Again, just as with sleep-interfering processes, an optimal understanding of the role of sleep-interpreting processes in insomnia requires an understanding of the nature of healthy functional sleep-interpreting processes. Table 6.2 suggests some examples of functional ways of thinking about sleep and sleeping problems. To some extent, psychoeducational methods may help to address such issues, for example by informing patients about research findings that show that a poor night's sleep tends to be compensated for by deeper and more refreshing sleep (i.e., increased delta sleep) during subsequent nights (e.g., Horne, 2010)—informing patients that a sleepless night, therefore, is no catastrophe.

TABLE 6.2   Some Themes in a Functional Way of Thinking About Sleep and Sleep Problems

---

1. Sleep and rest are important aspects of life, and people need to find a well-functioning balance between active, goal-directed strivings and rest/sleep.

2. Sleep fluctuates as the result of various kinds of external and internal events (stressful events, emotional concerns, and the like).

3. Sleep is not under voluntary control, and there are no methods that can be used efficiently in order to fall asleep, so these fluctuations have to be accepted.

4. A sleepless night is no catastrophe. "Even if I will get no sleep at all tonight, I will still manage tomorrow."

5. A poor night's sleep is generally compensated for by deeper and more refreshing sleep (i.e., increased delta sleep) during subsequent nights.

6. Sleep may be improved by learning new skills and habits, but this is a process that leads to effects over time and is not a matter of using techniques in order to fall asleep.

Common to psychoeducational methods and cognitive techniques (e.g., Socratic questioning) is that these *directly* address patients' way of thinking about sleep and their way of interpreting signs of poor sleep and poor daytime functioning. Acceptance and mindfulness techniques may, however, also play a potentially important role here by affecting patients' sleep-interpreting processes in a more indirect way. The development of increased mindfulness and acceptance skills can, for example, contribute to an experiential relearning about sleep and the contingencies of falling asleep, which may lead to more functional ways of thinking about sleep. For example, mindful observation of pre-sleep processes may lead to an increasing realization that these processes, as well as the quality of sleep, fluctuate naturally as the result of various kinds of external and internal events (stressful events, emotional concerns, and the like). Such mindful observation may then lead to a more elaborate understanding that sleep is not under voluntary control and that such fluctuations have to be accepted.

Dysfunctional beliefs about how to improve one's sleep may be a suitable target for ACT-derived techniques. In Hayes et al.'s (1999) acceptance and commitment therapy (ACT), the therapist begins the process by focusing on three primary questions: (1) What does the client want? (2) What has the client tried? (3) How has that worked? This often leads to the identification of a class of futile control strategies that have not worked, and the broader "unworkable change agenda" underlying these strategies. The next goal is to introduce an alternative to these control strategies, formulated in terms of "acceptance." This kind of approach may be particularly suitable in the treatment of insomnia, because sleep problems represent a paradigm example of a problem where control strategies are bound to fail. Applied to insomnia, this means that the assessment might include a detailed review of all kinds of techniques that the client has tried in order to improve his or her sleep. This will most probably lead to an identification of a class of goal-directed control strategies that have not worked very well and which can be the starting point for looking at alternatives of another kind. Various metaphors may also be used for the same purpose.

Techniques from ACT may also be used to address issues related to people's *valuing* processes—for example, how they value sleep and other forms of rest, in comparison with various kinds of activity-based strivings and accomplishments. A process of values clarification (Hayes et al., 1999), whereby the individual gets the opportunity to reflect on what he or she values in life, and which explicitly includes questions about sleep and rest, may set the occasion for changes that contribute to a better balance in the person's life between activity and rest, sleep and wakefulness, and, more generally, being and doing. Such modification of values may be expected to have direct effects on a person's way of thinking about sleep, so that (a) sleep is valued more optimally than before and (b) sleep is seen as something that occurs naturally as part of being, and not achieved as the result of doing.

Empirical Studies

Empirical evidence showing that mindfulness predicts sleep-related self-regulation and well-being has been presented by Howell, Digdon, and Buro (2010), who found that mindfulness was associated with less pre-sleep arousal, sleep effort, and daytime sleepiness and with better sleep hygiene and sleep quality. Moreover, structural equation analyses suggested that mindfulness predicted well-being in part through its association with adaptive sleep functioning. Although these findings were based on cross-sectional data, which do not allow causal inferences, they are highly consistent with the present model of insomnia and suggest that mindfulness-based interventions carry promise in the treatment of insomnia.

Attempts to apply mindfulness techniques to insomnia have begun to emerge, although mostly in uncontrolled studies with a weak pre-post design. In some of these studies, mindfulness techniques have been combined with other CBT methods, like stimulus control and sleep restriction (Bootzin & Stevens, 2005; Ong, Shapiro, & Manber, 2008, 2009). In other studies, pure mindfulness-based treatments, either mindfulness-based stress reduction (MBSR) or mindfulness-based cognitive therapy (MBCT), have been adapted for insomnia patients (Gross et al., 2009; Heidenreich, Tuin, Pflug, Michal & Michalak, 2006; Shapiro, Bootzin, Figueredo, Lopez, & Schwartz, 2003; Yook et al., 2008).

The larger treatment packages have generally shown promising results, although it is difficult to know if the mindfulness techniques have contributed to the overall treatment effects beyond the traditional CBT methods. Bootzin and Stevens (2005), for example, used an uncontrolled pre-post design to investigate a multicomponent intervention that included mindfulness meditation along with several sleep and stress management techniques for fifty-five adolescents who complained of insomnia and daytime sleepiness and had a substance-abuse history. Participants who completed the program (only 42 percent of the sample) reported improvements in sleep onset latency, sleep efficiency, number of awakenings, total sleep time, and sleep quality, as well as reductions in daytime sleepiness and worry, but there is no information about the possible contribution of mindfulness techniques to the outcome.

Ong, Shapiro, and Manber (2008) also carried out an uncontrolled study to examine the effects of an intervention that combined mindfulness meditation with ordinary CBT for insomnia (CBT-I) for thirty nonclinical subjects who met diagnostic criteria for psychophysiological insomnia. The treatment was delivered in six weekly sessions of 90 to 120 minutes duration. Sessions two through five consisted of a combination of mindfulness meditations, sleep restriction, and stimulus control. Meditation exercises conducted during the session included breathing meditation, body scan, walking meditation, and eating meditation. Participants were also instructed to practice meditation for at least thirty minutes per day, five days per week. Initially, during the skill acquisition phase, participants were instructed to practice the meditation no later than two hours before bedtime. Once regular daytime practice had been established, the application of mindfulness meditation during sleepless periods at night was discussed and encouraged. The results showed a significant reduction in sleep onset latency (from thirty-nine to twenty-one minutes) and a significant increase in sleep efficiency* (from 79 percent to 88 percent), but no increase in total sleep time. The results also showed significant reductions in pre-sleep arousal, sleep effort, and dysfunctional sleep-related cognitions. Interestingly, a significant correlation was found between the number of meditation sessions and changes on a trait measure of arousal.

Ong, Shapiro, and Manber (2009) conducted a naturalistic follow-up of twenty-one of the participants in Ong et al.'s (2008)

---

* Sleep efficiency is defined as the ratio of total sleep time to time spent in bed.

study at six and twelve months post-treatment. The results showed that the sleep-related benefits of the combined CBT-I and mindfulness treatment were generally maintained during the twelve-month follow-up period. In addition, they revealed that (a) higher presleep arousal and sleep effort at end of treatment were associated with worse long-term outcome (experience of at least one insomnia episode of one month or longer during the follow-up) and (b) participants with higher mindfulness skills reported less daytime sleepiness at each of the three time points (although there was no correlation between mindfulness skills and nocturnal symptoms of insomnia). It would be of interest to use a dismantling design to compare the combined treatment package with CBT-I only, in order to see if the mindfulness component adds to the efficacy of CBT-I.

With the studies of single mindfulness-based treatments, the evidence is also promising but inconclusive. Shapiro et al. (2003) applied MBSR to sleep problems in a group of women with breast cancer. Although there was no significant difference between the mindfulness group and a control group on sleep measures after treatment, the results showed that participants who reported greater mindfulness practice reported significantly improved sleep quality. It should be noted that this treatment was not adapted for sleep problems but involved a general training focused especially on mindful breathing.

More promising results were found by Heidenreich et al. (2006) in a small uncontrolled pilot study of MBCT in sixteen patients suffering from persistent insomnia at the Department of Sleep Medicine, Frankfurt University, in Germany. All participants met DSM-IV criteria for primary insomnia, had been suffering from insomnia for more than one year, and had been treated with a variety of both pharmacological and psychological methods without improvement for at least six months prior to intake. The patients also showed high rates of comorbidity (recurrent depression, personality disorders). The treatment protocol followed Segal et al.'s (2002) MBCT manual, but with the cognitive elements tailored to insomnia rather than depression. On sleep diary measures, the results showed a significant increase in total sleep time (from an average of 5 hours 36 minutes to 6 hours 41 minutes), but no significant change in sleep onset latency (from 30 minutes to 26 minutes).

The participants also reported significantly less focusing on sleep-related content and significantly less worry after treatment. Because the study suffered from a lack of control group, it cannot be concluded that these changes were due to the treatment. Taking into account the treatment-refractory nature and severity of the patients' sleep disorders, however, Heidenreich et al. considered it unlikely that all effects could be attributed to spontaneous recovery.

Yook et al. (2008) carried out an uncontrolled pilot study to examine the usefulness of MBCT for treating insomnia symptoms in patients with anxiety disorder. Nineteen patients with anxiety disorders were assigned to eight weeks of MBCT. Participants showed significant improvement in sleep quality, worry, rumination, anxiety, and depression at the end of the eight-week program, as compared with baseline.

The first controlled study of a mindfulness-based treatment for insomnia has been reported by Gross et al. (2009), although only preliminary results have been reported so far. Gross et al. randomized thirty patients with primary insomnia to eight weeks of either MBSR or pharmacotherapy, in two waves. Preliminary results, after wave one, showed no differences between MBSR and pharmacotherapy (PCT) arms on insomnia measures, but all patients who had attended more than five MBSR classes (ten of eleven patients) reached criteria for improvement on at least one established self-assessment measure of sleep.

It should be noted that all published attempts so far to apply mindfulness and acceptance techniques to insomnia have relied on existing treatments, like MBSR and MBCT, which have been adapted to insomnia. Another possibility would be to develop a mindfulness- and acceptance-inspired treatment that is tailor-made for insomnia. In our own research group, we have tried this along three different lines: (1) a modified form of Jacobson's (1938) progressive relaxation in "a mindfulness context" has been tried in some case studies; (2) the above-mentioned study by Lundh and Hindmarsh (2002) with the cognitive-emotional self-observation task (CEST) also produced some treatment-relevant results—the administering of a nighttime version of the CEST during one week was, in fact, associated with decreased sleep latencies, longer sleep time, and better sleep satisfaction, as compared with a baseline week; (3) a series of pilot studies have been carried out of an ACT-inspired treatment for insomnia. In the first of these (Åkerlund, Bolanowski, & Lundh, 2005), ten participants received five sessions of an acceptance- and mindfulness-based treatment for insomnia. At post-treatment, the results showed a significant decrease from pre- to post-test on insomnia severity, as measured by the Insomnia Severity Index (ISI; Bastien, Vallières, & Morin, 2001). Before treatment, all ten participants passed the cutoff (>15) for clinical insomnia on the ISI; after treatment, only two of the ten participants scored above this cutoff. There was also a large reduction of cognitive pre-sleep arousal, as measured by the cognitive subscale of the Pre-Sleep Arousal Scale (PSAS; Nicassio, Mendlowitz, Fussell, & Petras, 1985). On sleep diaries, there was a nonsignificant reduction in sleep latency from an average of 41 minutes before treatment to 27 minutes after treatment, and a nonsignificant increase of total sleep time from an average of 6 hours and 29 minutes to 6 hours and 52 minutes. Seven of the patients were reached for a follow-up after six months. On the ISI, only one of these patients at follow-up scored above the cutoff for insomnia; also, the patients' cognitive pre-sleep arousal had been further reduced from the post-test. On sleep diary measures, however, the effects were not similarly impressive.

Summary

This chapter advocated the inclusion of acceptance and mindfulness techniques in the treatment of insomnia. It proposed that two categories of psychological processes are involved in the development and maintenance of insomnia: sleep-interfering arousal processes, and dysfunctional interpretations of sleep and sleeplessness. Further, it argued that acceptance- and mindfulness-related methods can be used to modify both of these processes, in the following ways: (1) by means of mindfulness training, the individual may develop skills of cognitive deactivation that, when automatized in the pre-sleep situation, can counteract sleep-interfering arousal; (2) by means of acceptance- and mindfulness-related techniques, the individual may also modify his or her way of valuing sleep and rest as compared with more activity-based strivings and accomplishments (and, in a more general sense, being as compared with doing), as well as dysfunctional beliefs about sleep and sleeplessness. It is important to note, however, that these are still hypotheses with very limited empirical evidence so far. What is needed is more research on how to apply mindfulness and acceptance techniques in the most efficient way to insomnia. This research may also benefit from the development of reliable measures of cognitive activation and deactivation.

References

American Psychiatric Association. (1994). *Diagnostic and statistical manual of mental disorders* (4th ed.). Washington, DC: Author.

Ancoli-Israel, S., Cole, R., Alessi, C., Chambers, M., Moorcroft, W., & Pollak, C. P. (2003). The role of actigraphy in the study of sleep and circadian rhythms. *Sleep, 26,* 342–392.

Åkerlund, R., Bolanowski, I., & Lundh, L. G. (2005). Unpublished data.

Baer, R. A., Smith, G. T., Hopkins, J., Krietemeyer, J., & Toney, L. (2006). Using self-report assessment methods to explore facets of mindfulness. *Assessment, 13,* 27–45.

Bastien, C. H., Vallières, A., & Morin, C. M. (2001). Validation of the Insomnia Severity Index as an outcome measure for insomnia research. *Sleep Medicine, 2,* 297–307.

Bishop, S. R., Lau, M., Shapiro, S., Carlson, L., Anderson, N. C., Carmody, J., et al. (2004). Mindfulness: A proposed operational definition. *Clinical Psychology: Science and Practice, 11,* 230–241.

Bolge, S. C., Doan, J. F., Kannan, H., & Baran, R. W. (2009). Association of insomnia with quality of life, work productivity, and activity impairment. *Quality of Life Research, 18,* 415–422.

Bonnet, M. H., & Arand, D. L. (1995). Twenty-four-hour metabolic rate in insomniacs and matched normal sleepers. *Sleep, 18,* 581–588.

Bootzin, R. R. (1972). Stimulus control treatment for insomnia. *Proceedings of the American Psychological Association, 7,* 395–396.

Bootzin, R. R., & Stevens, S. J. (2005). Adolescents, substance abuse, and the treatment of insomnia and daytime sleepiness. *Clinical Psychology Review, 25*, 629–644.

Borbély, A. A. (1982). A two process model of sleep regulation. *Human Neurobiology, 1*, 195–204.

Borkovec, T. D. (1994). The nature, function, and origins of worry. In G. Davey & F. Tallis (Eds.), *Worrying: Perspectives on theory, assessment and treatment.* New York: Wiley.

Broomfield, N. M., & Espie, C. A. (2003). Initial insomnia and paradoxical intention: An experimental investigation of putative mechanisms using subjective and actigraphic measurement of sleep. *Behavioural and Cognitive Psychotherapy, 31*, 313–324.

Dinges, D. F., Pack, F., Williams, K., Gillen, K. A., Powell, J. W., Ott, G. E., et al. (1997). Cumulative sleepiness, mood disturbance, and psychomotor vigilance performance decrements during a week of sleep restricted to 4–5 hours per night. *Sleep, 20*, 267–277.

Drake, C. L., Roehrs, T. A., Burduvali, E., Bonahoom, A., Rosekind, M., & Roth, T. (2001). Effects of rapid versus slow accumulation of eight hours of sleep loss. *Psychophysiology, 38*, 979–987.

Espie, C. A. (2002). Insomnia: Conceptual issues in the development, persistence, and treatment of sleep disorders in adults. *Annual Review of Psychology, 53*, 215–243.

Espie, C. A., Broomfield, N. M., MacMahon, K. M. A., Macphee, L. M., & Taylor, L. M. (2006). The attention-intention-effort pathway in the development of psychophysiological insomnia: A theoretical review. *Sleep Medicine Reviews, 10*, 215–245.

Espie, C. A., & Lindsay, W. R. (1985). Paradoxical intention in the treatment of chronic insomnia: Six case studies illustrating variability in therapeutic response. *Behaviour Research and Therapy, 23*, 703–709.

Espie, C. A., Lindsay, W. R., Brooks, D. N., Hood, E. M., & Turvey, T. (1989). A controlled comparative investigation of psychological treatments for chronic sleep-onset insomnia. *Behaviour Research and Therapy, 27*, 79–88.

Gross, C., Cramer-Bornemann, M., Kreitzer, M. J., Reilly, M., Wall, M., & Winbush, N. (2009). A trial of mindfulness versus pharmacotherapy for primary chronic insomnia. *EXPLORE: The Journal of Science and Healing, 5*, 157.

Harvey, A. G. (2001). I can't sleep, my mind is racing! An investigation of strategies of thought control in insomnia. *Behavioural and Cognitive Psychotherapy, 29*, 3–11.

Harvey, A. G. (2002). A cognitive model of insomnia. *Behaviour Research and Therapy, 40*, 869–893.

Harvey, A. G. (2003). The attempted suppression of presleep cognitive activity in insomnia. *Cognitive Therapy and Research, 27*, 593–602.

Harvey, A. G. (2008). Insomnia, psychiatric disorders, and the transdiagnostic perspective. *Current Directions in Psychological Science, 5*, 299–303.

Harvey, A. G., & Tang, N. K. Y. (2003). Cognitive behaviour therapy for primary insomnia: Can we rest yet? *Sleep Medicine Reviews, 7*, 237–262.

Hayes, S. C., Strosahl, K. D., & Wilson, K. G. (1999). *Acceptance and commitment therapy: An experiential approach to behavior change.* New York: Guilford Press.

Heidenreich, T., Tuin, I., Pflug, B., Michal, M., & Michalak, J. (2006). Mindfulness-based cognitive therapy for persistent insomnia: A pilot study. *Psychotherapy and Psychosomatics, 75*, 188–189.

Horne, J. (2010). Sleepiness as a need for sleep: When is enough, enough? *Neuroscience and Biobehavioral Reviews, 34*, 108–118.

Howell, A. J., Digdon, N. L., & Buro, K. (2010). Mindfulness predicts sleep-related self-regulation and well-being. *Personality and Individual Differences, 48*, 419–424.

Jacobson, E. (1938). *Progressive relaxation: A physiological and clinical investigation of muscular states and their significance in psychology and medical practice.* Chicago: University of Chicago Press.

Kabat-Zinn, J. (1994). *Wherever you go, there you are: Mindfulness meditation in everyday life.* New York: Hyperion.

Lundh, L. G. (2005). The role of acceptance and mindfulness in the treatment of insomnia. *Journal of Cognitive Psychotherapy, 19*, 29–39.

Lundh, L. G., & Broman, J. E. (2000). Insomnia as an interaction between sleep-interfering and sleep-interpreting processes. *Journal of Psychosomatic Research, 49,* 1–12.

Lundh, L. G., & Hindmarsh, H. (2002). Can meta-cognitive observation be used in the treatment of insomnia? A pilot study of a cognitive-emotional self-observation task. *Behavioural and Cognitive Psychotherapy, 30,* 239–242. (This is a brief summary of an extended report that is available from the first author.)

Lundh, L. G., Lundqvist, K., Broman, J. E., & Hetta, J. (1991). Vicious cycles of sleeplessness, sleep phobia, and sleep-incompatible behaviours in patients with persistent insomnia. *Scandinavian Journal of Behaviour Therapy, 20,* 101–114.

Morin, C. M. (1993). *Insomnia: Psychological assessment and management.* New York: Guilford Press.

Nelson, J., & Harvey, A. G. (2002). The differential functions of imagery and verbal thought in insomnia. *Journal of Abnormal Psychology, 111,* 665–669.

Nelson, J., & Harvey, A. G. (2003). Pre-sleep imagery under the microscope: A comparison of patients with insomnia and good sleepers. *Behaviour Research and Therapy, 41,* 273–284.

Nicassio, P. M., Mendlowitz, D., Fussell, J., & Petras, L. (1985). The phenomenology of the pre-sleep state: The development of the Pre-Sleep Arousal Scale. *Behaviour Research and Therapy, 23,* 263–271.

Nolen-Hoeksema, S. (2000). The role of rumination in depressive disorders and mixed anxiety/depressive symptoms. *Journal of Abnormal Psychology, 109,* 504–511.

Ohayon, M. M., & Reynolds, III, C. F. (2009). Epidemiological and clinical relevance of insomnia diagnosis algorithms according to the DSM-IV and the International Classification of Sleep Disorders (ICSD). *Sleep Medicine, 10,* 952–960.

Ong, J. C., Shapiro, S. L., & Manber, R. (2008). Combining mindfulness meditation with cognitive-behavior therapy for insomnia: A treatment-development study. *Behavior Therapy, 39,* 171–182.

Ong, J. C., Shapiro, S. L., & Manber, R. (2009). Mindfulness meditation and cognitive behavioural therapy for insomnia: A naturalistic twelve-month follow-up. *EXPLORE: The Journal of Science and Healing, 5*, 30–36.

Posner, M. I., & Rothbart, M. K. (2000). Developing mechanisms of self-regulation. *Development and Psychopathology, 12*, 427–441.

Ratcliff, R., & Van Dongen, H. P. A. (2009). Sleep deprivation affects multiple distinct cognitive processes. *Psychonomic Bulletin & Review, 16*, 742–751.

Segal, Z., Williams, M., & Teasdale, J. (2002). *Mindfulness-based cognitive therapy for depression: A new approach to preventing relapse.* New York: Guilford Press.

Shapiro, S. L., Bootzin, R. R., Figueredo, A. J., Lopez, A. M., & Schwartz, G. E. (2003). The efficacy of mindfulness-based stress reduction in the treatment of sleep disturbance in women with breast cancer. An exploratory study. *Journal of Psychosomatic Research, 54*, 85–91.

Shiffrin, R. M., & Schneider, W. (1977). Controlled and automatic human information processing: II. Perceptual learning, automatic attending, and a general theory. *Psychological Review, 84*, 129–190.

Spielman, A. J., Saskin, P., & Thorpy, M. J. (1987). Treatment of chronic insomnia by restriction of time in bed. *Sleep, 10*, 45–56.

Steinmark, S. W., & Borkovec, T. D. (1974). Active and placebo treatment effects on moderate insomnia under counterdemand and positive demand instructions. *Journal of Abnormal Psychology, 83*, 157–163.

Stickgold, R., & Walker, M. P. (2007). Sleep-dependent memory consolidation and reconsolidation. *Sleep Medicine, 8*, 331–343.

Thomsen, D. K., Mehlsen, M. Y., Christensen, S., & Zachariae, R. (2003). Rumination—relationship with negative mood and sleep quality. *Personality and Individual Differences, 34*, 1293–1301.

Tryon, W. W. (2004). Issues of validity in actigraphic sleep assessment. *Sleep, 27*, 158–165.

Turner, R. M., & Ascher, L. M. (1979). A controlled comparison of progressive relaxation, stimulus control and paradoxical intention therapies for insomnia. *Journal of Consulting and Clinical Psychology, 47*, 500–508.

Woolfolk, R. L., Carr-Kaffashan, L., McNulty, T. F., & Lehrer, P. M. (1976). Meditation training as a treatment for insomnia. *Behavior Therapy, 7,* 359–365.

Woolfolk, R. L., & McNulty, T. F. (1983). Relaxation training for insomnia: A component analysis. *Journal of Consulting and Clinical Psychology, 51,* 495–503.

Yook, K., Lee, S. H., Ryu, M., Kim, K. H., Choi, T., Suh, S. Y., et al. (2008). Usefulness of mindfulness-based cognitive therapy for treating insomnia in patients with anxiety disorders: A pilot study. *Journal of Nervous and Mental Disease, 196,* 501–503.

7 Mindfulness for Cancer and Terminal Illness

Linda E. Carlson

Division of Psychosocial Oncology, Department of Oncology, Faculty of Medicine, University of Calgary; Department of Psychosocial Resources, Tom Baker Cancer Centre, Alberta Cancer Board, Calgary, Alberta, Canada

Joan Halifax

Director, Upaya Institute, Project on Being with Dying, Santa Fe, New Mexico

The diagnosis of cancer is a traumatic event for every person who receives such news, and for their family members and support system. Cancer continues to be a leading cause of death in developed countries. The World Health Organization (WHO) estimates that new worldwide cases of cancer will jump from 11.3 million in 2007 to 15.5 million in 2030, and the number of global cancer deaths will increase from 7.9 million to 11.5 million (a 45 percent increase) in this same period, influenced in part by an increasing and aging global population (World Health Organization, 2008).

Even though today approximately two-thirds of all people diagnosed with cancer in developed countries will survive long term (at least five years post-diagnosis) (Altekruse et al., 2009), associations of the word "cancer" with an acute life threat, hair loss, disfigurement, nausea, vomiting, potential long-term disability, and premature death still spring readily to mind. For this reason, although cancer has in many cases become a chronic illness, the psychological impact of cancer is still greater than for many other similarly life-threatening conditions.

Psychological Sequelae of Cancer Diagnosis and Treatment

It has been well recognized that instances of depression, anxiety, and general distress are high for people diagnosed with cancer, with anywhere from 45 to 65 percent of patients reporting elevated levels of general distress at the time of diagnosis (Carlson, Groff, Maciejewski, & Bultz, in press). For many, this distress persists over time and can be exacerbated by specific problems such as sleep difficulties, lingering fatigue, pain, and symptoms such as nausea and vomiting. A survey of a representative cross-section of cancer patients attending a large treatment center found that almost half of all patients reported fatigue as a problem, followed by pain (26.4 percent), managing emotions/stress (24.8 percent), depression (24.0 percent), and anxiety (24.0 percent) (Carlson, Angen, et al., 2004). People of lower income, those of minority ethnicities, and those who were on active treatment were more vulnerable to distress than others.

Other, more existential issues also often predominate for people struggling with cancer. For example, people may ask themselves the question "Why me? Why did I get cancer?" They may be trying to make sense of the illness or find some meaning in it. If they have a type of cancer that has clear causal factors, such as lung cancer caused by smoking, people may blame themselves and become disheartened, feeling guilty and depressed. They may feel they "deserve" to have cancer and may put little effort into their own healing; some just give up. On the other hand, if they feel that they have lived a healthy lifestyle and taken care of their body, some may feel betrayed by the development of cancer. They may wonder if they are being punished for some deed or thought they perpetrated in the past. Others may find meaning in their sickness by concluding that "everything happens for a reason" and make the best of the situation or just accept that it wasn't their fault—that cancer can strike anyone. These people often turn the popular question on its head, asking "Why *not* me? What makes me so special?"

Other realities are brought into light through a cancer diagnosis, such as the fact that things are largely not controllable. This challenges a belief many people hold that they have of control over their lives, which is difficult to sustain in the face of a cancer crisis. In fact, most people have much less control than they would like to believe, and having to face this illusion of control can be very uncomfortable and cause increased distress. A similar issue is the lack of certainty that is highlighted in dealing with cancer and its treatments. Even the most highly trained oncologists can only provide a range of probabilities of the success of any particular treatment or of how long a patient will survive. In many ways this is always the case for all of us—we never know when we will die. However, most people are not confronted with this uncertainty as starkly as those dealing with a life-threatening and unpredictable illness such as cancer. The only certainty is that each of us will in fact pass away; anguish sometimes comes from not knowing when or how that will come to pass.

All of these issues, from the practical problems of coping with day-to-day stressors of treatment including the frequent financial burden, to the larger existential questions of living and dying, control, and uncertainty, take a huge toll on persons living with cancer and their supporters. In the next sections we will discuss how mindfulness-based approaches can help address a wide range of these problems.

Application of Mindfulness in Cancer Patients

At the Tom Baker Cancer Centre in Calgary, Alberta, Canada, we have been offering mindfulness-based stress reduction (MBSR) since

1996, and other groups across Canada, the United States, Australia, and Great Britain have more recently begun clinical and research programs also aimed at cancer patients. Clinical work with palliative patients based on the mindfulness training of Joan Halifax has been ongoing for several decades. Below we summarize some background information pertaining to these applications and provide a brief literature review of the research evaluating their impact.

Origins and Definition of Mindfulness

"Mindfulness" is a term that originates from Buddhist writings and is often translated as a combination of the Pali words *sati* and *sampajañña*, which as a whole can be translated as "awareness, circumspection, discernment, and retention." In the book *The Art and Science of Mindfulness: Integrating Mindfulness into Psychology and the Helping Professions* (Shapiro & Carlson, 2009), the authors defined mindfulness as "The awareness that arises through intentionally attending in an open, caring, and nonjudgmental way" (p. 4). This definition was meant to take into account mindfulness both as a way of being in the world and as a process or practice. We refer to these two components as (1) mindful awareness, an abiding presence or awareness, a deep knowing that contributes to freedom of the mind, and (2) mindful practice, the systematic practice of intentionally attending in an open, caring, and discerning way, which involves both knowing and shaping the mind. We developed a model of mindfulness that involves three components: intention, attention, and awareness—called the IAA model (Shapiro, Carlson, Astin, & Freedman, 2006). Other scholars have also attempted to define mindfulness; the operational definition proposed by Bishop and colleagues (2004) includes two components, similar to the attention and awareness elements of the IAA model above: (1) self-regulation of attention maintained on immediate experience, allowing for increased recognition of mental events in the present moment, and (2) adopting an orientation that is characterized by curiosity, openness, and acceptance.

Mindfulness-Based Cancer Recovery Program Description

Mindfulness practice has most frequently been offered and introduced to people, and to medical patients specifically, in the form of the Mindfulness-Based Stress Reduction (MBSR) program developed by Jon Kabat-Zinn and colleagues (Kabat-Zinn, 1990), already briefly described in this volume. Although many other venues for the transmission of mindfulness meditation theory and practice are widely available, particularly through meditation centres, which specialize in specific types of meditation, the MBSR approach, developed in a medical setting, is largely independent of the teachings of any particular school of Buddhism. This secular approach initially focused on stress reduction as its central aspect, and mindfulness was presented as a tool to achieve this goal.

The program that we have been offering to cancer patients and their family members since 1996 at the Tom Baker Cancer Centre in Calgary is now referred to as Mindfulness-Based Cancer Recovery (MBCR) to acknowledge both its debt to the MBSR program and its unique aspects specific to people coping with this condition. Michael Speca and the first author published a self-help book detailing the specifics of this program, which is targeted at a lay audience and takes a practical, step-by-step approach (Carlson & Speca, 2010).

The MBCR program, similar to MBSR, is an eight-week program with a six-hour retreat during the day between classes six and seven. Weekly classes are shorter in MBCR, typically 1.5 hours each, and are roughly divided into three sections: introduction and discussion, yoga, and meditation. The class begins with a short sitting meditation to help orient participants and encourage a present-moment stance, followed by discussion of home practice and group problem solving around any issues that have arisen. Participants are encouraged to share how they may have approached similar problems and what insights or solutions, if any, they were able to find. Group facilitators take the stance of deferring to participants as the experts on their own bodies and practice, providing guidance but refraining from providing quick answers or solutions. Various educational topics are introduced as the weeks progress, including discussion of the stress and relaxation responses, diaphragmatic breathing, mindful coping, and balance in the autonomic nervous system. Exercises such as eating a raisin mindfully are included to highlight certain attitudes and approaches to meditation that are helpful. There is a heavy emphasis on the importance of the attitudinal component of how one approaches practice. Attitudes of nonjudging, patience, beginner's mind, trust, nonstriving, acceptance, and nonattachment as described by Kabat-Zinn (1990) are highlighted.

The second main component of the program is the practice of mindful yoga, or mindful movement, as it is sometimes called. Postures derived from those used in MBSR are also utilized in MBCR, with modifications made for individual participants as necessary. If people are unable to lie on a mat on the floor, they are encouraged to participate while sitting in a chair, for example. After the movement component, a different form of meditation practice is introduced each class. These begin with the body scan, followed by sitting meditation, walking meditation, mountain meditation, choiceless awareness, and loving-kindness practices. Mini meditation exercises are also introduced, and informal practice is encouraged throughout the program. Home practice is crucial to fully adopting mindfulness as a central part of one's life and is emphasized throughout. Participants are encouraged to make a commitment to themselves of forty-five minutes each day for practice during the program.

The question remains: why would mindfulness or MBCR, as described above, be especially helpful to people coping with cancer? As it turns out, many of the issues cancer patients face are best dealt with through approaches that emphasize acceptance and awareness, as well as nonattachment. Nonattachment arises from an understanding of impermanence, the constantly changing nature of all things. With an understanding of impermanence, patients are able to loosen their stranglehold on needing things to be or stay a certain way, or needing to know exactly the outcomes of their treatments and their prognosis for the future. With a present-moment stance and through the practice of seeing things clearly as they are, simply allowing acceptance of circumstances, patients are able to stop struggling with questions of "why" and simply dwell in the "what" of each moment. Worry often arises from questions around the future—these can be attenuated through focus on the present moment and learning to allow events to unfold moment by moment.

Mindfulness is also a useful tool for regulating emotions and encourages acceptance rather than avoidance of one's experiences. It can decrease rumination about past and future events (Berceli & Napoli, 2006) through the experience of increased self-awareness and can help to counteract the tendency to avoid painful experiences, which often leads to an amplification in the very feelings that avoidant-coping individuals are hoping to control (Barlow, Allen, & Choate, 2004). Through the body scan, for example, the experience of mindfulness can cultivate body awareness and allow individuals who have been exposed to traumatic or stressful events to learn how to accept physical sensations related to stress without judgment.

Efficacy of Mindfulness-Based Interventions for Cancer Patients

There is a growing body of research into the application of mindfulness-based approaches for treating a wide range of problems facing cancer patients and their family members. Recent years have seen a spike in interest in this area, and enough individual research studies have been published to encourage several review papers. Previous review papers from our group provided rationale and background of mindfulness in cancer (Carlson, Labelle, Garland, Hutchins, & Birnie, 2009; Carlson & Speca, 2007; Mackenzie, Carlson, & Speca, 2005; Speca, Carlson, Mackenzie, & Angen, 2006) and others included narrative summary reviews of the literature in this area (Lamanque & Daneault, 2006; Matchim & Armer, 2007; Ott, Norris, & Bauer-Wu, 2006; Smith, Richardson, Hoffman, & Pilkington, 2005). In this section we divide the research based on the outcomes studied as a way to organize the review. A select overview of each area is provided.

PSYCHOLOGICAL OUTCOMES

The majority of studies of mindfulness-based interventions in cancer patients have focused on psychological outcomes. One recent meta-analysis concluded that effects were medium sized for psychological outcomes such as decreases in stress and improved mood, and small sized for improvements in physical health parameters (Ledesma & Kumano, 2009). A recent book chapter in the text *Psycho-Oncology* highlights all the current studies published in a systematic review (Carlson, in press). Twenty-one studies are included, all of which have been published since the year 2000; ten stem from our research program at the Tom Baker Cancer Centre in Calgary, with the rest originating from different research groups primarily in the United States. Fifteen of the twenty-one studies were uncontrolled trials, usually simple pre-post assessments of one group of MBSR participants on a range of outcome measures, or qualitative interview studies. The other six studies were randomized controlled trials (RCTs) that compared MBSR (or a variation of it) to either a waiting list (4/6) or some other active form of therapy (2/6).

In one of several studies that looked at psychological outcomes, Tacon and colleagues conducted a small pre-post study with twenty-seven breast cancer survivors who showed improvements on measures of stress and anxiety, as well as less hopelessness and anxious preoccupation about cancer and greater internal locus of control (Tacon, Caldera, & Ronaghan, 2004). A larger study of forty women also showed less pain and distress related to symptoms post-MBSR (Tacon, 2007). In other uncontrolled trials, Spahn and colleagues found improvements in role function and fatigue in eighteen MBSR program participants (Spahn et al., 2003), and Brown and Ryan (2003) showed decreases in mood disturbance and stress levels that were associated with higher levels of mindfulness in forty-one breast and prostate cancer patients. Garland, Carlson, Cook, Lansdell, and Speca (2007) saw improvements on measures of post-traumatic growth and spirituality, as well as stress symptoms and mood disturbance, in a mixed group of sixty cancer patients taking MBSR.

In the first randomized controlled trial published, Speca, Carlson, Goodey, and Angen (2000) found that patients with heterogeneous cancers in MBSR improved significantly more on mood states and symptoms of stress than those in a wait-list control condition, with large improvements of approximately 65 percent on mood and 35 percent on stress symptoms. Patients reported less tension, less depression, less anger, fewer concentration problems, and more vigor, as well as fewer peripheral manifestations of stress (e.g., tingling in hands and feet), cardiopulmonary symptoms of arousal (e.g., racing heart, hyperventilation), central neurological symptoms (e.g., dizziness, faintness), gastrointestinal symptoms (e.g., upset stomach, diarrhea), habitual stress behavioral patterns (e.g. smoking, teeth grinding, overeating, insomnia), anxiety/fear, and emotional instability compared to those still waiting for the program. These patients, as well as the control group when they later completed treatment, were followed up six months later, and it was found that benefits in both groups were maintained over the follow-up period (Carlson, Ursuliak, Goodey, Angen, & Speca, 2001). In the combined group, more home practice was associated with greater decreases in overall mood disturbance. In a recent publication, we looked at both cancer patients and their partners who attended the program together (Birnie, Speca, & Carlson, in press) and found that both groups improved on total mood disturbance, muscle tension, neurological/GI and upper respiratory stress symptoms, and levels of mindfulness. Post-intervention, partners' mood disturbance scores were significantly positively correlated with patients' symptoms of stress and negatively correlated with patients' levels of mindfulness.

BIOLOGICAL AND SLEEP OUTCOMES

A number of uncontrolled studies have also been conducted investigating biological outcomes and health behaviors, such as sleep. Carlson et al. (Carlson, Speca, Patel, & Goodey, 2003, 2004; Carlson, Speca, Patel, & Faris, 2007) looked at measures of immune, endocrine, and autonomic function in fifty-nine breast and prostate cancer survivors. Immune function was investigated by looking at the counts and function of a number of lymphocyte subsets, including T cells and natural killer (NK) cells, through secretion of cytokines in response to cell stimulation. Cytokines were either of the pro-inflammatory or of the anti-inflammatory variety—pro-inflammatory processes have been associated with several poorer outcomes in both cardiovascular and cancer patients. T-cell production of interferon gamma (IFN-λ), a pro-inflammatory cytokine,

167

decreased. Patterns of change were also assessed over a full year following program participation, and levels of pro-inflammatory cytokines continued to decrease (Carlson et al., 2007). Although the exact meaning of these changes in relation to cancer progression is not known, in some studies elevated pro-inflammatory cytokines have been associated with poorer cancer outcomes (Costanzo et al., 2005).

Our research also looked at salivary cortisol, since daily salivary cortisol levels have been related to stress and health and are often dysregulated in cancer survivors; such dysregulation has been associated with shorter survival time (Sephton, Sapolsky, Kraemer, & Spiegel, 2000). Cortisol profiles also shifted pre- to post-intervention, with fewer evening cortisol elevations found post-MBSR and some normalization of abnormal diurnal salivary cortisol profiles occurring (Carlson, Speca, et al., 2004). Over the year of follow-up, continuing decreases in overall cortisol levels were seen, mostly due to decreases in evening cortisol levels (Carlson et al., 2007). In this same study, overall resting systolic blood pressure (SBP) decreased significantly from pre- to post-MBSR (Carlson et al., 2007). This is desirable, since high blood pressure (hypertension) is the most significant risk factor for developing cardiovascular disease, and cancer patients who have received common forms of chemotherapy are at higher risk for developing cardiac problems. In a wait-list controlled study, Van Wielingen, Carlson, and Campbell (2007) found that home blood pressure measured weekly while taking MBSR or waiting for the program decreased significantly only for those women who took the program. For those with initially elevated systolic BP, an average decrease of 15 mmHg was reported, which is similar in magnitude to decreases resulting from blood pressure medication.

Turning to sleep, Carlson and Garland (2005) found improvements on measures of sleep in a general sample of sixty-three cancer patients following MBSR. Before attending the MBSR program, sleep disturbance was closely associated with levels of self-reported stress and mood disturbance, and, when stress symptoms declined over the course of the MBSR program, sleep also improved. On average, sleep hours increased by one-half to one hour per night. One other sleep study, by Shapiro, Bootzin, Figueredo, Lopez, and Schwartz

(2003), found no statistically significant relationships between participation in an MBSR group and sleep quality for fifty-four women with breast cancer; however, within the MBSR group those who practiced more informal mindfulness reported feeling more rested.

QUALITATIVE RESEARCH

Mackenzie, Carlson, Munoz, and Speca (2007) conducted qualitative interviews with a specific subgroup of MBSR participants who attended weekly drop-in meditation groups. Five major themes were identified in the interviews: opening to change, self-control, shared experience, personal growth, and spirituality. This information was used to develop a specific theory concerning mechanisms whereby MBSR effects change for cancer patients. According to these cancer survivors, the initial participation in the eight-week program was only the beginning of an ongoing process of self-discovery, a slight shift in orientation that began the growth process. Although the participants didn't realize it at the time, the eight-week program was just the proverbial "tip of the iceberg." During the active treatment phase, MBSR provided these patients with concrete tools for self-regulation and the ability to better control fluctuating emotional responses. This resulted relatively quickly in reduced stress and less mood disturbance. The group was also crucial at this time, and later, to help meet their needs for social support from others going through a similar experience—a shared sense of humanity both in facing cancer and in learning a new world of mindfulness meditation. The program helped them feel less alone and introduced ways to look at the world they might not have previously considered. As practice progressed, people began to learn to be less reactive and exercise more diffuse self-regulation across a wider variety of life circumstances. They developed qualities of positive health beyond a focus on symptom reduction, and they focused more on finding meaning and purpose in their life and feeling increasingly interconnected with others. They consistently mentioned feeling more "spiritual," which for some meant a return to prayer in their own original tradition; for others this referred to feeling more connected to nature and other people. Over time, they were able to see cancer as only one part of their life story and no longer the predominant storyline.

Another recent qualitative and quantitative study was conducted with thirteen women who had completed breast cancer treatment (Dobkin, 2008). The women experienced decreases in perceived stress and medical symptoms as well as improvements on a measure of mindfulness. They took better care of themselves and viewed life as more meaningful and manageable. Themes identified by the women were similar to those identified in the previous study: (1) acceptance; (2) regaining and maintaining mindful control; (3) taking responsibility for what could change; and (4) cultivating a spirit of openness and connectedness.

ADAPTATIONS OF MBSR

There have also been adaptations of the traditional eight-week group MBSR program for special populations of cancer patients, particularly two studies that looked at mindfulness meditation for hospitalized patients undergoing bone-marrow or stem-cell transplantation (BMT). Bauer-Wu and Rosenbaum (2004) adapted MBSR for individual use in isolated hospitalized BMT patients, finding immediate effects on levels of pain and anxiety as measured on visual analogue scales immediately before and after meditation sessions. Horton-Deutsch, O'Haver Day, Haight, and Babin-Nelson (2007) also investigated MBSR in twenty-four BMT patients, providing six to eight biweekly individual sessions based on an adaptation of the group MBSR curriculum. In fifteen patients, less negative affect was reported after the intervention despite increasing symptoms of nausea and appetite loss, and patients found the program feasible, although they felt that training in mindfulness *before* hospitalization would have been optimal.

A unique modification of MBSR that has been applied to cancer patients is called Mindfulness-Based Art Therapy (MBAT), which combines the principles of MBSR with other creative modalities. Patients practice meditation, then express their experience through a number of visual arts outlets such as painting and drawing. In a randomized controlled trial (N = 111), researchers compared the eight-week MBAT intervention to a wait-list control in a heterogeneous cohort of women with mixed cancer types. MBAT participants had less depression, anxiety, somatic symptoms of stress, and hostility than control participants post-intervention (Monti et al., 2005).

An innovative study by Jim Carmody's group at the Centre for Mindfulness looked at the effects of combining a dietary intervention with MBSR on prostate-specific antigen (PSA) levels, an indicator of the level of activity of prostate cancer cells in men with active prostate cancer (Saxe et al., 2001). The combined program resulted in a slowing of the rate of PSA increase in a pilot sample of ten men. In 2008 they published the results of a larger randomized controlled trial of this intervention, measuring dietary intake of various nutrients and quality of life as well as PSA outcomes and time spent meditating (Carmody, Olendzki, Reed, Andersen, & Rosenzweig, 2008). Thirty-six men and their partners participated, and those in the intervention group showed targeted increases in the consumption of healthy nutrients such as plant-based protein, lycopene, and carotenoids three months after the program. They also decreased their consumption of fat and animal protein and had greater improvements in quality of life (QL) than those in the wait-list group. Although there were no overall group differences in PSA levels, those in the intervention group had increased their PSA doubling time from eighteen to fifty-nine months, while the waitlist participants remained steady around nineteen months. It is impossible to determine the role that the meditation practice versus the dietary change may have played in this outcome, but it may be that the meditation practice allowed the men to be more vigilant and mindful of their dietary choices, as time spent in meditation practice correlated with intake of vegetable protein.

In summary, empirical work on MBSR in cancer patients supports its usefulness for decreasing a wide range of psychological outcomes such as symptoms of stress, anxiety, anger, depression, and mood disturbance and improving quality of life and sleep outcomes. It may be effective both for patients who are undergoing treatment (including BMT) and for those who have completed treatment protocols. Effects on biological outcomes such as cortisol and immune function are suggested, but more research with controlled comparison groups is required. Few studies have compared MBSR directly to other supportive care interventions, so it is impossible to know which effects are specific to MBSR or if different types of interventions would produce similar positive results.

Mindfulness-Based Interventions for End of Life Care

This section is focused on the work of Joan Halifax in the area of mindfulness-based interventions for people in palliative care nearing the end of life. A rationale for why these types of interventions are helpful is followed by a description of some specific practices that can be applied as individuals near end of life.

Rationale

Those facing the end of their lives typically have diminished physical and social capacities. As a result of physical distress, psychological defense mechanisms are often lowered. Resilience, a dynamic process that arises through the experience of positive behavioral adaptations when an individual encounters significant adversity, is in part associated with one's ability to self-regulate one's emotions—another capacity strengthened by mindfulness practice and important for those who are gravely ill (Coffey & Hartman, 2008; Shapiro, Schwartz, & Bonner, 1998). Resilience can be enhanced through the development of a metacognitive perspective. This allows patients to monitor their thought processes, and it assists in focusing attention. More explicitly, metacognition is the ability of a patient to de-center from thought and to understand thought processes as transient events rather than as a direct representation of reality (Teasdale, Segal, & Williams, 1995; Teasdale et al., 2002). This capacity to see things from a more distal and relative perspective can be very beneficial for an individual suffering from a severe illness and facing complex questions with regard to treatment or the anticipated outcome of death.

For example, it is common for dying patients who have gone through many medical procedures to be very "sensitive" to their circumstances, to be frightened, anxious, or even angry at what they are going through, or to feel futility and experience depression. It has been our experience that dying people are often traumatized not only by their diagnosis but also by diagnostic procedures and medical interventions employed in an endeavor to extend life or alleviate symptoms. We have observed that a patient's effort to suppress or reduce the frequency of certain distressing thoughts in these circumstances can actually increase the occurrence of those thoughts. This phenomenon of the futility of thought suppression is borne out by research (Wegner & Smart, 1997). The utilization of a mindfulness-based practice can assist traumatized patients in dealing with the stresses encountered in their situation, and it can assist them in facing the realities of sickness, pain, dying, and death.

Over the past forty years, the work of the second author has focused on teaching contemplative interventions and mindfulness-based practices to clinicians and to dying individuals. We will address the benefits of these types of contemplative interventions for those facing death and those who have been diagnosed with a catastrophic illness.

Contemplative interventions in general refer to a type of process that trains the mind through working with concentration and inquiry. This again includes mindfulness, a way of perceiving the world that is based in the nonjudgmental experience of the present moment, as taught in the MBCR program and described above. Jon Kabat-Zinn further defines mindfulness as "the awareness that emerges through paying attention, on purpose, in the present moment, and nonjudgmentally to the unfolding of experience moment by moment" (Kabat-Zinn, 2003, p. 145). According to Kabat-Zinn, mindfulness practice not only induces the capacity to focus on the reality of the present moment but also makes it possible for an individual to accept what is happening in the present moment without being subject to rumination or emotional reactions in relation to challenging situations in the past, present, or future. These three features (present-moment awareness, acceptance, and nonreactivity) have the potential to enhance the quality of life of those who are dealing with a serious illness and those who are dying.

Earlier we mentioned the IAA model of mindfulness, in which three core qualities of mindfulness were identified: (1) intention, which focuses on a motivational component to one's attention and behavior; (2) present-centered attention and awareness; and (3) attitude, which reflects on how we attend, such as interest, curiosity, nonjudgment, acceptance, compassion, and receptiveness (Shapiro et al., 2006). Present-centered attention aids patients in not dwelling on the past or on an anticipated catastrophic future. The motivational component entails a top-down process for the gravely ill or dying person; in other words, there is greater engagement and commitment in the attentional process. The third component, for us, is especially interesting: how mindfulness can foster an attitude toward the dying process that shifts the experience from a catastrophe to a journey of a developmental nature for the one experiencing it.

Baer, Carmody, and others have described mindfulness as comprising five key skills. These include (1) acting with awareness; (2) observing; (3) describing; (4) nonreactivity to inner experience; and (5) nonjudging of inner experience (Baer, Smith, Hopkins, Krietemeyer, & Toney, 2006; Baer et al., 2008; Carmody & Baer, 2008). With a base in these skills, mindfulness allows for greater flexibility and accuracy in the perception of what is happening in the present moment, and greater acceptance and less reactivity to whatever is taking place on a somatic, cognitive, affective, or behavioral level. These mental processes can be beneficial for a patient who is facing or dealing with a catastrophic diagnosis, which is often accompanied by uncertainty and stress. These five skills can give a patient the grounding to positively appraise the situation, even discovering benefits; as one patient said, "My cancer has given me many gifts." Another patient said, "My diagnosis has given me my life back." A third patient noted, "I can accept my pain, as I now know that everything is impermanent." These words reflect an earned sense of acceptance, equanimity, and even wisdom about their situation. All three patients had done basic meditation practice as an endeavor to explore their illness.

For those with a catastrophic illness, mindfulness practices can have potential benefits in four core areas: (1) attentional balance, which includes fostering and sustaining vivid, stable, effortless, inclusive, and nonjudgmental attention; (2) emotional balance, meaning the cultivation of prosocial mental processes, including altruism, empathy, kindness, compassion and self-compassion, joy, and equanimity; (3) cognitive control, which includes the development of the capacity to guide thoughts and behaviors in accord with intention, to override and down-regulate habitual responses, and to cultivate mental flexibility, insight, and meta-cognition; and (4) resilience, which includes stress reduction, fostering relaxation, and enhanced immune response.

These four key areas enhance coping and resilience as well as insight and wisdom for those going through the experience of a catastrophic illness. From our experience, we have seen that training individuals who are gravely ill in mindfulness practice can assist them in becoming less reactive in the face of difficulties such as pain, the loss of capacities, relationships, means, and roles, and can assist them in facing loss and death. Patients can become more resilient and accepting of their situation, and develop a sense of meaning and balance, as they face the vicissitudes of illness.

Mindfulness Practices for End of Life

Mindfulness practice can be divided into three major types of reflective practices. One type enhances concentration, assisting an individual to stabilize her or his mental state; a second type entails receptive practices that broaden attention so it is panoramic, receptive, and reflective; and the third type includes practices that enhance insight as well as prosocial mental processes.

For example, when one is working with a person who is ill, and whose breathing is not compromised, a concentration exercise might consist of gently asking the patient to let his or her attention be anchored by the breath. One can suggest that the in-breath be accompanied by silently saying "accepting" and the out-breath be accompanied by the words "letting go." The person guiding this simple meditation practice can follow the patient's breath rhythm by breathing in the same rhythm as the patient, thus supporting his or her experience through attunement.

This first simple practice uses an attentional base that is focused. A practice that uses panoramic attention might consist of guiding the patient to first let the breath anchor the attention. After mindfully breathing in and out several times, the patient is encouraged to relax and simply let whatever arises be there, without clinging to sensory or mental phenomena, but rather letting thoughts, feelings, and sensations flow through him or her like a gentle stream.

A guided practice that develops a prosocial state involves a somewhat different approach. One usually begins with some simple instruction such as "All our lives, our innate wisdom tells us to let go, to relax, to relinquish unwise efforts to control. Our culture, conditioning, and personal history usually tell us to hold on, to attempt to cling to people, experiences, and accomplishments in order to be happy. Many times our lives are spent in a battle between our innate wisdom and the culture's message about clinging and control. Dying is above all the time to turn to, trust, and rest in the voice of truth within us. Here are some phrases that may be of help to you in this. They are phrases of loving-kindness practice. Be as comfortable as possible sitting or lying down. Take a few deep, soft breaths to let your body settle. Bring your attention to your breath, and begin to silently say your chosen phrases in rhythm with the breath. You can also experiment with just having your attention settle in the phrases, without using the anchor of the breath. Feel the meaning of what you are saying."

Then slowly and meaningfully repeat the phrases that are appropriate; here are some examples:

"May all those I leave behind be safe and peaceful."

"May I accept my pain, knowing that I am not my pain, not my body, not my illness."

"May I accept my suffering, knowing it does not make me bad or wrong."

"May I accept my anger, fear, and sadness, knowing that my heart is not limited by them."

"May I remain in peace and let go of expectations."

"I forgive myself for mistakes made and things left undone."

"May I remember my consciousness is much vaster than this body, as I let go of this body."

"May I open to the unknown, as I leave behind the known."

These examples are from the book entitled *Being with Dying: Cultivating Compassion and Fearlessness in the Presence of Death* (Halifax, 2009) which may serve as a useful manual for professionals working with dying patients. There is a wealth of clinical knowledge and experience regarding the benefits of these practices for dying patients, but to our knowledge no scientific studies have specifically investigated the efficacy of these approaches with terminally ill patients.

Summary

More research into the efficacy of mindfulness interventions for people who have cancer is warranted. However, the indications from existing research and experience lead us to surmise that mindfulness as an intervention has great potential benefits for those who are suffering from a catastrophic illness. MBCR is a group-based mindfulness training program that has empirical support for its benefits in terms of improving coping, improving quality of life, decreasing stress, improving mood, and enhancing qualities of spirituality and personal growth in the face of cancer diagnosis and treatment. The introduction of this type of intervention late in the illness process poses some particular challenges, and it is recommended that such interventions be applied as close to the time of diagnosis as possible, in order to reap maximum benefit. More empirical work with patients facing the end of life, too, is needed, to evaluate the application of mindfulness-based approaches at this time in the cancer journey.

References

Altekruse, S. F., Kosary, C. L., Krapcho, M., Neyman, N., Aminou, R., Waldron, W., et al. (Eds.). (2009). SEER Cancer Statistics Review, 1975–2007, National Cancer Institute, Bethesda, MD. Retrieved November 2009 from http://seer.cancer.gov/csr/1975_2007

Baer, R. A., Smith, G. T., Hopkins, J., Krietemeyer, J., & Toney, L. (2006). Using self-report assessment methods to explore facets of mindfulness. *Assessment, 13*(1), 27–45.

Baer, R. A., Smith, G. T., Lykins, E., Button, D., Krietemeyer, J., Sauer, S., et al. (2008). Construct validity of the Five Facet Mindfulness Questionnaire in meditating and nonmeditating samples. *Assessment, 15*, 329–342.

Barlow, D. H., Allen, L. B., & Choate, M. L. (2004). Toward a unified treatment for emotional disorders. *Behavior Therapy, 35*(2), 205–230.

Bauer-Wu, S. M., & Rosenbaum, E. (2004). Facing the challenges of stem cell/bone marrow transplantation with mindfulness meditation: A pilot study. *Psycho-Oncology, 13*, S10–S11.

Berceli, D., & Napoli, M. (2006). A proposal for a mindfulness-based trauma prevention program for social work professionals. *Complementary Health Practice Review, 11*(3), 153–165.

Birnie, K., Speca, M., & Carlson, L. E. (in press). Exploring self-compassion and empathy in mindfulness-based stress reduction (MBSR). *Stress and Health.*

Bishop, S. R., Lau, M., Shapiro, S., Carlson, L., Anderson, N. C., Carmody, J., et al. (2004). Mindfulness: A proposed operational definition. *Clinical Psychology: Science and Practice, 11*, 230-241.

Brown, K. W., & Ryan, R. M. (2003). The benefits of being present: Mindfulness and its role in psychological well-being. *Journal of Personality and Social Psychology, 84*, 822–848.

Carlson, L. E. (in press). Meditation and yoga. In J. Holland (Ed.), *Psycho-oncology* (2nd ed.). New York: Oxford University Press.

Carlson, L. E., Angen, M., Cullum, J., Goodey, E., Koopmans, J., Lamont, L., et al. (2004). High levels of untreated distress and fatigue in cancer patients. *British Journal of Cancer, 90*(12), 2297–2304.

Carlson, L. E., & Garland, S. N. (2005). Impact of mindfulness-based stress reduction (MBSR) on sleep, mood, stress, and fatigue symptoms in cancer outpatients. *International Journal of Behavioral Medicine, 12*, 278–285.

Carlson, L. E., Groff, S. L., Maciejewski, O., & Bultz, B. D. (in press). Screening for distress in lung and breast cancer outpatients: A randomized controlled trial. *Journal of Clinical Oncology.*

Carlson, L. E., Labelle, L. E., Garland, S. N., Hutchins, M. L., & Birnie, K. (2009). Mindfulness-based interventions in oncology. In F. Didonna (Ed.), *Clinical handbook of mindfulness* (pp. 383–404). New York: Springer.

Carlson, L. E., & Speca, M. (2007). Managing daily and long-term stress. In M. Feurrestein (Ed.), *Handbook of cancer survivorship* (pp. 339–360). New York: Springer.

Carlson, L. E., & Speca, M. (2010). *Mindfulness-based cancer recovery: A step-by-step MBSR approach to help you cope with treatment and reclaim your life.* Oakland, CA: New Harbinger Publications.

Carlson, L. E., Speca, M., Patel, K. D., & Faris, P. (2007). One year pre-post intervention follow-up of psychological, immune, endocrine and blood pressure outcomes of mindfulness-based stress reduction (MBSR) in breast and prostate cancer outpatients. *Brain, Behavior, and Immunity, 21,* 1038–1049.

Carlson, L. E., Speca, M., Patel, K. D., & Goodey, E. (2003). Mindfulness-based stress reduction in relation to quality of life, mood, symptoms of stress, and immune parameters in breast and prostate cancer outpatients. *Psychosomatic Medicine, 65*(4), 571–581.

Carlson, L. E., Speca, M., Patel, K. D., & Goodey, E. (2004). Mindfulness-based stress reduction in relation to quality of life, mood, symptoms of stress and levels of cortisol, dehydroepiandrosterone sulfate (DHEAS) and melatonin in breast and prostate cancer outpatients. *Psychoneuroendocrinology, 29*(4), 448–474.

Carlson, L. E., Ursuliak, Z., Goodey, E., Angen, M., & Speca, M. (2001). The effects of a mindfulness meditation-based stress reduction program on mood and symptoms of stress in cancer outpatients: Six-month follow-up. *Supportive Care in Cancer, 9,* 112–123.

Carmody, J., & Baer, R. A. (2008). Relationships between mindfulness practice and levels of mindfulness, medical and psychological symptoms and well-being in a mindfulness-based stress reduction program. *Journal of Behavioral Medicine, 31,* 23–33.

Carmody, J., Olendzki, B., Reed, G., Andersen, V., & Rosenzweig, P. (2008). A dietary intervention for recurrent prostate cancer after definitive primary treatment: Results of a randomized pilot trial. Manuscript submitted for publication.

Coffey, K. A., & Hartman, M. (2008). Mechanisms of action in the inverse relationship between mindfulness and psychological distress. *Complementary Health Practice Review, 13*(2), 79–91.

Costanzo, E. S., Lutgendorf, S. K., Sood, A. K., Anderson, B., Sorosky, J., & Lubaroff, D. M. (2005). Psychosocial factors and interleukin-6 among women with advanced ovarian cancer. *Cancer, 104*, 305–313.

Dobkin, P. L. (2008). Mindfulness-based stress reduction: What processes are at work? *Complementary Therapies in Clinical Practice, 14*(1), 8–16.

Garland, S. N., Carlson, L. E., Cook, S., Lansdell, L., & Speca, M. (2007). A non-randomized comparison of mindfulness-based stress reduction and healing arts programs for facilitating post-traumatic growth and spirituality in cancer outpatients. *Supportive Care in Cancer, 15*(8), 949–961.

Halifax, J. (2009). *Being with dying: Cultivating compassion and fearlessness in the presence of death.* Boston: Shambala Publications.

Horton-Deutsch, S., O'Haver Day, P., Haight, R., & Babin-Nelson, M. (2007). Enhancing mental health services to bone marrow transplant recipients through a mindfulness-based therapeutic intervention. *Complementary Therapies in Clinical Practice, 13*(2), 110–115.

Kabat-Zinn, J. (1990). *Full catastrophe living: Using the wisdom of your body and mind to face stress, pain, and illness.* New York: Delacorte.

Kabat-Zinn, J. (2003). Mindfulness-based interventions in context: Past, present, and future. *Clinical Psychology: Science and Practice, 10*, 144–156.

Lamanque, P., & Daneault, S. (2006). Does meditation improve the quality of life for patients living with cancer? *Canadian Family Physician, 52*, 474–475.

Ledesma, D., & Kumano, H. (2009). Mindfulness-based stress reduction and cancer: A meta-analysis. *Psycho-Oncology, 18*(571), 579.

Mackenzie, M. J., Carlson, L. E., Munoz, M., & Speca, M. (2007). A qualitative study of self-perceived effects of mindfulness-based stress reduction (MBSR) in a psychosocial oncology setting. *Stress and Health: Journal of the International Society for the Investigation of Stress, 23*(1), 59–69.

Mackenzie, M. J., Carlson, L. E., & Speca, M. (2005). Mindfulness-based stress reduction (MBSR) in oncology: Rationale and review. *Evidence Based Integrative Medicine, 2,* 139–145.

Matchim, Y., & Armer, J. M. (2007). Measuring the psychological impact of mindfulness meditation on health among patients with cancer: A literature review. *Oncology Nursing Forum, 34*(5), 1059–1066.

Monti, D. A., Peterson, C., Shakin Kunkel, E. J., Hauck, W. W., Pequignot, E., Rhodes, L., et al. (2005). A randomized, controlled trial of mindfulness-based art therapy (MBAT) for women with cancer. *Psycho-Oncology, 15*(5), 363–373.

Ott, M. J., Norris, R. L., & Bauer-Wu, S. M. (2006). Mindfulness meditation for oncology patients. *Integrative Cancer Therapies, 5,* 98–108.

Saxe, G. A., Hebert, J. R., Carmody, J. F., Kabat-Zinn, J., Rosenzweig, P. H., Jarzobski, D., et al. (2001). Can diet in conjunction with stress reduction affect the rate of increase in prostate specific antigen after biochemical recurrence of prostate cancer? *Journal of Urology, 166,* 2202–2207.

Sephton, S. E., Sapolsky, R. M., Kraemer, H. C., & Spiegel, D. (2000). Diurnal cortisol rhythm as a predictor of breast cancer survival. *Journal of the National Cancer Institute, 92*(12), 994–1000.

Shapiro, S. L., Bootzin, R. R., Figueredo, A. J., Lopez, A. M., & Schwartz, G. E. (2003). The efficacy of mindfulness-based stress reduction in the treatment of sleep disturbance in women with breast cancer: An exploratory study. *Journal of Psychosomatic Research, 54,* 85–91.

Shapiro, S. L., & Carlson, L. E. (2009). *The art and science of mindfulness: Integrating mindfulness into psychology and the helping professions.* Washington, DC: American Psychological Association Publications.

Shapiro, S. L., Carlson, L. E., Astin, J. A., & Freedman, B. (2006). Mechanisms of mindfulness. *Journal of Clinical Psychology, 62,* 373–386.

Shapiro, S. L., Schwartz, G. E., & Bonner, G. (1998). Effects of mindfulness-based stress reduction on medical and premedical students. *Journal of Behavioral Medicine, 21*, 581–599.

Smith, J. E., Richardson, J., Hoffman, C., & Pilkington, K. (2005). Mindfulness-based stress reduction as supportive therapy in cancer care: Systematic review. *Journal of Advanced Nursing, 52*, 315–327.

Spahn, G., Lehmann, N., Franken, U., Paul, A., Longhorst, J., Michalsen, A., et al. (2003). Improvement of fatigue and role function of cancer patients after an outpatient integrative mind-body intervention. *Focus on Alternative and Complementary Therapies, 8*(4), 540.

Speca, M., Carlson, L. E., Goodey, E., & Angen, M. (2000). A randomized, wait-list controlled clinical trial: The effect of a mindfulness meditation-based stress reduction program on mood and symptoms of stress in cancer outpatients. *Psychosomatic Medicine, 62*(5), 613–622.

Speca, M., Carlson, L. E., Mackenzie, M. J., & Angen, M. (2006). Mindfulness-based stress reduction (MBSR) as an intervention for cancer patients. In R. A. Baer (Ed.), *Mindfulness-based treatment approaches: A clinician's guide to evidence base and approaches* (pp. 239–-261). Burlington, MA: Elsevier.

Tacon, A. M. (2007). Mindfulness effects on symptoms of distress in women with cancer. *Journal of Cancer Pain and Symptom Palliation, 2*(2), 17–22.

Tacon, A. M., Caldera, Y. M., & Ronaghan, C. (2004). Mindfulness-based stress reduction in women with breast cancer. *Families, Systems, & Health, 22*, 193–203.

Teasdale, J. D., Moore, R. G., Hayhurst, H., Pope, M., Williams, S., & Segal, Z. V. (2002). Metacognitive awareness and prevention of relapse in depression: Empirical evidence. *Journal of Consulting and Clinical Psychology, 70*, 275–287.

Teasdale, J. D., Segal, Z., & Williams, J. M. (1995). How does cognitive therapy prevent depressive relapse and why should attentional control (mindfulness) training help? *Behaviour Research and Therapy, 33*, 25–39.

Van Wielingen, L. E., Carlson, L. E., & Campbell, T. S. (2007). Mindfulness-based stress reduction (MBSR), blood pressure, and psychological functioning in women with cancer. *Psychosomatic Medicine, 69*(Meeting Abstracts), A43.

Wegner, D. M., & Smart, L. (1997). Deep cognitive activation: A new approach to the unconscious. *Journal of Consulting and Clinical Psychology, 65*(6), 984–995.

World Health Organizaton. (2008). Ask the expert Online Q&A, 1 April 2008: Are the number of cancer cases increasing or decreasing in the world? Retrieved November 2009 from http://www.who.int/features/qa/15/en/

PART 3

Assessment Methods

8   ASSESSMENT OF ACCEPTANCE AND MINDFULNESS IN BEHAVIORAL MEDICINE

Ruth A. Baer & Jessica R. Peters
University of Kentucky

Mindfulness- and acceptance-based interventions have been developed for a wide range of problems and disorders and are increasingly available in a variety of settings. Within behavioral medicine, the empirical literature suggests that mindfulness- and acceptance-based approaches can be effective in helping participants manage pain in constructive ways, improve health-related behavior, and cope adaptively with diseases and health conditions. The two most commonly cited mindfulness-based interventions in the behavioral medicine literature are mindfulness-based stress reduction (MBSR; Kabat-Zinn, 1982) and acceptance and commitment therapy (ACT; Hayes, Strosahl, & Wilson, 1999). MBSR is a structured group intervention based on the intensive practice of mindfulness meditation exercises that cultivate present-moment awareness and nonjudgmental acceptance of the experiences of daily life. Reviews suggest that MBSR has clinically significant benefits for persons with a variety of health-related concerns (Baer, 2003; Grossman, Niemann, Schmidt, & Walach, 2004). ACT combines a wide range of mindfulness and acceptance exercises with behavior change methods and can be flexibly applied in individual or group formats. A growing literature supports the efficacy of ACT in many populations, including those with chronic pain, other illnesses, and other health-related problems (Hayes, Luoma, Bond, Masuda, & Lillis, 2006).

Assessment tools are important to the acceptance and mindfulness literature for several reasons (Bishop et al., 2004; Dimidjian & Linehan, 2003). Interventions that claim to teach mindfulness and acceptance skills cannot be thoroughly evaluated without assessing the extent to which participants learn these skills. Moreover, in order to understand how these interventions work and to improve their efficacy, it is important to investigate whether increases in levels of mindfulness and acceptance are responsible for the beneficial effects that are often observed, including reduced symptoms and improved well-being. The purpose of this chapter, therefore, is to provide an overview of the instruments that have been developed to assess mindfulness and acceptance and to review the literature on their application in behavioral medicine settings. First we provide a summary of the definitions and descriptions of mindfulness and acceptance on which these instruments are based.

Definitions and Descriptions of Mindfulness and Acceptance

"Mindfulness" is usually defined as attention to or awareness of present-moment experiences (Brown & Ryan, 2003), including internal stimuli (cognitions, emotions, bodily sensations, urges), external stimuli (sights, sounds, smells), and ongoing behavior. Mindfulness can be contrasted with "automatic pilot" (Segal, Williams, & Teasdale, 2002) in which behavior occurs mechanically or without awareness because attention is focused elsewhere. Many descriptions of mindfulness also include particular qualities of attention that are brought to bear on present-moment experiences, such as acceptance, openness, nonjudging, and nonreactivity. For example, Segal et al. (2002) note that "in mindfulness practice, the focus of a person's attention is opened to admit whatever enters experience, while at the same time, a stance of kindly curiosity allows the person to investigate whatever appears, without falling prey to automatic judgments or reactivity" (pp. 322–323).

Acceptance has been comprehensively discussed in the literature on dialectical behavior therapy (DBT; Linehan, 1993) and acceptance and commitment therapy (Hayes et al., 1999). These approaches usually define acceptance as willingness to experience unpleasant internal phenomena (thoughts and feelings) without attempting to avoid, escape, or terminate them, in the service of pursuing valued goals. For example, social interactions may lead to more satisfying relationships but can also elicit anxiety. Avoiding the anxiety by avoiding social occasions will be maladaptive if it leads to loneliness. Engaging in social interactions but attempting to eliminate the anxiety, perhaps by avoiding eye contact or using substances, may lead to ineffective behavior or harmful effects on health. Thus, the most adaptive approach may be to allow anxiety to be present while continuing with goal-consistent social interactions.

The nature of mindfulness and acceptance can also be understood through examination of the instructions used to teach these skills. Mindfulness training encourages participants to focus their attention on present-moment stimuli, such as the sensations of breathing or sounds in the environment. If cognitions or emotions arise, participants observe them carefully and often label them with descriptive, nonjudgmental words, such as "thinking," "a feeling of sadness," or "aching." They are encouraged to adopt a stance or attitude of acceptance, openness, allowing, willingness, nonjudging, friendliness, kindness, or compassion, even if the observed experiences are unpleasant or unwanted. In DBT, mindfulness has been operationalized as a set of six interrelated skills—three related to what to do while being mindful and three related to how to do it. The first three skills include observing (noticing or attending to current experience), describing (noting or labeling observed experience with words), and participating (focusing full attention on current activity). The second set includes being nonjudgmental (refraining from evaluation, allowing things to be as they are), being one-mindful (using undivided attention), and being effective (using skillful means or doing what works).

In most of the psychological literature, mindfulness and acceptance are such closely related constructs that it is difficult to articulate clear distinctions between them. Some authors suggest that acceptance is an outcome of practicing mindfulness (Bishop et al., 2004) or a stance that aids in the cultivation of mindfulness (Brown, Ryan, & Creswell, 2007). Others describe acceptance as an element or component of mindfulness. Most mindfulness questionnaires assess attention to or awareness of present-moment experiences as well as acceptance, willingness, or nonavoidance of these experiences. Mindfulness questionnaires have been written from several theoretical and clinical perspectives. In contrast, most measures of acceptance were developed within the ACT literature, which conceptualizes mindfulness and acceptance as components of psychological flexibility, a broader construct that also includes engaging in overt behavior consistent with values and goals. ACT-based acceptance measures typically include items assessing willingness to experience negative thoughts and feelings and ability to behave consistently with goals and values while unpleasant internal experiences are present.

Instruments for Measuring Mindfulness

In the following sections we describe the available instruments for measuring mindfulness and their application in behavioral medicine settings.

Freiburg Mindfulness Inventory (FMI)

The Freiburg Mindfulness Inventory (FMI; Buchheld, Grossman, & Walach, 2001) is a thirty-item measure assessing openness to and nonjudgmental observation of present-moment stimuli. It provides a single total score. Items include "I watch my feelings without becoming lost in them" and "I am open to experience in the present moment." The FMI was developed with experienced meditators in intensive meditation retreats and demonstrates high internal consistency within this sample (α = .93). Participants showed significant increases in FMI scores from pre- to post-retreat. A shorter form with fourteen items has been developed for nonmeditating samples (Walach, Buchheld, Buttenmuller, Kleinknecht, & Schmidt, 2006). This shorter version has adequate to good internal consistency and showed differences in the expected directions between meditators, nonmeditators, and clinical groups. Both forms of the FMI were positively correlated with private self-awareness and self-knowledge and negatively correlated with dissociation and psychological distress in meditating and general adult samples. The authors recommend the longer form of the FMI for respondents who have experience with mindfulness or Buddhist concepts and the shorter form for other populations.

Mindful Attention Awareness Scale (MAAS)

The Mindful Attention Awareness Scale (MAAS; Brown & Ryan, 2003) is a fifteen-item, single-factor measure assessing the general tendency to engage in present-oriented attention and awareness. Items are reverse scored and describe being preoccupied or inattentive and functioning on automatic pilot—for example, "I find it difficult to stay focused on what's happening in the present" and "I break or spill things because of carelessness, not paying attention, or thinking of something else." Brown and Ryan (2003) reported good internal consistencies for the MAAS in undergraduate and general adult samples (α = .82 and .87, respectively). Positive correlations with openness to experience, emotional intelligence, and well-being, negative correlations with rumination and social anxiety, and a nonsignificant relationship to self-monitoring provided evidence for convergent and discriminant validity. MAAS scores were significantly higher in Zen Buddhist meditators than in community controls.

Kentucky Inventory of Mindfulness Skills (KIMS)

The Kentucky Inventory of Mindfulness Skills (KIMS; Baer, Smith, & Allen, 2004) is based largely on the DBT conceptualization of mindfulness skills and provides separate scores for four facets of general mindful behavior: observing, describing, acting with awareness, and accepting without judgment. Items include "I notice when my moods begin to change" (observing), "I'm good at finding words to describe my feelings" (describing), "When I do things, my mind wanders and I am easily distracted" (acting with awareness, reverse scored), and "I tell myself I shouldn't be feeling the way I'm feeling" (accepting without judgment, reverse scored). The four-factor structure was supported by exploratory and confirmatory analyses, and the authors report internal consistencies ranging from .76 to .91 for the four subscales. Correlations were found in expected directions, with constructs including openness to experience, emotional intelligence, and experiential avoidance, providing evidence for convergent and discriminant validity.

Cognitive and Affective Mindfulness Scale – Revised (CAMS-R)

The Cognitive and Affective Mindfulness Scale – Revised (CAMS-R; Feldman, Hayes, Kumar, Greeson, & Laurenceau, 2007) is a twelve-item measure of attention, present focus, awareness, and acceptance of thoughts and feelings in general daily experience. Items include "I try to notice my thoughts without judging them" and "It is easy for me to concentrate on what I am doing." Ratings are summed to provide a total score. Internal consistency ranged from .74 to .77, and confirmatory factor analyses supported the proposed single factor model. The CAMS-R has been shown to be positively correlated with the FMI and the MAAS and with well-being, adaptive emotion regulation, cognitive flexibility, problem analysis, and plan rehearsal and negatively correlated with symptoms of distress, worry, rumination, brooding, thought suppression, and experiential avoidance (Feldman et al., 2007).

Southampton Mindfulness Questionnaire (SMQ)

The Southampton Mindfulness Questionnaire (SMQ; Chadwick, Hember, Mead, Lilley, & Dagnan, 2008) is a sixteen-item instrument assessing the tendency to respond mindfully to distressing thoughts and images. Although items describe several aspects of mindfulness (mindful observation, nonaversion, nonjudgment, and letting go), the authors recommend use of single total score. Items begin with "Usually when I have distressing thoughts or images" and continue with a mindfulness-related statement, such as "I am able to just notice them without reacting" or "They take over my mind for quite a while afterward" (reverse scored). The measure has demonstrated good internal consistency ($\alpha = .89$) and a significant correlation with the MAAS ($r = .57$). As expected, regular meditators scored significantly higher than nonmeditators. Scores were positively correlated with pleasant mood ratings and showed significant increases following participation in MBSR.

Philadelphia Mindfulness Scale (PHLMS)

The Philadelphia Mindfulness Scale (PHLMS; Cardaciotto, Herbert, Forman, Moitra, & Farrow, 2007) is a twenty-item measure assessing two elements of mindfulness that are scored separately. The awareness factor assesses the ongoing monitoring of internal and external experience (e.g., "I'm aware of thoughts I'm having when my mood changes"). The acceptance factor measures a nonjudgmental attitude and openness to experience, which includes refraining from attempts to avoid or escape experience (e.g., "I try to distract myself when I feel unpleasant emotions," reverse scored). In clinical and nonclinical samples, good internal consistency has been established, and most correlations with other constructs were significant in expected directions. Clinical samples generally produced lower scores than nonclinical samples.

Five-Facet Mindfulness Questionnaire (FFMQ)

The Five-Facet Mindfulness Questionnaire (FFMQ; Baer, Smith, Hopkins, Krietemeyer, & Toney, 2006) has thirty-nine items and is based on exploratory factor analysis of the combined item pool from five of the mindfulness questionnaires just summarized (all but the PHLMS, which was not yet available). This analysis yielded a five-factor solution. The "observing" factor measures the ability to observe one's inner experiences and responses to stimuli and contains items such as "I pay attention to how my emotions affect my thoughts and behavior." The "describing" factor assesses the ability to put words to one's thoughts and feelings (e.g., "I'm good at finding words to describe my feelings"). "Acting with awareness" measures the tendency to take conscious and deliberate actions as opposed to functioning automatically and without thought or reflection and contains items such as "It seems I am 'running on automatic' without much awareness of what I'm doing" (reverse scored). "Nonjudging of inner experiences" measures the tendency to accept one's inner state as opposed to judging thoughts and emotions as good or bad (e.g., "I tell myself I shouldn't be feeling the way I'm feeling"; reverse scored). "Nonreactivity to inner experiences" assesses the tendency to allow emotionally provocative stimuli to come and go without necessarily reacting to them (e.g., "When I have distressing thoughts or images, I am able to just notice them without reacting"). The factors demonstrated adequate to excellent internal consistency (α ranging from .75 to .91) and appear to be conceptually consistent with elements of mindfulness described in the published literature. Correlations between the facet scales and other variables were consistent with predictions in most cases. Most facet scores were higher in meditators than in nonmeditators, and several were shown to mediate the relationship between meditation experience and psychological well-being (Baer et al., 2008). They also suggest that a multifaceted approach to the assessment of mindfulness is useful because it may help to clarify which aspects of mindfulness are most important in accounting for the benefits of mindfulness training.

Toronto Mindfulness Scale (TMS)

The instruments discussed previously assess mindfulness as a traitlike general tendency to be mindful in daily life. Mindfulness has also been conceptualized as a statelike quality that occurs when attention is intentionally directed to present sensations, thoughts, and emotions, with an attitude of openness, curiosity, and acceptance (Bishop et al., 2004). The Toronto Mindfulness Scale (TMS: Lau et al., 2006) assesses attainment of a mindful state during an immediately preceding meditation session. Participants complete a fifteen-minute meditation exercise and then rate the extent to which they were aware and accepting of their experiences during the exercise. The TMS contains two factors. The "curiosity" factor assesses interest and curiosity about inner experience, including items such as "I was curious to see what my mind was up to from moment to moment." The "decentering" factor assesses awareness of experiences without identifying with them or being carried away with them and includes items such as "I experienced myself as separate from my changing thoughts and feelings." Good internal consistency for each factor and significant correlations with other measures of self-awareness were reported.

A trait version of the TMS has recently been developed (Davis, Lau, & Cairns, 2009) by making minor wording changes to the items so that respondents report on how they generally relate to their thoughts and feelings rather than on how they related to them in a particular meditation exercise. This version showed good internal consistency and significant correlations with other mindfulness measures, although correlations were higher for the decentering factor than for the curiosity factor. Scores on the decentering factor were also significantly higher in meditators than in nonmeditators.

Use of Mindfulness Measures in Behavioral Medicine Settings

Mindfulness questionnaires have been used in numerous behavioral medicine studies, often to test predictions about relationships between mindfulness and other clinically relevant variables. The MAAS has been used most frequently in the context of behavioral medicine, and associations have been demonstrated between MAAS scores and measures of physiological and psychological functioning in numerous populations. For example, Carlson and Brown (2005) reported that MAAS scores were negatively correlated with mood disturbance and stress in cancer outpatients. In chronic pain patients, higher MAAS scores were associated with lower levels of depression, pain-related anxiety, and disability, after controlling for pain intensity and pain-related acceptance (McCracken, Gauntlett-Gilbert, & Vowles, 2007). A similar study (McCracken & Keogh, 2009) found that anxiety sensitivity (fear of anxiety) was associated with greater pain, disability, and distress in chronic pain patients, but that acceptance of pain and general mindfulness (as measured by the MAAS) substantially reduced this relationship, suggesting that mindfulness and acceptance can counteract the effects of anxiety sensitivity on distress and disability in chronic pain patients. In a study of adults with HIV/AIDS, MAAS scores interacted with disengagement coping to predict anxiety. High MAAS scores and low levels of disengagement coping were associated with low levels of anxiety (Gonzalez, Solomon, Zvolensky, & Miller, 2009). In general, this body of findings suggests that high levels of mindfulness are associated with adaptive functioning in populations with significant medical concerns, even after controlling for potentially confounding or overlapping variables.

In an undergraduate student sample, MAAS scores moderated the relationship between dehydroepiandrosterone (DHEA), an endogenous steroid that is positively correlated with physiological health, and self-reports of physiological symptoms (O'Loughlin & Zuckerman, 2008). Individuals with higher MAAS scores showed greater concordance between their self-reported physical symptoms and their DHEA levels (measured with saliva samples), suggesting that more mindful individuals can more accurately perceive their physical symptoms. Although this study used a nonclinical sample, its findings imply that mindfulness may be adaptive in populations with health problems for whom more accurate perceptions of their own inner states may be related to more effective use of self-care or medical resources, such as seeking medical services when they need them.

Mindfulness instruments have also been used to investigate the outcomes of MBSR and other mindfulness-based interventions in behavioral medicine settings. Brown and Ryan (2003) studied cancer patients who completed MBSR and found that MAAS scores were negatively associated with measures of mood disturbance and stress before and after the intervention. Pre- to post-treatment increases in MAAS scores predicted decreases in measures of psychological disturbance. Carmody, Reed, Kristeller, and Merriam (2008) assessed levels of mindfulness before and after MBSR using the MAAS to assess trait mindfulness and the TMS to assess state mindfulness. Increases in MAAS scores, but not TMS scores, were associated with decreases in reported medical symptoms and psychological distress.

Other mindfulness instruments have also been used in mindfulness-based treatment studies. Carmody and Baer (2008) found significant increases in FFMQ scores from pre- to post-MBSR in a sample of adults complaining of illness-related stress, chronic pain, anxiety, and general stress. These increases were significant mediators of the relationship between meditation practice time and improvements in psychological symptoms, stress, and well-being (Carmody & Baer, 2008). Findings are consistent with the common assumption that the practice of mindfulness meditation leads to increased ability to be mindful in daily life and that this facilitates health and well-being; however, results were stronger for psychological than for medical symptoms. Forman, Butryn, Hoffman, and Herbert (2009) conducted a weight-loss intervention that included acceptance and mindfulness exercises. Mindfulness, as measured by the PHLMS, increased significantly from pre- to post-treatment. Although mediation analyses were not conducted, increases in PHLMS were significantly correlated with amount of weight lost at six-month follow-up, suggesting that increased mindfulness skills may be an important mechanism of change.

In some studies, mindfulness questionnaires have not shown significant changes over the course of mindfulness-based treatment. For example, Witek-Janusek and colleagues (2008) examined the effects of MBSR compared to a control group on immune function in a sample of patients recently diagnosed with early-stage breast cancer. Although the MBSR group reported significant improvements in immune function, coping effectiveness, and quality of life, as well as decreases in cortisol levels, no significant changes on MAAS scores were found after MBSR and no significant differences in MAAS scores were reported between the MBSR and control groups. Similarly, a mindfulness-based intervention targeting prenatal stress and mood during pregnancy produced significant reductions in anxiety, but only nonsignificant increases in mindfulness as measured by the MAAS (Vieten & Astin, 2008).

When increases in mindfulness scores following mindfulness-based treatment are found, they have not always been correlated with the intervention's positive outcomes. Kingston, Chadwick, Meron, and Skinner (2007) investigated the effect of mindfulness practice on pain tolerance in an asymptomatic sample and used the KIMS to assess mindfulness skills. The mindfulness intervention increased both pain tolerance and scores on the KIMS; however, the increase in pain tolerance was not correlated with the increase in mindfulness skills.

Overall, the current literature supports the utility of mindfulness measures in behavioral medicine contexts. Most studies show that mindfulness is significantly correlated with other important variables, and several suggest that increased mindfulness may be a mediator of change in mindfulness-based interventions. The MAAS has been used most widely in the behavioral medicine literature. However, the MAAS is unidimensional, and it is possible that elements of mindfulness not assessed by the MAAS, such as acceptance, nonjudging, and nonreactivity, may be important in behavioral medicine populations. Thus, more research with the other mindfulness measures is needed.

Instruments for Measuring Acceptance, Values, or Psychological Flexibility

Numerous instruments have been developed to assess constructs related to the ACT model of acceptance, such as experiential avoidance, psychological flexibility, and values-based action. The most commonly used is the Acceptance and Action Questionnaire (Hayes et al., 2004). In addition, several variants of the AAQ have been developed for use with specific populations.

Acceptance and Action Questionnaire (AAQ)

The Acceptance and Action Questionnaire (AAQ; Hayes et al., 2004) is the most generally applicable of the ACT-based measures and is available in several versions. The nine-item version (Hayes et al., 2004) has been widely used and assesses elements of experiential avoidance, including negative evaluation of and tendency to avoid or control aversive internal stimuli and inability to take constructive action while experiencing these stimuli. When reverse scored, it serves as a measure of acceptance. It has adequate internal consistency (α = .70) and is correlated with many forms of psychopathology. It predicts future mental health and has been shown to mediate the relationship between participation in ACT and improved well-being (Dalrymple & Herbert, 2007; Forman, Herbert, Moitra, Yeomans, & Geller, 2007). A sixteen-item version (Bond & Bunce, 2000) includes two subscales: "Willingness" and "Action." The Willingness subscale reflects openness to experiencing negative thoughts and feelings and includes items such as "I try hard to avoid feeling depressed or anxious" (reverse scored). The Action subscale reflects the ability to behave consistently with values and goals even when experiencing unpleasant thoughts and feelings and includes items such as "When I feel depressed or anxious, I am unable to take care of my responsibilities" (reverse scored). The most recent version, known as the AAQ-II (Bond et al., in press) has ten items and is conceptualized as a measure of psychological flexibility, the central construct in the most recent descriptions of ACT. Psychological flexibility includes full awareness of the present moment, including thoughts and feelings, while either changing behavior or persisting in ongoing behavior, depending on what is required to pursue valued goals (Hayes et al., 2006). Thus, the psychologically flexible individual is able to engage in constructive behavior consistent with deeply held values even when negative thoughts, emotions, and sensations are present. Preliminary findings suggest that the AAQ-II has good internal consistency, a single factor structure, and significant correlations with measures of mental health.

Within the behavioral medicine literature, versions of the AAQ have been used in several ways. Correlational studies consistently show that AAQ scores are significantly associated with many health-related variables. For example, in a medical rehabilitation population, Kortte, Veiel, Batten, and Wegener (2009) found that AAQ scores were negatively correlated with depression and negative affect and positively correlated with hope, positive affect, and spiritual well-being. AAQ scores also predicted level of handicap and life satisfaction at three-month follow-up. In a sample of older adults, Andrews and Dulin (2007) reported that AAQ scores partially moderated the relationship between self-reported health and both depression and anxiety. Poor physical health was associated with depression and anxiety, but this relationship was smaller for persons with high acceptance scores on the AAQ. Findings suggest that attempts to avoid the distressing thoughts and emotions associated with declining health in old age paradoxically contribute to higher levels of anxiety and depression.

A few studies have shown that AAQ scores predict responses to pain tolerance tasks in laboratory settings. A commonly used task is the cold pressor, in which participants submerge one hand in very cold water for as long as possible. Feldner and colleagues (2006) reported that persons whose AAQ scores reflected low levels of acceptance showed lower pain tolerance and longer recovery times than those whose scores were high in acceptance. Similar results have been reported by Zettle and others (2005).

Other studies have examined whether AAQ scores change with participation in a mindfulness- or acceptance-based intervention and, if so, whether the change in AAQ scores mediates the effect on treatment outcomes. A study of an ACT intervention for obesity (Lillis, Hayes, Bunting, & Masuda, 2009) found that AAQ scores (nine-item version) had increased significantly at three-month follow-up and mediated changes in psychological distress, quality of life, and stigma. However, Tapper and colleagues (2009) studied an ACT intervention for obesity and found no significant changes in the AAQ-II.

Overall, these studies suggest that assessment of general acceptance or psychological flexibility is helpful in clarifying relationships with other variables and mechanisms of change in mindfulness-based interventions. However, several authors have suggested that it may be useful to assess acceptance of specific types of experiences, such as unpleasant thoughts, emotions, and sensations related to particular health conditions. Accordingly, several variants of the AAQ designed for specific behavioral medicine populations have been developed. These are described next.

Chronic Pain Acceptance Questionnaire (CPAQ)

The Chronic Pain Acceptance Questionnaire (CPAQ; McCracken, 1998) is a twenty-item measure with two subscales (McCracken, Vowles, & Eccleston, 2004; Vowles, McCracken, McLeod, & Eccleston, 2008). The Activity Engagement subscale captures participation in important activities in the presence of pain (e.g., "I am getting on with the business of living no matter what my level of pain is"). The Pain Willingness subscale assesses allowing pain to be present without attempting to control or avoid it (e.g., "I would gladly sacrifice important things in my life to control this pain better"; reverse scored). Internal consistencies for the total score and subscales have ranged from .78 to .91. At least thirty-five studies using a variety of designs in assessment and treatment contexts demonstrate relationships between CPAQ scores and multiple measures of emotional, physical, and social functioning, providing strong support for construct validity and utility of the CPAQ (Cheung, Wong, Yap, & Chen, 2008; McCracken et al., 2004; Nicholas & Asghari, 2006; Vowles et al., 2008; Wicksell, Olsson & Melin, 2009).

Acceptance and Action Diabetes Questionnaire (AADQ)

This eleven-item instrument (Gregg, 2004) assesses psychological flexibility in relation to diabetes, including awareness, believability, and acceptance of diabetes-related thoughts and feelings. Items include "I try to avoid reminders of my diabetes" and "I do not take care of my diabetes because it reminds me that I have diabetes." Most items are reverse scored, so that higher scores represent higher levels of psychological flexibility. Preliminary evidence suggests that psychometric properties are good, with internal consistency of .88 (Gregg, 2004) and increases in scores after an intervention combining ACT with basic diabetes education (Gregg, Callaghan, Hayes, & Glenn-Lawson, 2007). The latter study also found that changes in the AADQ mediated the effect of treatment on outcome variables, including an objective measure of blood sugar. Thus, increased acceptance of diabetes-related thoughts and feelings appeared to lead to improved self-care that was reflected in blood glucose levels.

Acceptance and Action Epilepsy Questionnaire (AAEpQ)

This eight-item instrument (Lundgren, Dahl, & Hayes, 2008) measures psychological flexibility related to epilepsy. Items include "When I have upsetting feelings or thoughts about my epilepsy, I try to get rid of those feelings or thoughts" and "I cannot exercise regularly because it reminds me that I have epilepsy" (both items reverse scored). In a small sample, the Acceptance and Action Epilepsy Questionnaire (AAEpQ) demonstrated adequate internal consistency (.65–.76) and showed substantial changes in an ACT-based treatment for management of epilepsy. Changes in AAEpQ scores fully mediated the significant relationship between ACT-based treatment for epilepsy and the total seconds of seizures experienced per month (Lundgren et al., 2008). These findings suggest that acceptance of epilepsy-related thoughts and feelings is important in the effective management of this condition and that the AAEpQ is a useful assessment tool.

Avoidance and Inflexibility Scale (AIS)

The Avoidance and Inflexibility Scale (AIS; Gifford et al., 2004) has thirteen items and measures psychological flexibility related to smoking. Introductory statements note that sometimes people have thoughts and feelings that make them want to smoke. Respondents then rate their response to these thoughts and feelings—for example, "How likely is it that these thoughts will lead you to smoke?" and "How important is it to get rid of these feelings?" High scorers show a low level of willingness to experience the unpleasant sensations and emotions that arise in the absence of smoking. The AIS has high internal consistency (α = .93), was significantly associated with likelihood of quitting smoking after ACT-based treatment, and significantly mediated the effects of the treatment on smoking status (Gifford et al., 2004). This instrument has been adapted for use in overeating research, with the only difference that items refer to eating rather than smoking. Internal consistency of this version was good (α of .82 and .92). It was significantly correlated with the general AAQ and with body mass index (BMI) in an overweight population, and changes in the AIS significantly mediated the effects of an ACT intervention on weight loss over three months.

Tinnitus Acceptance Questionnaire (TAQ)

This twelve-item instrument (Westin, Hayes, & Andersson, 2008) assesses the tendency to accept thoughts and feelings related to tinnitus. It has two factors: activity engagement ("My tinnitus has led me to decrease my engagement in former activities") and tinnitus suppression ("I strive to suppress aversive thoughts and feelings related to tinnitus"; both items reverse scored). Internal consistency was good (α = .89). In patients seeking treatment for tinnitus, the activity engagement factor fully mediated the relationship between tinnitus distress at baseline and depression and quality of life at follow-up. Similar results were found for the total score (Westin et al., 2008). Results were less clear for the tinnitus suppression subscale. The general AAQ (nine-item version) had lower internal consistency in this sample and was not a significant mediator of treatment outcomes, suggesting the potential utility of assessment of tinnitus-specific acceptance. Overall, findings suggest that reduced engagement in rewarding activities because of tinnitus is maladaptive and that the TAQ may be a useful tool for measuring this tendency.

Acceptance and Action Questionnaire for Weight (AAQW)

This seventeen-item instrument (Lillis et al., 2009) assesses the extent to which weight-related thoughts and feelings interfere with valued behavior. Example items are "My eating urges control me" and "I try hard to avoid feeling bad about my weight or how I look" (both items reverse scored). The Acceptance and Action Questionnaire for Weight (AAQW) has good internal consistency (α = .88). A mindfulness- and acceptance-based intervention produced increases on scores on the AAQW compared to a control group, and this increase mediated improvement on all outcome measures, including BMI, stigma, psychological distress, and quality of life (Lillis et al., 2009). Findings suggest that weight-related acceptance is an important process of change and that the AAQW is a promising tool for assessing it.

Illness Cognitions Questionnaire (ICQ)

The Illness Cognitions Questionnaire (ICQ; Evers et al., 2001) assesses three categories of cognitions in persons with chronic diseases: helplessness, acceptance, and perceived benefits. Acceptance items include "I have learned to accept the limitations imposed by my illness" and "I have learned to live with my illness." In adults with rheumatoid arthritis or multiple sclerosis, internal consistency and test–retest reliability of all factors was strong. The acceptance factor was significantly related to lower levels of functional disability, physical complaints, and negative mood and higher levels of active coping and positive mood. Acceptance also predicted better physical and psychological health one year later. This instrument does not directly address mindfulness-related constructs captured by the instruments described earlier. However, it may be a useful tool in populations with a variety of chronic diseases.

Overall, the recent literature suggests that content-specific measures of acceptance are useful tools in the study of behavioral medicine conditions. In addition to the variants on the AAQ just described, several other measurement approaches have been introduced in the recent literature and are described in the following paragraphs. Although empirical support for their utility is still preliminary, they appear to warrant additional study.

Brief Pain Coping Inventory – 2 (BPCI-2)

This nineteen-item measure (McCracken & Vowles, 2007) assesses traditional cognitive behavioral methods of coping with pain, such as relaxation, distraction, and positive self-statements, as well as acceptance-based approaches consistent with psychological flexibility, such as awareness of pain without attempts to avoid it and acting in accordance with values even when pain is present. These two subscales, labeled pain management and psychological flexibility, have adequate internal consistency (α = .73 for each). Although both subscales were correlated with measures of patient functioning, correlations for the psychological flexibility subscale were much larger. After controlling for pain intensity, the psychological flexibility subscale predicted incremental variance in patient functioning, whereas the pain management subscale did not. Results provide additional support for the importance of psychological flexibility in understanding the functioning of persons with chronic pain and suggest that the Brief Pain Coping Inventory – 2 (BPCI-2) is useful in assessing it. However, it is not clear whether the BPCI-2 had advantages over the CPAQ, which has more research supporting its utility.

Psychological Inflexibility in Pain Scale (PIPS)

This sixteen-item measure (Wicksell, Renöfält, Olsson, Bond, & Melin, 2008) has two subscales: avoidance ("I avoid scheduling activities because of my pain") and cognitive fusion ("It is important to understand what causes my pain"). The Psychological Inflexibility in Pain Scale (PIPS) has adequate to good internal consistency (α = .75 to .90). Regression analyses indicated that both factors predict pain intensity and interference, physical and emotional functioning, and quality of life (Wicksell et al., 2008). The PIPS has not been directly compared to the CPAQ, and it is therefore not clear whether it has advantages over this instrument.

Chronic Pain Values Inventory (CPVI)

This twelve-item instrument (McCracken & Yang, 2006) measures six values domains: family, intimate relations, friends, work, health, and growth or learning. Respondents rate the importance of each domain and their success in meeting their goals in each domain. The importance subscale has a ceiling effect, with respondents tending to indicate that most domains are of high importance. The success subscale appears to be the more meaningful factor and predicts current and future functioning in individuals suffering from chronic pain (McCracken & Yang, 2006; McCracken & Vowles, 2008). Changes in the success subscale are associated with improvements in functioning at three months following an intervention (McCracken & Vowles, 2008), and increases were correlated with increases on the CPAQ (Vowles & McCracken, 2008).

Values Bull's-Eye

The Values Bull's-Eye (Lundgren et al., 2008) measures attainment of values and persistence in the face of barriers. Using worksheets with concentric circles to represent dartboards, participants place deeply held values at the center (the bull's-eye) and mark how closely their behavior accords with each value and how persistently they are pursuing values in the face of barriers. Distances on the dartboards provide scores for values attainment and persistence. Lundgren (2006) reported good test–retest reliability ($r = .86$) and Cronbach's α ranged from .65 to .76 (Lundgren et al., 2008). A combination of values attainment and persistence through barriers fully mediated the significant relationship between ACT-based treatment for epilepsy and measures of personal well-being, quality of life, and total seconds of seizures experienced per month (Lundgren et al., 2008).

Acceptance and Defusion Process Measure (ADPM)

The Acceptance and Defusion Process Measure (ADPM; Hesser, Westin, Hayes, & Andersson, 2009) is an observational measure of the extent to which verbal statements during ACT sessions are consistent with acceptance and defusion. Participants' verbalizations are rated by trained coders. In a study of ACT for tinnitus, in-session acceptance and defusion rated early in treatment predicted sustained positive treatment effects of ACT, even when symptom improvement prior to acceptance and defusion measurement was accounted for statistically (Hesser et al., 2009).

Conclusions

Some measures of mindfulness and acceptance are designed for general use, whereas others are intended for specific populations in behavioral medicine. The utility of general and specific instruments may depend on the population, problem, or intervention being studied. For example, MBSR cultivates the general capacity to be mindful in daily life and is often delivered to heterogeneous groups of patients with a wide variety of difficulties. In this context, it is important to assess whether participants are learning to be more generally mindful and whether increases in mindfulness are related to improvements in symptoms, stress levels, and overall well-being. However, both MBSR and ACT have been tailored for application to specific problems (chronic pain, obesity, self-care in diabetes, smoking cessation, coping with tinnitus, and so on). Because treatment in these contexts is likely to emphasize the application of acceptance and mindfulness skills to the specific difficulties of each population, the more-targeted assessment instruments may be more informative. Very few studies have included both general and content-specific measures of acceptance and mindfulness. McCracken and Keogh (2009) found that both acceptance of chronic pain (measured with the CPAQ) and general mindfulness (measured with the MAAS) contributed to the prediction of variance in distress and disability. These findings suggest that both may be important in cultivating overall well-being in people with chronic pain. Thus, continued work on both general and specific tools for the assessment of mindfulness and acceptance appears warranted.

Several issues require additional work. First, instruments differ on their use of reverse-scored or negatively worded items. Such items describe an absence of mindfulness or acceptance and ratings are reversed, whereas positively worded items directly describe an aspect of mindfulness or acceptance. Some questionnaires consist of all positively worded items, whereas others are all negatively worded, and some include both types of items. Although questions are sometimes raised about the validity of reverse-scored items, this issue has not been thoroughly examined in the mindfulness and acceptance literature. Overall, current research provides strong support for the reliability and validity of many mindfulness and acceptance measures, regardless of the items' scoring direction.

The number of elements or components of mindfulness and acceptance that should be measured separately is also unresolved. Strong efforts have been made to identify facets of mindfulness that contribute independently to the understanding of relationships with health and well-being. In the ACT literature, although the current model of psychological flexibility includes six elements, many instruments provide a single total score representing psychological flexibility as a unidimensional construct. Others provide two subscale scores. Specific elements of the ACT model, including cognitive defusion and self-as-context, are not scored separately. Whether it would be useful to do so is unclear.

Despite these issues, however, the available tools for measuring acceptance and mindfulness in behavioral medicine settings are very promising. They are contributing to increased understanding of the nature of mindfulness and acceptance and their important roles in enhancing health and well-being in persons with pain, illness, and other health-related problems.

References

Andrews, D., & Dulin, P. (2007). The relationship between self-reported health and mental health problems among older adults in New Zealand: Experiential avoidance as a moderator. *Aging and Mental Health, 11,* 596-603.

Baer, R. A. (2003). Mindfulness training as a clinical intervention: A conceptual and empirical review. *Clinical Psychology: Science and Practice, 10,* 125–143.

Baer, R. A., Smith, G. T., & Allen, K. B. (2004). Assessment of mindfulness by self-report: The Kentucky Inventory of Mindfulness Skills. *Assessment, 11,* 191–206.

Baer, R. A., Smith, G. T., Hopkins, J., Krietemeyer, J., & Toney, L. (2006). Using self-report assessment methods to explore facets of mindfulness. *Assessment, 13,* 27–45.

Baer, R. A., Smith, G. T., Lykins, E., Button, D., Krietemeyer, J., Sauer, S., et al. (2008). Construct validity of the Five Facet Mindfulness Questionnaire in meditating and nonmeditating samples. *Assessment, 15,* 329–342.

Bishop, S. R., Lau, M., Shapiro, S., Carlson, L., Anderson, N. C., Carmody, J., et al. (2004). Mindfulness: A proposed operational definition. *Clinical Psychology: Science and Practice, 11,* 230–241.

Bond, F. W., & Bunce, D. (2000). Mediators of change in emotion-focused and problem-focused worksite stress management interventions. *Journal of Occupational Health Psychology, 5,* 156-163.

Bond, F., Hayes, S. C., Baer, R. A., Carpenter, K. M., Orcutt, H. K., Waltz, T., et al. (in review). Preliminary psychometric properties of the Acceptance Action Questionnaire-II: a revised measure of psychological flexibility and acceptance.

Brown, K. W., & Ryan, R. M. (2003). The benefits of being in the present: Mindfulness and its role in psychological well-being. *Journal of Personality and Social Psychology, 84,* 822–848.

Brown, K. W., Ryan, R. M., & Creswell, J. D. (2007). Mindfulness: Theoretical foundations and evidence for its salutary effects. *Psychological Inquiry, 18,* 211–237.

Buchheld, N., Grossman, P., & Walach, H. (2001). Measuring mindfulness in insight meditation and meditation-based psychotherapy: The development of the Freiburg Mindfulness Inventory (FMI). *Journal for Meditation and Meditation Research, 1,* 11–34.

Cardaciotto, L., Herbert, J. D., Forman, E. M., Moitra, E., & Farrow, V. (2007). The assessment of present-moment awareness and acceptance: The Philadelphia Mindfulness Scale. *Assessment, 15,* 204–223.

Carlson, L. E., & Brown, K. W. (2005). Validation of the Mindful Attention Awareness Scale in a cancer population. *Journal of Psychosomatic Research, 58,* 29–33.

Carmody, J., & Baer, R.A. (2008). Relationships between mindfulness practice and levels of mindfulness, medical and psychological symptoms and well-being in a mindfulness-based stress reduction program. *Journal of Behavioral Medicine, 31,* 23–33.

Carmody, J., Reed, G., Kristeller, J., & Merriam, P. (2008). Mindfulness, spirituality, and health-related symptoms. *Journal of Psychosomatic Research, 64,* 393–403.

Chadwick, P., Hember, M., Mead, S., Lilley, B., & Dagnan, D. (2008). Responding mindfully to unpleasant thoughts and images: Reliability and validity of the Southampton Mindfulness Questionnaire. *British Journal of Clinical Psychology, 47,* 451–455.

Cheung, N. M., Wong, T. C. M., Yap, J. C. M., & Chen, P. P. (2008). Validation of the Chronic Pain Acceptance Questionnaire (CPAQ) in Cantonese-speaking Chinese patients. *Journal of Pain, 9,* 823–832.

Dalrymple, K. L., & Herbert, J. D. (2007). Acceptance and commitment therapy for generalized social anxiety disorder: A pilot study. *Behavior Modification, 31,* 543–568.

Davis, K. M., Lau, M. A., & Cairns, D. R. (2009). Development and preliminary validation of a trait version of the Toronto Mindfulness Scale. *Journal of Cognitive Psychotherapy, 23,* 185–197.

Dimidjian, S., & Linehan, M. (2003). Defining an agenda for future research on the clinical application of mindfulness practice. *Clinical Psychology: Science and Practice, 10,* 166–171.

Evers, A., Kraaimaat, F., van Lankveld, W., Jongen, P., Jacobs, J., & Bijlsma, J. (2001). Beyond unfavorable thinking: The illness cognition questionnaire for chronic diseases. *Journal of Consulting and Clinical Psychology, 69*, 1026–1036.

Feldman, G. C., Hayes, A. M., Kumar, S. M., Greeson, J. G., & Laurenceau, J. P. (2007). Mindfulness and emotion regulation: The development and initial validation of the Cognitive and Affective Mindfulness Scale-Revised (CAMS-R). *Journal of Psychopathology and Behavioral Assessment, 29*, 177–190.

Feldner, M. T., Hekmat, H., Zvolensky, M. J., Vowles, K., E., Secrist, Z., & Leen-Feldner, E. W. (2006). The role of experiential avoidance in acute pain tolerance: A laboratory test. *Journal of Behavior Therapy & Experimental Psychiatry, 37*, 146–158.

Forman, E. M., Butryn, M. L., Hoffman, K. L., & Herbert, J. D. (2009). An open trial of an acceptance-based behavioral intervention for weight loss. *Cognitive and Behavioral Practice, 16*, 223–235.

Forman, E. M., Herbert, J. D., Moitra, E., Yeomans, P. D., & Geller, P. A. (2007). A randomized controlled effectiveness trial of acceptance and commitment therapy and cognitive therapy for anxiety and depression. *Behavior Modification, 31*, 772–799.

Gifford, E. V., Kohlenberg, B. S., Hayes, S. C., Antonuccio, D. O., Piasecki, M. M., Rasmussen-Hall, M. L., et al. (2004). Acceptance-based treatment for smoking cessation. *Behavior Therapy, 35*, 689–705.

Gonzalez, A., Solomon, S. E., Zvolensky, M. J., & Miller, C. T. (2009). The interaction of mindful-based attention and awareness and disengagement coping with HIV/AIDS-related stigma in regard to concurrent anxiety and depressive symptoms among adults with HIV/AIDS. *Journal of Health Psychology, 14*, 403–413.

Gregg, J. (2004). *A randomized controlled effectiveness trial comparing patient education with and without acceptance and commitment therapy for type 2 diabetes self-management.* Unpublished doctoral dissertation, University of Nevada, Reno.

Gregg, J. A., Callaghan, G. M., Hayes, S. C., & Glenn-Lawson, J. L. (2007). Improving diabetes self-management through acceptance, mindfulness, and values: A randomized controlled trial. *Journal of Consulting and Clinical Psychology, 75*, 336–343.

Grossman, P., Niemann, L., Schmidt, S., & Walach, H. (2004). Mindfulness-based stress reduction and health benefits: A meta-analysis. *Journal of Psychosomatic Research, 57,* 35–43.

Hayes, S. C., Luoma, J., Bond, F., Masuda, A., & Lillis, J. (2006). Acceptance and commitment therapy: Model, processes and outcomes. *Behaviour Research and Therapy, 44,* 1–25.

Hayes, S. C., Strosahl, K., & Wilson, K. G. (1999). *Acceptance and commitment therapy: An experiential approach to behavior change.* New York: Guilford Press.

Hayes, S. C., Strosahl, K., Wilson, K. G., Bissett, R. T., Pistorello, J., Toarmino, D., et al. (2004). Measuring experiential avoidance: A preliminary test of a working model. *Psychological Record, 54,* 553–578.

Hesser, H., Westin, V., Hayes, S. C., & Andersson, G. (2009). Clients' in-session acceptance and cognitive defusion behaviors in acceptance-based treatment of tinnitus distress. *Behaviour Research and Therapy, 47,* 523–528.

Kabat-Zinn, J. (1982). An outpatient program in behavioral medicine for chronic pain patients based on the practice of mindfulness meditation: Theoretical considerations and preliminary results. *General Hospital Psychiatry, 4,* 33–47.

Kingston, J. L., Chadwick, P., Meron, D., & Skinner, T. C. (2007). The effect of mindfulness practice on pain tolerance, psychological well-being and physiological activity: A randomised, single blind, active control trial. *Journal of Psychosomatic Research, 62,* 297–300.

Kortte, K. B., Veiel, L., Batten, S., & Wegener, S. T. (2009). Measuring avoidance in medical rehabilitation. *Rehabilitation Psychology, 54,* 91–98.

Lau, M. A., Bishop, S. R., Segal, Z. V., Buis, T., Anderson, N. D., Carlson, L., et al. (2006). The Toronto Mindfulness Scale: Development and validation. *Journal of Clinical Psychology, 62,* 1445–1467.

Lillis, J., Hayes, S. C., Bunting, K., & Masuda, A. (2009). Teaching acceptance and mindfulness to improve the lives of the obese: A preliminary test of a theoretical model. *Annals of Behavioral Medicine, 37,* 58–69.

Linehan, M. M. (1993). *Cognitive-behavioral treatment of borderline personality disorder.* New York: Guilford Press.

Lundgren, T. (2006, July). *Validation and reliability data of the Bull's-Eye*. Presentation at the second world conference on ACT/RFT, London.

Lundgren, T., Dahl, J., & Hayes, S. C. (2008). Evaluation of mediators of change in the treatment of epilepsy with acceptance and commitment therapy. *Journal of Behavioral Medicine, 31*, 225–235.

McCracken, L. M. (1998). Learning to live with the pain: Acceptance of pain predicts adjustment in persons with chronic pain. *Pain, 74*, 21–27.

McCracken, L. M., Gauntlett-Gilbert, J., & Vowles, K. E. (2007). The role of mindfulness in a contextual cognitive-behavioral analysis of chronic pain-related suffering and disability. *Pain, 131*, 63–69.

McCracken, L. M., & Keogh, E. (2009). Acceptance, mindfulness, and values-based action may counteract fear and avoidance of emotions in chronic pain: An analysis of anxiety sensitivity. *Journal of Pain, 10*, 408–415.

McCracken, L. M., & Vowles, K. E. (2007). Psychological flexibility and traditional pain management strategies in relation to patient functioning with chronic pain: An examination of a revised instrument. *Journal of Pain, 8*, 700–707.

McCracken, L. M., & Vowles, K. E. (2008). A prospective analysis of acceptance and values in patients with chronic pain. *Health Psychology, 27*, 215–220.

McCracken, L. M., Vowles, K. E., & Eccleston, C. (2004). Acceptance of chronic pain: Component analysis and a revised assessment method. *Pain, 107*, 159–166.

McCracken, L. M., & Yang, S. (2006). The role of values in a contextual cognitive-behavioral approach to chronic pain. *Pain, 123*, 137–145.

Nicholas, M. K., & Asghari, A. (2006). Investigating acceptance in adjustment to chronic pain: Is acceptance broader than we thought? *Pain, 124*, 269–279.

O'Loughlin, R. E., & Zuckerman, M. (2008). Mindfulness as a moderator of the relationship between dehydroepiandrosterone and reported physical symptoms. *Personality and Individual Differences, 44*, 1193–1202.

Segal, Z. V., Williams, J. M., & Teasdale, J. D. (2002). *Mindfulness-based cognitive therapy for depression: A new approach to preventing relapse*. New York: Guilford Press.

Tapper, K., Shaw, C., Ilsley, J., Hill, A. J., Bond, F. W., & Moore, L. (2009). Exploratory randomised controlled trial of a mindfulness-based weight loss intervention for women. *Appetite, 52*, 396–404.

Vieten, C., & Astin, J. (2008). Effects of a mindfulness-based intervention during pregnancy on prenatal stress and mood: Results of a pilot study. *Archives of Women's Mental Health, 11*, 67–74.

Vowles, K. E., & McCracken, L. M. (2008). Acceptance and values-based action in chronic pain: A study of effectiveness and treatment process. *Journal of Consulting and Clinical Psychology, 76*, 397–407.

Vowles, K. E., McCracken, L. M., McLeod, C., & Eccleston, C. (2008). The Chronic Pain Acceptance Questionnaire: Confirmatory factor analysis and identification of patient subgroups. *Pain, 140*, 284–291.

Walach, H., Buchheld, N., Buttenmuller, V., Kleinknecht, N., & Schmidt, S. (2006). Measuring mindfulness—the Freiburg Mindfulness Inventory (FMI). *Personality and Individual Differences, 40*, 1543–1555.

Westin, V., Hayes, S. C., & Andersson, G. (2008). Is it the sound of your relationship to it? The role of acceptance in predicting tinnitus impact. *Behaviour Research and Therapy, 46*, 1259–1265.

Wicksell, R. K., Olsson, G. L., & Melin, L. (2009). The Chronic Pain Acceptance Questionnaire (CPAQ)—further validation including a confirmatory factor analysis and a comparison with the Tampa Scale of Kinesiophobia. *European Journal of Pain, 13*, 760–768.

Wicksell, R. K., Renöfält, J., Olsson, G. L., Bond, F. W., & Melin, L. (2008). Avoidance and cognitive fusion—central components in pain related disability? Development and preliminary validation of the Psychological Inflexiblity in Pain Scale (PIPS). *European Journal of Pain, 12*, 491–500.

Witek-Janusek, L., Albuquerque, K., Chroniak, K. R., Chroniak, C., Durazo-Arvizu, R., & Mathews, H. L. (2008). Effect of mindfulness based stress reduction on immune function, quality of life and coping in women newly diagnosed with early stage breast cancer. *Brain, Behavior, & Immunity, 22*, 969–981.

Zettle, R. D., Hocker, T. L., Mick, K. A., Scofield, B. E., Petson, C. L., Song, H., & Sudarijanto, R. P. (2005). Differential strategies in coping with pain as a function of level of experiential avoidance. *Psychological Record, 55*, 511–524.

PART 4

Related Clinical Methods

9 Acceptance and Commitment Therapy and Motivational Interviewing for Health Behavior Change

David Gillanders
University of Edinburgh and NHS Lothian

Living with a chronic health problem is not easy. Many, if not all, chronic conditions require adaptation and adjustment both emotionally and behaviorally. Many health conditions require changes to diet, exercise, self-monitoring, medication adherence, and self-regulation. Such behavior change may need to be lifelong. Across almost all conditions, when one is helping people to change health-related behavior, issues of resistance, "denial," setbacks, relapses, frustration, and negative feelings are the norm rather than the exception. Health behavior change also occurs in an interpersonal context. Significant others and health professionals can interact with patients in ways that can promote or undermine health behavior change.

Since the 1980s, considerable clinical and research work has gone into investigating and describing a clinical method known as Motivational Interviewing (MI) (Miller, 1983; Miller & Rollnick, 1991, 2002). Many practitioners working in health care fields will have heard of MI. For many it is still associated with the substance-misuse treatment field, though MI has been applied to issues of changing health-related behaviors for some time (Rollnick, Mason, & Butler, 1999; Rollnick, Miller, & Butler, 2008). The purpose of this chapter is to examine similarities and differences between MI and acceptance and commitment therapy (ACT) and to consider how these approaches can be integrated.

Key Features of MI

MI is "a collaborative, person-centred form of guiding to elicit and strengthen motivation for change" (Miller & Rollnick, 2009). In other statements about MI, the authors also mention that it seeks to do so by helping the individual to resolve ambivalence, or conflicting motivations, about change (e.g., Hettema, Steele, & Miller, 2005). These statements give a clear description of what MI is: a clinical method or form of interacting that is designed to increase the likelihood that an individual will make adaptive behavior changes in relation to his health. There are two important elements to the practice of MI: the interpersonal style of the interviewer (sometimes referred to as "the spirit of MI") and the technical tools of the motivational interview (Miller & Rose, 2009).

The first element, the spirit of MI, reflects its origins in the humanistic psychology movement, particularly in the Client Centred Therapy of Carl Rogers (Rogers, 1951). The spirit of MI is an interpersonal style characterized as "collaborative, evocative and honouring patient autonomy" (Rollnick et al., 1999, p. 6). By "collaborative," it is meant that the clinician behaves in a way so as to put himself on an equal footing with the patient. He does not lecture, persuade, or give advice. There is an active collaboration and joint decision making between clinician and patient. The clinician tries to avoid acting like the expert.

The spirit of MI is evocative as it aims to evoke and clarify the patient's own perceptions, reasons, and motivations for change. The motivational interview does not "provide" skills, knowledge, or motivation that the patient is thought to be lacking in some manner. Instead, the motivational interview elicits and evokes the patient's own reasons for making adaptive health behavior changes. In honoring patient autonomy, clinicians are encouraged to recognize that the individual has a right to choose whether or not to change. While being encouraged to care about the choices that the patient makes, clinicians are also reminded to have "a certain detachment from outcomes" (Rollnick et al., 1999, p. 7). These three cornerstones of the spirit of MI represent a mind-set for clinicians in approaching the work. The interpersonal style of MI is also characterized by accurate empathy, encouragement of hope and optimism, listening closely, and appreciating the patients' own motivations, concerns, reasons to change or not change, and struggles they have had in trying to effect change.

Regarding the technical tools of MI, where MI departs from traditional Client Centered Therapy is that it is consciously goal oriented (Miller & Rollnick, 2009). During the motivational interview, the clinician listens carefully to the different types of talk that the client makes about the behavior changes being considered. The client's verbal behavior is categorized as "sustain talk" and "change talk." Sustain talk represents verbalizations of ambivalence about change, resistance to change, difficulties or struggles that are associated with the change, reasons not to change, predictions of failure regarding change, and the like. In contrast, change talk is verbal behavior that suggests a potential to change, the benefits of change, confidence to make changes, and beliefs that change will be initiated.

Although the clinician will respond with empathy to sustain talk, over the course of the interview she will differentially reinforce change talk. She does this by eliciting, encouraging, rolling with resistance, and focusing on the client's own cares, concerns, and reasons for change. By selectively responding to the patient's change talk, the clinician sees more change talk and less sustain talk appearing over the course of the motivational interview.

MI was first developed as a clinical method in the substance-misuse field. MI has been adapted for use in other health care settings since the early 1990s and now an impressive array of evidence testifies to its efficacy, including several systematic reviews and meta-analyses (e.g., Dunn, DeRoo, & Rivara, 2001; Hettema et al., 2005; Martins & McNeil, 2009; see also Emmons & Rollnick, 2001). These reviews show positive results of MI in a wide range of health problems, including cardiac problems, diabetes, dietary change, exercise, hypertension, hyperlipidemia, asthma, oral health, HIV risk, and smoking (see, however, Knight, McGowan, Dickens, & Bundy, 2006, for a more critical review).

It is clear from the evidence that MI has a lot to offer in helping people to change health-related behaviors. It is also clear that many of the underlying concepts that are important in MI, such as the explicit acknowledgment of the therapeutic stance, the focus on behavior change, and the "normalization" of patient resistance, are also common threads in ACT. The originators of MI have recently written that MI might also have synergistic effects when added as a component to an existing active treatment (Miller & Rose, 2009). Given the apparent sympathy of ACT and MI in terms of therapeutic stance and behavioral focus, it is unsurprising that this method (MI) can be easily incorporated into an ACT model for working with people who have chronic health problems. The rest of this chapter outlines areas of compatibility and divergence between ACT and MI, covering clinical issues in health behavior change as well as philosophical and theoretical underpinnings.

Similarities Between ACT and MI

There are substantial areas of sympathy between ACT and MI. These are outlined in the following section.

The Therapeutic Stance

Just as the originators of MI have spelled out the stance required of the clinician to successfully implement MI, so the originators of the ACT model have provided detailed guidance regarding the therapeutic stance in ACT (e.g., Hayes, Strosahl, & Wilson, 1999; Luoma, Hayes, & Walser, 2007; Pierson & Hayes, 2007; Wilson & Dufrene, 2008).

The therapeutic stance in ACT is one of equality. The therapist and patient are both human beings who have "minds." They are both people who have at times known struggle, heartache, joy, sadness, longing, and hurt. They are both people who have acted in ways that they regret, and they both get caught in rules of how we "should" be living and what we "should" do in any given moment (particularly as therapists). The ACT therapist welcomes this shared humanity and makes attempts to establish equality in the relationship. This might involve selected self-disclosure, in the service of the client's values or struggles. A successful ACT therapist is likely to create a mindful, defused, flexible space, in which anything can be discussed in the room, especially ongoing, moment-to-moment, psychological experiences occurring in session, including those occasioned by the therapeutic relationship itself, for both parties.

At the same time, the ACT therapist is relatively directive or guiding, in that he is there for the service of the client's more successful valued living. Clients may need a lot of encouragement and therapeutic influence to give up old patterns, try new things, and sit with difficult material. The ACT therapist is active and goal oriented, though if the goal is to be better able to sit willingly with painful material, the therapist may sit quietly, empathizing, encouraging gently, allowing space for emotion to be strongly present, and helping the client to cultivate an accepting, flexible, defused, and present-focused stance toward that painful material. If, on the other hand, the immediate therapeutic goal is to hold a difficult thought more lightly, the therapist may be playful, using humor, games, and exercises that allow the client to experience the thought as a thought, and may be quite irreverent toward the thought. This will always depend upon the client and the nature of the relationship and is never done in a spirit of belittling the client. The ACT model is explicit in that therapists are most likely to perform effectively from their own direct experience in learning to apply the ACT model and methods to their own behavior. In particular, this includes the therapist's ability to work effectively in the context of potential fusion and avoidance, to respond flexibly when the therapist could otherwise become drawn into unproductive "mind chatter" or stuck in a literal level of analyzing and reanalyzing events, such as in response to the patient's painful experiences or the therapist's own reactions to these.

Given such a therapeutic stance, it is not surprising that motivational interviewing might easily be incorporated into an ACT-consistent treatment.

In MI, the therapist is guided to "roll with resistance" when it shows up in the work. The therapist's own self-awareness, through the use of mindfulness and experiential learning, helps her to notice the kinds of thoughts that would be likely to get in the way of her capacity to roll with resistance. When therapists buy thoughts such as "This client is unmotivated," or "This client is using me," or "I must help this client change his behavior," the result is likely to be a loss of empathy and potentially an increase in therapist lecturing, telling, persuading, and so on. Therapists who are aware of such thoughts in a defused, flexible manner are likely to be more able to respond to the client in any given moment in a way that is flexible and empathic. Therapists who are able to step back from their own thoughts about what they "should" be doing will be more likely to be able to create a defused, flexible, noncoercive space in which the client's capacity to make choices in his life becomes the central focus.

Focus on Behavior Change

Both ACT and MI have a focus on overt behavior change as the primary goal. ACT and MI also share an underpinning theoretical background in behavior analysis. These shared roots lead directly to some of the theoretical concepts in ACT and MI and also to therapist behaviors.

In both ACT and MI the therapist will use principles of contingency management to shape the client's behavior in the direction of the client's goals for therapy. In the first phase of MI, for instance, the client's "change talk" is selectively attended to by the therapist and differentially reinforced, relative to "sustain talk." The reinforcement is in the form of therapist encouragement, praise, interest, sustained attention, and enthusiasm. Sustain talk, by contrast, is responded to with empathy and flexibility, and the therapist gently encourages further exploration of themes relevant to the change talk.

Similarly, ACT therapists seek to ascertain which of the six ACT processes may need to be instigated to help make a behavioral change (based upon an ACT-based functional analysis of the problem behavior). In any given therapeutic moment, the ACT therapist is monitoring her own and her client's processes to determine what kinds of interventions might be useful. She will try to shape the client's behavior toward greater willingness, a more defused stance, and being in the here and now, as a means to the client taking specific actions toward his chosen values. Each therapeutic moment might involve the therapist modeling the required behavior, instigating the behavior in the client, or reinforcing the successive approximations of behavior as the client, produces them (Luoma et al., 2007, p. 233). The notion that the therapist actively shapes the client's behavior in the therapy context by use of selective reinforcement and contingency management is a shared underpinning of ACT and MI. Use of homework assignments and commitment to behavioral goals are methods by which such shaping generalizes beyond the immediate therapy context.

Philosophical Issues

Looking beyond technique or theory, a number of philosophical underpinnings are shared between ACT and MI. First, both are clearly rooted in the tradition of scientific clinical psychology (Hayes et al., 1999, Miller & Rollnick, 2009). They both assume that clinical psychology is best progressed by empirical clinical science, direct observation, a focus on measurable behavior, and the derivation of principles that can be generalized across a broad range of problems rather than be specific to narrowly defined behavioral targets. The same principles, for instance, should be helpful in reducing smoking behavior and also in encouraging a person with diabetes to self-monitor for blood glucose. Within the tradition of empirical clinical psychology, both ACT and MI have encouraged the use of mediational analyses to determine if their methods are effective due to the processes they hypothesize (e.g., Hayes, Luoma, Bond, Masuda, & Lillis, 2006; Miller & Rose, 2009). Finally, there is a good degree of harmony between the philosophy and values that underpin these approaches, though there are also some areas of divergence.

ACT is based upon a philosophy of science known as "functional contextualism" (see Pepper, 1942; Hayes, Hayes, & Reese, 1988; Hayes, Hayes, Reese, & Sarbin, 1993). Functional contextualism is a worldview that explains any given phenomenon in terms of its function in context. Behavioral scientists working from a functional contextual perspective do not seek hypothetical causes of behaviors such as thoughts or motivation but see the "act in context" as the unit of analysis. In addition, functional contextual analyses do not assume that the universe exists as an independent "thing" waiting to be discovered. Instead, the behavior of the scientist is part of the analysis of the phenomena being investigated. For these reasons, functional contextualism is said to be "a-ontological" (meaning not ontological) (Hayes et al., 1999, p. 20). In any functional contextual analysis, the truth value of a given statement is defined as its usefulness. From these philosophical assumptions flow the ACT focus on workability and on sensitivity to function and context.

The functional contextual stance also allows the originators of the ACT model to deal with the notion of whether the model or theory is "accurate" or "true." Such notions, from a mainstream scientific perspective, assume an ontological reality, within which the role of a scientist is to "discover" the principles by which that reality works—a position sometimes known as mechanism (Pepper, 1942) or, more recently, "elemental realism" (Hayes, 2009). As functional contextual analyses do not share such ontological assumptions, the question of empirical validity is transformed into "usefulness" or "workability." The ACT model is deemed true insofar as its predictions lead to workable solutions and as interventions derived from an ACT model are useful in relation to the goals of such specified interventions.

The philosophical underpinnings of MI must be understood in relation to the social and historical context that gave rise to the humanistic movement in psychology. Humanism as a psychological movement developed as a counter thread in psychology to the then-dominant schools of psychological thought: psychoanalysis and methodological behaviorism (Wertz, 1998). Whereas behaviorism was viewed as reductionist and dehumanizing, the humanistic movement in psychology emphasizes human wholeness, regards human experience as irreducible, and seeks to understand human concepts such as values, personal growth, selfhood and self-actualization.

Humanism in psychology draws from the philosophical schools of humanism, phenomenology, and existentialism. The humanist philosophical school assumes the value of human ethics, reason, and virtue. Phenomenological philosophy represents an attempt to understand human conscious experience, while existentialism is concerned with the notion of being, in broad terms. At the level of theory, such philosophical underpinnings pose no difficulty for the ACT model. ACT as a clinical model also concerns itself with here-and-now human experience, the importance of human values, the meaning of self, and notions of being. There exists then, in MI, sufficient philosophical and technical sympathy with the ACT model in terms of clinical goals and pragmatic view of human concerns that these two ways of working are readily compatible.

Differences Between ACT and MI

As well as the substantial similarities or sympathies between ACT and MI, there are important areas of difference between them. These areas of divergence between ACT and MI are mainly at the level of concept and explanation, rather than technique, goals, or focus.

Explanatory Concepts

Arising principally from the phenomenological underpinnings of humanism, MI makes the assumption that certain mentalistic constructs exist and that MI acts on these to effect behavior change. For instance, MI works by increasing "intrinsic motivation" to change. In this way, it is easy for the practitioner to regard and treat motivation as almost "substancelike." The goal of the therapist becomes to increase such intrinsic motivation by encouraging change talk. While the notion of intrinsic motivation may not be problematic per se, from a functional contextualist perspective it is an unnecessary explanatory construct. Speaking of "motivation" in this view becomes a causal mechanism that lies beyond the "act in context" and therefore more properly belongs to a different worldview. Similarly, MI seeks to increase intrinsic motivation to change by resolving ambivalence toward behavior change.

Again, from a functional contextual perspective, ambivalence is a hypothetical explanatory construct and therefore an attempt to analyze beyond the act in context. A functional contextual analysis of "ambivalence" would be an analysis of the act in context. This might look something like this: in a context where behavior change is a desired outcome, excessive focus on regulating contrary private events as a prerequisite to behavior change is likely to lower the probability of the behavior change being initiated. In a broader functional contextual analysis, the usefulness of continuing to seek to regulate behavior using verbal behaviors (such as thoughts and rules) would be questioned according to its usefulness.

While we could compare empirically whether MI or ACT is more useful, or works better in a given field of health behavior change, to compare their underpinning philosophies would be to little purpose. This has been likened to comparing two journeys, such as starting from "New York and heading as far west as possible on foot, versus starting from New Orleans and heading as far north as possible by boat. Neither journey is correct or better in any absolute sense" (Hayes, Strosahl, Bunting, Twohig, & Wilson, 2004, p. 18).

Model Development

There are some other conceptual areas where MI and ACT diverge. ACT is a clinical model, derived from a basic, experimentally derived theory of human cognition and language called relational frame theory (RFT; Hayes, Barnes-Holmes, & Roche, 2001). Though a review of RFT is beyond the scope of this chapter, RFT is a behavior-analytic account of human language and cognition that has been derived from systematic scientific endeavor within a consistent functional contextual philosophy of science. As such, ACT represents a clinical model with detailed basic theoretical underpinnings and coherent philosophical assumptions.

MI, by contrast, is a clinical method, rather than a theory. The authors describe their post hoc theorizing regarding why MI might be effective (e.g., Miller & Rollnick, 2002), citing concepts such as cognitive dissonance (Festinger, 1957), self-perception theory (Bem, 1972), and psychological reactance (Brehm & Brehm, 1981). There have also been successful post hoc attempts to explain the clinical method according to other theories in social psychology (e.g., Leffingwell, Neumann, Babitzke, Leedy, & Walters, 2007). While such an approach provides MI with a theoretical underpinning, it could be argued that such a post hoc "rationalization" could easily be susceptible to confirmatory bias. In addition, although MI can be understood in terms of a particular theory, it is not known whether MI's effects are due to those explanatory concepts. Of course, the same is true of the ACT model, though the functional contextual underpinning suggests that determining whether or not ACT actually works via these routes is not the goal of the analysis. The goal of the analysis is to determine whether the explanatory behavioral processes lead to useful analyses of target problems.

In a recent article, Miller and Rose begin to articulate a theory of MI (Miller & Rose, 2009). This paper describes mediational analyses and component studies that provide evidence that MI works due to the specific mechanism of each of its proposed processes. Studies conducted on problem drinkers show that therapist empathic interpersonal style predicts a substantial proportion of the variance in drinking outcomes at six, twelve, and twenty-four months after intervention (Miller, Taylor, & West, 1980; Miller & Baca, 1983). In terms of the specific behavioral factors in MI, the use of MI has been shown to increase the proportion of change talk within session (e.g., Miller, Benefield, & Tonigan, 1993; Moyers & Martin, 2006; Moyers et al., 2007). In-session change talk furthermore predicts the strength of the client's utterances in favor of behavior change, termed "strength of commitment language," and the change in commitment language over the latter part of the interview directly predicts subsequent behavior change (Amrhein, Miller, Yahne, Palmer, & Fulcher, 2003).

This "dismantling" approach convincingly provides evidence that MI works via its postulated component processes. It could be argued, however, that while this level of scientific rigor is welcome, useful, and indeed necessary in behavior change research, it is more of an elaboration and test of the mechanics of the method than actual theory building. Such mediational analyses are also characteristic of the literature on ACT (e.g., Hayes et al., 2006). Where these scientific endeavors differ, however, is in the fact that the mediational analyses offered by the ACT scientific community are based upon hypothesized relationships between psychological processes that are derived from abstracted general principles and basic theory. The mediational analyses offered by the MI community are based on clinical observation of therapist effects, pragmatic formulation of such effects, systematic testing of interventions derived from these formulations, component dismantling, and mediational analyses. Although this brings a richness and rigor to a well-defined clinical method, such scientific activity could lead to a theory with relatively narrow scope. Indeed, MI could look to other theories to explain its effects and in that regard ACT, RFT, and functional contextualism could be a useful addition to MI. The philosophical background of MI (i.e., humanism and phenomenology) lends itself to the development of the kind of inductive theorizing described by Miller and Rose (2009). ACT has developed from a combination of inductive and deductive processes, based upon clinical observation and earlier attempts to apply behavior analyses to language and cognition (see Zettle, 2005, for an account of the development of ACT).

Clinical Issues

So how do ACT and MI conceptualize and approach the kinds of issues involved in health behavior changes, outlined in the introduction to this chapter? Awareness of a "need" to change behavior will often bring up resistance, ambivalence, avoidance, struggle, nonacceptance, and other thoughts and feelings about change. As well as experience such intrapsychic aspects of health behavior change, people may find themselves communicating with others about the need for change. ACT and MI can both be used to understand these multiple issues that arise in response to a "need" to change health-related behaviors.

Ambivalence and Resistance to Change

While MI recognizes that for many individuals change occurs naturally and without intervention (Miller & Rollnick, 2002, p. 4), both ACT and MI share the concept that resistance to change can be a natural part of being human. Both approaches suggest analyses of why this is. In ACT, for example, resistance to change would be viewed as a quality of behavior reflecting psychological inflexibility, most likely coordinated by the presence of unwanted private events (thoughts, feelings, urges) that occur in a context that signals behavior change is required. The ACT analysis would seek to specify that the behavior change in question is dominantly under the control of such private events, such that when they are present the probability of behavior change is relatively low. When one details the ACT analysis further, the psychological processes that are specified by the ACT model would be used to perform a functional analysis of behavior, including identification of behaviors that continue occurring even though it is a goal to reduce them, and identification of behaviors that do not occur or persist even though it is a goal to strengthen them—each a constituent part of the observed "resistance to change."

Consider, for example, the individual with heart disease who is given advice to reduce weight and increase exercise. In ACT, the therapist would investigate what kinds of internal events show up when the individual contemplates a specified behavior, such as going to the gym. The ACT therapist would consider the functional relations between thoughts, feelings, urges, and behavior. Key questions would be "What is being avoided?" "How fused is the client with private events as literal truths and as reasons for action or inaction?" "How strongly is the behavior change connected with the client's values?" This analysis would likely begin at the specific behavior change level, though it may quickly extend to how these functional processes apply to the rest of the client's life. In particular, the ACT therapist would wish to clarify how central the required behavior change is to this client's overall values, what the person's experience of change efforts has been, and how workable those strategies have been in terms of living a valued life. A functional assessment such as this would seek to identify the processes that are interfering with the client taking committed action.

Resistance to change in ACT is seen as based in behavioral processes, such as those leading to avoidance of difficult private events, for example contacting feelings of failure, feelings of fear about negative health outcomes, and feelings of loss related to lifestyle, fitness, or health. In this analysis, the avoidance of change is likely underpinned by fusion with thoughts such as "It's too difficult," "I can't," and "I don't want to," and in particular fusion with thoughts such as these as reasons for action or inaction. When processes such as these occur, behavior is likely to be dominantly under the control of these aversive stimuli, creating narrow and inflexible behavioral repertoires that function to allow avoidance of the aversive stimuli. Such stimuli might be others' expressions of the need to change behavior, the person's own thoughts about behavior change, symptoms of a medical condition, and so on. The client may also be attached to a relatively narrowly defined view of the self, and the client's behavior may be overly regulated by verbal events related to a feared future and/or a certain view of the past. Such processes are conceptualized in ACT as normal and supported by the verbal community that has reinforced verbal regulation of behavior as a desirable outcome in many areas of life (Hayes et al., 1999, p. 11). The cost of such excessive verbal regulation of behavior, however, is that a behavior change that may lead to desired outcomes is avoided, due to its participation in relational framing related to difficulty, struggle, imposition, fear, and loss, among other experiences.

A motivational interviewing stance would also accept resistance as a normal part of health behavior change. Leffingwell et al. (2007) describe how resistance can be understood as "psychological reactance" (Brehm & Brehm, 1981), "a process in which an individual will behave in ways that preserve a sense of autonomous freedom when choice is perceived to be threatened by others' directions or mandates, such as when others demand behaviour change" (Leffingwell et al., 2007, p. 32). Resistance to change can also be understood in terms of an individual's need to minimize discrepancies between behavior and attitudes, a process known as cognitive dissonance (Festinger, 1957). Such theoretical analyses are somewhat post hoc. MI is more concerned with the pragmatic business of specifying functional relationships between therapist behavior and the increase or decrease in verbal processes in the client that signal resistance to change (i.e., sustain talk).

MI practitioners would further work with resistance or ambivalence by developing the discrepancy between current behaviors and desired outcomes. Several strategies are available for this, such as exploring the pros and cons of a particular course of action or status quo, more fully exploring the client's values (e.g., Wagner & Sanchez, 2002) or larger life goals and how the behavior change fits (or does not fit), asking the client to clarify or elaborate on an already suggested reason for change, and the use of scaling questions.

Scaling questions can be used to explore reasons for change. Typically, an interviewer will inquire of the client how important the behavior change being considered is. For example, if a client were to rate the importance of increasing exercise as only two out of ten, the therapist would acknowledge that and inquire, "What is it that makes you rate that as two and not zero, for example?" As the client begins to talk about these reasons, he is making verbal statements that support reasons for change. After some exploration of these reasons, the interviewer might ask, "What kinds of things would need to happen to make your rating of the importance of this move from two to, say, a three or four?" This kind of question elicits more reasons for change and allows the client to further make the case for change.

These types of interventions are intended to help the client resolve ambivalence about change. Ambivalence about change is seen as a normal part of human experience, and its resolution is a critical task in MI (Leffingwell et al., 2007). While certain elements of this, particularly at the level of technique, are highly ACT consistent (e.g., exploration of values and life goals, developing discrepancy between workability of current behavior and life goals, enhancing willingness to change), the concept of resolution of ambivalence is not ACT consistent. From an ACT perspective, encouraging change talk helps the client to experience thoughts and feelings about change that have typically been avoided and could thus be seen as an acceptance strategy. While MI might be a better alternative than struggling with or avoiding reasons for change, ACT attempts to undermine verbal events, ambivalent thoughts, and reasons in general as regulators of behavior. The idea that ambivalence must be resolved before a person can move in the direction of his or her life goals is not consistent with an ACT approach. Instead, ACT might ask the client to "make room for" or "be willing to have" mixed feelings and thoughts about behavior change and commit to those changes anyway. Such a strategy is considered to have more generalized benefits, reducing the strength of behavioral regulation by private events, thus allowing individuals greater and greater contact with the direct contingencies operating in support of more adaptive behavior.

Self-Efficacy

In MI, much is made of self-efficacy, particularly at the level of technique (e.g., Miller & Rollnick, 2002, pp. 111–125). Self-efficacy refers to the belief that one is capable of achieving a particular goal (Bandura, 1997). In the context of MI for health behavior change, this translates into belief and expectation of success in producing the required behavior change. This is discussed in somewhat more concrete terms under the heading "Enhancing Confidence" (Miller & Rollnick, 2002, p. 111). In MI, the same scaling questions technique that is used for exploring reasons for change can also be used to explore confidence in one's ability to produce a specified behavioral change. This technique helps a client to verbalize aspects that support or enhance confidence to make changes, while also pointing to strategies that will further enhance self-efficacy.

In MI, self-efficacy is seen as an important prerequisite to change and a cognitive-affective factor that can greatly influence the likelihood of clients changing their behavior. Self-efficacy has both cognitive and affective elements. The cognitive elements include beliefs about one's capacity to make a behavioral change, appraisals of how difficult the behavior change will be, and judgments regarding probable outcomes. In addition to these cognitive aspects, self-efficacy contains their affective associates, such as hopefulness, optimism, confidence, and determination, or their counterparts. In essence, the motivational interviewer is operating from the principle of shaping these cognitive and affective elements as both a prerequisite to behavior change and a method of supporting and sustaining behavior change. While MI is explicitly "not a form of cognitive-behavior therapy" (Miller & Rollnick, 2009, p. 134), the element of modifying cognitions and affects as a prerequisite to behavior change is similar in principle to cognitive behavioral therapy.

In ACT for health behavior change, self-efficacy is an explanatory construct that refers to various private events (thoughts, judgments, appraisals, predictions, urges, and emotions). The collection of these covert behaviors into a functional class of private events might be useful in a functional analysis of behavior change, but the drawing of these together into a hypothetical construct would be considered unnecessary in an ACT model (see Wilson, 2001). More fundamentally, the requirement to have the client's thoughts and feelings all in line and positive about behavior change as a prerequisite to making such a change would not be ACT consistent. ACT proposes a more radical notion, of reducing the power of thoughts and feelings as behavioral regulators in general. Such a notion is radically countercultural and can be difficult for many clients and therapists to appreciate and use (Hayes et al., 1999, pp. 3–12).

ACT therapists might approach the issue of self-efficacy from multiple perspectives—for example, increasing the client's willingness to be in contact with his thoughts and feelings about behavior change, without having to resolve these. Another example might be to draw attention to the familiarity and "oldness" of the feeling of struggling with such thoughts and feelings and the ultimate "unworkability" in the client's experience of such attempts to "think right" or "feel good" about behavior change. Various defusion exercises might also be employed regarding feelings of confidence being required before committing to behavior change. The therapist could deconstruct words to show the unintended behavioral effects of language (Blackledge, 2007). For example, a client may say, "I would go to the gym to exercise, but I don't feel confident." An ACT therapist might respond by exploring with the client the nature of the word "confidence." The word comes from the Latin word *confidere*, meaning "to have trust or faith in." The client might be asked, "What would going to the gym with faith in yourself be like?" In such a dialogue, the therapist is trying to help the client see that "feeling confident" does not have to be present to do something with faith in oneself (Sonja Batten, personal communication, July 2008). By pointing at the hidden effects of language, the therapist is trying to reduce language-based processes, such as needing to feel good and think right as primary sources of behavior regulation. ACT and MI overlap more in terms of the focus on values and importance of behaviors. An ACT therapist might also explore with a client how the behavior change is linked to what he really cares about, and this kind of talk would be highly consistent with both ACT and MI. In the example above, defining clearly what going to the gym "with fidelity" would mean would help the client to contact what was important about the behavior change, thereby enhancing values as a behavioral regulator, relative to other private events. In summary, ACT is permissive of self-efficacy but simply sees it as an explanatory hypothetical construct that can lead to potential problems of a scientific and philosophical nature. It is ACT-inconsistent to say that self-efficacy is a necessary condition for change, but it is not ACT-inconsistent to say that speaking of self-efficacy is permitted, as long as it is clear that self-efficacy is actually shorthand for a functional class of beliefs and feelings.

Motivation to Change

While in MI the notion of intrinsic motivation is central, in ACT it is a further example of a hypothetical explanatory construct. Motivation to change may be a very convenient way for therapists and clients to talk about behavioral intentions. More concretely, when a client is talking in a way that might suggest a high level of motivation to change, we might view these verbal behaviors as precursors to actual behavior change that may strengthen the probability of behavior. We may also see them merely as collateral events that reflect already-present strength of behavior.

There is some interesting research from the MI literature that sheds light on the relations between verbal behaviors and actual behavior change. Amrhein and colleagues (2003) performed linguistic analysis on audio recordings of motivational interviews with substance-misusing clients. They were able to identify patterns of client talk during the motivational interview that reliably correlated with change or maintenance of drug-taking behavior at long-term follow-up. The detail of the linguistic analysis also revealed that clients' change talk in the early part of the interview predicted strength of commitment talk in the later part of the interview and that it is the change in strength of commitment talk over the course of the interview that reliably predicts behavioral outcomes (Amrhein et al., 2003; Miller & Rose, 2009).

The study by Amrhein and colleagues (2003) is clearly supportive of MI's basic principles: that client change talk leads to enhanced commitment to change, which leads to actual behavior changes. Within ACT, much is made of encouraging clients to make statements of commitment toward specific actions, as a way of initiating behavior change (Hayes et al., 1999; Luoma et al., 2007). While these methods show similarity at the level of technique, the value of "motivation to change" would be questioned in ACT.

From an ACT perspective, the danger of motivation to change is that (in an oversimplified form) the therapist must help the client to "think right and feel good" about behavior change prior to making actual changes. Contrary thoughts and impulses are unlikely to be removed by MI, so, when they appear, their influence on behavior remains as powerful as prior to MI. In ACT, by contrast, the nature of intervention has been to reduce the behavioral regulatory functions of private events on behavior, particularly those that present unhelpful influences. Thus, when contrary urges, thoughts, and feelings show up, the intervention has been designed to ensure that behavioral persistence is maximized.

Maintenance of Behavior Changes

The literature on motivational interviewing per se has less to say about maintenance of behavior change, though its close cousin the transtheoretical model of change (TTM) does address this (DiClemente & Velasquez, 2002). A full exploration of the TTM is beyond the scope of this chapter, though interested readers are referred to Prochaska and DiClemente, 1984. Briefly, the TTM sets out a stagelike model of behavior change. Individuals progress (or fail to progress) through the stages of the model in any behavioral change. These stages are described as Precontemplation, Contemplation, Action, Maintenance, and Relapse. In Precontemplation, the individual is not actively considering behavior change. In Contemplation, the individual is considering a certain change, though has not yet progressed to making changes. In the Action stage, the individual initiates the behavior change. Once a behavior change has become established, the individual is considered to be in a Maintenance stage, where continued commitment to the behavior change and persistence is necessary. The final stage, Relapse, may be entered from any stage of the TTM and is common in any behavior change.

MI can be a useful method at any of the stages of the TTM (DiClemente & Velasquez, 2002). With regard to maintaining behavior changes in the arena of health behaviors, MI can be useful in dealing with slips and relapses of health behavior. The provision of accurate empathy and genuine understanding for the individual in danger of relapse can be helpful in providing the kind of supportive environment that will help the individual to turn relapse around and make further commitments to change. Similarly, scaling questions on importance and confidence can be used to help the client explore continued reasons for maintaining behavior change while also enhancing efficacy for the maintenance of behavior change. Similarly, empathic responding to some of the obstacles that arise during long-term commitment to health behaviors can usefully reduce resistance to health behavior maintenance.

In ACT, maintenance of behavior change is seen as continued commitment to values and to committed action. Where an individual experiences problems with maintenance of health behaviors, a functional analysis based upon the ACT model would attempt to describe which of the six overlapping ACT processes are most useful in understanding and intervening with the problem of behavior maintenance. For example, the client may be unwilling to be in contact with thoughts, feelings, and urges, and this may present a barrier to behavior change. In such circumstances, willingness to experience such events would be encouraged via metaphor, experiential exercises such as the "Contents on Cards" exercise (Hayes et al., 1999, p. 162), examining workability, or other methods. The client may be fused with such thoughts and beliefs or with feelings of resentment toward the behavior change. In this instance, defusion exercises might be used, such as visualizing what the feelings of resentment would look like if they could be seen "out there" in the therapy room (Hayes et al., 1999, pp. 170, 171).

The person may be living relatively in the "conceptualized past" in which, perhaps, health behaviors were not necessary and spontaneity of living was very attractive. It may be helpful for clients to practice mindfulness of the present moment and to take an alternate perspective on the self, one in which the memories of the past are experienced within the context of the self, rather than the self being overidentified with such memories. Examples of ways of working with this material include the "good cup / bad cup" exercise (Hayes et al., 1999, p. 169), the "Chessboard metaphor" (Hayes et al., 1999, p. 191), or the "Observer self" exercise (Hayes et al., 1999, p. 193). These exercises are described under specific chapters by Hayes and colleagues (1999), in relation to their functional elements (willingness, defusion, self-as-context, and so on). In reality, however, each exercise targets multiple psychological processes, and theoretical statements about the ACT model describe them as "overlapping and interrelated" (Hayes et al., 2006, p. 9).

For the client in relapse, ACT therapists would (in common with MI practitioners) take an empathic and validating stance. They would also encourage the client to be willing to experience all of her thoughts and feelings about relapse as fully as possible. Client and therapist may work together to encourage the client to adopt a kind, accepting, and forgiving stance toward herself in the context of the relapse. It is likely that they would reaffirm commitments to values, exploring how the health behavior links with these. Finally, client and therapist would be likely to reestablish commitment to health behavior change, while enhancing psychological flexibility to work skillfully with the numerous obstacles that can continue to be present.

Summary

In the arena of health behavior change, ACT and MI share many similarities in technique, stance, behavioral goals, behavioral concepts, science values, and view of humanity. They differ principally in scope, theoretical constructs, and philosophical assumptions. Despite some of the divergence between ACT and MI at the level of philosophy and concept, the two methods are highly compatible. MI provides a very ACT-consistent strategy within which therapist stance and language can be usefully developed. As such, methods from MI could be seen as useful elements in the ACT therapist's toolkit.

The ACT model allows clinicians to conceptualize the different problems and obstacles that are likely to arise in any health behavior change enterprise and to develop strategies to work with these. One element of the ACT model that is particularly useful in this regard is the notion that the six core ACT processes apply equally to clinicians as they do to clients (Luoma et al., 2007, p. 221). MI exhorts the practitioner to be able to "roll with resistance…by avoiding arguing for change and not directly opposing resistance" (Miller & Rollnick, 2002, p. 40). Where an ACT model could enhance this key MI skill is in helping therapists to develop greater self-awareness, greater ability to be present, greater awareness of how their own "mind" might draw them into exactly the kinds of behaviors that are not consistent with MI. The therapist's own judgments, beliefs about the client and about therapy, beliefs about his training, and his own (lack of) willingness to sit with difficult feelings are all examples of private content that might draw a therapist away from behaving in an MI-consistent way. ACT provides a framework and explicit training agenda that therapists can use to develop their own psychological flexibility, in the service of responding to clients in a way that will maximize the client's capacity to change. Such a stance is highly consistent with both motivational interviewing and acceptance and commitment therapy.

References

Amrhein, P. C., Miller, W. R., Yahne, C. E., Palmer, M., & Fulcher, L. (2003). Client commitment language during motivational interviewing predicts drug use outcomes. *Journal of Consulting and Clinical Psychology, 71,* 862–878.

Bandura, A. (1997). *Self-efficacy: The exercise of control.* New York: Freeman.

Bem, D. J. (1972). Self-perception theory. In L. Berkowitz (Ed.), *Advances in experimental social psychology* (Vol. 6, pp. 1–62). New York: Academic Press.

Blackledge, J. T. (2007). Disrupting verbal processes: Cognitive defusion in acceptance and commitment therapy and other mindfulness-based psychotherapies. *Psychological Record, 57,* 555–576.

Brehm, S. S., & Brehm, J. W. (1981). *Psychological reactance: A theory of freedom and control.* New York: Academic Press.

DiClemente, C. C., & Velasquez, M. M. (2002). Motivational interviewing and the stages of change. In W. R. Miller & S. Rollnick (Eds.), *Motivational interviewing: Preparing people for change* (2nd ed.). New York: Guilford Press.

Dunn, C., DeRoo, L., & Rivara, F. P. (2001). The use of brief interventions adapted from motivational interviewing across behavioral domains: A systematic review. *Addiction, 96,* 1725–1742.

Emmons, K. M., & Rollnick, S. R. (2001). Motivational interviewing in healthcare settings: Limitations and opportunities. *American Journal of Preventive Medicine, 20,* 68–74.

Festinger, L. (1957). *A theory of cognitive dissonance.* Evanston, IL: Row, Peterson.

Hayes, S. C. (2009, July). *The importance of RFT to the development of contextual behavioral science.* Presidential address at the Association for Contextual Behavioral Science Third World Congress, University of Twente, Netherlands.

Hayes, S. C., Barnes-Holmes, D., & Roche, B. (Eds.). (2001). *Relational frame theory: A post-Skinnerian account of human language and cognition.* New York: Plenum Press.

Hayes, S. C., Hayes, L. J., & Reese, H. W. (1988). Finding the philosophical core: A review of Stephen C. Pepper's World Hypotheses. *Journal of the Experimental Analysis of Behavior, 50,* 97–111.

Hayes, S. C., Hayes, L. J., Reese, H. W., & Sarbin, T. R. (Eds.). (1993). *Varieties of scientific contextualism.* Reno, NV: Context Press.

Hayes, S. C., Luoma, J. B., Bond, F. W., Masuda, A., & Lillis, J. (2006). Acceptance and commitment therapy: Model, processes and outcomes. *Behaviour Research and Therapy, 44,* 1–25.

Hayes, S. C., Strosahl, K. D., Bunting, K., Twohig, M., & Wilson, K. G. (2004). What is acceptance and commitment therapy? In S. C. Hayes & K. D. Strosahl (Eds.), *A practical guide to acceptance and commitment therapy.* New York: Springer.

Hayes, S. C., Strosahl, K. D., & Wilson, K. G. (1999). *Acceptance and commitment therapy: An experiential approach to behavior change.* New York: Guilford Press.

Hettema, J., Steele, J., & Miller, W. R. (2005). Motivational interviewing. *Annual Review of Clinical Psychology, 1,* 91–111.

Knight, K. M., McGowan, L., Dickens, C., & Bundy, C. (2006). A systematic review of motivational interviewing in physical health care settings. *British Journal of Health Psychology, 11,* 319–332.

Leffingwell, T. R., Neumann, C. R., Babitzke, A. C., Leedy, M. J., & Walters, S. T. (2007). Social psychology and motivational interviewing: A review of relevant principles and recommendations for research and practice. *Behavioural and Cognitive Psychotherapy, 35,* 31–45.

Luoma, J. B., Hayes, S. C., & Walser, R. (2007). *Learning ACT: An acceptance and commitment therapy skills-training manual for therapists.* Oakland, CA: New Harbinger Publications.

Martins, R. K., & McNeil, D. W. (2009). Review of motivational interviewing in promoting health behaviours. *Clinical Psychology Review, 29,* 283–293.

Miller, W. R. (1983). Motivational interviewing with problem drinkers. *Behavioural Psychotherapy, 11,* 147–172.

Miller, W. R., & Baca, L. M. (1983). Two-year follow up of bibliotherapy and therapist-directed controlled drinking training for problem drinkers. *Behavior Therapy, 14,* 441–448.

Miller, W. R., Benefield, R. G., & Tonigan, J. S. (1993). Enhancing motivation to change in problem drinking: A controlled comparison of two therapist styles. *Journal of Consulting and Clinical Psychology, 61,* 455–461.

Miller, W. R., & Rollnick, S. (1991). *Motivational interviewing: Preparing people to change addictive behavior.* New York: Guilford Press.

Miller, W. R., & Rollnick, S. (Eds.). (2002). *Motivational interviewing: Preparing people for change* (2nd ed.). New York: Guilford Press.

Miller, W. R., & Rollnick, S. (2009). Ten things that motivational interviewing is not. *Behavioural and Cognitive Psychotherapy, 37,* 129–140.

Miller, W. R., & Rose, G. S. (2009). Toward a theory of motivational interviewing. *American Psychologist, 64,* 527–537.

Miller, W. R., Taylor, C. A., & West, J. C. (1980). Focused versus broad-spectrum behavior therapy for problem drinkers. *Journal of Consulting and Clinical Psychology, 48,* 590–601.

Moyers, T. B., & Martin, T. (2006). Therapist influence on client language during motivational interviewing sessions: Support for a potential causal mechanism. *Journal of Substance Abuse Treatment, 30,* 245–251.

Moyers, T. B., Martin, T., Cristopher, P. J., Houck, J. M., Tonigan, J. S., & Amrhein, P. C. (2007). Client language as a mediator of motivational interviewing efficacy: Where is the evidence? *Alcoholism: Clinical and Experimental Research, 31*(Suppl. 3), 40–47.

Pepper, S. C. (1942). *World hypotheses: Prolegomena to systematic philosophy and a complete survey of metaphysics.* Berkeley, CA: University of California Press.

Pierson, H., & Hayes, S. C. (2007). Using acceptance and commitment therapy to empower the therapeutic relationship. In P. Gilbert & R. Leahy (Eds.), *The therapeutic relationship in cognitive behaviour therapy.* London: Routledge.

Prochaska, J. O., & DiClemente, C. C. (1984). *The transtheoretical approach: Crossing traditional boundaries of therapy.* Homewood, IL: Dow/Jones Irwin.

Rogers, C. (1951). *Client-centered therapy: Its current practice, implications and theory.* London: Constable.

Rollnick, S., Mason, P., & Butler, C. C. (1999). *Health behavior change: A guide for practitioners.* New York: Churchill Livingstone.

Rollnick, S., Miller, W. R., & Butler, C. C. (2008). *Motivational interviewing in health care.* New York: Guilford Press.

Wagner, C. C., & Sanchez, F. P. (2002). The role of values in motivational interviewing. In W. R. Miller & S. Rollnick (Eds.), *Motivational interviewing: Preparing people for change* (2nd ed.). New York: Guilford Press.

Wertz, F. J. (1998). The role of the humanistic movement in the history of psychology. *Journal of Humanistic Psychology, 38,* 42–70.

Wilson, K. G. (2001). Some notes on theoretical constructs: Types and validation from a contextual behavioural perspective. *International Journal of Psychology and Psychological Therapy, 1,* 205–215.

Wilson, K. G., & Dufrene, T. (2008). *Mindfulness for two: An acceptance and commitment therapy approach to mindfulness in psychotherapy.* Oakland, CA: New Harbinger Publications.

Zettle, R. (2005). The evolution of a contextual approach to therapy: From comprehensive distancing to ACT. *International Journal of Behavioral Consultation and Therapy, 1,* 77–89.

10 INTEGRATION OF EXPOSURE-BASED AND OTHER TRADITIONAL CBT METHODS WITH ACCEPTANCE AND MINDFULNESS

Rikard K. Wicksell
Behavior Medicine Pain Treatment Services,
Astrid Lindgren Children's Hospital,
Karolinska University Hospital; Department of Clinical
Neuroscience, Karolinska Institute

Over the last three decades there have been many changes in the cognitive and behavioral therapies (CBT). The integration of methods from different traditions within CBT has been an important part of the developmental process. Recently, acceptance-oriented interventions, especially in relation to acceptance and commitment therapy (ACT), have gained increasing empirical support (Hayes, Masuda,

Bissett, Luoma, & Guerrero, 2004; McCracken & Eccleston, 2005; Wicksell, Melin, Lekander, & Olsson, 2009) but it is not always clear how such strategies can be utilized and implemented in relation to existing clinical models. This chapter will specifically examine relationships between methods from ACT and those from the wider CBT tradition, and it will consider how they can be integrated in treatments for chronic medical conditions. Although the focus is on specific treatment methods, a discussion of theoretical assumptions and therapeutic processes is provided as a framework for this analysis.

Background and Theoretical Framework

Treatments based broadly on CBT are today well established, particularly within the field of behavioral medicine (Compas, Haaga, Keefe, Leitenberg, & Williams, 1998; Keefe et al., 2002; Morley, Eccleston, & Williams, 1999). These treatments can, however, vary extensively with regard to theoretical assumptions, treatment objectives, and methods (Turk & Okifuji, 2002). This has perhaps become more apparent with the relatively recent arrival of acceptance- and mindfulness-based forms of CBT, commonly described as part of the "third wave" (Hayes, 2004), such as acceptance and commitment therapy (ACT), dialectical behavior therapy (DBT), functional analytic psychotherapy (FAP), behavioral activation (BA, and mindfulness-based cognitive therapy (Hayes, Follette, & Linehan, 2004).

Among the "third wave" therapies, ACT has perhaps the most-developed and well-integrated theoretical framework. Acceptance and mindfulness strategies, as part of an ACT approach, are based on a functional analysis of behavior. "Behavior" here is defined broadly as everything the individual does, including thinking. For example, engaging in behaviors to postpone or inhibit an aversive event such as pain, fatigue, or fear is classified as avoidance and is understood as resulting from processes of respondent and operant conditioning. Importantly, although the topographical form of such behaviors may differ, as in not lifting a heavy box or staying home from school, the function of the behavior—avoidance—is the same. Avoidance is seen as central to disability and is developed and sustained through reinforcing consequences that are usually short term, such as less discomfort, or possibly more attention or assistance from others. However, avoidance is likely to result in a passive, nonvital lifestyle. The detrimental effects of avoidance patterns on health include problems like reduced muscle strength, increased cardiovascular risk, and depression. In ACT, avoidance behaviors are considered to occur in relation to undesirable private experiences, such as sensations, feelings (shame, fear, guilt), or thoughts. This emphasis on psychological experiences as the occasions for avoidance has led to the use of the term "experiential avoidance."

ACT is based on functional contextualism (Hayes, 2004) where the unit of analysis is the act in context. Hence, whether these "acts" are thoughts, emotional reactions, or overt behaviors, they are not psychologically meaningful events unless considered in relation to the situation where they occur and the individual's history related to that situation. Thus, although acts and contextual features can be examined separately, the whole contextually situated act remains the primary unit. Clinically, this is illustrated in the functional analysis where contextual factors that have preceded and followed the target behaviors in the past are identified in order to understand the function of it. The psychological experience of a situation is contained not just in what is seen, heard, and felt in the moment but in what these experiences mean and the influences they engender by virtue of the individual's experiences in the past. Functional contextualism can be contrasted with a more mechanistic view, where behaviors are primarily regarded as a result of formal properties of a situation and processes occurring within the person, with relatively minor consideration to the distinction between form and function and the role of history. These differences have practical implications. A conceptualization based on cognitive theories focuses on the form and content of thoughts because of two main reasons. First, the mere presence of negative thoughts is considered important for psychological well-being. Second, thoughts are seen as causes of ineffective behaviors and poor self-management. In cognitive interventions, thoughts are explored to identify underlying cognitive schemata and core beliefs, with the intention to reduce or alter the frequency and content of the thoughts, including pain beliefs, inaccurate predictions about future events, and appraisals of self-efficacy. Cognitive processes are thus, within this theoretical frame, considered to be central mediators of change and should therefore be targeted in order for behavior change to occur.

In contrast, ACT deemphasizes the explanatory value of internal events considered alone, or the direct causal relationship between psychological experiences and behavioral actions. Instead, behaviors are seen as coordinated by thoughts and other experiences in interactions with contextual factors. When symptoms are not easily changed, a functional contextual approach may be aimed at altering the context in which symptoms occur, with the objective to reduce the negative impact of symptoms on behaviors. For example, when chronic pain is experienced within a context characterized by a focus on pain reduction, situations associated with pain are likely to be avoided. In an alternative context, characterized by willingness, where symptoms are allowed to remain, the presence of pain will no longer lead to avoidance, and pain will not present the same barrier to physical and social functioning.

An important aspect of ACT is the pragmatic approach to truth, where the validity of an analysis or intervention is measured by how well it works in relation to a specified goal. This can be contrasted with how the idea corresponds with reality or fits a certain theory. In other words, "workability" is emphasized as a truth criterion and the person's own life values are used as the criteria to assess the workability of a particular strategy.

ACT is based on processes of learning and cognition as conceptualized in relational frame theory (RFT) (Hayes, Barnes-Holmes, & Roche, 2001). In short, RFT clarifies why reducing the frequency of negative thoughts may not be an adequate therapeutic goal or even necessary to achieve overt behavior change. RFT is discussed elsewhere in this volume, and a complete description of it is otherwise beyond the scope of this chapter.

Case Conceptualization

For patients where cure or complete symptom alleviation is not readily attainable, as is typical in chronic medical conditions, improved self-management becomes central to functioning and quality of life. In most clinical models influenced by CBT, dysfunctional behaviors as well as negative thoughts and emotions are considered central targets in treatment. However, depending upon the theoretical framework, the conceptualization of the problem can vary (Lappalainen et al., 2007). In pain management, for example, the predominant focus might include catastrophizing, pain beliefs, anxiety sensitivity, pain-specific fear, or kinesiophobia (Turk, Meichenbaum, & Genest, 1983; Turk & Okifuji, 2002; Vlaeyen & Linton, 2000). Even a single construct can be conceptualized in different ways. Catastrophizing can be conceptualized as a category of negative automatic thoughts that evoke fear and avoidance or as a dysfunctional covert operant behavior (rumination) that is reinforced through anxiety-reducing functions. The fear-avoidance model of chronic pain and disability comprises respondent and operant conditioning as well as cognitive mechanisms. In accord with a cognitive conceptualization of pain behaviors, inaccurate predictions about future events are given a central role in explaining avoidance behaviors (Vlaeyen & Linton, 2000).

In general, ACT as a functional analytic approach considers catastrophic thoughts, pain beliefs, or negative predictions about reinjury to be, essentially, verbal responses with stimulus qualities. In ACT, aversive thoughts, emotions, or bodily sensations alone are not conceptualized as being the problem. Instead, the problem is based in these experiences and, for example, the context of needing to control them as a way to achieve quality of life and health.

Treatment Objectives and Processes

Although symptom reduction has traditionally been seen as the primary outcome variable, most clinical models of chronic condition management, including ACT, emphasize improved functioning and quality of life. However, the means to get there vary. In fact, even among treatments associated with CBT, there are differing goals and proposed processes of change, including but not restricted to reduction in symptoms, reduction in symptom-related distress, increased self-efficacy, decreases in muscle tension, alteration in dysfunctional thought patterns, and reduced pain-specific fear (Morley et al., 1999; Turk et al., 1983). ACT does not predominantly target reduction or control of symptoms, or changes in frequency or content of thoughts, and it raises concerns regarding the utility of these processes (Hayes, Strosahl, & Wilson, 1999). Instead, improvements in functioning and quality of life are considered to be a result of increased psychological flexibility, defined in part as the ability to act in alignment with values whether in the presence of interfering symptoms or feelings of distress or not. Although ACT and more traditional CBT methods are different in many respects, overlaps may be noted. For example, self-efficacy and psychological flexibility appear to be somewhat related in that both constructs involve the ability to perform relevant activities in the presence of interfering private experiences such as pain or distress. However, they differ in whether or not this ability must be based in a positive belief that this is possible; self-efficacy requires this belief, while psychological flexibility does not.

Implementing ACT Interventions with Traditional Methods

Recent findings show that methods to promote psychological flexibility, such as those involving acceptance and mindfulness, may be particularly useful to increase the ability to live vitally in the presence of symptoms such as pain, fatigue, or emotional distress. However, it is not always clear how traditional forms of CBT can integrate principles and processes from approaches such as ACT. In the following discussion, it will be illustrated that implementing acceptance and related methods can be done in degrees, without necessarily requiring extensive or wholesale changes of a treatment program. In fact, rather small differences may be useful to enhance treatment effectiveness. Due to the variety of CBT strategies, ACT-based processes will be discussed in relation to some central interventions. Some familiarity with these processes and methods is assumed, and these will only be described to illustrate similarities, differences, and possible implementation.

Acceptance

Acceptance has long been a focus in psychological treatments, but wide differences exist in definition and interventions. As acceptance is a core process in ACT, it is worth clarifying. In ACT, acceptance is seen as the abandonment of strategies to control or avoid negative private events (emotions, thoughts, and bodily sensations) and the process of opening up to experience them as they are. It should be noted that acceptance is not a goal in and of itself. Instead, acceptance is seen as a critical process of behavior change, particularly lending a quality of engagement in valued activities in the presence of potentially interfering and typically undesirable physical or emotional experiences. Thus, acceptance represents a process of relating to negative experiences, rather than a formal exercise or a specific technique. As such, acceptance may be addressed through a range of methods. Importantly, acceptance is not passive but involves detecting experiential avoidance and increasing awareness of psychological experiences to reduce their impact, choosing actions with a different function than avoidance, and staying present with the previously avoided private events. There are many specific procedures considered useful to facilitate acceptance (Hayes et al., 1999).

Cognitive Restructuring and Defusion

CBT commonly includes interventions aimed at cognitive restructuring to correct inaccurate predictions about avoided situations (e.g., "I might injure myself if I exercise") and ultimately alter dysfunctional schemata or core beliefs. To accomplish these goals, several cognitive techniques are used, such as testing the thought, Socratic questioning, and cognitive disputation. In contrast, among the many methods available within ACT, one approach would be to notice and accept the thought as a hypothesis rather than as a fact, in order to "disentangle" from the literal meaning of the thought and facilitate an awareness of the thinking itself as an ongoing process. Negative thoughts would be analyzed from a functional perspective, such as by looking at the behavior that emerges when a thought is believed or followed. In other words, the function of the thought is assessed in relation to what the patient defines as valued living. As an example, it is of less interest whether or not a particular thought (such as "If I go to the party, pain might increase") is true in the sense that it corresponds with reality. Instead, it is evaluated based on whether acting on that thought facilitates engaging in valued living.

Cognitive defusion techniques are performed with the intent to reduce the excessive and restricting impacts of private events on behaviors. In essence, following a successful defusion process, the patient could conceivably continue to have catastrophic thoughts or inaccurate predictions with the same frequency, duration, and intensity, without buying into the content or acting on them. There are numerous ways of working with defusion, including the use of metaphor or experiential tasks. Essentially, cognitive defusion is about repeatedly creating the distinction between the process of thinking and the content of thinking. Therefore, the functional analysis is in itself an important part of the defusion process. Just noticing the thoughts as thoughts, as they occur, is one particularly useful defusion strategy that may easily be implemented in mindfulness-oriented exercises. Other techniques include ways to make the process of thinking separate and objective, such as writing the thoughts on cards and carrying them for a day, acting like the patient's "chattering mind" while taking a walk, and the like (Hayes et al., 1999).

It may be argued that techniques labeled cognitive restructuring or cognitive defusion may both facilitate similar processes. Indeed, a cognitive defusion process may eventually alter frequency and form of the thoughts, and cognitive restructuring is likely to create greater awareness and reduce inappropriate impact on behaviors. In fact, this is ultimately an empirical question, which points out the importance of exploring change processes in these types of interventions.

Exposure

Exposure-based methods, including systematic desensitization, flooding, graded in vivo exposure, and the like, have a long history within CBT. Exposure is generally understood as a procedure characterized by the making or increasing of contact with previously avoided experiences such as particular social situations, bodily sensations, pain, and emotional experiences. Most treatment models based on CBT include some form of exposure, and it can be performed in many different ways—for example by gradually increasing the time spent in a previously avoided situation (in vivo), thinking of or discussing a catastrophic event or planning for future events (imaginative), and attending to bodily sensations (interoceptive). On a topographical level, exposure methods may be relatively similar across various CBT approaches, including ACT, DBT, and BA. However, the rationale and treatment objective may differ substantially. For example, in vivo exposure may be used in a desensitization process to reduce symptoms of pain and distress, such as in low back pain or complex regional pain syndrome (De Jong et al., 2005). Also, graded exposure to symptom-inducing procedures can be conducted in order to practice control strategies such as relaxation, breathing, and mental activities (distraction) with the objective to increase the sense of control and self-efficacy. These examples illustrate a functional difference between some approaches within more traditional forms of CBT and ACT. ACT does not predominantly utilize exposure procedures to reduce symptoms, improve skills aimed at controlling them, or alter the content of thoughts or beliefs. Instead, exposure within ACT is primarily conducted to expand the behavior repertoire in the presence of symptoms, to promote willingness, contact with the present moment, and actions that are values-based and have a committed quality. In short, for ACT, exposure is meant to promote flexibility around what is felt and thought, not to change what is felt and thought.

It is possible that some groups of patients may respond less well to more traditional forms of exposure due to high levels of cognitive fusion and subtle forms of experiential avoidance. If so, it may be beneficial to apply cognitive defusion methods and to target the control agenda. For some patients, the bodily sensations that their medical conditions engender can provoke fear and catastrophic thoughts. For these patients, exposure can be combined with mindfulness; bodily sensations may be attended to interoceptively while promoting acceptance and an observing, defused perspective on these reactions, in a process aimed at increased psychological flexibility. Thus, exposure-based methods can be applied with differing purposes, and some of these can include the promotion of acceptance, mindfulness, defusion, and flexibility.

Mindfulness and Relaxation

Mindfulness is complex and can be defined in different ways. It was recently suggested that mindfulness should be conceptualized as broadly multifaceted, including nonreactivity to inner experience, observing sensations, acting with awareness, describing with words, and nonjudging of experiences (Baer, Smith, Hopkins, Krietemeyer, & Toney, 2006). As seen, there is a large overlap between mindfulness and processes found in ACT. Mindfulness has also been described as a set of skills to reduce psychological symptoms and improve health (Baer et al., 2006). Such mindfulness skills can be practiced in several ways, from shorter exercises as commonly done in ACT and DBT to longer, formal meditation (see chapters 7 and 12).

The term "mindfulness" refers to both method and process, which can be confusing. Treatments to promote acceptance and psychological flexibility do not necessarily have to include explicit mindfulness exercises. With ACT, for example, mindfulness may be enhanced by a range of procedures aimed at promoting the process of contact with the present moment and staying present with potentially negative psychological experiences. Mindfulness procedures resemble, in some ways, exposure procedures, in that the patient is encouraged to engage in activities that elicit uncomfortable reactions. When this is done without attempts to escape or modify the experience, this can promote acceptance. Furthermore, mindfulness procedures commonly include observing and describing sensations facilitating a defusion process.

Mindfulness practice may share many features with relaxation training and, undoubtedly, meditation or formal mindfulness exercises are typically conducted in a way that can lead to a more relaxed state. However, the functions, or target processes, are normally quite different. While relaxation is typically aimed at reducing symptoms and/or increasing control over experiences, the primary goal of mindfulness has been described as developing a "moment-to-moment effort to perceive a phenomenon...with full awareness... without gross distortion of the bare percept from associated and second-order meanings" (Kabat-Zinn, Lipworth, & Burney, 1985, p. 165).

Relaxation is used in many different forms and in combination with several different methods, such as desensitization, biofeedback training, hypnosis, and yoga. More specifically, a central aim is normally to reduce symptoms by decreasing muscle tension, or to control pain by learning to recognize early signals of pain or stress and discriminating between a relaxed and an aroused state. Sometimes relaxation is used as part of a skill-building program to inhibit learned behavioral responses and reduce physiological reactions, as well as to promote more effective actions in difficult situations. As such, relaxation can be used to facilitate exposure by enhancing the individual's ability to stay with a distressing situation, both to reduce symptoms and to expand the behavior repertoire. If the bracing and guarding quality of muscular tension functions as a form of experiential avoidance and appears dysfunctional in relation to certain values, relaxation may indeed be seen as de facto exposure and an act of willingness. Depending upon the context, however, it should be noted that relaxation may sometimes reduce contact with the aversive stimuli and thus function as an avoidance strategy. Hence, rather than as a means for symptom reduction, an ACT therapist may use relaxation to enhance acceptance and contact with the present moment, as well as to explore symptoms in a process of defusion. Thus, although relaxation and mindfulness can be compared in form, similarities and differences should also be considered at the level of function.

Distraction

A patient who withdraws from activities due to symptoms tends to reduce the amount of external stimulation and thereby restrict attention to private events, which may amplify the focus on negative thoughts and emotions as well as exacerbate the perception of the symptoms. Accordingly, it makes obvious sense to make use of techniques to redirect attention away from painful stimuli, a process that can be referred to as distraction. In functional terms, distraction is a type of avoidance behavior that may or may not be beneficial depending upon the context. Pain caused by potentially injurious stimulation should normally, at least in the acute phase, be attended to in order to take appropriate actions. From an ACT perspective, not attending to this pain would illustrate insensitivity to the actual contingencies in the situation.

Procedures such as vaccination inflict pain that is brief. Most times we might just as well look away or focus on something else, because there is no obvious value in staying present with this pain and distress. However, when pain is not informative and is constantly present, strategies characterized by avoidance may need to be reevaluated. Ultimately, it is not a question of right or wrong but rather of workability, particularly in relation to valued living. Distraction in traditional CBT has been used as a coping skill to master or alter pain and to increase the sense of control. There are good reasons to believe that a control agenda like this may backfire if patients experience that it does not work, that it is effective for only a short period of time, or that it is insufficient with regard to increases in functioning and quality of life.

Interventions such as distraction are normally based on the idea that the goal is to reduce the perception of symptoms or to increase control of it. However, noticing the unpleasant symptoms and related distress, followed by identifying values and taking appropriate actions, would be considered psychologically flexible. The latter may appear similar to distraction in form but would not be considered avoidance because it is not exclusive and the function is not primarily to escape from an unpleasant feeling. Emotion regulation—as used in, for example, DBT—utilizes distraction techniques in similar ways. A functional comparison between acceptance and distraction raises questions such as when each is appropriate, how they operate when they are useful, and how they may be integrated into patterns of behavior that optimize flexible and effective functioning.

Imagery

Strategies based on different forms of imagery, such as hypnosis or guided imagery, are normally aimed at reducing pain and distress. These may also provide the patient with a sense of self-control, which, in turn, may facilitate increases in social activities, for example. Typically, these methods are combined with relaxation techniques, can be more or less structured, and are taught as a self-management skill. If the explicit target is to teach the patient how to divert attention away from symptoms in order to reduce pain and distress, imagery, like distraction, can be conceptualized as avoidance. As such, it can be contrasted with acceptance, mindfulness, and contact with the present moment.

However, imagery techniques may also be used with different objectives. Following a short mindfulness exercise to facilitate contact with the present moment, imagery may be useful to elicit emotionally painful stimuli in the form of traumatic memories. This is clearly not avoidance, but rather imaginative exposure. Also, rather than targeting a reduction in emotional distress, this type of intervention may be used to practice different behaviors in relation to the painful stimuli, namely behaviors with a quality of willingness, mindfulness, and defusion. Consequently, relaxation and imagery may be conducted in order to facilitate exposure and can promote processes emphasized in ACT.

From the above, it should be clear that what ultimately characterizes an intervention is not primarily its topographical form but its function. An intervention that "looks like" imagery and relaxation may be functionally similar to either experiential avoidance or acceptance, and this depends upon the rationale, quality of delivery, and treatment objective. Interestingly, it may be that relaxation, distraction, mindfulness, and acceptance methods result in similar experiences of increased control but through distinctly different processes: from having increased skills in controlling pain, or from the experience that pain does not need to be controlled in order to control life.

Education

Although the experiential aspect of learning is emphasized in ACT, formal education can play an important role because it is neither particularly meaningful nor necessary to accept or defuse from wrong information or misunderstandings. Most chronic condition management programs include some form of education to help patients understand the nature of their condition. As with other methods, the purpose may be described differently depending upon the theoretical framework, such as to alter dysfunctional thought patterns or reduce anxiety, versus to alter the context in which such symptoms occur. From an ACT perspective, education can help set the stage for exposure and acceptance, with the ultimate purpose to facilitate an increase in activity, by clarifying that exposure may increase symptoms without being harmful. Accordingly, useful education may tap into relevant aspects such as values, acceptance, and short- and long-term effects of behavioral choices, and it may address issues that relate to motivation for change.

Values Clarification and Goal Setting

An important aspect of CBT is the goal-setting process, where treatment objectives are clarified. Target behaviors and goals are normally defined in a way that makes it possible for the patient to note the progress and achievement of the goal, by assuring that they have certain qualities, that they are specific, measurable, action oriented, realistic, time limited, desirable, and the like. An important aspect of goals lies with their ability to "motivate" action. However, the motivational aspect can be limited due to the delay between the behavior (e.g. going for a walk) and goal achievement (participate in a hiking trip with friends), which may potentially diminish the reinforcing properties of the goal. In addition, progress in behavior change may slow down after the goal is reached until the goal setting is repeated. When behavior change is explicitly related to a defined goal in the future, this may draw attention away from the inherent value of the behavior itself in the moment and toward other types of extraneous contingencies, possibly arbitrary, social or otherwise. Thus, a focus on the performance and goal achievement may increase behavior change in the short term but also divert attention away from the vital quality of the activity, potentially reducing the reinforcing properties of the activity itself, and hindering its integration into a long-term pattern of new behaviors.

In ACT, values work resembles the goal setting in most CBT-oriented treatment programs but has a wider focus. Values clarification, in ACT, is concerned with questions such as "What do you want your life to be about?" Or, "Who do you want to be in relation to the people you care about?" Technically, values are qualities of actions and represent verbal constructions of desired future contingencies. As such, these verbal representations of future events are experienced in the present and may therefore have a significant influence on behaviors.

Commonly, values are metaphorically described as a direction, such as east, in contrast to a destination, such as Stockholm, and the traveling as a lifelong process. What matters is not only the reaching of a certain destination but also the traveling in a valued direction in itself. Accordingly, a distinction can be made between values as a life orientation, such as being a good friend or learning new ideas; and goals, such as calling friends twice a week or attending school. Especially, the values work appears essential when one is targeting behavior change in patients with chronic pain or other symptoms that are unlikely to be reduced. The discussion of values provides a shift in focus from symptom alleviation to vital living in the presence of those symptoms, a context in which exposure and behavior activation is legitimized. Expressed differently, the values work is motivational in the sense that it illuminates the incentives to repeatedly engage in behaviors that are likely to increase pain and distress. However, ACT is ultimately about behavior change, and values are subsequently operationalized and described in behavioral terms. Thus, the more traditional form of goal setting can be usefully combined with the values work as described in ACT.

It is important to note that values work engenders more than goal setting and motivation. Most patients experience their life as far from values-oriented. Discussing values may elicit various negative reactions such as disappointment, fear, and frustration. The psychological functions present in these discussions may reveal patterns of experiential avoidance, unwillingness, and cognitive fusion. Talking about values provides in itself a context for exposure and an opportunity to address pain and distress associated with vital living. Likely, emotional barriers have contributed to experiential avoidance, for example not planning the future because that is frightening. If so, acceptance may be used to facilitate engagement in values clarification and goal setting. Also, when discussing values and long-term goals, patients are sometimes considerably fused with ideas such as "There is no use," which may call for exercises aimed at defusing from the content of these thoughts.

Physical Exercise and Behavioral Activation

In chronic medical condition management, physical exercise is usually considered important and serves a number of purposes: first, to increase strength and mobility and prevent negative effects of inactivity and, second, to increase self-efficacy, or the perceived ability to perform certain physical activities. Although physical exercise is considered important by most patients, it is not uncommon that this type of intervention meets comments such as "I see the point in doing that, and I will try as soon as my pain is under control." From an ACT perspective, this response may reflect two potentially contrasting agendas: to improve strength and to decrease symptoms. Here, strategies to undermine the need for experiential avoidance are likely to be useful because they directly address barriers to behavior change. For example, exercises aimed at defusion may promote a more flexible contact with the thought "I shouldn't do what increases my symptoms" and may facilitate active exposure even in the presence of these thoughts. The therapist may also benefit from directly addressing willingness to have symptoms as a means to undermine their influence on behaviors. If the physical activity is not initially rewarding in itself, a discussion of values may prove useful. Furthermore, physical exercises that elicit negative thoughts, emotions, and bodily sensations provide an excellent opportunity to increase awareness of, and alter the relationship to, private events through mindfulness-oriented interventions.

Closely related to physical exercise is behavioral activation, which, similar to the above, may be conducted in different ways and for different purposes. Behavioral activation of various forms is commonly included in CBT and is sometimes aimed at symptom reduction or performed to test and ultimately change dysfunctional thoughts. Behavioral activation can also be done in the service of increasing values-oriented activities and to expand and enrich a behavioral repertoire. Behavioral activation as described by Martell, Addis, and Jacobson (2001) resembles ACT in many aspects—for example, it is similarly based on ongoing functional analyses. It is important to note that both approaches emphasize the behavior–context interaction, rather than the content of the private experience, such as pain or feelings of distress. However, there are also differences, such as ACT's basis in RFT as the theoretical framework. Also, specific techniques differ somewhat. For example, the behavioral activation model is more oriented toward goal setting and graded activities and emphasizes skills acquisition to a larger extent. ACT, on the other hand, focuses more on the patient's willingness to experience pain and distress, cognitive defusion strategies, values work, and increased psychological flexibility.

Skills Training in and Between Sessions

CBT has traditionally emphasized self-management skills, including stress coping, problem solving, communication, and activity management strategies, to increase the ability to behave effectively in difficult situations. ACT does not reject the importance of skill acquisition when the functional analysis calls for this type of intervention. However, it is often identified that individuals already have requisite skills and that these are suppressed or blocked in aspects of psychological inflexibility. In fact, if progress in skills acquisition is less than expected, a functional analysis may reveal experiential avoidance and cognitive fusion. Thus, increased success in a particular context may require behavior change, such as increased assertive behavior, in the presence of previously avoided anxiety, frustration, fear of being let down, and similar experiences. When avoidance of emotional reactions appears to be a central barrier to effective actions, the control agenda and emotional struggles may be targeted through acceptance and defusion. Skills training may then become more similar to a vehicle for the work of exposure.

Both mindfulness-based approaches and ACT include skills-training methods such as instruction, feedback, rehearsal, and daily home practice. In ACT, skills training is appropriate whenever a treatment goal includes behavior patterns that are not yet developed or within the patient's current behavior repertoire. In addition, implementing values work may be particularly beneficial to increase the sense of vitality in the skills training.

Interventions aimed at skills improvement for young people may also include teaching and training parents in contingency management. However, if parents are taught these principles but experience problems with adopting the new strategies, the analysis may reveal experiential avoidance and cognitive fusion that prevent the utilization of contingency management. Under these circumstances the skills training may usefully be combined with ACT-oriented strategies. The emotional turmoil that is elicited in critical situations may be directly addressed with exposure, acceptance, and defusion strategies to increase psychological flexibility. Similarly, when experiential avoidance is identified and addressed by exposure, a certain amount of skills training may increase the likelihood that new behaviors are reinforced.

ACT and other forms of third-wave CBT emphasizes the functional similarity between behaviors occurring inside and outside sessions. Target behaviors are therefore addressed directly in session, to shape a more adaptive behavior pattern. Accordingly, experiential exercises play an important role in detecting and altering behaviors characterized by cognitive fusion and experiential avoidance. However, the effectiveness of these interventions is obviously enhanced if the patient is also encouraged to engage in relevant behaviors between sessions. Well-structured CBT normally includes more or less formal homework assignments, and this is true also for ACT and other third-wave therapies.

Medication Use

It is not uncommon for clinicians, normally physicians, to ask if and how ACT can be combined with strategies that are primarily aimed at reducing symptoms, such as medication use. Again, such discussion should include not just the topographical form of the intervention but also the function of it. An important distinction in relation to medical therapies is that some are designed to manage underlying disease processes, such as inflammatory arthritis, cancer, diabetes, hypertension, and congestive heart failure; some are designed to change what symptoms feel like, or to palliate, such as in management of chronic nonmalignant pain, anxiety symptoms, or such problems as insomnia.

It is not uncommon for medications, prescribed to manage a potentially harmful underlying condition, to be associated with significant side effects. Under such conditions, psychological methods may be applied to promote medication-use behaviors in the service of long-term health. In fact, not using effective medication may be a psychologically inflexible behavior pattern that results from experiential avoidance and cognitive fusion (for example, "Only weak people use medications," "Taking pills means admitting I can't handle this," and "I'm not sick"). In these situations, acceptance-oriented strategies may be implemented to further enhance adherence and effectiveness.

When medication is aimed at symptom management only, not at treating an underlying condition, the situation is different. Obviously, medications that reduce symptoms without side effects, and also increase the ability to live vitally, appear worth continuing. However, medications are often ineffective or only partially effective in this regard. Habituation, and possibly even addiction, or other kinds of therapeutic failure can occur among people suffering from chronic conditions, and for some patients it can become necessary for long-term health to reduce medications. CBT has a lot to offer when medications fail or must be reduced, including education and scheduling of medication intake (in contrast to on a need basis) (Turk et al., 1983). Possibly, ACT can provide additional strategies based on processes such as willingness and defusion when trying to wean patients from medication. When one is reducing medication, resistance may be due to fear and concerns regarding a return of symptoms. Thus, it is quite likely that patients will face several problems such as withdrawal effects, psychological distress, and increased symptoms, and it appears likely that acceptance would be particularly useful to prevent discontinuation of the weaning process. Also, exaggerated thoughts, such as "I'm not strong enough to do this," "They don't understand I am really suffering—that I really need the medication," and "It will never be better," can be addressed by defusion techniques to decrease their impact on actions. Similarly, incorporating discussions of values may help the patient to clarify the incentives for engaging in behaviors that will, most likely, not be immediately rewarding and yet are defined as values-oriented.

Thus, it may be useful to alter the context in which the medication-use behavior occurs by addressing the fact that medication intake can be aligned with different purposes: for instance, "I must have medication to feel better" or "I take medication because when I do so I find that I can successfully do more of the activities that are important to me." Building flexibility around the medication-use behavior may be a useful step in a process aimed at optimizing the long-term effectiveness of the medication use.

Acceptance of Therapist Distress

All therapists have encountered situations where emotional barriers emerge as potential blocks in their delivery of services for patients. When patients get stuck, lack motivation, or experience doubt, this may raise significant distress within the therapist.

Clearly it can be as hard for the therapist to notice, accept, and defuse from painful or nonconstructive private experiences as for anyone, and it is natural for us to try to protect ourselves from feeling incompetent, mean, or ignorant. Thus, cognitive fusion and experiential avoidance are likely to play an important role when therapists experience distress in relation to patients' possible failures. As a result, we may engage in behaviors aimed at avoiding feelings of incompetence, rather than behaviors characterized by a commitment to successful patient behavior change or therapy progress. In these situations, we may find ourselves working harder, doing more exercises, extending sessions, or trying to motivate, without any clear rationale or effect on therapy progress. Indeed, a sense of control over uncomfortable experiences is as attractive to the therapist as to the patient. However, to let go of control means that we, from time to time, have to sit with experiences of worry, frustration, and disappointment. To willingly expose ourselves to such feelings of distress, in the service of therapy progress, and apply acceptance and defusion strategies to deal with these situations, appears highly relevant to maximize the quality of the therapeutic work.

Summary

Traditional CBT is known for being a well-structured psychotherapeutic approach. Likewise, a clear rationale and structure is as relevant when acceptance and mindfulness strategies are implemented, although this should not be at the cost of a flexible and patient-centered format. On a related point, validation, emotional disclosure, and compassion are all important ingredients in ACT. However, success will rely on the ability to adequately utilize certain therapeutic techniques, and this in turn is dependent on our ability to effectively manage our own private experiences. Clearly, there is an infinite number of different therapeutic styles. Nevertheless, poorly performed technique is not a "style." Just as we should act with compassion, for example, we should act with skillfulness. There are several methods for therapy training firmly established within the wider tradition of CBT that can, and should, be used, including regular and structured supervision, self-observation, and role-playing.

In future development of increasingly effective treatments for patients with chronic medical conditions, it is suggested that acceptance and mindfulness processes can readily be implemented in various ways within more standard CBT programs. This is likely to be useful especially for patients with such problems as ineffective self-management behaviors, a sense of being dominated by their condition, low compliance with necessary medical advice, and other psychologically inflexible behavior patterns resulting from cognitive fusion, experiential avoidance, and the like. The utility of different strategies as well as combinations of strategies is ultimately an empirical question. In part because of its broad definition, the processes by which CBT is effective are still relatively unclear. Rather than exclusively comparing treatment packages based on ACT and the more familiar CBT, we may find it useful to also pursue comparative process and treatment component analyses. Such analyses may provide a focus for continuing development involving more or less related theoretical frameworks (Wicksell, Lekander, Sorjonen, & Olsson, in press; Wicksell, Olsson, & Hayes, in press; Vowles, McCracken, & Eccleston, 2008).

There is a process of change and refinement that carries on implicitly, and in some ways imperfectly, in clinical practice in behavioral medicine. Shifts between theories, models, and methods are often not quick and clean. It is worth considering how well the family of CBT approaches provides a tolerant and permissive space for developments to occur. Theories and technologies of ACT, mindfulness, and other "third wave" therapies are beginning to meet the larger mass of clinicians and researchers, and this chapter has attempted to show that integration is possible and that there is much to learn in doing this. It is also suggested here that a truly progressive field of behavioral medicine will emerge from a primary focus on function and processes rather than on "brands" of therapy or methods.

References

Baer, R. A., Smith, G. T., Hopkins, J., Krietemeyer, J., & Toney, L. (2006). Using self-report assessment methods to explore facets of mindfulness. *Assessment, 13*(1), 27–45.

Compas, B. E., Haaga, D. A., Keefe, F. J., Leitenberg, H., & Williams, D. A. (1998). Sampling of empirically supported psychological treatments from health psychology: Smoking, chronic pain, cancer, and bulimia nervosa. *Journal of Consulting and Clinical Psychology, 66*(1), 89–112.

De Jong, J. R., Vlaeyen, J. W., Onghena, P., Cuypers, C., den Hollander, M., & Ruijgrok, J. (2005). Reduction of pain-related fear in complex regional pain syndrome type I: The application of graded exposure in vivo. *Pain, 116*, 264–275.

Hayes, S. C. (2004). Acceptance and commitment therapy, relational frame theory, and the third wave of behavioral and cognitive therapies. *Behavior Therapy, 35*, 639–665.

Hayes, S. C., Barnes-Holmes, D., & Roche, B. (Eds.). (2001). *Relational frame theory: A Post-Skinnerian account of human language and cognition.* New York: Plenum Press.

Hayes, S. C., Follette, V. M., & Linehan, M. M. (Eds.). (2004). *Mindfulness and acceptance: Expanding the cognitive-behavioral tradition.* New York: Guilford Press.

Hayes, S. C., Masuda, A., Bissett, R. T., Luoma, J., & Guerrero, L. F. (2004). DBT, FAP and ACT: How empirically oriented are the new behavior therapy technologies? *Behavior Therapy, 35*, 35–54.

Hayes, S. C., Strosahl, K. D., & Wilson, K. G. (1999). *Acceptance and commitment therapy: An experiential approach to behavior change.* New York: Guilford Press.

Kabat-Zinn, J., Lipworth, L., & Burney, R. (1985). The clinical use of mindfulness meditation for the self-regulation of chronic pain. *Journal of Behavioral Medicine, 8*(2), 163–190.

Keefe, F. J., Smith, S. J., Buffington, A. L., Gibson, J., Studts, J. L., & Caldwell, D. S. (2002). Recent advances and future directions in the biopsychosocial assessment and treatment of arthritis. *Journal of Consulting and Clinical Psychology, 70*(3), 640–655.

Lappalainen, R., Lehtonen, T., Skarp, E., Taubert, E., Ojanen, M., & Hayes, S. C. (2007). The impact of CBT and ACT models using psychology trainee therapists: A preliminary controlled effectiveness trial. *Behavior Modification, 31*(4), 488–511.

Martell, C., Addis, M., & Jacobson, N. (2001). *Depression in context. Strategies for guided action.* New York: Norton & Company.

McCracken, L. M., & Eccleston, C. (2005). A prospective study of acceptance of pain and patient functioning with chronic pain. *Pain, 118*(1–2), 164–169.

Morley, S., Eccleston, C., & Williams, A. (1999). Systematic review and meta-analysis of randomized controlled trials of cognitive behaviour therapy and behaviour therapy for chronic pain in adults, excluding headache. *Pain, 80*(1-2), 1–13.

Turk, D. C., Meichenbaum, D., & Genest, M. (1983). *Pain and behavioral medicine: A cognitive-behavioral perspective.* New York: Guilford Press.

Turk, D. C., & Okifuji, A. (2002). Psychological factors in chronic pain: Evolution and revolution. *Journal of Consulting and Clinical Psychology, 70*(3), 678–690.

Wicksell, R. K., Lekander, M., Sorjonen, K., & Olsson, G. L. (in press). The Psychological Inflexibility in Pain Scale (PIPS)—statistical properties and model fit of an instrument to assess change processes in pain related disability. *European Journal of Pain.*

Wicksell, R. K., Melin, L., Lekander, M., & Olsson, G. L. (2009). Evaluating the effectiveness of exposure and acceptance strategies to improve functioning and quality of life in longstanding pediatric pain—a randomized controlled trial. *Pain, 141*(3), 248–257.

Wicksell, R. K., Olsson, G. L., & Hayes, S. C. (in press). Processes of change in ACT-based behavior therapy—psychological flexibility as mediator of improvement in patients with chronic pain following whiplash injuries. *European Journal of Pain.*

Vlaeyen, J. W., & Linton, S. J. (2000). Fear-avoidance and its consequences in chronic musculoskeletal pain: A state of the art. *Pain, 85*(3), 317–332.

Vowles, K. E., McCracken, L. M., & Eccleston, C. (2008). Patient functioning and catastrophizing in chronic pain: The mediating effects of acceptance. *Health Psychology, 27*(Suppl. 2), S136–143.

PART 5

Training and Education of Health Care Providers

11 BIAS, PREJUDICE, AND DISPARITIES IN HEALTH CARE

Miles Thompson

Bath Centre for Pain Services, Royal National Hospital for
Rheumatic Diseases, Bath, United Kingdom

We live in a world of divisions and inequalities—including in the area of health care. These divisions present across many categories, including socioeconomic status, nationality, ethnicity, age, gender, diagnosis, mental health status, and the like. Tied into these divisions and the inequalities they engender are fundamentally psychological processes of language, cognition, emotion, and behavior. These processes contribute to what we refer to when we use the words "bias" and "prejudice." This chapter offers insights into these processes from the evidence-based framework of relational frame theory (RFT) and acceptance and commitment therapy (ACT). It is worth highlighting at the outset that the possible varieties and locations of disparities that exist within health care are vast. The entire chapter, indeed an entire book, could be spent detailing the instances where disparities have been reported. Rather than do this, this chapter will provide the reader with a perspective that he or she can use to aid his or her conceptualization of disparity wherever it is found.

The chapter is structured to first touch on the extent of global health care inequality and then to provide a more detailed overview of the evidence for health care disparity in just one area, namely that experienced by racial and ethnic minority groups in the United States. It will then outline interventions in this area, particularly those targeted at health care professionals. Next it will outline how insights from RFT may add to our understanding of the possible roots of bias and prejudice. Then it will detail the attempts of ACT to influence such processes and highlight other potential applications of this framework.

Global Health Care Disparities

Researchers note that the terms "health disparity," "health inequality," and "health equity" are used somewhat interchangeably (Braveman, 2006). Writing about "health equity" for the World Health Organization, Margaret Whitehead notes that "equity in health implies that ideally everyone should have a fair opportunity to attain their full health potential and, more pragmatically, that no one should be disadvantaged from achieving this potential, if it can be avoided" (Whitehead, 1990, p. 7).

At a global level, disparities are not hard to find. For example, the World Health Organization reports that the United States has just 10 percent of the global burden of disease, but 37 percent of the world's health workers and 50 percent of the world's health financing. Conversely, the African region has 24 percent of the burden but only 3 percent of health workers and less than 1 percent of world health expenditure (World Health Organization, 2006, pp. xviii–xix). Other disparities are just as easy to highlight. Regarding overall life expectancy at birth, the Population Division of the Department of Economic and Social Affairs of the United Nations Secretariat (2009) reports that the current global average life expectancy is 67.6 years, with the life expectancy for the top three countries ranging from 82.7 to 81.8 years (Japan, China, and Switzerland), while the bottom three range from just 43.8 to 45.2 years (Afghanistan, Zimbabwe, and Zambia). Figures on child mortality indicate that progress is being made, but much more work is required before we approach health equity. The number of yearly deaths in the under-five age range stood at 10.4 million in 2000 and 8.8 million in 2009 (You, Wardlaw, Salama, & Jones, 2010). Based on the 2000 data, Black, Morris, and Bryce (2003) calculated that most deaths were due to neonatal disorders, diarrhea, pneumonia, and malaria. Working with this data, and based on an understanding of the forty-two countries where 90 percent of these deaths occurred, Jones, Steketee, Black, Bhutta, & Morris (2003) conclude that roughly two-thirds of these deaths could have been prevented by applying simple prevention- or treatment-based interventions that are feasible but not widely available in low-income countries.

Racial and Ethnic Minority Disparity in Health Care in the United States

Research in the area of racial and ethnic minority disparity in health care in the United States is not new. In the early 1900s, W. E. B. DuBois (2003) along with fellow academics refuted the findings of Frederick L. Hoffman (1896), who claimed that death rates in African Americans were a reflection of underlying physical vulnerability. DuBois instead argued that such disparity was a result of social and economic conditions. Decades later, Swedish economist, politician, and Nobel laureate Gunnar Myrdal wrote, "area for area, class for class, Negroes cannot get the same advantages in the way of prevention and care of disease that whites can" (1944, pp. 171–172).

Throughout the latter half of the twentieth century, research in this area continued to grow, with the first review being published in 2000 by Mayberry, Mili, and Ofili. Parallel to this, in 1999, the United States Congress asked the Institute of Medicine (IOM) to examine the evidence for disparity in health care services for racial and ethnic minorities. In 2002 the IOM published "Unequal Treatment: Confronting Racial and Ethnic Disparities in Health Care" (Smedley, Stith, & Nelson, 2002). The report limits its data, only including studies that provided some form of control or adjustment for the influence of insurance status, yet it still cites evidence for possible disparity in analgesia, asthma, cancer, cardiovascular disease, cerebrovascular disease, children's health care, diabetes, emergency services, eye care, gallbladder disease, HIV/AIDS, maternal and infant health, mental health, peripheral vascular disease, pharmacy, physician perceptions, patients' perceptions, radiographs, rehabilitative services, renal care and transplantation, (general) use of services and procedures, vaccination, and women's health (see Smedley et al., 2002, appendix B, pp. 285–383).

The chief finding of the IOM report was significant variation in health care practices toward white and nonwhite individuals. The authors state that "racial and ethnic disparities in health care exist and, because they are associated with worse outcomes in many cases, are unacceptable" (Smedley et al., 2002, Finding 1-1, p. 6). The nongovernmental organization Physicians for Human Rights also reviewed the existing data and both confirmed and extended the conclusions of the IOM report, stating that "the evidence is robust, beyond reasonable doubt, of a pervasive and troubling finding in the health care system, and a cause for deep concern" (Physicians for Human Rights, 2003, p. 1).

Perhaps the strongest evidence for disparity comes from the field of cardiovascular disease, where "the consistency of findings from these studies, many using large sample sizes, is striking" (Smedley et al., 2002, p. 43). Evidence in this area includes research from administrative databases where, for example, white patients were four times more likely than African Americans to be given a coronary artery bypass graft (n = 86,000; Goldberg, Hartz, Jacobsen, Krakauer, & Rimm, 1992). Evidence from clinical data is also included where, for example, in prospective research, researchers found that African Americans were less likely than whites to receive bypass surgery even when the researchers adjusted for comorbidities and disease severity, among other factors (Peterson, Shaw, & Califf, 1997; Taylor, Meyer, Morse, & Pearson, 1997). In other health areas, the IOM report found lower levels of diagnostic and therapeutic procedures among African Americans with cerebrovascular disease (Oddone et al., 1999; Mitchell, Ballard, Matchar, Whisnant, & Samsa, 2000). In the field of renal transplantation, despite a higher prevalence of renal disease in African Americans, the evidence suggests that disparities exist (Kasiske, London, & Ellison, 1998; Young & Gaston, 2000). Regarding HIV/AIDS, the evidence again suggests disparity for racial and ethnic minorities (Moore, Stanton, Gopalan, & Chaisson, 1994; Shapiro et al., 1999).

In the years since the IOM and PHR reports, evidence has continued to accumulate. Klonoff (2009) has selectively reviewed the latest research in the area and reports that, in the field of vascular disease, recent evidence suggests that African Americans and other ethnic groups still receive less or different treatments for myocardial infarction and different anticoagulants (Sonel et al., 2005; Bhandari, Wang, Bindman, & Schillinger, 2008). Research also suggests that new technologies such as implantable cardioverter defibrillators (ICD) are used less for African Americans than for whites (Stanley, DeLia, & Cantor, 2007). Hernandez and colleagues (2007) found that the adjusted odds of ICD use in black men were 0.73 and in black women 0.56 when compared to white men. In surgery, those of racial and ethnic minorities are less likely to undergo kidney transplants (Stolzmann et al., 2007), and similar disparity has been found in African Americans awaiting liver transplants (Reid, Resnick, Chang, Buerstatte, & Weissman, 2004). Similar patterns of disparities also appear to exist in orthopedic surgery (Skinner, Weinstein, Sporer, & Wennberg, 2003). Skinner, Zhou, and Weinstein (2006) report racial disparity in the area of total knee arthroplasty, where, compared to white men, the adjusted odds ratio for surgery was 0.36 for black men and 0.28 for Asian men. Klonoff also reports disparity in breast cancer, where, for example, Mandelblatt and colleagues (2002) report that, compared to white women, black women are more likely to receive a mastectomy rather than breast conservation, odds ratio 1.36, and more likely to receive breast conservation without radiation treatment, odds ratio 1.48. Finally, when at risk of developing breast cancer, African American women were less likely to have genetic counseling for breast cancer genes BRCA1/2 testing than equivalent white women (odds ratio 0.22; Armstrong, Micco, Carney, Stopfer, & Putt, 2005).

The IOM report is more than seven hundred pages long. It contains the findings of hundreds of research articles, and many dozens more have been written since. If disparities toward racial and ethnic minorities exist in health care, two important issues arise: where do they come from, and how can they be countered?

Reasons and Solutions

The IOM report suggests a number of reasons why disparities may exist. The report is clear that differences in patient biology or behavior across race (along with many other possible explanatory factors) cannot explain the disparities (Smedley et al., 2002). Understandably, the authors situate their explanation for disparity in health care within the much broader context of wider racial and ethnic minority inequality and discrimination that has existed in the United States and throughout the world in both the past and the present. However, on top of this, they conclude that the disparity found in health care may also be maintained as a result of influences and interactions among health systems, health professionals, and patients.

While systemic factors such as the fragmentation of health care systems, lower-cost health plans, and incentives for health care professionals to limit the services they offer may play a role, the IOM is also clear that factors within the encounter between patient and health care professional may contribute to disparities. Again, there was an acknowledgment that any relationship between a health care professional and his or her patient involves a complex interaction drawing on the history and context of each individual. It was noticeable, however, that the IOM highlighted the possible role of "bias, stereotyping, prejudice, and clinical uncertainty" on the part of the health care professional (Smedley et al., 2002, Finding 4-1, p. 178). The IOM committee concluded that there is "strong but circumstantial evidence" (Smedley et al., 2002, p. 178) for this and encouraged more research.

The role of prejudice in the health care profession and its relationship to disparity is not merely hypothesized; it has also been investigated empirically. In one study, Schulman and colleagues (1999) investigated the possible role of prejudice on physicians' recommendations for cardiac catheterization. The research surveyed 720 physicians using a computer program that modeled the assessment of patients suffering from chest pain. Physicians watched a scripted interview with "patients" (played by one of eight actors) who were either fifty-five or seventy years old, were either white or black, were of either gender, and also varied according to chest pain type and stress-test results. Physicians assessed one of 144 possible combinations and were asked if they wanted to order more cardiac evaluations or to refer the patient for cardiac catheterization. Results indicated that, while patient race made no significant difference in physicians' assessment of the probability of coronary artery disease, both women and blacks were less likely to be referred for cardiac catheterization, with black women being significantly less likely than white men to be referred for the procedure (odds ratio 0.4). These results remained even after the researchers adjusted for variations in symptoms and for physicians' perceptions of patient personality. The authors rightly acknowledge that their study used actors and videos and accordingly may lose some ecological validity. However, other studies investigating similar topics have used actual clinical data.

Van Ryn and Burke (2000) published research investigating the effect of patient race and socioeconomic status (SES) on physicians' perceptions of patients. They collected data from 618 physician encounters with post-angiogram patients, collecting information on patient race and SES, along with various physician reports of patient ability and likelihood of patient behavior. The authors controlled statistically for many factors in the physician (including age, sex, race, and specialty), the patient (including age, sex, and health risk status), and variously for patient race or SES. The results suggested that black patients were perceived to be less intelligent and physicians liked them less. They were also perceived to be more non-compliant, more likely to abuse substances, and more likely to have poorer levels of social support than white patients. Equally, patients of lower SES were seen to have less self-control and less responsibility for family members; to be less physically active, less intelligent, and more irrational; and as more likely to be noncompliant.

Ways Forward

If, as above, evidence suggests that bias and prejudice in the behavior of physicians or other health care providers is a contributing factor in the levels of disparity that racial and ethnic minorities experience in health care, what can be done about it? Examination of the contemporary literature suggests that the related notions of patient-centered care and cultural competence are in the vanguard of current attempts to address the issue.

Patient-centered care and cultural competence are related concepts with both shared and unique aspects (Beach, Saha, & Cooper, 2006). Central to both is the appreciation of the individual patient. The phrase "patient-centered medicine" was coined by Balint, who highlighted the importance of understanding the patient "as a unique human-being" (Balint, 1969, p. 269). More generally, patient-centered care seeks to facilitate more individualized interaction and communication between professional and patient (Mead & Bower, 2000). Work in cultural competence began with increasing awareness of different cultural contexts and traditions but has since expanded to include notions such as being aware of one's own biases and stereotypes. Cultural competence is defined as "the ability of individuals to establish effective interpersonal and working relationships that supersede cultural differences" (Cooper & Roter, 2002, p. 554). The IOM report recommends the integration of crosscultural education into all future training and all current professional development programs (Smedley et al., 2002).

Beach and colleagues (2005) conducted a systematic review of research published between 1980 and 2003 in the area of cultural competence. The authors found 34 eligible studies and applied a preexisting system to rate the quality of the research collected from A (strongest) to D (weakest) (West et al., 2002). These studies were divided into those who reported on provider knowledge, provider attitudes, and provider skills. The best evidence (grade A) came from studies demonstrating improvements in knowledge on cultural concepts, improved in 17 of 19 studies. Out of 25 studies, 21 demonstrated a change in attitudes—for example, cultural self-efficacy (grade B). Regarding skills, such as communication and social interaction, 14 out of 14 demonstrated improvements (again grade B). Despite the apparent success of this research stream, only 3 studies measured patient outcomes and all of these measured patient satisfaction; no study examined health-related outcomes. It is important to note that, despite evidence that training can improve knowledge and attitudes related to cultural competence, it appears that there is not yet any evidence that an increase in cultural competence has any impact on disparity.

Regarding patient-centered care, a brief cohort study of 177 third-year medical students found that all students performed equally well interacting with a white patient but students with higher levels of person-centered attitude performed significantly, but modestly, better when interacting with an African American patient (Beach et al., 2007). While evidence such as this supports a relationship between patient-centered attitudes and interactions, large, as yet unanswered, questions remain regarding how to manipulate person-centered attitudes themselves. In other literature in this area, researchers propose broader frameworks to educate professionals and improve patient-centered care (Cooper, Beach, Johnson, & Inui, 2006; Burgess, van Ryn, Dovidio, & Saha, 2007). They highlight the importance of factors such as appropriate emotional expression and regulation.

Research that has focused on understanding and influencing health professionals' potential impact on racial and ethnic minority disparities in health care appears to be at an early stage. Despite the intuitive importance of notions such as cultural competence and patient-centered care, there is little or no data suggesting how to enhance these processes or suggesting that doing so leads directly to improvements in health or disparity-related outcomes. Perhaps looking closer at psychological processes at the core of prejudice is a means toward a better solution.

Psychological Accounts of Prejudice

The word "prejudice" comes from the Latin *praejudicium*, suggesting advance (*prae*) judgment (*judicium*). The compact *Oxford English* dictionary defines prejudice as preconceived opinion that is not based on reason or experience, or unjust behavior formed on such a basis (AskOxford, n.d). In traditional psychological accounts, prejudice is often seen as an "extreme" attitude containing a cognitive, an evaluative/affective, and a behavioral component. Theories about the origins of prejudice differ. Personality theorists propose explanations rooted in the personality of the individual; examples include the authoritarian personality (Adorno, 1950), the open and closed mind (Rokeach, 1960), and tough/tender mindedness (Eysenck, 1954). Social psychologists place more of an emphasis within society; for example, on intergroup conflict (Sherif, 1966) and social identity theory/minimal groups (Tajfel, Bilig, & Bundy, 1971). More recently, social cognitive theory has emphasized the role of social schema (Macrae & Bodenhausen, 2000) and implicit and explicit prejudice (Devine, 1989). Many also conclude that, despite obvious drawbacks, prejudice serves a function and can provide cognitive shortcuts by reducing the need for problem solving particularly in novel or threatening situations (Macrae, Milne, & Bodenhausen, 1994).

Popular ideas for prejudice reduction fall into three main categories. First is equal-status contact, which involves interacting with others on an even footing (Aronson, 1980). A second approach is the pursuit of successful cooperation toward interdependent goals (Sherif, Harvey, White, Hood, & Sherif, 1961). A third approach, as illustrated above, is education. However, results in these areas have been mixed. Classic research into equal-status contact found that behavior changed only toward the individual(s) concerned and not toward the group generally (Hewstone & Brown, 1986) and also found that prejudice was reduced only in certain social settings (Minard, 1952). Similarly, research into intergroup contact suggests that positive results might not have long-term impact; however, extensions of this research continue (Hewstone, Rubin, & Willis, 2002). The education literature produces similarly mixed results, with both positive and mixed evidence, alongside questions over the risks of paradoxical or rebound effects—where providing information appears to make prejudice worse (Macrae, Bodenhausen, Milne, & Jetten, 1994). Numerous studies in the area of education have been undertaken in the field of mental health (Corrigan et al., 2001; Corrigan, Watson, Warpinski, & Gracia, 2004).

The evidence above suggests that new and more effective approaches to reduce the adverse impacts of prejudice are clearly needed (Lillis & Hayes, 2007, p. 390). The remainder of this chapter will attempt to provide an account of prejudice as seen from the perspective of relational frame theory (RFT) and acceptance and commitment therapy (ACT). The former (RFT) provides a basic psychological theory on which the therapeutic approach (ACT) is based.

Relational Frame Theory

Relational frame theory (RFT) provides a scientific understanding of human language and cognition. The framework is consistent with and builds on the foundations of behavioral analysis. It is important to note that RFT aids not only our understanding of language and cognition in isolation but also our understanding of how these processes contribute to complicated human interactions, such as bias and prejudice and other behaviors that are often described under the umbrellas of psychopathology, developmental psychology, and social psychology (Hayes, Barnes-Holmes, & Roche, 2001). A growing research base demonstrates that human language is dependent on the processes described below and, although it is beyond the scope of this chapter to provide a complete introduction to RFT, readers can seek this information elsewhere (Hayes et al., 2001; Ramnerö & Törneke, 2008).

The R of RFT highlights the central importance of relations to human language and cognition, but it is important to clarify what this means, as nonhumans can also act in accordance with relations. Rhesus monkeys, for example, can select the "taller" of two stimuli in experimental settings. They can continue to do so even if the shorter of the current choices was previously the tallest (Harmon, Strong, & Pasnak, 1982). This suggests that they are behaving on the basis of the relationship between stimuli, meaning that they are making a relational response. It is important to note that in the above experiment, one stimulus is physically different from the other—the relationship exists in the world. Humans, on the other hand, can also act on the basis of relations that do not depend on the formal properties of objects. We can build relations that are independent of the physical properties of stimuli and that exist merely because of social context or our own individual history. Because of this, we can bring virtually anything into a relationship with anything else; this ability is known as "arbitrarily applicable relational responding."

The acquisition of relational responding starts when we are very young. As infants we are taught to relate objects to names (for example an object like a "teddy" and its corresponding name, "t-e-d-d-y"). Curious as it sounds, the words we use to relate to objects are arbitrary. The word "t-e-d-d-y" relates to the object "teddy" only because of history, context, and social convention. The relationship seems natural to us only because our history has paired the two things together on many occasions. When we are first learning these relationships, each relationship is explicitly taught and reinforced, but over time, "generalized relational responding" emerges. This means that each individual relationship no longer has to be taught, as responding has become generalized and can emerge indirectly.

Of course, relations are formed not just between words and objects, but between words and words, objects and objects, people and words, and so on. What is more, these relations do not need to be trained; they can be "derived," often without awareness. The notion of "derived stimulus relations" expands on the notion of stimulus equivalence (Sidman, 1971). In Sidman's classic experiment, a subject with learning disabilities was taught to match spoken words to pictures and also taught to match spoken words to printed words. On top of this, despite the fact that the relationship was never directly taught, the subject became able to match printed words to pictures. This last relationship, between printed words and pictures, had formed spontaneously. In other words, the stimuli had become equivalent to each other without training or reinforcement. Put simply, a derived stimulus relation is a relationship between two or more stimuli that is not directly trained or taught.

There are three important properties of human language and cognition that are key to RFT: mutual entailment, combinatorial entailment, and the transformation of stimulus functions. In mutual entailment, if a relationship from "a" to "b" is learned and reinforced, then the reverse relationship, from "b" to "a," is also derived despite never being reinforced itself. Combinatorial entailment involves three or more stimuli. Here, if the relationships from "a" to "b" and "b" to "c" are established, relationships from "a" to "c" and "c" to "a" are again derived without direct learning taking place. The third property concerns the transformation of stimulus functions; here stimuli exchange properties and stimuli become "functionally equivalent" to other stimuli they are related to. This means, for example, that if stimulus "a" is aversive to an individual, and the individual learns that "a" is similar to "b," then "b" also becomes aversive as the function is transformed from "a" to "b."

When stimuli become related to each other, they are said to exist in a "relational frame." If the object "teddy" is in a relational frame with the word "teddy," they are said to be in a frame of co-ordination (or sameness) with each other. The "a" to "b" examples given above are also in frames of coordination. Other families of relational frames also exist, such as opposition (for example, "a" is the opposite of "b"), distinction ("a" is not "b"), comparison ("a" is bigger/smaller than "b" or better/worse). Hierarchical, temporal, spatial, and deictic relational frames also exist along with relations concerning conditionality and causality (see Hayes, Fox, et al., 2002). Remember, the workings of these frames are initially trained and reinforced, but the capacity of relating eventually becomes generalized and elaborated automatically and outside of awareness.

Taken together, these processes lead to the many efficiencies (and problems) of living with human language. Because of arbitrarily applicable relational responding, derived stimulus relations, and relational frames, "words" (spoken language and thoughts) allow our behavior to be shaped without direct contact with the environment. Experience of words alone can change what we think, feel, and do, because the words alone are all that is necessary to bring us into contact with the function of the objects that they relate to. Not only that, but these functions can change and continue to be changed without our ever needing to directly contact the objects themselves due to the transformation of stimulus functions. The working of such processes is perhaps best illustrated with an example:

Imagine that as a child you learn that "men and women are opposite sexes" (a relational frame of opposition) and also that "men are strong" (a frame of coordination). From this you may derive that "women are weak" (coordination) without it ever being taught. If you later learn that "strength comes with age," you may again derive that "younger women are weaker than older women" and that "younger women are weaker still than older men" (adapted from Roche, Barnes-Holmes, Barnes-Holmes, & Stewart, 2002, p. 76).

The implications of these processes are vast. The verbal relationships that structure our world and guide our behavior can be formed automatically and without our control. In addition, researchers suggest that such processes are self-sustaining and make us insensitive to the world outside of our network of relational frames (Hayes, Niccolls, Masuda, & Rye, 2002; Roche et al., 2002).

RFT and Prejudice

We saw earlier how prejudice has been multiply understood and targeted from within the psychological literature. Let us now look at it from the perspective of RFT. Researchers propose that RFT, "a theory and technology of language, provides the empirical and conceptual tools for the analysis of such modes of social discourse and their roles in the establishment, maintenance, and amelioration of prejudice" (Dixon, Dymond, Rehfeldt, Roche, & Zlomke, 2003, p. 134). Other RFT researchers have defined human prejudice as "objectification and dehumanization of human beings because of their participation in verbal evaluative categories" (Hayes, Niccolls, et al., 2002, p. 298). What this means is that through the processes described above, individuals or groups of people are arbitrarily and automatically placed within taught and derived relational frames. It is then possible that our behavior toward these individuals or groups is influenced by the transfer of stimulus functions within relational frames and becomes entangled in verbally based processes. Sadly, the more our behavior comes under the control of verbal categories and the arbitrary functions they carry, the more we lose contact with aspects of the world that are not structured by these verbal processes. Notice that RFT does see prejudice as not an abnormal process—more an understandable overextension of human language. Indeed it can be seen as being inherent in "human beings, because it is built into language itself" (Hayes, Niccolls, et al., 2002, p. 297).

RFT also provides possible explanations for the results of previous prejudice research. Reasons why equal-status contact appears to have benefits that do not extend more widely than the individual can be hypothesized through RFT. It may be that equal-status contact adds multiple features to the relational frame associated with only the individual and not the group itself. Indeed, the contact may also inadvertently loosen the connection between the individual and the group through the transformation of stimulus functions, while leaving the relational frame associated with the group untouched. RFT also suggests that some well-meaning educational techniques designed to reduce prejudice may be counterproductive. Some researchers working in health disparities already raise concerns that promoting specific cultural information might promote rather than reduce stereotyping (Beach et al., 2005), and other research suggests that using education to confront and correct prejudicial attitudes is not always helpful (Thornton & Wahl, 1996; Wahl & Leftkowits, 1989). RFT helps explain this by noting that providing information about prejudiced groups might simply increase the strength of the discriminating relational frame that contains the group by, first, referring to it and, second, by adding to its features (Dixon et al., 2003; Roche et al., 2002). Important research parallel to RFT also suggests that telling people not to think certain things can make thoughts occur more frequently and increase their influence on behavior (Wenzlaff & Wegner, 2000).

Much of the recent work concerning RFT and prejudice has been as a result of the events and ramifications of the terrorist attacks on September 11, 2001 (Dixon et al., 2003; Dixon, Zlomke, & Rehfeldt, 2006; Hayes, Niccolls, et al., 2002). An example from this literature provides another illustration of how easily prejudice can be established and spread:

> An American witnesses the attacks of 9/11 (A), in so doing he experiences emotions of rage and hate (B). A little later the media also broadcasts images of terrorists (C) suspected of being responsible for the attack (A). Notice that A relates to B and A separately also relates to C. However, derived relations may also come to exist between B and C so that images of terrorists now give rise to feelings of rage and hate. The distinctive features of the terrorist group (C) include their race, skin color, religion, and country of origin. RFT illustrates how easy and automatic it will be for the feelings of hate to be felt not just toward the terrorists but toward

all individuals of Middle Eastern descent (D) who share the same characteristics as the terrorist group. (Adapted from Dixon et al., 2003, p. 135)

RFT Interventions

RFT is a bottom-up, data-driven approach to understanding human language and cognition, and much of its research takes place in laboratory conditions. One of the key processes relevant to RFT and prejudice is the transformation of stimulus functions. It is this process that explains how the feelings associated with the falling of the Twin Towers can come to be associated with individuals of Middle Eastern descent in the example above, or how a doctor may make different choices when treating a black woman and a white man, for example. Researchers have investigated whether a transformation of stimulus functions could occur between stimuli associated with obesity and arbitrary, neutral stimuli. Subjects participated in a "matching-to-sample" preparation where they were indirectly trained to respond to horizontal and vertical lines as if these were stimuli associated with obesity or thinness. The results suggest that the neutral stimuli acquired the functions of obese stimuli through derived training. Moreover, the research provided evidence that transformations of this kind require only a very brief training history (Weinstein, Wilson, & Kellum, 2008).

Basic research provides support for the RFT conceptualization of prejudice, and laboratory-based protocols may reveal ways to undermine it. Key to this might be the ability to loosen relational networks, perhaps by adding to the functions of groups or by making the relational frames of stereotyped groups overlap or merge with the other groups (Dixon et al., 2006). However, doing this under laboratory conditions has proven difficult.

In stimulus equivalence experiments, researchers noted that in Northern Ireland surnames often distinguished one religious background (i.e., Protestant or Catholic) from another (Watt, Keenan, Barnes, & Cairnes, 1991). They conducted a study using subjects from both Northern Ireland and England. Subjects were trained to relate three Catholic surnames to three nonsense syllables and later to relate the nonsense syllables to three Protestant symbols. Subjects were then tested to see if relations of equivalence had been established. They were presented with the Protestant symbols and given the options of selecting a Catholic name from training or a new, novel Protestant surname. All of the English subjects followed their experimental training and chose the Catholic name, but twelve of the nineteen subjects from Northern Ireland chose the new, novel Protestant name. It seems that the laboratory-based training was weaker than the preexisting relationships that had already been established for the Northern Irish subjects. Results such as this are not uncommon. Responding to the events of September 11, 2001, researchers tried to form frames of coordination between terrorist and American images in subjects in an effort to reduce prejudice (Dixon et al., 2006). However, across two experiments most participants did not form such frames and the researchers concluded that the training within the laboratory-based experiment was not yet sufficient.

It appears that, as yet, laboratory-based procedures related to RFT are not sufficient to counter real-world examples of prejudice. However, fruitful research has already taken place using a clinical, behavioral approach that is "consciously derived from RFT" (Wilson, Hayes, Gregg, & Zettle, 2002, p. 231), namely ACT.

Acceptance and Commitment Training

While RFT provides the basic psychological theory to explain how prejudice can arise from human language, ACT may provide the behavioral antidote. In brief, the ACT model suggests that six interrelated, double-sided processes are key to much human suffering or, conversely, psychological flexibility (in other words, the ability to sustainably move toward that which truly matters to you, in full contact with the present moment). The ACT model has been written about extensively (Luoma, Hayes, & Walser, 2007; Hayes, Luoma, Bond, Masuda, & Lillis, 2006; Hayes, Strosahl, & Wilson, 1999). In short, ACT can give us the ability not to stop prejudicial thoughts or feelings but to have the flexibility to let our mind do what it will and at the same time live life in accordance with that which we value most. It can provide personal, experiential insight into what our mind does, how this can dictate our behavior, and how awareness of this can allow us more control over what we do, moment to moment, in everyday life.

ACT, unlike other psychological approaches, does not set out to change the form or content of thoughts (including prejudicial ones) but aims to change their function or context—including the influence they have on us and our behavior. Typically, when we become entangled with thoughts, we may respond in accordance with them or do what they say. Prejudicial thoughts are seen as a natural part of human existence, but this does not mean that our behavior needs to be directed by them. Instead of trying to change the thought (either its occurrence or what it says), we may find it more useful, ACT would suggest, to change our *relationship* with the thought. ACT encourages flexibility in the face of such events including the willingness to experience. Such work includes becoming more aware of our own prejudices, biases, and intolerances.

It may seem odd to work with prejudicial thoughts without trying to change and challenge them, but evidence for successfully working in this way existed before ACT existed as an approach. In one experiment, children in one room were told that a disabled child was in the next. The children were then asked to name any prejudicial thoughts they had. One group of children had their thoughts acknowledged; the other had them corrected. Then both groups were taken into the room where the disabled child was. The group of children who had had their thoughts corrected avoided the disabled child more than the group who had had such thoughts acknowledged (Langer, Bashner, & Chanowitz, 1985). As well as providing support for an ACT way of working, the results of research such as this might again help us consider the potential for accidental detrimental side effects of some forms of education.

The research evidence for using ACT as a therapeutic approach is growing steadily in both mental health and behavioral medicine (Hayes et al., 2006); there is also evidence that it is useful in organizational settings (Bond & Hayes, 2002). A small but growing evidence base is demonstrating its use in the amelioration of prejudice. Although it may seem a leap, researchers in this area argue that the thoughts that might potentially be involved in prejudice (such as "The poor are undeserving") are not dissimilar to thoughts that potentially bring people into therapy (such as "I am undeserving") (adapted from Lillis and Hayes, 2007).

ACT Interventions

Below are the details of three illustrative interventions that use ACT to reduce (1) racial and ethnic minority prejudice in students, (2) stigma associated with individuals with mental health problems, and (3) drug and alcohol counselors' prejudice toward clients. In these group-based interventions, the T in ACT, which usually stands for "therapy," is replaced by a T for "training."

From the perspective of ACT and RFT, in all three cases, the core of bias, prejudice, and stigma is felt to be the objectification and dehumanization of human beings because of their participation in verbal evaluative categories, and it is these processes that studies of ACT have been designed to address.

In 2007, Lillis and Hayes published a study that applied ACT to the reduction of prejudice toward racial and ethnic minorities (Lillis & Hayes, 2007). The research compared the effectiveness of an ACT intervention to one based on education. The study used a counterbalanced within-group design, and subjects included thirty-two undergraduates, all of whom participated in both the ACT and the education condition. A new questionnaire was designed for the study and was called the "Prejudicial Biases Awareness, Defusion, and Action Questionnaire." It contained items that examined positive action intention and other relevant domains within the ACT model (awareness and acknowledgment of bias, acceptance and flexibility, thought control, and general defusion skills). The questionnaire was administered five times (before the first session, after the first session, before and after the second session, and at follow-up one week later). Each session lasted seventy-five minutes.

The education intervention was based on material from a popular psychology textbook on crosscultural counseling. It explored the characteristics of three different racial groups (African Americans, Asian Americans, and Hispanic or Latino Americans), particularly their strengths and common stereotypes. Time was also spent identifying and correcting one's own biases and seeing the unique aspects of others. The ACT intervention aimed to raise awareness of personal private prejudicial events (thoughts, feelings, and behaviors), increase acceptance of these, increase ability to notice other general evaluative language processes, and increase ability to act in accordance with personal values.

The ACT intervention improved the primary outcome—positive action intention—significantly at post-treatment and at one-week follow-up. It produced an average improvement of between 18 and 19 percent. Education produced no significant overall change in positive action intention. In terms of process change, "acceptance and flexibility" as measured by the questionnaire produced the largest differences at all time points. In a subsequent analysis, acceptance and flexibility were shown to partially mediate the impact of the ACT intervention on positive outcomes.

Also in 2007, another study investigated the impact of an ACT intervention on the stigma associated with psychological disorders (Masuda et al., 2007). The study utilized ninety-five undergraduates, of whom half were assigned to an ACT condition and half to education. Both interventions lasted two and one-half hours. The study used the Community Attitudes Toward the Mentally Ill—CAMI questionnaire (Taylor & Dear, 1981), which was redesigned for a college population, and the Acceptance and Action Questionnaire—AAQ (Hayes, Strosahl, et al., 2004). Scores on the AAQ were used to determine whether subjects were psychologically inflexible (≤ 66) or psychologically flexible (≥ 67). Before the training, 30 percent of those in the ACT condition and 26 percent of those in the education condition were classified as psychologically inflexible. Measures were taken at pre- and post-intervention and at one-month follow-up.

The education condition included group activities, discussion, and didactic presentation. The material was delivered in a nonconfrontational manner to avoid paradoxical effects but still aimed to replace subjects' stigmatizing thoughts with new, nonstigmatizing ones. Conversely, the ACT condition emphasized that stigma is built into natural language and instead drew its material from a series of experiential tasks based on a classic ACT textbook (Hayes et al., 1999).

Subjects with higher levels of psychological flexibility at pre-treatment reported less stigmatizing on the CAMI compared to those with lower levels of psychological flexibility. At post-treatment, results indicated that the ACT intervention reduced stigma scores in people with both high and low psychological flexibility. The education condition reduced stigma only for people with high levels of psychological flexibility at pre-treatment. At follow-up, all scores showed slight but nonsignificant drops.

Finally, a third study included an ACT intervention designed to affect stigmatizing attitudes within drug and alcohol abuse counselors (Hayes, Bissett, et al., 2004). The study contained three conditions: control, multicultural training, and ACT. Taking part were 93 counselors (30 in the ACT condition, 34 in the multicultural training, and 29 in the control). The training took place on one day, and all interventions lasted six hours.

Measures were taken at pre-treatment (the start of the day) and post-treatment (the end of the day), and follow-up data was collected three months later. The primary measure for the study was the Community Attitudes Toward Substance Abusers (CASA), an adapted version of the CAMI (Taylor & Dear, 1981), the Maslach Burnout Inventory (MBI) (Maslach, Jackson, & Leiter, 1996), and an ACT measure called "Stigmatizing Attitudes—Believability" (SAB) constructed for the study. The SAB contained twenty common thoughts about individuals with substance-use problems and asked subjects to rate the believability of such thoughts.

The control group received education on drugs which, among other things, emphasized the biological factors involved in addiction and treatment. The multicultural training condition contained information on culture, race, ethnicity, family structure, spirituality, and language—with the latter focusing on making subjects more aware of the stigmatizing effects of cultural bias. Similar to the above studies, the ACT condition explored the role of natural language processes within the counselor–client relationship.

The results suggest that in terms of stigma (as measured by the CASA), compared to pre-intervention the control condition did not produce a significant change at either post-treatment or follow-up. The multicultural intervention was found to produce a significant change at post-intervention but not at follow-up, and ACT showed no change at post-treatment but a significant improvement at follow-up. In terms of burnout, again the control condition showed no change at either time point. The multicultural intervention showed change at post-treatment but not at follow-up, while ACT produced a significant change at both post-treatment and follow-up. Regarding process, ACT altered the believability of stigmatizing thoughts (as measured by the SAB) and it was this that appeared to mediate the ACT condition's influence on stigma and burnout scores.

Taken together, these studies suggest a significant future role for both RFT and ACT in our understanding and amelioration of prejudice and its possible role in health care disparities. The research above does need to be placed in context and treated modestly. Some of the studies had relatively small sample sizes, all used measures constructed for the purposes of the study, and none contained direct measures of behavior (only self-report). That being said, the suggestion that useful changes can be achieved as a result of such brief interventions hints at the possible potency of such approaches. Researchers are clear that these studies should not be taken to suggest that multicultural and educational approaches should not be used; instead it might be more useful to combine them with ACT interventions in order that the ACT-related material might prevent the "psychological misuse" of the educational information (Hayes, Bissett, et al., 2004).

Widening the Scope

This chapter focuses its attention at the level of the health care professional; at the same time, the IOM and PHR reports discuss the need for awareness and changes at many levels (such as general public, patients, insurance companies, policy makers, and health care professionals). Each of these levels involves human beings subject to the same processes of language and thinking that have been described and investigated by RFT. All of us have similar potential to be caught in the prejudicial traps that are set by human language. Accordingly, wide-ranging benefits could be achieved from wide application of ACT-consistent methods designed to help individuals live alongside and not at the beck and call of their psychological experiences. Research in this area is just beginning, and much more is needed both to substantiate these initial findings and to fully investigate the potential scope of the methods described above.

This chapter deliberately focused its attention on bias and prejudice within U.S. health care toward racial and ethnic minorities. Indeed, within the United States, the term "health disparities" tends to have such a focus (Braveman, 2006). However, it is hopefully clear that this is not the only place where prejudice in health care can be found, nor the only place where the application of ACT and RFT might be useful. Bias, prejudice, and therefore potential disparity in one form or another are likely to be found wherever we are prepared to look, wherever the categorical qualities imposed on people dominate over their individual human qualities. In these instances, human beings can become objectified and dehumanized because of their participation in processes of normal, automatic, verbal evaluation.

Disparities have been documented in many other health areas. In chronic pain, for example, research used to suggest that apparent racial and ethnic minority differences in pain perception might reflect underlying differences in biology (Edwards, Fillingim, & Keefe, 2001), although research now increasingly reports that differences may be reduced or eliminated when subjects are matched more closely on different variables (Edwards, Moric, Husfeldt, Buvanendran, & Ivankovich, 2005; McCracken, Matthews, Tang, & Cuba, 2001). However, disparities in the treatment for chronic pain echo the story told repeatedly above (Bonham, 2001; Carey & Garrett, 2003), which is also echoed in mental health research (Cook, McGuire, & Miranda, 2007; McGuire et al., 2008; Zito, Safer, Zuckerman, Gardner, & Soeken, 2005). There are many areas of division and inequality, and researchers are now even examining the role of multiple disparities. Here individuals may have to contend with the combined impact of belonging to two or more powerful verbal evaluative categories, for example a racial and ethnic minority group and a lower socioeconomic class (Williams & Jackson, 2005; Chu, Miller, & Springfield, 2007), or categories related to "medically unexplained" chronic pain, those considered to be "somatizing" patients, and those regarded as "mentally ill."

Of course, racial and ethnic minorities are not the only area within which disparity has been investigated. Other domains include socioeconomic status (Braveman, 2006; Morenoff et al., 2007; Krupski, Kwan, Afifi, & Litwin, 2005), gender (Healy, 1991; Orth-Gomer, 2000), and multiple disparities, such as gender and disability (McCarthy et al., 2006). Indeed, the list of personal differences that can provide the basis for disparities is practically unending. Presenting illness, comorbid condition, race, ethnic origin, gender, age, weight, height, accent, religion, intelligence, job status, job title, social class, sexual orientation, mental health, emotional state, disability, perceived attractiveness, and dress are but a tiny selection of words that arbitrarily relate to other events or experiences that might, on occasion, come to influence our behavior toward others.

Braveman (2006) notes that pursuance of fair and equally accessible health care is not a matter of ethics but a matter of human rights and states that the "right to health can be operationalized as the right of all social groups...to attain the level of health enjoyed by the most privileged in society" (Braveman & Gruskin, 2003; Braveman, 2006, p. 184). Increasingly, researchers are looking not just within national boundaries but across national boundaries to explore the disparities and inequalities in health (Wallace, 2008).

Disparities in health care are rooted in multifaceted, complex historical causes. They are built into natural processes of language, categorization, and judgment. These processes are acting on your behavior now as you read this chapter. Addressing inequalities of service access and health is no less important than addressing effects of infection, heart disease, cancer, or other diseases, and yet the challenge may be greater in some ways. Our methods of detecting, understanding, and treating the root causes of health disparities are in their infancy. It appears, however, that there is a clear role for the use of RFT and ACT to help examine the innumerable accumulating individual choices, the actions and contexts that constitute disparities in health care, and to use this knowledge to help reduce inequalities in health care at local, national, and global levels.

References

Adorno, T. W. (1950). *The authoritarian personality.* New York: Harper.

Armstrong, K., Micco, E., Carney, A., Stopfer, J., & Putt, M. (2005). Racial differences in the use of BRCA1/2 testing among women with a family history of breast or ovarian cancer. *Journal of the American Medical Association, 293*(14), 1729–1736.

Aronson, E. (1980). *The social animal.* San Francisco: W. H. Freeman.

AskOxford. (n.d). Prejudice. Retrieved December 24, 2009, from http://www.askoxford.com/concise_oed/prejudice

Balint, E. (1969). The possibilities of patient-centered medicine. *Journal of the Royal College of General Practitioners, 17*(82), 269–276.

Beach, M. C., Price, E. G., Gary, T. L., Robinson, K. A., Gozu, A., Palacio, et al. (2005). Cultural competence: A systematic review of health care provider educational interventions. *Medical Care, 43*(4), 356–373.

Beach, M. C., Rosner, M., Cooper, L. A., Duggan, P. S., & Shatzer, J. (2007). Can patient-centered attitudes reduce racial and ethnic disparities in care? *Academic Medicine, 82*(2), 193–198.

Beach, M. C., Saha, S., & Cooper, L. A. (2006). *The role and relationship of cultural competence and patient-centeredness in health care quality.* New York: The Commonwealth Fund.

Bhandari, V. K., Wang. F., Bindman, A. B., & Schillinger, D. (2008). Quality of anticoagulation control: Do race and language matter? *Journal of Health Care for the Poor and Underserved, 19*(1), 41–55.

Black, R., Morris, S., & Bryce, J. (2003). Where and why are 10 million children dying every year? *Lancet, 361*(9376), 2226–2234.

Bond, F. W., & Hayes, S. C. (2002). Acceptance and commitment therapy at work. In F. W. Bond and W. Dryden (Eds.), *Handbook of brief cognitive behaviour therapy.* Chichester, UK: John Wiley & Sons.

Bonham, V. L. (2001). Race, ethnicity, and pain treatment: Striving to understand the causes and solutions to the disparities in pain treatment. *Journal of Law, Medicine & Ethics, 29*(1), 52–68.

Braveman, P. (2006). Health disparities and health equity: Concepts and measurement. *Annual Review of Public Health, 27,* 167–194.

Braveman, P., & Gruskin, S. (2003). Poverty, equity, human rights and health. *Bulletin of the World Health Organization, 81*(7), 539–545.

Burgess, D., van Ryn, M., Dovidio, J., & Saha, S. (2007). Reducing racial bias among health care providers: Lessons from social-cognitive psychology. *Journal of General Internal Medicine, 22*(6), 882–887.

Carey, T. S., & Garrett, J., M. (2003). The relation of race to outcomes and the use of health care services for acute low back pain. *Spine, 28*(4), 390–394.

Chu, K. C., Miller, B. A., & Springfield, S. A. (2007). Measures of racial/ ethnic health disparities in cancer mortality rates and the influence of socioeconomic status. *Journal of the National Medical Association, 99*(10), 1092–1104.

Cook, B. L., McGuire, T., & Miranda, J. (2007). Measuring trends in mental health care disparities, 2000–2004. *Psychiatric Services, 58*(12), 1533–1540.

Cooper, L. A., Beach, M. C., Johnson, R. L., & Inui, T. S. (2006). Delving below the surface. Understanding how race and ethnicity influence relationships in health care. *Journal of General Internal Medicine, 21*(Suppl. 1), 21–27.

Cooper, L. A., & Roter, D. L. (2002). Patient-provider communication: The effect of race and ethnicity on process and outcomes of healthcare. In B. D. Smedley, A. Y. Stith, & A. R. Nelson (Eds.), *Unequal treatment: Confronting racial and ethnic disparities in health care.* Washington, DC: National Academy of Sciences (Institute of Medicine).

Corrigan, P. W., River, L. P., Lundin, R. K., Penn, D. L., Uphoff-Wasowski, K., Campion, et al. (2001). Three strategies for changing attributions about severe mental illness. *Schizophrenia Bulletin, 27*(2), 187-95.

Corrigan, P. W., Watson, A. C., Warpinski, A. C., & Gracia, G. (2004). Stigmatizing attitudes about mental illness and allocation of resources to mental health services. *Community Mental Health Journal, 40*(4), 297–307.

Devine, P. G. (1989). Stereotypes and prejudice: Their automatic and controlled components. *Journal of Personality & Social Psychology, 56*(1), 5–18.

Dixon, M. R., Dymond, S., Rehfeldt, R. A., Roche, B., & Zlomke, K. R. (2003). Terrorism and relational frame theory. *Behavior and Social Issues, 12,* 129–147.

Dixon, M. R., Zlomke, K. R., & Rehfeldt, R. A. (2006). Restoring Americans' nonequivalent frames of terror: An application of relational frame theory. *Behavior Analyst Today, 7*(3), 275–289.

DuBois, W. E. B. (2003). The health and physique of the Negro American. 1906. *American Journal of Public Health, 93*(2), 272–276.

Edwards, C. L., Fillingim, R. B., & Keefe, F. (2001). Race, ethnicity and pain. *Pain, 94*(2), 133–177.

Edwards, R. R., Moric, M., Husfeldt, B., Buvanendran, A., & Ivankovich, O. (2005). Ethnic similarities and differences in the chronic pain experience: A comparison of African American, Hispanic, and White patients. *Pain Medicine, 6*(1), 88–98.

Eysenck, H. J. (1954). *The psychology of politics.* London: Routledge & Kegan Paul.

Goldberg, K. C., Hartz, A. J., Jacobsen, S. J., Krakauer, H., & Rimm, A. A. (1992). Racial and community factors influencing coronary artery bypass graft surgery rates for all 1986 Medicare patients. *Journal of the American Medical Association, 267*(11), 1473–1477.

Harmon, K., Strong, R., & Pasnak, R. (1982). Relational responding in tests of transposition with rhesus monkeys. *Learning and Motivation, 13,* 495–504.

Hayes, S. C., Barnes-Holmes, D., & Roche, B. (Eds.). (2001). *Relational frame theory: A post-Skinnerian account of human language and cognition.* New York: Kluwer Academic/Plenum Publishers.

Hayes, S. C., Bissett, R., Roget, N., Padilla, M., Kohlenberg, B. S., Fisher, G., et al. (2004). The impact of acceptance and commitment training and multicultural training on the stigmatizing attitudes and professional burnout of substance abuse counselors. *Behavior Therapy, 35,* 821–835.

Hayes, S. C., Fox, E., Gifford, E., Wilson, K. G., Barnes-Holmes, D., & Healy, O. (2002). Derived relational responding as learned behavior. In S. C. Hayes, D. Barnes-Holmes, & B. Roche (Eds.), *Relational frame theory: A post-Skinnerian account of human language and cognition.* New York: Kluwer Academic/Plenum Publishers.

Hayes, S. C., Luoma, J., Bond, F., Masuda, A., & Lillis, J. (2006). Acceptance and commitment therapy: Model, processes, and outcomes. *Behaviour Research and Therapy, 44*(1), 1–25.

Hayes, S. C., Niccolls, R., Masuda, A., & Rye, A. K. (2002). Prejudice, terrorism, and behavior therapy. *Cognitive and Behavioral Practice, 9,* 296–301.

Hayes, S. C., Strosahl, K. D., & Wilson, K. G. (1999). *Acceptance and commitment therapy: An experiential approach to behavior change.* New York: Guilford Press.

Hayes, S. C., Strosahl, K. D., Wilson, K. G., Bissett, R. T., Pistorello, J., Toarmino, D., et al. (2004). Measuring experiential avoidance: A preliminary test of a working model. *Psychological Record, 54,* 553–578.

Healy, B. (1991). The Yentl syndrome. *New England Journal of Medicine, 325* (4), 274–276.

Hernandez, A. F., Fonarow, G. C., Liang, L., Al-Khatib, S. M., Curtis, L. H., LaBresh, K. A., et al. (2007). Sex and racial differences in the use of implantable cardioverter-defibrillators among patients hospitalized with heart failure. *Journal of the American Medical Association, 298* (13), 1525–1532.

Hewstone, M., & Brown, R. (1986). Contact is not enough: An intergroup perspective on the contact hypothesis. In M. Hewstone & R. Brown (Eds.), *Contact and conflict in intergroup encounters,* Oxford: Blackwell.

Hewstone, M., Rubin, M., & Willis, H. (2002). Intergroup bias. *Annual Review of Psychology, 53,* 575–604.

Hoffman, F L. (1896). *Race traits and tendencies of the American negro.* New York: American Economic Association.

Jones, G., Steketee, R. W., Black, R. E., Bhutta, Z. A., & Morris, S. S. (2003). How many child deaths can we prevent this year? *Lancet, 362*(9377), 65–71.

Kasiske, B. L., London, W., & Ellison, M. D. (1998). Race and socioeconomic factors influencing early placement on the kidney transplant waiting list. *Journal of the American Society of Nephrology, 9*(11), 2142–2147.

Klonoff, E. A. (2009). Disparities in the provision of medical care: An outcome in search of an explanation. *Journal of Behavioral Medicine, 32*(1), 48–63.

Krupski, T. L., Kwan, L., Afifi, A. A., & Litwin, M. S. (2005). Geographic and socioeconomic variation in the treatment of prostate cancer. *Journal of Clinical Oncology, 23*(31), 7881–7888.

Langer, E., Bashner, R., & Chanowitz, B. (1985). Decreasing prejudice by increasing discrimination. *Journal of Personality and Social Psychology, 49*, 113–120.

Lillis, J., & Hayes, S. C. (2007). Applying acceptance, mindfulness, and values to the reduction of prejudice: A pilot study. *Behavior Modification, 31*(4), 389–411.

Luoma, J. B., Hayes, S. C., & Walser, R. D. (2007). *Learning ACT: An acceptance and commitment therapy skills-training manual for therapists.* Oakland, CA: New Harbinger Publications.

Macrae, C. N., & Bodenhausen, G. V. (2000). Social cognition: Thinking categorically about others. *Annual Review of Psychology, 51*, 93–120.

Macrae, C. N., Bodenhausen, G. V., Milne, A. B., & Jetten, J. (1994). Out of mind but back in sight: Stereotypes on the rebound. *Journal of Personality and Social Psychology, 67*, 808–817.

Macrae, C. N., Milne, A. B., & Bodenhausen, G. V. (1994). Stereotypes as energy-saving devices: A peek inside the cognitive toolbox. *Journal of Personality and Social Psychology, 66*, 37–47.

Mandelblatt, J. S., Kerner, J. F., Hadley, J., Hwang, Y. T., Eggert, L., Johnson, L. E., et al. (2002). Variations in breast carcinoma treatment in older Medicare beneficiaries: Is it black or white. *Cancer, 95*(7), 1401–1414.

Maslach, C., Jackson, S. E., & Leiter, M. P. (1996). *Maslach burnout inventory manual* (3rd ed.). Palo Alto, CA: Consulting Psychologists Press.

Masuda, A., Hayes, S. C., Fletcher, L. B., Seignourel, P. J., Bunting, K., Herbst, S. A., et al. (2007). Impact of acceptance and commitment therapy versus education on stigma toward people with psychological disorders. *Behaviour Research and Therapy, 45*(11), 2764–2772.

Mayberry, R. M., Mili, F., & Ofili, E. (2000). Racial and ethnic differences in access to medical care. *Medical Care Research and Review, 57*(Suppl. 1), 108–145.

McCarthy, E. P., Ngo, L. H., Roetzheim, R. G., Chirikos, T. N., Li, D., Drews, R. E., et al. (2006). Disparities in breast cancer treatment and survival for women with disabilities. *Annals of Internal Medicine, 145*(9), 637–645.

McCracken, L. M., Matthews, A. K., Tang, T. S., & Cuba, S. L. (2001). A comparison of blacks and whites seeking treatment for chronic pain. *Clinical Journal of Pain, 17*(3), 249–255.

McGuire, T. G., Ayanian, J. Z., Ford, D. E., Henke, R. E. M., Rost, K. M., & Zaslavsky, A. M. (2008). Testing for statistical discrimination by race/ethnicity in panel data for depression treatment in primary care. *Health Services Research, 43*(2), 531–551.

Mead, N., & Bower, P. (2000). Patient-centredness: A conceptual framework and review of the empirical literature. *Social Science & Medicine, 51*(7), 1087–1110.

Minard, R. D. (1952). Race relations in the Pocahontas coalfield. *Journal of Social Issues, 8*, 29–44.

Mitchell, J. B., Ballard, D. J., Matchar, D. B., Whisnant, J. P., & Samsa, G. P. (2000). Racial variation in treatment for transient ischemic attacks: Impact of participation by neurologists. *Health Services Research, 34*(7), 1413–1428.

Moore, R. D., Stanton, D., Gopalan, R., & Chaisson, R. E. (1994). Racial differences in the use of drug therapy for HIV disease in an urban community. *New England Journal of Medicine, 330*(11), 763–768.

Morenoff, J. D., House, J. S., Hansen, B. B., Williams, D. R., Kaplan, G. A., & Hunte, H. E. (2007). Understanding social disparities in hypertension prevalence, awareness, treatment, and control: The role of neighborhood context. *Social Science & Medicine, 65*(9), 1853–1866.

Myrdal, G. (1944). *An American dilemma. Vol 1.* New York: Harper and Brothers Publishers.

Oddone, E. Z., Horner, R. D., Sloane, R., McIntyre, L., Ward, A., Whittle, J., et al. (1999). Race, presenting signs and symptoms, use of carotid artery imaging, and appropriateness of carotid endarterectomy. *Stroke, 30*(7), 1350–1356.

Orth-Gomer, K. (2000). New light on the Yentl syndrome. *European Heart Journal, 21*(11), 874–875.

Peterson, E. D., Shaw, L. J., & Califf, R. M. (1997). Risk stratification after myocardial infarction. *Annals of Internal Medicine, 126*(7), 561–582.

Physicians for Human Rights. (2003). *The right to equal treatment: An action plan to end racial and ethnic disparities in clinical diagnosis and treatment in the United States.* Boston: Author.

Population Division of the Department of Economic and Social Affairs of the United Nations Secretariat. (2009). *World population prospects: The 2008 revision. Highlights.* New York: United Nations.

Ramnerö, J., & Törneke, N. (2008). *The ABCs of human behavior: Behavioral principles for the practicing clinician.* Oakland, CA: New Harbinger Publications.

Reid, A. E., Resnick, M., Chang, Y., Buerstatte, N., & Weissman, J. S. (2004). Disparity in use of orthotopic liver transplantation among blacks and whites. *Liver Transplantation, 10*(7), 834–841.

Roche, B., Barnes-Holmes, Y., Barnes-Holmes, D., & Stewart, I. (2002). Relational frame theory: A new paradigm for the analysis of social behavior. *Behavior Analyst, 25*(1), 75–91.

Rokeach, M. (1960). *The open and closed mind: Investigations into the nature of belief systems and personality systems.* New York: Basic Books.

Schulman, K. A., Berlin, J. A., Harless, W., Kerner, J. F., Sistrunk, S., Gersh, B. J., et al. (1999). The effect of race and sex on physicians' recommendations for cardiac catheterization. *New England Journal of Medicine, 340*(8), 618–626.

Shapiro, M. F., Morton, S. C., McCaffrey, D. F., Senterfitt, J. W., Fleishman, J. A., Perlman, J. F., et al. (1999). Variations in the care of HIV-infected adults in the United States: Results from the HIV cost and services utilization study. *Journal of the American Medical Association, 281*(24), 2305–2315.

Sherif, M. (1966). *Group conflict and co-operation: Their social psychology.* London: RKP.

Sherif, M., Harvey, O. J., White, B. J., Hood, W. R., & Sherif, C. W. (1961). *Intergroup cooperation and competition: The robbers cave experiment.* Norman, OK: University Book Exchange.

Sidman, M. (1971). Reading and auditory-visual equivalences. *Journal of Speech and Hearing Research, 14*, 5–13.

Skinner, J., Weinstein, J. N., Sporer, S. M., & Wennberg, J. E. (2003). Racial, ethnic, and geographic disparities in rates of knee arthroplasty among Medicare patients. *New England Journal of Medicine, 349*(14), 1350–1359.

Skinner, J., Zhou, W., & Weinstein, J. (2006). The influence of income and race on total knee arthroplasty in the United States. *Journal of Bone and Joint Surgery, 88*(10), 2159–2166.

Smedley, B. D., Stith, A. Y., & Nelson, A. R. (Eds.). (2002). *Unequal treatment: Confronting racial and ethnic disparities in health care.* Washington, DC: National Academy of Sciences (Institute of Medicine).

Sonel, A. F., Good, C. B., Mulgund, J., Roe, M. T., Gibler, W. B., Smith, S. C., Jr., et al. (2005). Racial variations in treatment and outcomes of black and white patients with high-risk non-ST-elevation acute coronary syndromes: Insights from CRUSADE. *Circulation, 111*(10), 1225–1232.

Stanley, A., DeLia, D., & Cantor, J. C. (2007). Racial disparity and technology diffusion: The case of cardioverter defibrillator implants, 1996–2001. *Journal of the National Medical Association, 99*(3), 201–207.

Stolzmann, K. L., Bautista, L. E., Gangnon, R. E., McElroy, J. A., Becker, B. N., & Remington, P. L. (2007). Trends in kidney transplantation rates and disparities. *Journal of the National Medical Association, 99*(8), 923–932.

Tajfel, H., Bilig, M. G., & Bundy, R. P. (1971). Social categorization and intergroup behaviour. *European Journal of Social Psychology, 1*(2), 149–178.

Taylor, S. M., & Dear, M. J. (1981). Scaling community attitudes toward the mentally ill. *Schizophrenia Bulletin, 7*(2), 225–240.

Taylor, A. J., Meyer, G. S., Morse, R. W., & Pearson, C. E. (1997). Can characteristics of a health care system mitigate ethnic bias in access to cardiovascular procedures? Experience from the Military Health Services System. *Journal of the American College of Cardiology, 30*(4), 901–907.

Thornton, J. A., & Wahl, O. F. (1996). Impact of a newspaper article on attitudes toward mental illness. *Journal of Community Psychology, 24,* 17–25.

Van Ryn, M., & Burke, J. (2000). The effect of patient race and socio-economic status on physicians' perceptions of patients. *Social Science & Medicine, 50*(6), 813–828.

Wahl, O. F., & Leftkowits, J. Y. (1989). Impact of a television film on attitudes toward mental illness. *American Journal of Community Psychology, 17,* 521–528.

Wallace, B. C. (Ed.). (2008). *Toward equity in health: A new global approach to health disparities.* New York: Springer.

Watt, A., Keenan, M., Barnes, D., & Cairns, E. (1991). Social categorization and stimulus equivalence. *Psychological Record, 41*(1), 33–50.

Weinstein, J. H., Wilson, K. G., & Kellum, K. K. (2008). A relational frame theory contribution to social categorization. *Behavior and Social Issues, 17,* 39–64.

Wenzlaff, R. M., & Wegner, D. M. (2000). Thought suppression. *Annual Review of Psychology, 51,* 59–91.

West, S., King, V., Carey, T. S., Lohr, K. N., McKoy, N., Sutton, S. F., et al. (2002). *Systems to rate the strength of scientific evidence.* Evidence report/technology assessment no. 47 (prepared by the Research Triangle Institute-University of North Carolina Evidence-based practice center under contract No. 290-97-0011). Rockville, MD: Agency for Healthcare Research and Quality.

Whitehead, M. (1990). *The concepts and principles of equity and health.* Copenhagen: World Health Organization.

Williams, D. R., & Jackson, P. B. (2005). Social sources of racial disparities in health. *Health Affairs, 24*(2), 325–334.

Wilson, K. G., Hayes, S. C., Gregg, J., & Zettle, R. D. (2002). Psychopathology and psychotherapy. In S. C. Hayes, D. Barnes-Holmes, & B. Roche (Eds.), *Relational frame theory: A post-Skinnerian account of human language and cognition.* New York: Kluwer Academic/Plenum Publishers.

World Health Organization. (2006). *The world health report 2006: Working together for health.* Geneva, Switzerland: World Health Organization Press.

You, D., Wardlaw, T., Salama, P., & Jones, G. (2010). Levels and trends in under-five mortality, 1990–2008. *Lancet, 375*(9709), 100–103.

Young, C. J., & Gaston, R. S. (2000). Renal transplantation in black Americans. *New England Journal of Medicine, 343*(21), 1545–1552.

Zito, J. M., Safer, D. J., Zuckerman, I. H., Gardner, J. F., & Soeken, K. (2005). Effect of Medicaid eligibility category on racial disparities in the use of psychotropic medications among youths. *Psychiatric Services, 56*(2), 157–163.

12 MINDFULNESS-BASED TRAINING FOR HEALTH CARE PROFESSIONALS

Nicole L. Kangas & Shauna L. Shapiro
School of Education and Counseling Psychology,
Santa Clara University

Intense demands faced by health care professionals are associated with increased stress and burnout, which in turn have negative consequences for clinicians' physical and mental health and the quality of care that is provided to patients. Accordingly, health care professionals must find ways to manage stress so they can increase their own well-being and deliver meaningful and empathetic patient care.

The literature emphasizes the importance of self-care for students, trainees, and professionals engaged in helping others (see Larson, 1993; Rothschild, 2006; Shapiro & Carlson, 2009), and increasingly, faculty in training programs are addressing self-care issues. Nonetheless, few training programs specifically integrate self-care in their curricula, and most health care professionals are left to their own devices and strategies to promote their personal care (Shapiro & Carlson, 2009). Consequently, compassion fatigue, vicarious traumatization, burnout, distress, and dissatisfaction remain problems for many clinicians.

Health care professionals need support in coping with the myriad of stressors they face at work. Training in mindfulness may be especially relevant for this purpose. Although researchers and clinicians initially focused on how mindfulness can benefit patients with physical or psychological conditions, there is now recognition that mindfulness is an effective means for health care professionals to reduce their own stress (Shapiro & Carlson, 2009).

In addition to helping health care professionals manage stress, mindfulness practice also cultivates specific professional skills and qualities essential to clinical work (Shapiro & Carlson, 2009). Clinicians can bring mindfulness into their practice in a variety of ways. They can engage personally in mindfulness practice to enhance their presence and attention during clinical work (referred to as the "mindful therapist"); they can use a theoretical orientation with their patients that is informed by mindfulness teachings ("mindfulness-informed therapy"); or they can explicitly teach their patients mindfulness skills ("mindfulness-based therapy") (Germer, Siegel, & Fulton, 2005; Shapiro & Carlson, 2009).

This chapter explicates how mindfulness can be utilized by health care professionals to improve their own health and to enhance patient care. The first part of the chapter examines mindfulness as a self-care technique. It begins by providing an overview of the stresses and health problems clinicians face. Drawing on existing literature, it details how mindfulness can be used to help minimize or reduce these problems. The second part of the chapter explores how mindfulness enhances the professional effectiveness of health care providers. Specifically, it details the integration of mindfulness into therapeutic work through therapist mindfulness, mindfulness-informed therapy, and mindfulness-based therapy, and it explains how each approach can benefit patients.

Mindfulness and Self-Care for Health Care Professionals

Being engaged in a helping profession often means encountering extensive stress and suffering. On a regular basis, health care professionals expend substantial energy, time, and resources trying to reduce other people's suffering. At the same time, they can fail to give themselves the same kind of care and attention. Putting their patients' welfare above their own can have negative consequences for clinicians, and ultimately for patients (Shapiro & Carlson, 2009).

Consequences of Clinician Stress

Health care professionals are vulnerable to adverse effects from exposure to their patients' negative emotions and experiences. Indeed, research indicates that, at some point in their careers, a substantial portion of health care providers will experience a decline in their professional performance that results in practice that is consistently below what is customary for them (Barnett & Cooper, 2009; Smith & Moss, 2009; Coster & Schwebel, 1997). Health care professionals are likely to suffer from a variety of problems, such as "compassion fatigue" (Figley, 2002; Weiss, 2004), "vicarious traumatization" (Trippany, Kress, & Wilcoxon, 2004; Baird & Kracen, 2006); "secondary traumatic stress" (Baird & Kracen, 2006); and "burnout" (Rosenberg & Pace, 2006; Taylor & Barling, 2004). Stress-related psychological problems are especially likely among health care providers working in demanding settings like hospitals and community agencies (Rosenberg & Pace, 2006; Vredenburgh, Carlozzi, & Stein, 1999) and among those working with populations that present special emotional challenges, such as patients who have experienced abuse (Cunningham, 2003) or trauma (Bride, 2007; Collins & Long, 2003) and those with personality disorders (Linehan, Cochran, Mar, Levensky, & Comtois, 2000).

There is evidence that the stress inherent in health care leads to increased depression, emotional exhaustion, and anxiety (Gilroy, Carroll, & Murra, 2001, 2002; Radeke & Mahoney, 2000; Tyssen, Vaglum, Gronvold, & Ekeberg, 2001). In Gilroy, Carroll, and Murra's (2002) study of 452 psychologists, for example, 62 percent reported experiencing depressive symptoms while working as clinicians. Similarly, in their 2001 study of female psychologists, 76 percent reported that they suffered from some form of depression, with the most frequent diagnosis being dysthymia (Gilroy et al., 2001).

Social distancing or isolation (Baranowski, 2006), decreased job satisfaction (Flanagan & Flanagan, 2002), disrupted personal relationships (Myers, 2001), loneliness (Lushington & Luscri, 2001), reduced self-esteem (Butler & Constantine, 2005), suicide (Pompili et al., 2006; Reimer, Trinkaus, & Jurkat, 2005), and increased substance abuse (Cicala, 2003) are also problems for health care professionals. In his summary report of substance abuse among physicians, for instance, Cicala (2003) reported that, while the exact rate of physician substance abuse is uncertain, even by the most conservative estimates between 8 and 12 percent of physicians (more than the population in general) will develop a substance-abuse problem at some point during their career (Brewster, 1986; Boisaubin & Levine, 2001). That is, at any given time, one out of every fourteen practicing physicians is an active substance abuser (Talbott, Gallegos, & Angres, 1998).

Research also shows a link between the stress that health care professionals endure and their physical health. Specifically, job stress has been associated with fatigue, insomnia, heart disease, obesity, hypertension, infection, carcinogenesis, diabetes, and premature aging (Melamed, Shirom, Toker, Berliner, & Shapira, 2006; Melamed, Shirom, Toker, & Shapira, 2006; Spickard, Gabbe, & Christensen, 2002).

It is important to note that the stresses associated with providing health care may also harm professional effectiveness. For example, stress decreases clinicians' attention and concentration (Braunstein-Bercovitz, 2003; Mackenzie, Smith, Hasher, Leach, & Behl, 2007; Skosnik, Chatterton, Swisher, & Park, 2000), weakens decision-making and communication skills (Shanafelt, Bradley, Wipf, & Back, 2002), decreases empathy (Beddoe & Murphy, 2004; Thomas et al., 2007), reduces patient trust in health care providers (Meier, Back, & Morrison, 2001), and reduces professionals' abilities to engage in meaningful patient relationships (Enochs & Etzbach, 2004). These problems are not rare or unusual: up to 60 percent of psychologists report that they have practiced when they were distressed to the point of ineffectiveness (Pope, Tabachnik, & Keith-Spiegel, 1987), and three-quarters of social workers report burnout at some point in their career (Siebert, 2005). Taken together, this research suggests that, if health care professionals do not care for themselves, they risk their own health and well-being as well as their patients'.

Mindfulness Practice as a Means of Self-Care

Existing literature posits that the cultivation of mindfulness can enhance mental and physical health (see Baer, 2003, and Grossman, Niemann, Schmidt, & Walach, 2004, for reviews). Most mindfulness research has focused on patient benefits. Recently, however, researchers have begun exploring mindfulness for other populations. They have found that mindfulness training may be particularly useful for health care professionals and trainees as a means of managing stress and promoting self-care (see Irving, Dobkin, & Park, 2009, for a review of empirical studies. See also Krasner et al., 2009, for a recent study of mindfulness among primary care physicians).

What Is Mindfulness?

Mindfulness can be defined as the "awareness that arises through intentionally attending in an open, kind, and discerning way" (Shapiro & Carlson, 2009, p. 15). Thus, mindfulness can be defined as both the awareness (mindful awareness) and the practice (mindful practice). Mindful awareness is a way of being that allows us to be deeply aware of what is happening in the present and to experience life as it arises and passes in each moment. This awareness involves freedom from striving and wanting things to be different than they are, and it entails relating to all experiences in an open and receptive way, resting in the natural presence that is already here (Shapiro & Carlson, 2009).

Mindfulness practices involve formal exercises that focus on the specific and purposeful training of attention with openness, acceptance, and curiosity. Without mindfulness training, people spend much of their time engaged in "mindlessness." That is, rather than being present in the moment, they get caught up in distracting thoughts or opinions about what is happening, what happened in the past, or what might happen in the future. Mindful practice enables individuals to cultivate mindful awareness, helping one to develop the capacity to dwell in this place of natural presence more often. In mindful meditation, practitioners allow a state of "fluid attention" to emerge, rather than focusing on any specific object or sensation (Irving et al., 2009). Cognitions are observed and accepted as they are, without being judged or manipulated. The most well-known form of mindfulness meditation training is Mindfulness-Based Stress Reduction (MBSR), a psychoeducational program developed by Jon Kabat-Zinn and colleagues at the University of Massachusetts Medical Center. MBSR and other mindful practices are discussed in more detail in the section on mindfulness-based psychotherapy below.

Why Is Mindfulness Practice Especially Useful for Health Care Professionals?

Although there are a number of self-care and stress-reduction techniques that could benefit health care professionals, mindfulness practice is particularly useful for this purpose. Mindfulness offers the dual benefit of teaching practitioners how to manage their own stress as well as teaching them basic and essential qualities necessary to be an effective clinician (Shapiro & Carlson, 2009). Research demonstrates that mindfulness training significantly increases the capacity to cope with stress and increases one's sense of well-being (Newsome, Christopher, Dahlen, & Christopher, 2006; Shapiro, Astin, Bishop, & Cordova, 2005). Further, mindfulness practice is associated with qualities that are critical to effective therapy, such as attention, empathy, emotion regulation, and affect tolerance. When we become comfortable with our psyches, we become better able to explore our patients' inner worlds (Shapiro & Carlson, 2009). We see that emotions and cognitions are impermanent experiences that can be seen as they arise and depart. We develop a capacity to be with our experience, with a caring acceptance. In this way, we cultivate the ability to be with and know another's experience (Shapiro & Carlson, 2009).

Mindfulness practice helps clinicians develop an attitude of nonstriving and acceptance. Many health care professionals become singularly focused on "fixing" patients, which can prevent clinicians from remaining attuned to their patients in the present. Mindfulness teaches clinicians how to be with their patient in the moment, without striving toward an end goal, and it enables them to accept things as they are, at that particular time and place (Shapiro & Carlson, 2009). This helps them to focus their energy and decreases the stress associated with always trying to change or remedy things for the patient.

Mindfulness also teaches self-compassion, allowing health care professionals to accept themselves as imperfect, or "perfectly human" (Shapiro & Carlson, 2009, p. 111). It is important for health care professionals to recognize that, despite their best intentions, things will sometimes go wrong. Instead of becoming self-critical and condemning in these situations, clinicians can use mindfulness to treat themselves with the same care and compassion they want to bring to their patients. As Germer (2009) explains in his book on mindfulness and self-compassion, "the more openhearted we are with ourselves, the closer we feel toward the rest of life" and the more empathy we feel for others (p. 87). This idea is supported by research, which shows that therapists who lack self-compassion are more critical and controlling of their patients and have poorer therapeutic outcomes (Henry, Schacht, & Strupp, 1990).

A final reason mindfulness can be particularly helpful for health care professionals is that it can be applied to all types of life situations, not only during duress. In other words, in addition to helping health care professionals through stressful times, mindfulness also allows them to be more aware and present for joyful, positive moments, both in their own lives (see, e.g., Roy, 2007) and in the lives of their patients (Shapiro & Carlson, 2009).

Review of Research

A growing body of existing research supports the usefulness of mindfulness training for health care professionals. Numerous studies have investigated the impact of mindfulness training on students or trainees in the medical and nursing fields. For instance, Shapiro, Schwartz, and Bonner (1998) investigated the effects of an eight-week MBSR program, which met two hours per week, on symptoms of anxiety, depression, empathy, and spiritual experience among seventy-eight medical and premedical students. Results of this randomized, wait-list controlled study revealed decreased anxiety and depression and increased empathy and spirituality in the MBSR group compared to the wait-list control group. These findings continued through a stressful final examination period and were replicated when the wait-list control group received the MBSR intervention.

Several additional recent studies build on this research. Specifically, Jain and colleagues (2007), in a controlled trial of premedical students, determined that students receiving an MBSR intervention experienced increases in positive mood states and significant decreases in rumination and stress, compared with a control group. Notably, effect sizes for the MBSR group were moderate to large in mood state increases, whereas the effect size for the control group was virtually zero. Furthermore, the rumination effect size was moderate for the MBSR group and small to moderate in the opposite direction for the control group. In other words, for the controls, rumination actually increased over time.

Similarly, Rosenzweig, Reibel, Greeson, Brainard, and Hojat (2003) found that medical students who participated in an MBSR course experienced significant decreases in mood disturbance and distress compared with a control group. Particularly, mean scores on the Total Mood Disturbance Scale (TMD) decreased 18 percent in overall psychological distress for the MBSR group and increased 38 percent for the control group during the ten-week observation period.

Within nursing, Young, Bruce, Turner, and Linden (2001) found significant decreases in self-reported psychological symptoms in third-year nursing students who received MBSR training compared to a control group, and Beddoe and Murphy (2004) found significant improvements in empathy, stress, and anxiety measures among undergraduate nursing students who received MBSR training in a pre-post study. In the later study, 75 percent of participants reported greater self-confidence after the training, 88 percent indicated that they were more hopeful, 69 percent reported that they were better able to express their feelings and needs, 63 percent reported changes in their relationships to thoughts and feelings and their reactions to them, and 88 percent reported that they knew how to take better care of themselves and that they were actually doing it.

Researchers have also examined the effects of MBSR on therapists in training. Shapiro, Brown, and Biegel (2007), for example, examined the effects of MBSR on graduate counseling psychology students. Their study compared students in an MBSR course to matched-cohort control participants enrolled in didactic courses. Students in the MBSR course showed significant pre-post decreases in perceived stress, negative affect, rumination, and state and trait anxiety and significant increases in positive affect and self-compassion. Christopher, Christopher, Dunnagan, and Schure (2006) conducted a qualitative study of the impact of mindfulness meditation practice upon counseling psychology students' self-care practices. The study found student improvement in interpersonal functioning and coping with stress. Participants also reported that the program enhanced their clinical training.

Research on the effects of MBSR has also been extended to professionals engaged in clinical work. For example, Shapiro and colleagues (2005) explored how health care workers were affected by an eight-week MBSR intervention at a Department of Veterans Affairs Hospital. From their prospective controlled study, they determined that the intervention reduced stress and increased quality of life and self-compassion among health care professionals. Particularly, they found that 88 percent of participants in the MBSR group improved their stress scores, while 90 percent increased in terms of self-compassion. Compared to controls, MBSR participants reported higher life satisfaction (19 percent vs. 0 percent), decreased stress (23 percent vs. 11 percent), and decreased job burnout (10 percent vs. 4 percent). Using a pre-post study of employees from a university hospital, including those involved in direct patient care, Galantino, Baime, Maguire, Szapary, and Farrar (2005) also found decreases in emotional exhaustion and improvements in mood after employees completed an eight-week MBSR program.

A number of studies of practicing nurses support these findings. Specifically, Mackenzie, Poulin, and Seidman-Carlson (2006) found decreases in symptoms of burnout and increased relaxation and life satisfaction among nurses and nursing aides, compared to wait-listed control participants, after they participated in a shortened four-week MBSR program. Despite a small sample ($N = 16$), effect sizes were large, indicating that the intervention had a powerful effect on participants. Numerous other studies support the benefits of providing nurses with MBSR training. For instance, nurses in an MBSR program reported significant improvements in aspects of burnout (personal accomplishment and emotional exhaustion) compared with the wait-listed control group (Cohen-Katz, Wiley, Capuano, Baker, & Shapiro, 2004, 2005; Cohen-Katz, Wiley, Capuano, Baker, Deitrick, et al., 2005). These results were maintained up to three months after the intervention (Cohen-Katz, Wiley, Capuano, Baker, & Shapiro, 2005; Cohen-Katz, Wiley, Capuano, Baker, Deitrick, et al., 2005). Qualitative results revealed that nurses found the program useful for promoting relaxation and self-care and for improving relationships at work and home (Cohen-Katz, Wiley, Capuano, Baker, & Shapiro, 2005; Cohen-Katz, Wiley, Capuano, Baker, Deitrick, et al, 2005). The nurses identified increases in feelings of self-acceptance and self-compassion, self-awareness, and self-reliance. They also reported that their relationships were enhanced via improved communication, increased presence and empathy, and decreased reactivity.

A recent study of the association between a mindfulness educational program and burnout, empathy, and attitudes among primary care doctors (Krasner et al., 2009) highlights the usefulness of mindfulness training for practicing physicians. In this pre-post study, seventy primary care doctors participated in an intensive eight-week mindfulness course and a ten-month maintenance phase (2.5 hours per month). Participation was associated with medium-sized improvements in burnout, depersonalization, empathy, total mood disturbance, consciousness, and emotional stability. It was also associated with improvements in attitudes toward patient-centered care. In combination, the body of research cited above makes a strong case for teaching mindfulness to health care professionals, and those in training, as a means of promoting self-care. Below we move to discussion of how mindfulness can be incorporated into therapy to enhance professional effectiveness and patient outcomes.

Incorporating Mindfulness in Therapy to Enhance Professional Effectiveness and Patient Outcomes

In addition to improving patient care through professional self-care, health care professionals can use mindfulness practice to benefit patients in numerous other ways. Germer and colleagues (2005) distinguish three ways of integrating mindfulness into therapeutic work to increase professional effectiveness. First, by practicing mindfulness meditation in their own lives, health care professionals can learn to cultivate mindful presence with their patients. Second, practitioners can utilize a theoretical frame of reference informed by theories and research about mindfulness to enhance care. Third, they can explicitly teach patients mindfulness skills and practices to enhance the patients' mindfulness.

In their recent book on integrating mindfulness into psychology and the helping professions, Shapiro and Carlson (2009) elaborate on Germer and colleagues' (2005) conceptualization of the three pathways for integrating mindfulness into psychotherapy, referred to as (1) the mindful therapist, (2) mindfulness-informed therapy, and (3) mindfulness-based therapy.

The Mindful Therapist

Existing research suggests that a number of "common factors"— such as the therapist–client relationship—account for a significant portion of therapy outcomes (Weinberger, 2002). The therapeutic relationship, in fact, has been shown to be the strongest predictor of therapeutic outcomes across all types of therapeutic intervention; within this category empathy, unconditional positive regard, and congruence between therapist and client have proven especially beneficial (Bohart, Elliott, Greenberg, & Watson, 2002). Given that mindfulness promotes these same qualities, it is not surprising that mindfulness is now receiving attention as a common factor for successful therapy, regardless of therapists' theoretical orientation (Martin, 1997; Germer, Siegel, & Fulton, 2005; Shapiro & Carlson,

2009), and that meditation training is recommended to help clinicians learn skills to enhance the therapeutic alliance (Anderson, 2005; Shapiro & Izette, 2008).

Simply put, the idea is that, by practicing mindfulness in their own lives, clinicians can become "mindful therapists," thereby enhancing the therapeutic relationship and improving therapy outcomes. Two recent research studies by Grepmair and his colleagues support this relationship (Grepmair, Mitterlehner, Loew, Bachler, et al., 2007; Grepmair, Mitterlehner, Loew, & Nickel, 2007). In the first study, the researchers conducted a nonrandomized sequential cohort pilot study comparing the outcomes of 196 patients treated by therapists-in-training, some of whom were practicing Zen meditation. They determined that patients of trainees who were practicing meditation reported better understanding of their own internal processes, difficulties, and goals. They also reported better progress overcoming their problems and symptoms and developing new adaptive behaviors to use in their daily lives.

In Grepmair and colleagues' second study, they used a tighter randomized control design. Specifically, 18 therapists-in-training were randomly assigned either to learn Zen meditation or to a control group, which lacked such training. One hundred and twenty-four patients with various mood and anxiety disorders were randomly assigned the therapists for individual and group therapy sessions. Patients did not know which therapists were meditating. They rated the quality of each individual therapy session and their overall well-being pre- and post-treatment course. Notably, patients treated by meditating therapists rated the therapeutic processes of "clarification" and "problem solving" higher and reported that they better understood the structure and characteristics of their problems and the potential and goals for their development. They also described greater improvements in symptoms of anxiety, depression, hostility, somatization, and obsessions and compulsions.

Shapiro and Carlson (2009) postulate that mindfulness training can help practitioners across theoretical orientations develop particular qualities that enhance the therapeutic relationship. Particularly, mindfulness can strengthen clinicians' attentional capacity and presence; the attitudes they apply during therapy; their ability to be self-compassionate and self-attuned; their empathy and attunement toward the patient; and their ability to regulate their emotions and handle countertransference.

PRACTITIONER ATTENTION AND PRESENCE

According to Germer and colleagues (2005), mindful practice is "like a firm handshake with one object at a time in the field of experience. Mindfulness neither squeezes the object nor is casual in its grip, but the object is distinctly perceived" (Germer, Siegel, & Fulton, 2005, p. 14).

It is widely accepted among therapists from diverse theoretical orientations that successful psychotherapy requires that therapists pay attention and sustain attention during therapy sessions. While the capacity to be mindfully present is inherent in all therapists, systematic practice may be required to hone this skill. Existing research reveals that mindful presence and attention develop through formal mindfulness meditation practice.

For example, researchers found greater cortical thickness in areas of the brain associated with sustained attention and awareness in practitioners experienced in mindful meditation, compared to non-meditating participants (Lazar et al., 2005). Moreover, by measuring response times on the Attention Network Test (ANT) after eight weeks of mindfulness meditation training for novices, and a month-long retreat for more experienced meditators, Jha, Krompinger, and Baime (2007) found improvements in overall attention. Specifically, those who participated in the eight-week training were more able to direct focused attention when required, and those who attended the one-month retreat showed an increased ability to retain their focus when faced with distractions. Similarly, in a qualitative study of mindfulness training with counseling graduate students, students reported being more attentive and aware in therapy sessions, and feeling more comfortable with silence during sessions, after they completed mindfulness training (Schure, Christopher, & Christopher, 2008).

Research has also shown that mindfulness meditation can enhance control over how attention is distributed. For example, if too much attention is focused on one stimulus, another stimulus might be missed. Mindfulness training can help distribute attention so that the second stimulus is not ignored (see, e.g., Slagter et al., 2007). This is particularly important when clinicians need to deal with subtle and rapid patient information.

PRACTITIONER ATTITUDES

While paying attention is essential, *how* practitioners pay attention is also critical to patient outcomes. Attention can be cold and hard, with a clinical emphasis that can hinder the therapeutic relationship. This is contrasted with the attitudes of acceptance, letting go, nonattachment, nonstriving, nonjudging, patience, trust, warmth, friendliness, and kindness, which characterize mindfulness practice (Kabat-Zinn, 1990; Shapiro & Schwartz, 2000; Segal, Williams, & Teasdale, 2002). While these attitudes are not exhaustive, they underscore the type of attention that is likely to enhance the therapeutic alliance. These attitudes allow patients to feel safe and cared for, to pace themselves, and to disclose thoughts and experiences that may be shameful or deeply troubling.

Preliminary evidence supports a relationship between the attitudes cultivated through mindfulness and enhanced therapeutic encounters. Brown and Ryan (2003), for example, found that increased mindfulness is associated with "greater openness to experience," a measure of general personality characteristics measured on the NEO-Five Factor Index. Similarly, Thompson and Waltz (2007) found that higher trait mindfulness was related to less neuroticism and more agreeableness and consciousness on the same measure. As Shapiro and Carlson (2009) point out, these qualities of openness should cultivate unconditional positive regard and a stronger therapeutic relationship, though there are no existing studies that explore these relationships.

SELF-COMPASSION AND ATTUNEMENT

Compassion, which is a cornerstone of effective therapy, is also enhanced through mindfulness. Compassion incorporates both the ability to empathize with the suffering of oneself or others and the desire to act upon this empathy to reduce the suffering.

Attunement is a precursor to compassion, as it involves being in touch with the inner experience of oneself (self-attunement) or another. Being self-attuned entails developing a "witness consciousness," which observes the content of one's experience from a distance and accepts it without judgment or interpretation, as something that simply is. When clinicians find themselves being self-critical, they can practice observing the thoughts without labeling them as truth or reacting to them.

Mindfulness practice is one way health care professionals can strengthen their self-attunement and self-compassion. Indeed, a central tenet of mindfulness practice is to learn to let go of self-judgment and to relate to oneself with compassion and kindness. Through mindfulness meditation, we begin to see that our personal suffering is not unique but part of the universality of being human (Shapiro & Carlson, 2009).

One mindfulness meditation that can be particularly helpful in cultivating self-compassion is the loving-kindness meditation (see Kornfield, 2008; Shapiro & Carlson, 2009). This meditation asks participants to repeat four or five phrases of well-wishing, like "May I be peaceful and happy. May I be healthy." While reciting these phrases, participants are asked to feel the quality of loving-kindness in the body and heart. After many repetitions, love for oneself is established. The loving-kindness practice is then extended to others (family, friends, neutral people, and eventually difficult people).

Research supports the relationship between mindfulness and increased self-compassion. For instance, Shapiro and colleagues (2005) conducted a randomized controlled study of health care professionals working in a Veterans Hospital. They found significant increases in self-compassion among health care professionals after the professionals engaged in mindfulness training, compared to pre-training. Similarly, a study of counseling psychology graduate students revealed that MBSR resulted in significant improvements in self-compassion pre- to post-intervention, compared to a matched control group (Shapiro et al., 2007). Notably, improvements in mindfulness directly mediated changes in self-compassion following the intervention. As noted above, therapist self-acceptance is particularly important, as research shows that therapists who are the most critical of themselves are also the most hostile, controlling, and critical toward their patients (Henry et al., 1990). Thus, practitioner self-acceptance is critical to engaging clients in supportive and accepting relationships.

Empathy and Attunement with Others

Empathy, or the ability to "sense the [patient's] private world as if it were your own, but without losing the 'as if' quality" has been considered essential for effective therapy (Rogers, 1957, p. 95; Arkowitz, 2002; Bohart et al., 2002). Research suggests that meditation can significantly enhance clinician empathy. Lesh (1970), for instance, determined that counseling psychology students showed significantly more empathy after a Zen meditation intervention, compared to a wait-list control group. Empathy was measured by students' ability to accurately determine emotions expressed by a videotaped patient. Similarly, a randomized controlled trial by Shapiro and colleagues (1998) found increased empathy in pre-medical and medical students after an eight-week MBSR intervention, compared to the wait-list control group. More recent research on counseling psychology graduate students determined that eight weeks of MBSR training significantly increased empathic concern for others pre- to post-intervention (Shapiro et al., 2007). Further, increases in mindfulness correlated with increases in empathy, suggesting that students may have increased their empathetic concern for others because they became more mindful.

Results from a qualitative study of counseling psychology graduate students support these quantitative findings (Schure et al., 2008). After receiving mindfulness training, students reported feeling more empathic toward patients' suffering. For example, one student reported, "I think that this results in me being able to be more present, and being able to have more empathy for experiences they share with me."

Research from neurobiology has revealed the existence of what are called mirror neurons, or neurons that mirror the behavior of another, as though the observer were acting. One day it may be demonstrated that these neurons provide the basis for empathy and related processes within mindfulness. This line of research started with direct observation of primates (Di Pellegrino, Fadiga, Fogassi,

Gallese, & Rizzolatti, 1992; Rizzolatti, Fadiga, Gallese, & Fogassi, 1996; Rizzolatti & Criaghero, 2004). Subsequently, researchers showed brain activity consistent with mirror neurons in the anterior insula, anterior cingulate cortex, and inferior parietal cortex of humans (Botvinivk et al., 2005; Cheng, Yang, Lin, Lee, & Decety, 2008).

Although research on mirror neurons in humans is less well established, and the functional significance of mirror neurons in human emotion is still being contested (see, e.g., Lingnau, Gesierich, & Caramazza, 2009), a large number of experiments using functional MRI, electroencephalography, and magnetoencephalography have determined that particular brain regions are active when a person experiences an emotion *and* when he or she sees another person experiencing the emotion (Botvinivk et. al., 2005; Cheng et al., 2008; Morrison, Lloyd, Di Pellegrino, & Roberts, 2004; Wicker et al., 2003; Singer et al., 2004; Lamm, Batson, & Decety, 2007). Jabbi, Swart, and Keysers (2006) have also demonstrated that individuals who are more empathic based on self-report questionnaires have stronger activations in the mirror system for emotions, providing additional support for the idea that mirror neurons are associated with empathy.

Mirror neurons often fire at less intense levels in the observer than in the initial communicator of the emotion (Goleman, 2006). Mindful awareness may play a role here in enhancing one's receptivity even to small signals, thereby increasing attunement between two people. Daniel Siegel refers to this type of attunement as the "heart of therapeutic change" (Siegel, 2007).

EMOTIONAL REGULATION

Positive therapeutic relationships require that health care professionals know how to regulate their emotions and know when to avoid expressing their own emotions to patients. Strong emotions can often arise during therapy sessions. By attending to and regulating their own emotional reactions, practitioners can be more present and accepting of patients across a range of emotionally charged therapy scenarios, thereby enhancing the patient–professional relationship.

Recently, researchers have focused considerable attention on how mindfulness practice can benefit patients with emotion regulation disorders, such as those with borderline personality disorder and major depression (Linehan, 1993a, 1993b; Segal et al., 2002). While less attention has been paid to clinicians' emotional regulation, researchers are beginning to emphasize the importance of mindfulness training to help practitioners tolerate and hold emotions and to prevent emotional reactivity to what the patient presents (McCartney, 2004; Shapiro & Carlson, 2009). Because mindfulness training helps health care professionals become familiar with their minds and bodies, they are able to see their personal responses to a patient's behavior and regulate their emotions, which could otherwise hamper their relationships with patients.

Mindfulness-Informed Therapy

Mindfulness-informed therapy refers to integrating mindfulness into psychotherapy without teaching patients formal meditation practice (Germer, Siegle, & Fulton, 2005). It offers a framework for integrating wisdom and insights from Buddhist literature, the psychological mindfulness literature, and one's own mindfulness practice into psychotherapy. To date, there are no explicit instructions for how to develop a mindfulness-informed health care practice, nor is there research explicating the relationship between mindfulness-informed care and clinical outcomes for patients. Shapiro and Carlson (2009) and others, however, provide examples of how insights and teachings of mindfulness can be incorporated into clinical practice to enhance the therapeutic relationship. The ideas presented here are not comprehensive but are intended to introduce a few of the themes that clinicians might draw on as part of a mindfulness-informed approach.

IMPERMANENCE

Impermanence, or the reality of constant change, is central to Buddhism. As Bien (2006) explains, it is inevitable that we all have to face impermanence. The real question is whether we will come to terms with it. When we resist reality, our suffering increases. Thus, helping patients to accept impermanence can have important clinical implications. Clinicians can do this by presenting examples of impermanence and using language that highlights the ever-changing nature of human experience. They can invite patients to investigate the changing nature of their own lives and experiences and to focus on changing thoughts, emotions, and sensations (Shapiro & Carlson, 2009).

> Ed, a prominent businessman, was struggling with gastrointestinal problems. Sometimes he experienced abdominal bloating and nausea; other times he had constipation alternating with diarrhea. Ed underwent several medical evaluations, which failed to identify a disease or structural cause for his problems. Ed was persistently concerned that his symptoms would surface at inopportune or embarrassing times, and he carefully monitored what he ate, hoping to discover a correlation between what he ate and his symptoms. Ed became fixated on finding a cure for his condition. In therapy, Ed learned to mindfully observe his anxious thoughts about his symptoms and to embrace a nonrejecting attitude toward his condition. Without trying to correct his symptoms, Ed worked on "being with" his emotions, thoughts, and symptoms. Eventually, Ed came to see that his search for a cure was futile and had kept him preoccupied with his gastrointestinal system. In time, Ed let his symptoms come and go as they would, and he was able to begin to eat normally again. Importantly, he learned that his extreme desire for control was the root of his suffering. (adapted from Germer, Siegel, & Fulton, 2005)

No Self

Buddhist psychology also emphasizes impermanence of the self. This does not mean that people are not real, but rather that there is a sense in which they are constantly changing. Given the focus in much of the modern world on individualism, many people have difficulty with this idea. As Bien explains (2006), we typically think of ourselves as individual entities that move through time and space accumulating experiences but remaining fundamentally the same.

In reality, however, there is nothing solid for people to hold on to that they can call the self. One's body, feelings, thoughts, and perceptions are all flowing and changing moment to moment. While at first hard to grasp, the idea of "no self" is liberating because it allows us to see that we are larger than any of our transient experiences. Emotions are just emotions; thoughts are just thoughts. They are not "us." In therapy, clinicians can help patients recognize these ideas by talking about emotions and thoughts as ephemeral, "like guests who visit and then leave" (Goodman & Greenland, 2008, p. 422).

> During therapy, Richard was having a difficult time rewriting his personal narrative. Disturbing images of his partner and her former boyfriend continued to haunt him, and he was experiencing painful emotions associated with his partner's betrayal. Richard's therapist, together with meditation, helped Richard understand that these reactions existed outside of the reality of the present moment—bodily sensations, the colors in nature, the smell and taste of food. Richard came to see that the images and emotions he was struggling with were simply thoughts and fantasies, not the "final word" on him or his life. (adapted from Germer, Siegel & Fulton, 2005)

ACCEPTANCE

Acceptance refers to a way of receiving experiences without judgment or preference, with kindness and curiosity. Buddhist teachings on acceptance suggest that suffering arises when people desire things to be different than they are. Simply put, when people resist rather than accept things, they suffer.

It is important to note that acceptance is a skill that can be cultivated. Practitioners can encourage patients to "relax into" or "soften into" an experience of acceptance (Germer et al., 2005). Goldstein (1993) proposes using mantras such as "Let it be," or "It's okay, just let me feel this" (pp. 39–40). Regardless of specific verbiage, it is important that practitioners help patients embrace their range of emotions. People often want to push away negative thoughts and emotions. Mindfulness teaches us to acknowledge and attend to our pain so that we can respond consciously, with wisdom and clarity.

Juan had been a gang member since he was twelve years old, and he had learned not to trust anyone. When another gang member tried to kill him, Juan started having panic attacks. Consequently, he entered therapy, telling his psychologist that he wanted the panic attacks to stop, but he did not want to talk about his anxiety. Using a mindful approach, the psychologist taught Juan to respond effectively by seeing problems clearly. She asked Juan if a group of guys was coming at him from behind, would he prefer to be ambushed or to turn to face them and see their weapons. Juan said he would want to see them. The psychologist explained that the same was true of the panic attacks—he could either be ambushed or understand clearly what is actually happening. The first step was to acknowledge and accept what was happening in the moment it was happening. Although Juan's therapy focused on cognitive-behavioral treatment for anxiety, using a mindful approach to accepting what was present helped Juan to open up and cooperate in therapy. (adapted from Shapiro & Carlson, 2009)

Conscious Responding

A central teaching of Buddhism is that suffering arises from habitual ways of reacting. Modern neuroscience tells us that our past reactions are engraved onto synapses that send messages to one another, making the same reactions likely in the future. If we pay attention, we can see how often our experiences are followed by automatic reactions. Mindfulness gives us an option to choose a healthier response. When we are able to see clearly, an appropriate response is more likely to arise.

In therapy, Jeremy explained that whenever he saw his former friend, Zach, who betrayed him in a business deal, he felt angry, sad, worried, and unhappy. Just seeing Zach brought up the memory of the betrayal, causing his body and mind to automatically contract in pain. Jeremy and his therapist explored the concept of reactivity, and Jeremy learned to become mindful of his reactions to Zach. Eventually, Jeremy would stop and respond differently when he saw Zach. As he felt the pain, he would look deeper inside himself. Although there was hurt, Jeremy had taken the steps needed to protect himself from further loss. There was no new problem and the worries in his mind were seen as the result of past conflict. Over time, Jeremy learned how to acknowledge the betrayal without dwelling in an unhappy state. Instead of anger he was able to experience peace and relief. (adapted from Kornfield, 2008)

INTERDEPENDENCE

A central Buddhist tenet is that all things are connected or interdependent. That means our happiness or unhappiness affects others, and their happiness or unhappiness affects us. This is why a one-hour therapy session with a profoundly depressed person can leave a clinician feeling drained. Indeed, we are not as separate as we generally think.

When people live their lives as though they are separate from others, confusion, despair, conflict, and loneliness can result (Shapiro & Carlson, 2009). This is true on a global level as well. For example, a country might adopt friendly relationships with particular oil-rich nations and consequently enjoy a cheap energy supply. Their being on friendly terms with such regimes, however, may seem threatening to others. These others may react with fear or hatred, and some may choose to direct a campaign of criticism, aggression, or terrorist tactics against them (Bien, 2006). Simply put, the global community, and the individuals who compose it, are interdependent.

During therapy, practitioners explore with their patients how things unfold in a mutually dependent web of complex interconnections. Patients' thoughts, ideas, and behaviors have consequences that inform future moments. As patients begin to uncover small examples of interconnectedness in their own lives, they will come to appreciate how everything in the universe is mutually interdependent, which will generate feelings of responsibility and connectedness to all beings.

Jane was having marital problems and felt isolated and disconnected from her husband. In therapy, Jane learned about interdependence and the idea that her husband might also feel alone and isolated, and that he wanted to be happy, just as she did. Jane committed to offering greater kindness and affection to her husband, without expecting anything back. Jane openheartedly carried through on her intention most days and at the end of the week, her husband brought home a bouquet of flowers and a card on which he wrote, "I love you." He hadn't done anything like that in years. Jane realized that her actions and intentions, however small, had an effect. By showing greater love and kindness to her husband, she was able to alter the entire system. (adapted from Shapiro & Carlson, 2009)

Mindfulness-Based Therapy

"Mindfulness-based therapy" refers to therapies in which mindfulness meditation practices are explicitly taught as a central treatment plan component. In recent decades, traditional mindfulness practices have been incorporated into numerous well-researched, empirically supported treatment approaches. These include mindfulness-based stress reduction (MBSR; Kabat-Zinn, 1990), mindfulness-based cognitive therapy (MBCT; Segal et al., 2002), dialectical behavior therapy (DBT; Linehan, 1993a, 1993b), and acceptance and commitment therapy (ACT; Hayes, 2005; Hayes, Strosahl, & Wilson, 1999). (See Baer, 2006, for a guide to evidence base and applications of numerous mindfulness-based treatment approaches.)

As previously noted, MBSR is the most widely used mindfulness-based therapy. It entails a highly experiential eight-week program of up to thirty-five participants who meet weekly for 2.5 to 3 hours. There is also a 6-hour silent meditation retreat between classes six and seven. Through MBSR, participants are taught a variety of meditation practices, including body scan, sitting meditation, walking meditation, gentle yoga, loving-kindness meditation, and informal daily mindfulness practice. (For details, see Kabat-Zinn, 1990, and Shapiro & Carlson, 2009.) These practices are used during classes, and participants are required to practice meditation and gentle yoga at home for forty-five minutes, six days per week. Mindfulness attitudes of nonjudging, patience, acceptance, beginner's mind, nonstriving, letting go, nonattachment, and trust are modeled and applied throughout the training program.

A multitude of controlled studies highlight the efficacy of MBSR with clinical populations for conditions such as chronic pain and illness, including cancer, and psychiatric disorders, such as depression and generalized anxiety (Kaplan, Goldenberg, & Galvin, 1993; Williams, Teasdale, Segal, & Soulsby, 2000; Randolph, Caldera, Tacone, & Greak, 1999; Goldenberg et al., 1994; Kabat-Zinn et al., 1998; Speca, Carlson, Goodey, & Angen, 2000; Carlson, Ursuliak, Goodey, Angen, & Speca, 2004). Numerous studies are also investigating the impact of mindfulness-based therapies for healthy populations and those wishing to minimize stress and enhance well-being. These studies reveal an association between MBSR and increases in immune function, cognition, and attention, and decreases in stress (Chiesa & Serretti, 2009; Irving et al., 2009; see also Shapiro & Carlson, 2009.)

MBCT was developed by John Teasdale, Mark Williams, and Zindel Segal, who are experts on treating depression using cognitive behavioral therapy (CBT; Segal et al., 2002). This formal therapy, which integrates CBT and MBSR, is particularly important for helping recovered depressed people avoid relapse. It emphasizes the notion that thoughts are not truth or reality, but passing "mind-moments" that will arise and pass if not elaborated upon.

The therapy is conducted over eight weeks, with a group of up to twelve participants. Like MBSR, MBCT includes the body scan, sitting meditation, walking meditation, and informal daily mindfulness practices. It does not, however, include loving-kindness meditation, and it focuses more on understanding depression than on the stress response, as in MBSR. It also includes a "three-minute breathing space" technique as well as other elements of cognitive therapy. (See Segal et al., 2002, and Shapiro & Carlson, 2009, for more detailed discussions of these techniques.)

Two randomized clinical trials provide strong empirical support for the efficacy of MBCT for the treatment of depression relapse (Teasdale et al., 2000; Ma & Teasdale, 2004). Smaller research studies have also shown MBCT's effectiveness in treating people with bipolar disorder and unipolar major depressive disorder (MDD; Williams et al., 2008) and generalized anxiety disorder (Evans et al., 2008). Other diverse MBCT applications are appearing as abstracts, dissertations, or case reports.

In addition to MBCT, a range of other therapies modeled after MBSR are also gaining traction in the behavioral health fields. These therapies have just begun developing an evidence base for their effectiveness. (For a review of existing research on these therapies, see Shapiro & Carlson, 2009.)

One such therapy is Mindfulness-Based Eating Awareness Training (Kristeller, Baer, & Quillian-Wolever, 2006), which integrates MBSR and CBT elements with guided eating meditations to help people with binge-eating disorder and obesity. Similarly, Mindfulness-Based Relapse Prevention (Marlatt & Gordon, 1985; Marlatt & Witkiewitz, 2005) is patterned after MBCT and integrates mindfulness with principles from a well-established risk-avoidance therapy for substance-abuse relapse prevention. Mindfulness-Based Relationship Enhancement (MBRE; Carson, Carson, Gil, & Baucom, 2006) was developed to enhance the relationships of relatively well-functioning couples. Similar to MBSR in terms of format and techniques, MBRE has modified several elements into dyadic exercises for couples. Finally, Mindfulness-Based Art Therapy (Monti et al., 2005) has been developed for use in medical populations and was piloted in women with breast cancer. By combining art and creativity with traditional MBSR elements, this approach aims to increase the supportive and expressive treatment aspects. Many other mindfulness-based therapies are emerging that have not yet been tested empirically. Future studies will be needed to assess the effectiveness of these approaches.

In addition to the mindfulness-based therapies, dialectical behavioral therapy (DBT; Linehan, 1993a, 1993b) and acceptance and commitment therapy (ACT; Hayes, 2005; Hayes et al., 1999) apply mindfulness to therapies with different theoretical roots. These therapies use shorter, less formal, and more focused mindfulness exercises, compared to the therapies discussed above, and they include an explicit emphasis on change-based strategies. Moreover, ACT is typically done individually and DBT includes both individual and group components.

Despite these differences from other mindfulness-based therapies, DBT and ACT incorporate key mindfulness components. Specifically, DBT, which is focused on the balance of opposing ideas like emotion and reason, utilizes mindfulness skills to help patients develop this balance. DBT includes a specific "mindfulness module" that introduces an array of mindfulness skills. The other three DBT modules are also influenced by the core mindfulness practices and are intimately connected with the mindfulness module.

ACT, like MBCT, posits that processes emerging from language lead patients to engage in futile attempts to control their inner lives. Mindfulness exercises are one way patients learn to contact and identify thoughts and feelings they have feared and avoided. The idea is that by exposing patients to feared inner experiences through mindfulness practices, patients will learn to accept these inner events, one of the core therapeutic processes of ACT.

Summary

Mindfulness has a variety of useful applications for health care providers, including personal care, professional effectiveness, and specific therapeutic interventions. This chapter considered the integration of mindfulness into health care in terms of (1) the mindful therapist; (2) mindfulness-informed therapy; and (3) mindfulness-based therapy. It also explored the topic of mindfulness as a means of self-care for the health professional. Finally, it offered pioneering models that could be used to integrate mindfulness into training programs for practitioners. There are a number of important future directions and research paths that warrant attention in each of these areas.

Regarding the mindful therapist, research is needed to investigate the extent to which mindfulness can be used to help health professionals develop core clinical skills. Research is also needed to determine the relationship between provider mindfulness and clinical outcomes. As noted above, preliminary research suggests that mindful therapists have increased empathy and attention, which are important in the clinical context. We also know from Grepmair and colleagues' studies that mindful therapists may have improved patient outcomes. However, rigorous scientific studies on how health professionals' mindfulness skills affect patients' perceptions of treatment or their symptomatology are sparse. Toward that end, we need research across a broad range of measures including patient self-report, behavioral observation, and clinician rating scales (Grepmair, Mitterlehner, Loew, Bachler, et al., 2007; Grepmair, Mitterlehner, Loew, & Nickel, 2007). Also important is research investigating the mechanisms through which these effects occur.

Mindfulness-informed therapy has not been tested empirically. Thus, apart from the accounts of individual clinicians who incorporate mindfulness into their practices, we know little about how mindfulness-informed therapy benefits patients. Studies that investigate the outcomes associated with incorporating different mindfulness techniques in the therapeutic setting are needed, as is more literature about how treatment providers can integrate different ideas and teachings from Buddhism and other psychological literature on mindfulness into clinical practice.

Future research on mindfulness-based approaches will require evaluation of all newly introduced therapies, as well as adding to the existing research on the effectiveness of mindfulness-based therapies for a variety of populations, including healthy ones. Moreover, studies of different types of clinical training and the impact of clinicians' self-meditation practices will be important as the debate over provider qualifications for mindfulness-based treatments continues.

Finally, we know that self-care is critical for health professionals, both for protecting practitioners' own health and well-being and for optimizing outcomes for patients. Accordingly, it is important to expand existing research on how mindfulness affects health care professionals' mental and physical health. A more systematic approach to self-care and mindfulness training in educational programs, and in continuing education programs for professionals, is also needed. This includes directing attention toward the integration of mindfulness training into education curricula (Shapiro & Carlson, 2009).

The potential applications of mindfulness for health care professionals are far reaching. We are hopeful that continued research and exploration in this area will benefit both health care professionals who work under stressful and difficult conditions and their patients who are searching for greater health and happiness in their own lives.

References

Anderson, D. T. (2005). Empathy, psychotherapy integration, and meditation: A Buddhist contribution to the common factors movement. *Journal of Humanistic Psychology, 45,* 483–502.

Arkowitz, H. (2002). Toward an integrative perspective on resistance to change. *Psychotherapy in Practice, 58,* 219–227.

Baer, R. A. (2003). Mindfulness training as clinical intervention: A conceptual and empirical review. *Clinical Psychology: Science and Practice, 10,* 125–143.

Baer, R. A. (Ed.). (2006). *Mindfulness-based treatment approaches: Clinician's guide to evidence base and applications.* San Diego: Elsevier.

Baird, K., & Kracen, A. (2006). Vicarious traumatization and secondary traumatic stress: A research synthesis. *Counseling Psychology Quarterly, 19,* 181–188.

Baranowski, K. P. (2006, March). Stress in pediatric palliative and hospice care: causes, effects, and coping strategies. NHPCO (National Hospice and Palliative Care Organization). Children's Project on Palliative/Hospice Services (CHIPPS). CHIPPS Newsletter.

Barnett, J. E., & Cooper, N. (2009). Creating a culture of self-care. *Clinical Psychology: Science and Practice, 16,* 16–20.

Beddoe, A. E., & Murphy, S. O. (2004). Does mindfulness decrease stress and foster empathy among nursing students? *Journal of Nursing Education, 43,* 305–312.

Bien, T. (2006). *Mindful therapy: Guide for therapists and helping professionals.* Boston: Wisdom Publications.

Bohart, A. C., Elliott, R., Greenberg, L. S., & Watson, J. C. (2002). Empathy. In J. C. Norcross (Ed.), *Psychotherapy relationships that work: Therapist contributions and responsiveness to patients* (pp. 89–108). New York: Oxford University Press.

Boisaubin, E. V., & Levine, R. E. (2001). Identifying and assisting the impaired physician. *American Journal of the Medical Sciences, 322,* 31–36.

Botvinivk, M., Jha, A. P., Bylsma, L. M., Fabian, S. A., Solomon, P. E., & Prkachin, K. M. (2005). Viewing the facial expressions of pain engages cortical areas involved in the direct experience of pain. *NeuroImage*, 25, 312–319.

Braunstein-Bercovitz, H. (2003). Does stress enhance or impair selective attention? The effects of stress and perceptual load on negative priming. *Anxiety, Stress and Coping, 16*, 345–357.

Brewster, J. (1986). Prevalence of alcohol and other drug problems among physicians. *Journal of the American Medical Association, 255*, 1913–1920.

Bride, B. E. (2007). Prevalence of secondary traumatic stress among social workers. *Social Work, 52*, 63–70.

Brown, K., & Ryan, R. (2003). The benefits of being present. Mindfulness and its role in psychological well-being. *Journal of Personality and Social Psychology, 84*, 822–848.

Butler, S. K., & Constantine, M. G. (2005). Collective self-esteem and burnout in professional school counselors. *Professional School Counseling, 9*, 55–62.

Carlson, L. E., Ursuliak, Z., Goodey, E., Angen, M., & Speca, M. (2004). The effects of a mindfulness meditation-based stress reduction program on mood and symptoms of stress in cancer outpatients: Six-month follow-up. *Supportive Care in Cancer, 9*, 112–123.

Carson, J. W., Carson, K. M., Gil, K. M., & Baucom, D. H. (2006). Mindfulness-based relationship enhancement. *Behavior Therapy, 35*, 471–494.

Cheng, Y., Yang, C. Y., Lin, C. P., Lee, P. R., & Decety, J. (2008). The perception of pain in others suppresses somatosensory oscillations: a magnetoencephalography study. *NeuroImage, 40*, 1833–1840.

Chiesa, A., & Serretti, A. (2009). Mindfulness-based stress reduction for stress management in healthy people: A review and meta-analysis. *Journal of Alternative and Complementary Medicine, 15*, 593–600.

Christopher, J. C., Christopher, S. E., Dunnagan, T., & Schure, M. (2006). Teaching self-care through mindfulness practices: the application of yoga, meditation, qigong to counselor training. *Journal of Humanistic Psychology, 46*, 494–509.

Cicala, R. S. (2003). Substance abuse among physicians: What you need to know. *Hospital Physician, 39*, 39–46.

Cohen-Katz, J., Wiley, S., Capuano, T., Baker, D. M., Deitrick, L., & Shapiro, S. (2005). The effects of mindfulness-based stress reduction on nurse stress and burnout: A qualitative and quantitative study, part III. *Holistic Nursing Practice, 19,* 78–86.

Cohen-Katz, J., Wiley, S., Capuano, T., Baker, D. M., & Shapiro, S. (2004). The effects of mindfulness-based stress reduction on nurse stress and burnout: A qualitative and quantitative study. *Holistic Nursing Practice, 18,* 302–308.

Collins, S., & Long, A. (2003). Working with the psychological effects of trauma: Consequences for mental health-care workers: A literature review. *Journal of Psychiatric and Mental Health Nursing, 10,* 417–424.

Coster, J. S., & Schwebel, M. (1997). Well-functioning in professional psychologists. *Professional Psychology: Research and Practice, 28,* 5–13.

Cunningham, M. (2003). Impact of trauma work on social work clinicians: Empirical findings. *Social Work, 48,* 451–459.

Di Pellegrino, G., Fadiga, L., Fogassi, L., Gallese, V., & Rizzolatti, G. (1992). Understanding motor events: a neurophysical study. *Experimental Brain Research, 91,* 176–180.

Enochs, W. K., & Etzbach, C. A. (2004). Impaired student counselors: Ethical and legal considerations for the family. *Family Journal, 12,* 396–400.

Evans, S., Ferrando, S., Fidler, M., Stowell, C., Smart, C., & Haglin, D. (2008). Mindfulness-based cognitive therapy for generalized anxiety disorder. *Journal of Anxiety Disorders, 22,* 716–721.

Figley, C. R. (2002). Compassion fatigue: Psychotherapists' chronic lack of self-care. *Journal of Clinical Psychology, 58*(11, Suppl. 1), 1433–1441.

Flanagan, N. A., & Flanagan, T. J. (2002). An analysis of the relationship between job satisfaction and job stress in correctional nurses. *Research in Nursing and Health, 25,* 282–294.

Galantino, M. L., Baime, M., Maguire, M. Szapary, P. O., & Farrar, J. T. (2005). Short-communication: Association of psychological and physiological measures of stress in health-care professionals during an eight-week mindfulness meditation program: Mindfulness in practice. *Stress and Health, 21,* 255–261.

Germer, C. K. (2009). *The mindful path to self-compassion: Freeing yourself from destructive thoughts and emotions.* New York: Guilford Press.

Germer, C. K., Siegel, R. D., & Fulton, P. R. (Eds.). (2005). *Mindfulness and psychotherapy.* New York: Guilford Press.

Gilroy, P. J., Carroll, L., & Murra, J. (2001). Does depression affect clinical practice? A survey of women psychotherapists. *Women & Therapy, 23*(4), 13–30.

Gilroy, P. J., Carroll, L., & Murra, J. (2002). A preliminary survey of counseling psychologists' personal experiences with depression and treatment. *Professional Psychology: Research and Practice, 33*, 402–407.

Goldenberg, D. L., Kaplan, K. H., Nadeau, M. G., Brodeur, C., Smith, S., & Schmid, H. C. (1994). A controlled study of a stress-reduction, cognitive-behavioral treatment program in fibromyalgia. *Journal of Musculoskeletal Pain, 2*, 53–66.

Goldstein, J. (1993). *Insight meditation: The practice of freedom.* Boston: Shambhala.

Goleman, D. (2006). *Emotional intelligence: Why it can matter more than IQ* (10th ed.). New York: Bantam Books.

Goodman, T. A., & Greenland, S. K. (2008). Mindfulness with children: Working with difficult emotions. In F. Didonna (Ed.), *Clinical handbook of mindfulness* (pp. 417–430). New York: Springer.

Grepmair, L., Mitterlehner, F., Loew, T., Bachler, E., Rother, W., & Nickel, M. (2007). Promoting mindfulness in psychotherapists in training influences the treatment results of their patients: A randomized, double-blind, controlled study. *Psychotherapy and Psychosomatics, 76*, 332–338.

Grepmair, L., Mitterlehner, F., Loew, T., & Nickel, M. (2007). Promotion of mindfulness in psychotherapists in training: Preliminary study. *European Psychiatry, 22*, 485–489.

Grossman, P., Niemann, L., Schmidt, S., & Walach, H. (2004). Mindfulness-based stress reduction and health benefits. A meta-analysis. *Journal of Psychosomatic Research, 57*, 35–43.

Hayes, S. C. (2005, July). Training. Retrieved February 10, 2009, from Association for Contextual Behavioral Science website: http://www.contextualpsychology.org/act_training

Hayes, S. C., Strosahl, K., & Wilson, K. G. (1999). *Acceptance and commitment therapy: An experiential approach to behavior change.* New York: Guilford Press.

Henry, W. P., Schacht, T. E., & Strupp, H. H. (1990). Patient and therapist introject, interpersonal process, and differential psychotherapy outcome. *Journal of Consulting and Clinical Psychology, 58,* 768–774.

Irving, J. A., Dobkin, P. L., & Park, J. (2009). Cultivating mindfulness in health care professionals: A review of empirical studies of mindfulness-based stress reduction. *Complementary Therapies in Clinical Practice, 15,* 61–66.

Jabbi, M., Swart, M., & Keysers, C. (2006). Empathy for positive and negative emotions in the gustatory cortex. *NeuroImage, 34,* 1744–1753.

Jain, S., Shapiro, S. L., Swanick, S., Roesch, S. C., Mills, P. J., Bell, et al. (2007). A randomized controlled trial of mindfulness meditation versus relaxation training: Effects on distress, positive states of mind, rumination, and distraction. *Annals of Behavioral Medicine, 33,* 11–21.

Jha, A. P., Krompinger, J., & Baime, M. J. (2007). Mindfulness training modifies subsystems of attention. *Cognitive, Affective and Behavioral Neuroscience, 7,* 109–119.

Kabat-Zinn, J. (1990). *Full catastrophe living: Using the wisdom of your body and mind to face stress, pain and illness.* New York: Delacorte.

Kabat-Zinn, J., Wheeler, E., Light, T., Skillings, A., Scharf, M. S., Cropley, T. G., et al. (1998). Influence of a mindfulness meditation-based stress reduction intervention on rates of skin clearing in patients with moderate to severe psoriasis undergoing phototherapy (UVB) and photochemotherapy (PUVA). *Psychosomatic Medicine, 60,* 625–632.

Kaplan, K. H., Goldenberg, D. L., & Galvin, N. M. (1993). The impact of a meditation-based stress reduction program on fibromyalgia. *General Hospital Psychiatry, 15,* 284–289.

Kornfield, J. (2008). *The wise heart: A guide to the universal teachings of Buddhist psychology.* New York: Bantam Books.

Krasner, M. S., Epstein, R. M., Beckman, H., Suchman, A. L., Chapman, B., Mooney, C. J., et al. (2009). Association of an educational program in mindful communication with burnout, empathy, and attitudes among primary care physicians. *Journal of the American Medical Association, 302,* 1284–1293.

Kristeller, J. L., Baer, R. A., & Quillian-Wolever, R. (2006). Mindfulness-based approaches to eating disorders. In R. A. Baer (Ed.), *Mindfulness-based treatment approaches: Clinician's guide to evidence base and applications* (pp. 75–91). London: Academic Press.

Lamm, C., Batson, C. D., & Decety, J. (2007). The neural substrate of human empathy: Effects of perspective-taking and cognitive appraisal. *Journal of Cognitive Neuroscience, 19,* 42–58.

Larson, D. G. (1993). *The helper's journey.* Champaign, IL: Research Press.

Lazar, S. W., Kerr, C. E., Wasserman, R. H., Gray, J. R., Greve, D. N., Treadway, M. T., et al. (2005). Meditation experience is associated with increased cortical thickness. *Neuroreport, 16,* 1893–1897.

Lesh, T. V. (1970). Zen meditation and the development of empathy in counselors. *Journal of Humanistic Psychology, 10,* 39–74.

Lingnau, A., Gesierich, B., & Caramazza, A. (2009). Asymmetric fMRI adaptation reveals no evidence for mirror neurons in humans. *Proceedings of the National Academy of Sciences, 106,* 9925–9930.

Linehan, M. M. (1993a). *Cognitive-behavioral treatment of borderline personality disorder.* New York: Guilford Press.

Linehan, M. M. (1993b). *Skills training manual for treating borderline personality disorder.* New York: Guilford Press.

Linehan, M. M., Cochran, B. N., Mar, C. M., Levensky, E. R., & Comtois, K. A. (2000). Therapeutic burnout among borderline personality disordered clients and their therapists: Development and evaluation of two adaptations of the Maslach Burnout Inventory. *Cognitive and Behavioral Practice, 7,* 329–337.

Lushington, K., & Luscri, G. (2001). Are counseling students stressed? A cross-cultural comparison of burnout in Australian, Singaporean and Hong Kong counseling students. *Asian Journal of Counseling, 8,* 209–232.

Ma, S. H., & Teasdale, J. D. (2004). Mindfulness-based cognitive therapy for depression: Replication and exploration of differential relapse prevention effects. *Journal of Consulting and Clinical Psychology, 72,* 31–40.

Mackenzie, C. S., Poulin, P. A., & Seidman-Carlson, R. (2006). A brief mindfulness-based stress reduction intervention for nurses and nurse aides. *Applied Nursing Research, 19,* 105–109.

Mackenzie, C. S., Smith, M. C., Hasher, L. Leach, L., & Behl, P. (2007). Cognitive functioning under stress: Evidence from informal caregivers of palliative patients. *Journal of Palliative Medicine, 10,* 749–758.

Marlatt, G. A., & Gordon, J. R. (Eds.). (1985). *Relapse prevention: maintenance strategies in the treatment of addictive behaviors.* New York: Guilford Press.

Marlatt, G. A., & Witkiewitz, K. (2005). Relapse prevention for alcohol and drug problems. In G. A. Marlatt & D. M. Donovan (Eds.), *Relapse prevention* (pp. 1–44). New York: Guilford Press.

Martin, J. R. (1997). Mindfulness: A proposed common factor. *Journal of Psychotherapy Integration, 7,* 291–312.

McCartney, L. (2004). *Counsellors' perspectives on how mindfulness meditation influences counsellor presence within the therapeutic relationship.* Unpublished master's thesis, University of Victoria, British Columbia, Canada.

Meier, D. E., Back, A., & Morrison, S. (2001). The inner life of physicians and the care of the seriously ill. *Journal of the American Medical Association, 286,* 3007–3014.

Melamed, S., Shirom, A., Toker, S., Berliner, S., & Shapira, I. (2006). Burnout and risk of cardiovascular disease: Evidence, possible causal paths, and promising research directions. *Psychological Bulletin, 32,* 327–353.

Melamed, S., Shirom, A., Toker, S., & Shapira, I. (2006). Burnout and risk of type 2 diabetes: A prospective study of apparently healthy employed persons. *Psychosomatic Medicine, 68,* 863–869.

Monti, D. A., Peterson, C., Kunkel, E. J., Hauck, W. W., Pequignot, E., Rhodes, L., et al. (2005). A randomized, controlled trial of mindfulness-based art therapy (MBAT) for women with cancer. *Psycho-Oncology, 15,* 363–373.

Morrison, I., Lloyd, D., Di Pellegrino, G., & Roberts, N. (2004). Vicarious responses to pain in anterior cingulate cortex: Is empathy a multisensory issue? *Cognitive and Affective Behavioral Neuroscience, 4,* 270–278.

Myers, M. F. (2001). The well-being of physician relationships. *Western Journal of Medicine, 174*, 30–33.

Newsome, S., Christopher, J. C., Dahlen, P., & Christopher, S. (2006). Teaching counselors self-care through mindfulness practices. *Teachers College Record, 108*, 1881–1900.

Pompili, M., Rinaldi, G., Lester, D., Girardi, P. Ruberto, A., & Tatarelli, R. (2006). Hopelessness and suicide risk emerge in psychiatric nurses suffering from burnout and using specific defense mechanisms. *Archives of Psychiatric Nursing, 20*, 135–143.

Pope, K. S., Tabachnik, B. G., & Keith-Spiegel, P. (1987). Ethics of practice: The beliefs and behaviors of psychologists as therapists. *American Psychologist, 42*, 993–1006.

Radeke, J. T., & Mahoney, M. J. (2000). Comparing the personal lives of psychotherapists and research psychologists. *Professional Psychology: Research and Practice, 31*, 82–84.

Randolph, P. D., Caldera, Y. M., Tacone, A. M., & Greak, M. L. (1999). The long-term combined effects of medical treatment and a mindfulness-based behavioral program for the multidisciplinary management of chronic pain in West Texas. *Pain Digest, 9*, 103–112.

Reimer, C., Trinkaus, S., & Jurkat, H. B. (2005). Suicidal tendencies of physicians—an overview. *Psychiatric Praxis, 32*, 381–385.

Rizzolatti, G., & Criaghero, L. (2004). The mirror-neuron system. *Annual Review of Neuroscience, 27*, 169–192.

Rizzolatti, G., Fadiga, L., Gallese, V., & Fogassi, L. (1996). Premotor cortex and the recognition of motor actions. *Cognitive Brain Research, 3*, 131–141.

Rogers, C. R. (1957). The necessary and sufficient conditions of therapeutic personality change. *Journal of Consulting Psychology, 21*, 95–103.

Rosenberg, T., & Pace, M. (2006). Burnout among mental health professionals: Special considerations for the marriage and family therapist. *Journal of Marital and Family Therapy, 32*, 87–99.

Rosenzweig, S., Reibel, D. K., Greeson, J. M. Brainard, G. C., & Hojat, M. (2003). Mindfulness-based stress reduction lowers psychological distress in medical students. *Teaching and Learning in Medicine, 15*, 88–92.

Rothschild, B. (2006). *Help for the helper: Self-care strategies for managing burnout and stress.* New York: W. W. Norton & Company.

Roy, D. (2007). *MOMfulness: Mothering with mindfulness, compassion, and grace.* San Francisco: Jossey-Bass.

Schure, M. B., Christopher, J., & Christopher, S. (2008). Mind-body medicine and the art of self-care: Teaching mindfulness to counseling students through yoga, meditation, and qigong. *Journal of Counseling & Development, 86,* 47–56.

Segal, Z. V., Williams, M. G., & Teasdale, J. D. (2002). *Mindfulness-based cognitive therapy for depression: A new approach to preventing relapse.* New York: Guilford Press.

Shanafelt, T. D., Bradley, K. A., Wipf, J. E., & Back, A. L. (2002). Burnout and self-reported patient care in an internal medicine residency program. *Annals of Internal Medicine, 136,* 358–367.

Shapiro, S. L., Astin, J. A., Bishop, S. R., & Cordova, M. (2005). Mindfulness-based stress reduction for health care professionals: Results from a randomized trial. *International Journal of Stress Management, 12,* 164–176.

Shapiro, S. L., Brown, K. W., & Biegel, G. M. (2007). Teaching self-care to caregivers: Effects of mindfulness-based stress reduction on the mental health of therapists in training. *Training and Education in Professional Psychology, 1,* 105–115.

Shapiro, S. L., & Carlson, L. E. (2009). *The art and science of mindfulness: Integrating mindfulness into psychology and the helping professions.* Washington, DC: American Psychological Association.

Shapiro, S. L., & Izette, C. (2008). Meditation: A universal tool for cultivating empathy. In D. Hick & T. Bien (Eds.), *Mindfulness and the therapeutic relationship* (pp. 161–175). New York: Guilford Press.

Shapiro, S. L., & Schwartz, G. E. (2000). Intentional systemic mindfulness: An integrative model for self-regulation and health. *Advances in Mind-Body Medicine, 16,* 128–134.

Shapiro, S. L., Schwartz, G. E., & Bonner, G. (1998). Effects of mindfulness-based stress reduction on medical and pre-medical students. *Journal of Behavioral Medicine, 21,* 581–599.

Siebert, D. C. (2005). Personal and occupational factors in burnout among practicing social workers: Implications for researchers, practitioners, and managers. *Journal of Social Service Research, 32*, 25–44.

Siegel, D. (2007). *The mindful brain: Reflection and attunement in the cultivation of well-being.* New York: Norton.

Singer, T., Seymour, B., O'Doherty, J., Kaube, H., Dolan, R. J., & Frith, C. D. (2004). Empathy for pain involves the affective but not sensory components of pain. *Science, 303*, 1157–1162.

Skosnik, P. D., Chatterton, R. T., Swisher, T., & Park, S. (2000). Modulation of attentional inhibition by norepinephrine and cortisol after psychological stress. *International Journal of Psychophysiology, 36*, 59–68.

Slagter, H. A., Lutz, A., Greischar, L. L., Francis, A. D., Nieuwenhuis, S., Davis, J. M., et al. (2007). Mental training affects distribution of limited brain resources. *PLoS Biology, 5*, e138.

Smith, P. L., & Moss, S. B. (2009). Psychologist impairment: What is it, how can it be prevented, and what can be done to address it? *Clinical Psychology: Science and Practice, 16*, 1–15.

Speca, M. Carlson, L. E., Goodey, E., & Angen, M. (2000). A randomized, wait-list controlled clinical trial: The effect of a mindfulness meditation-based stress reduction program on mood and symptoms in cancer outpatients. *Psychosomatic Medicine, 62*, 613–622.

Spickard, A., Gabbe, S. G., & Christensen, J. F. (2002). Mid-career burnout in generalist and specialist physicians. *Journal of the American Medical Association, 288*, 1447–1450.

Talbott, G. D., Gallegos, K. V., & Angres, D. H. (1998). Impairment and recovery in physicians and other health professionals. In A. W. Graham & T. K. Schultz (Eds.), *Principles of addiction medicine* (2nd ed., pp. 1263–1279). Chevy Chase, MD: American Society of Addiction Medicine.

Taylor, B., & Barling, J. (2004). Identifying sources and effects of career fatigue and burnout for mental health nurses: A qualitative approach. *International Journal of Mental Health Nursing, 13*, 117–125.

Teasdale, J. D., Segal, Z. V., Williams, J. M., Ridgeway, V. A., Soulsby, J. M., & Lau, M. A. (2000). Prevention of relapse/recurrence in major depression by mindfulness-based cognitive therapy. *Journal of Consulting and Clinical Psychology, 68*, 615–623.

Thomas, M. R., Dyrbye, L. N., Huntington, J. L., Lawson, K. L., Novotny, P. J., Sloan, J. A., et al. (2007). How do distress and well-being relate to medical student empathy? A multicenter study. *Journal of General Internal Medicine, 22*, 1525–1497.

Thompson, B. L., & Waltz, J. (2007). Everyday mindfulness and mindfulness meditation: Overlapping constructs or not? *Personality and Individual Differences, 43*, 1875–1885.

Trippany, R. L., Kress, V. E. W., & Wilcoxon, S. A. (2004). Preventing vicarious trauma: What counselors should know when working with trauma survivors. *Journal of Counseling & Development, 82*, 31–37.

Tyssen, R., Vaglum, P., Gronvold, N. T., & Ekeberg, O. (2001). Suicidal ideation among medical students and young physicians: A nationwide and prospective study of prevalence and predictors. *Journal of Affective Disorders, 64*, 69–79.

Vredenburgh, L. D., Carlozzi, A. F., & Stein, L. B. (1999). Burnout in counseling psychologists: Type of practice setting and pertinent demographics. *Counseling Psychology Quarterly, 12*, 293–302.

Weinberger, J. (2002). Short paper, large impact: Rosenzweig's influence on the common factors movement. *Journal of Psychotherapy Integration, 12*, 67–76.

Weiss, L. (2004). *Therapist's guide to self-care.* New York: Routledge.

Wicker, B., Keysers, C., Plailly, J., Royet, J. P., Gallese, V., & Rizzolatti, G. (2003). Both of us disgusted in my insula: the common neural basis of seeing and feeling disgust. *Neuron, 40*, 655–664.

Williams, J. M., Alatiq, Y., Crane, C., Barnhofer, T., Fennell, M. J., Duggan, D. S., et al. (2008). Mindfulness-based cognitive therapy (MBCT) in bipolar disorder: Preliminary evaluation of immediate effects on between-episode functioning. *Journal of Affective Disorders, 107*, 275–279.

Williams, J. M. G., Teasdale, J. D., Segal, Z., & Soulsby, J. (2000). Mindfulness-based cognitive therapy reduces over general autobiographical memory in formerly depressed patients. *Journal of Abnormal Psychology, 109*, 150–155.

Young, L. E., Bruce, A., Turner, L., & Linden, W. (2001). Evaluation of a mindfulness-based stress reduction intervention. *Canadian Nurse, 97*, 23–26.

13 Team Working and the Social Contexts of Health Care

Jeremy Gauntlett-Gilbert

Bath Centre for Pain Services, Royal National Hospital for
Rheumatic Diseases, Bath, United Kingdom

Where acute medicine is performing well and assuring good health, clinicians with skills in acceptance and commitment therapy (ACT) are unlikely to be needed. However, some clinical problems do not respond to contemporary medical approaches. These problems can defy clear medical diagnosis; they can be chronic and only partially respond to medications or other interventions; they can also require substantial behavioral change on the part of the patient, such that failure in this change will result in failure of the therapy (for example, adherence to a diabetic diet). This book has described ACT and mindfulness approaches to a number of medical problems that fit these categories.

In medical settings, success in ACT interventions often requires the whole medical team to either implement some ACT principles or at least understand and make room for ACT approaches. This can be difficult to achieve. Decades of research have shown how hard it can be to disseminate psychological therapy approaches to mental health clinicians, who should have the interest and aptitude to adopt new psychotherapies (Andrews & Titov, 2009; Shafran et al., 2009). Achieving dissemination of ACT into medical teams, and teaching staff who are trained and acculturated for acute medical roles, is likely to be more difficult still. Also, the ACT trainer will often be from a mental health or psychology background and may not fully understand the realities of acute medicine and the attitudes and cultures of medical teams.

However, ACT offers potential benefits to health professionals who are more accustomed to acute medical approaches. It can be genuinely liberating for a physician to deal with medication adherence within a framework of values and acceptance, particularly when the limits of simply attempting to persuade patients to take their pills have been painfully obvious. Physiotherapists and other rehabilitation clinicians are often relieved to be able to work toward valued functioning for its own sake, rather than tying exercise and rehabilitation to the agenda of symptom control. The intent of this chapter is to help the training and implementation of ACT approaches happen smoothly. Experience shows that certain misunderstandings and communication problems can occur where ACT trainers do not come from an acute medical background but are trying to communicate with acute medical staff. These barriers can be overcome. Also, teams and services are already embedded in cultures and ways of thinking, and team members are often already responding to intense clinical and financial pressures. This chapter tries to explain some aspects of current medical culture and some of the ways that these aspects will aid or hinder (or appear to aid or hinder) an ACT approach. Some of the issues discussed will be common to introducing any behavioral or psychosocial perspective into an acute medical setting, but many will be specific to ACT. I will not consider in detail generic issues in behavioral medicine such as the engagement of patients who are suspicious of psychological professionals. However, it is hoped that specific barriers to ACT implementation can be understood and negotiated with the help of the material below.

ACT makes many demands of the patient and the therapist, and these can often appear foreign or counterintuitive in medical settings.

The ACT model has been described elsewhere in this book; however, the ACT therapist stance can contrast sharply with the attitudes expected from medical professionals. For example, the following ACT themes can cause difficulty: a noncontrolling therapist stance; willingness to be uncertain; high levels of emotional expression; respect for the patient's inherent ability to change, even in difficult moments; studied skepticism about information giving and reassurance; willingness to accept chronic symptoms and "do nothing" about them; and defining therapeutic success as living in accordance with one's values rather than symptom relief. All of these ideas can be explained and implemented in medical settings, but it requires persistence and a genuine appreciation of the mind-set of colleagues who have been trained to combat illness, save lives, apply hazardous technical treatments, and deal with immediate risk. We will consider the backgrounds of our colleagues first. With regard to terminology, this chapter requires a term that applies to all non-mental-health clinicians who work in acute medicine and in the management of chronic medical conditions. While these settings may differ sharply, this chapter will address them generically and refer to "physical health" settings and colleagues, for lack of a better term.

Professional Training and Cultures

"The best kind of patient for this purpose is one who from great suffering and danger of life or sanity responds quickly to a treatment that interests his doctor and thereafter remains completely well; but those who recover only slowly or incompletely are less satisfying" (Main, 1957, p. 129).

Wherever an author attempts to characterize a "culture" or the mind-set of an entire group of professionals, there is a risk of unwise generalization. However, timidity in this regard does not help, and nursing and medical professionals are often unembarrassed in acknowledging the strength and style of their own professional cultures. To generalize, individuals join the physical health professions because they want to help people—they want to help by application of sophisticated and skilled means, based on expert understandings for which they are accorded professional status. People choose to become nurses, doctors, or physiotherapists, as opposed to voluntary workers, chaplains, or stockbrokers. In professional training, they are exposed to an understanding of their clinical work that has been characterized, and stereotyped, as the "medical model" (Engel, 1989).

In psychology and sociology there has been a tradition of criticizing the medical model of illness and disability. Rather than join this tradition, one might find it useful to understand this concept and recognize its utility as a framework for treating the more common medical conditions. Authors have attempted a number of different descriptions; the following is my own. According to the medical model:

> *The patient has an intrinsic condition, for which they are blameless, which underlies their visible symptoms. An expert is required to characterize this condition and actively treat it, as the patient's life is unlikely to improve before the condition is addressed. If the problem is impossible to diagnose, it may be psychological. The patient needs information about his or her condition; this information will lead the patient toward taking the correct action with regard to treatment and management. The patient will want to take the correct action, in order to know that it will lead to a good outcome. Psychosocial factors and the patient's behavior may be important, but they are secondary to the primary task of dealing with the condition. Mental health problems exist, but they tend to be rare and extreme, also requiring rapid expert evaluation and treatment.*

This framework saves countless lives every year. Training in this model leads to clinicians who behave in certain ways. These clinicians

- Try to achieve clarity of diagnosis and approach, and presume it is achievable.

- Act rather than doing nothing; take control of the situation.

- Treat to reduce symptoms and suffering.

- Educate patients to increase their understanding and reduce anxiety.

- Provide or suggest solutions based on expert knowledge.

Other nonmedical therapeutic and rehabilitation professionals have characterized their clinical urges as "to fix," "to reassure," and "to advise." These urges have received some research attention. For example, a study was carried out where a "patient" (an actor) who complained of a headache but had no other worrying symptoms asked for an MRI. Physicians were generally able to resist demands for the inappropriate and expensive test, but many nonetheless referred the "patient" to a specialist. It seems that physicians were keen to "do something" in the face of the patient's difficulties (Gallagher, Lo, Chesney, & Christensen, 1997).

As noted above, these clinical urges are valid much of the time but are not useful where conditions are idiopathic, are chronic, or require difficult patient behavior change. An ACT stance allows identification of where these behavior patterns are unworkable, and it introduces principled alternative courses of action.

Having characterized the "medical model" and styles of response, one finds it equally useful to acknowledge the styles of psychological therapy professionals. Many of the readers of this chapter will have professional or post-qualification training in talk therapies. From an external perspective—for example, from a financial service, military, or medical perspective—the culture around talk therapies is quite odd. The fact that six hours of individual therapist contact time can be regarded (by therapists) as a "brief" intervention hints at these cultural differences. The therapy "model" might be generalized as follows:

There is lots of time to give an individual person attention, and generally problems are long term and require long interventions. There is a lot of autonomy, and not much managerial or supervisory oversight, within the therapeutic relationship. Diagnoses are often unclear—this doesn't matter too much—and when they are clear they can be downright unhelpful. High levels of emotional expression—for example, prolonged crying—can be positively healthy. Awkward or challenging people should be given the benefit of the doubt, as they are often expressing vulnerability. When the patient repeatedly fails to change or find motivation, this should be met with sympathy and further analysis.

It is useful for ACT trainers to be aware of their own "model" of problems and therapy when approaching physical health colleagues, as many of the assumptions above can be seen as a luxury or indulgence.

Medical Imperatives

In order to operate in medical settings and influence medical staff, ACT clinicians need to understand the antecedents and genuine benefits of these "medical cultures." In acute medicine and on inpatient wards, precision, diligence, procedural adherence, and risk aversion are genuine virtues (Gawande, 2007). While these virtues may also be present in mental health and other psychosocial work, on inpatient medical wards they save lives and prevent tragedy at a frequency that is unfamiliar to mental health clinicians. In psychotherapeutic work, clinician errors lead to possible therapeutic alliance rupture, and where patient behavior change fails it can lead to further stasis. However, on an inpatient medical ward, clinician error can kill, and patient nonadherence can be similarly hazardous. Acute medical settings are fundamentally more procedurally and technically complicated than mental health settings.

Information giving and skills training also have a different weight in acute medicine. ACT contends that they are often insufficient for behavioral change, and this remains true in medicine. However, information about a drug regimen, or skills training in managing a stoma or Hickman line, has a different weight from its counterpart in psychotherapeutic work. Again, neglect in information giving and skills training in acute medicine can have far more rapid and dangerous effects.

In this context, ACT clinicians can better understand resistance to ACT approaches and training. Reluctance may be due to standard worries about learning new skills, or the emotional contact implied in ACT (these are analyzed further below); however, it is also true that if some ACT principles were inflexibly applied in the wrong medical settings they would be dangerous. ACT techniques are appropriate for their pragmatic goals in behavior change, and the theory behind ACT acknowledges that different forms of thinking and working are appropriate for different goals. The most resolute ACT fan would probably agree that, if he or she were watching a relative being resuscitated, tolerance of ambiguity and frank emotional expression should not be primary goals. Understanding this can aid communication with acute medical colleagues.

Attitudes Toward Distress

Clinicians from physical health backgrounds can tolerate different levels and types of distress compared to mental health clinicians. While certain experiences are invariably upsetting, physical health training and mental health training inure professionals to different types of experience. Understanding this allows mental health clinicians to pitch training more accurately and understand clinicians' fears better.

In general, acute medical staff have the repeated experience of patients dying or rapidly deteriorating, and of rapid and untimely death. They have usually dealt with grieving relatives and frequently have to deal with acutely furious, frightened, and confused patients and relatives. Perhaps obviously, they have a higher level of tolerance for bodily fluids and visible disfigurement. When mental health clinicians move into this area, they often have to adjust to the reality of patient death, and the distressing sights and smells that go along with acute medicine.

In contrast, mental health professionals are more used to a range of experiences that can frighten and distress their acute medical colleagues. They are more used to high levels of emotional distress. They have usually dealt with suicide risk regularly and are used to going home and going to sleep knowing that a patient they care for is at risk of self-harm. Most have heard disclosures of childhood abuse, adult assault, and appalling psychosocial deprivation and risk.

It is perhaps obvious to say that both physical and mental health clinicians can become uncomfortable when encountering the other's type of work-related distress. On many medical wards, staff are genuinely disturbed by a patient who carries on crying uncontrollably even after comfort and reassurance are given. Medical staff who can calmly lay out a dead body or deal with grieving relatives can find themselves overwhelmingly upset or angry by a disclosure of sexual abuse or at hearing a distressing life story. Alternatively, they can act in a dismissive fashion when faced with ongoing distress and failure to make behavioral changes. Where ACT clinicians are training acute medical staff, it is essential to recall that these colleagues may be distressed by things that a mental health professional takes for granted; equally, they may appear unperturbed by sights and events that a psychotherapist would find horrifying.

Professional Cultures: Summary

Acute medical colleagues are trained, to some degree, to view clinical problems according to a "medical model." This is valid and essential in physical medicine. However, it leads to specific clinical urges—for example, to seek diagnostic clarity, or to initiate repeated treatments—that may not be workable in certain situations. ACT clinicians involved in training and dissemination need to understand this mind-set and to respect its validity while asserting the value of ACT in addressing idiopathic, chronic, or self-management challenges. The genuine differences of inpatient ward culture should be understood and respected, as well as differing levels of tolerance of emotional distress seen in physical and mental health professionals.

Organization and Systems Cultures

As Menzies-Lyth (1960) wrote, "The success and viability of a social institution are intimately connected with the techniques it uses to contain anxiety" (p. 120).

When ACT is introduced into medical teams, it is never being introduced into an organizational vacuum. Many medical settings are pressured, demanding contexts that value some attitudes and outcomes while discouraging others. This is at times a problem and at times an advantage for the ACT approach. It is unlikely that a single ACT clinician, or bout of ACT training, will prevail where it is opposed by a team culture or organizational imperative. Understanding systems is essential.

Outcomes and Payments

Physical health settings and organizations tend to value certain categorical, medical outcomes. Medical journals favor analyses in terms of odds ratios relating to outcomes such as "remitted/relapsed" or, at its most simple, "alive/dead." While there is a bracing directness to such outcomes, this can pose a problem for an approach that values vital, valued living in the presence of distress. Medical teams and organizations are often assessed and paid according to categorical, medical outcomes.

Pain management and pain clinics provide an organizational case study for this difficulty. For example (see chapter 2), patients with chronic pain can benefit from avoiding fresh interventional treatments and medications while focusing on self-management of their condition in the service of valued living. However, ACT clinicians attempting to implement this approach are frequently situated within a pain clinic that is led by an anesthetist and focuses on interventions such as medication management and anesthetic injections. Often, these clinics receive payment by the number of procedures they perform—that is, the clinicians' salaries are paid, indirectly, by the number of injection procedures performed. Clearly, careful organizational consultation and understanding of desired outcomes is needed in these situations.

ACT interventions can succeed when clinicians are unabashed about their focus and desired outcomes. While there may be a financial pressure for intervention, pain research regularly demonstrates that medical and interventional approaches to chronic pain seldom lead to better living (Turk & Burwinkle, 2005). The evidence on this point is uncomfortably clear and could hardly be disputed by the most ardent exponent of injection therapies. However, ACT is again up against difficulties in medical scientific culture. Despite attempts to introduce broad-based outcome assessment in trials of pain therapies (Dworkin et al., 2005), authoritative reviews usually report only results for pain relief and neglect results for functioning. For example, recent reviews of spinal cord stimulation for pain, and of opioids for chronic pain, highlight pain relief and include minimal data on functioning and disability (Deshpande, Furlan, Mailis-Gagnon, Atlas, & Turk, 2007; National Institute for Health and Clinical Excellence, 2008). In ACT we are reminded to be sharply aware of how attempts to prevent suffering do not always lead to valued living; thus, the ACT community can have a positive impact on scientific and clinical thinking.

It is critical for ACT trainers to clarify where their intervention fits into team and organizational priorities. ACT trainers need to publicly assert and defend how they see therapeutic outcome and how this fits with, and can complement, other medical approaches. Equally, ACT therapists should not be surprised when their approach is neglected as not relevant to the "bottom line" of organizational outcome measurement or financial imperative. ACT trainers should always try to establish how outcomes are measured, and how payment is made, in the settings they hope to influence.

Working and Management Cultures

Being a nurse on a medical ward can be very different from delivering psychological therapy in an outpatient mental health clinic. Working cultures and expectations are quite different, time pressures differ, and attitudes toward training and management are highly specific. An ACT trainer cannot neglect these differences if he or she hopes to disseminate the approach.

To generalize once again, physical health cultures tend to be fast paced and activist, with a pressure to achieve a high number of medical/nursing tasks in a short space of time. Supervision is often not routine or not sustained. Training budgets can be minimal, and training time is often taken up with an annual mandatory training syllabus (such as refreshers on basic life support training and infection control procedure). Also, training is often in the form of teaching individuals to adhere to a particular, concrete protocol. As noted above, these protocols are essential for safety in a complex environment. However, they can also serve psychological functions.

Working in an anecdotal, psychodynamic model in the 1960s, Menzies-Lyth and others provided a vivid picture of how procedures and routines acted as a defense against anxiety for pressured nurses, and how increased job stress led to progressive depersonalization of the patient and reliance on routine (Menzies-Lyth, 1960). While concrete evidence for this is lacking, ACT clinicians will be able to identify the functional relationship between reliance on rules and experiential avoidance in their own settings. Obviously, where ACT trainers enter these cultures, they will encounter expectations about what training usually constitutes, and potential anxiety about a style of education that is more experientially based. Trainers will often encounter the question "But how do I actually do this?" This usually reflects a mixture of a healthy insistence on concrete skills training plus a more ambiguous desire to quickly feel confident about technique, in the service of mastering anxiety.

Medical settings also have their own cultures around blame, reporting error, and admitting personal weakness. These are not specific to health care organizations, but the repeated attempts to improve medical error reporting and to raise awareness of staff health and functioning attest to the fact that these are ongoing problems in hospitals and clinics (Waring, 2005). There are sophisticated and potent responses to these problems both organizationally (such as in "whistle-blowing" procedures) and in the literature, but all start from the premise that it remains hard to admit error or personal failing. The candor expected of ACT clinicians is difficult for every ACT therapist; it can be particularly hard when it is not supported by the broader context.

Working and Management Culture: Summary

In medical settings, there are potential disincentives for ACT outcomes and ACT-oriented therapist behaviors. To disseminate the approach, it is useful to have someone senior in the health care team who will support ACT outcomes and take the first step in modeling candor and emotional openness. Even when this happens, staff may need time to adjust to a less protocol-driven approach. However, ACT benefits from being an evidence-based approach, and the evidence often clarifies the limitations of routine medical treatment for some conditions.

Patient Assumptions and Expectations

"They can send a probe to Mars. Why can't they give me something that will reduce my pain?"

Patient expectations again highlight the differences between physical and mental health settings. Few patients go to a psychiatrist or psychologist expecting to be rapidly and effortlessly freed from suffering; however, this expectation is prevalent in acute medicine. This expectation is formed by the media, by direct marketing, by ambitious professional bodies, and by well-meaning international agencies. For example, the World Health Organization chooses to define health not only as the absence of symptoms but as a condition of thriving personal abundance (World Health Organization, 2006). While this may echo the ACT emphasis on vital living, it is more likely to fuel expectations of miraculous cure through medicine. ACT is based on a premise that suffering is normative, and this perspective echoes a biomedical view that sees death as evolutionarily beneficial and regards benign biological systems (the immune system, for example) as intrinsically prone to malfunction and attack of their host. However, these perspectives can be in sharp contrast to what patients expect of their doctors.

Patient satisfaction is regularly recorded and studied. For example, it is known that it declines slightly as the patient's socioeconomic status increases (Kravitz, 2001). Specific clinician acts are studied; failure to send a patient for a desired investigation can be interpreted as failure of the clinician to care. Studies of media portrayal of medicine are informative. For example, modern medical TV dramas contain more realism and emotional content than their predecessors did. However, the main change over time seems to have been to portray the failings and emotional lives of medical staff, rather than to increase realism about the limitations of medicine and its funding pressures (Strauman & Goodier, 2008). The emphasis remains, for understandable dramatic reasons, on heroic intervention for acute problems, which result in either cure or death. Episodes of *ER* that followed long-term living with diabetes would probably have encountered low ratings. However, this affects the public perception of medical intervention. The move to an ACT model that emphasizes self-management, personal efficacy, the limits of medicine, and living with long-term conditions is not made any easier by the media. One study has indicated that, when doctors decide not to carry out certain tests or investigations, patients are frequently unhappy and interpret this as a failure to care, rather than a principled decision or empirical approach to treatment (Kravitz & Callahan, 2000).

Patients also operate within families and social networks that support a particular view of sickness. This has been described as the "sick role," an implicit societal consensus about illness (Wade & Halligan, 2007) that can be summarized as follows:

> *Illness is an external factor over which the individual has no control. There is an underlying pathology to illness for which the person bears no responsibility. A person is either ill or well. If they are ill, they can be legitimately excused some responsibilities. However, they are expected to be interested in getting better as soon as possible.*

Evidently, many of the conditions described in this book contravene these assumptions. Some clinicians outside of the ACT tradition have noted how "sick role" thinking restricts patients by implying that they are helpless while ill and expected to return to full responsibilities when well. Wade and Halligan (2007) have recommended a return to "convalescence," an understood period of healing, personal recuperation, and useful but limited effort. ACT interventions have to find a way of helping patients explain how they are trying to help themselves yet are not responsible for their condition; how they are not (in some cases) dangerously unwell yet are limited and cannot "return to normal."

Finally, in Western societies sickness confers legitimate privileges (including financial) and reductions in demands, such as to work. It can also play a part in the assignment of blame; the reality and severity of a condition can be part of assigning blame and calibrating punishment toward, for example, a person involved in a patient's injury. ACT's invitation to behavioral change and valued living can be perceived as a threat to the sick role, its benefits, and the external assignation of blame. ACT clinicians have a range of useful tools to address these issues. If engagement is handled sensitively, then work on values, reason giving, and workability are all potentially potent.

Training ACT and Leading Implementation

"This stuff is fantastic. Obviously it would be great if I could communicate with kids like this...but I think you're trying to turn me into a psychologist. That's not my job. I'd love to do it but I'll never be able to do it the way you do it."—Senior pediatrician at a motivational interviewing workshop

Training mental health professionals in evidence-based treatments is a substantial challenge. Dissemination of high-quality practice is known to be difficult and rare; professionals often find reasons to persist in their previous practice. To implement ACT in medical settings, professionals with no background in the talk therapies need to be helped to absorb and implement ACT skills and the appropriate therapeutic stance.

When carrying out ACT with patients, the professional's emphasis is on experiential change, proceeding at the patient's pace, and avoiding persuasion or coercion. Information and skills training are thought to be important but often insufficient in themselves for behavioral change. However, when one is training colleagues it remains tempting to educate them about the ACT model, persuade them of its merits, and drive the process of change in a team. However, changing clinical practice is not a matter of skills training; clinical behavior is complex, is performed under pressure, and can be driven by highly personal thoughts and emotions. Thus, ACT therapeutic principles will apply to training.

The initial aim of training need not be to convince; rather, it can provide trainees the opportunity to witness the workability of ACT, both in their clinical practice and also as applied to their own private experiences. Trainers can have faith in experiential learning and confidently model the ACT therapeutic stance. If trainers try to "persuade" trainees of the necessity of experiential learning, trainees will respond to the behavior being modeled (persuasion) rather than the verbal message. As noted above, physical health professionals can find experiential training quite foreign, but experience also shows that they respect the practical and empirical emphasis of training that encourages workability and direct experience.

Before one considers the format of training, it is important to note that there are some concerns that may affect trainee engagement. Acute medical colleagues may fear that they are being pushed into a psychological role that they are not prepared for. There is also a basic fear of psychology and emotional expression; trainees may fear that trainers will be emotionally exposing and unpredictable. ACT trainers sometimes live up to this reputation, and they need to ensure that their willingness to create emotional exposure is matched by their diligence in seeking and monitoring trainee consent. Trainees can also be put off by the use of mental health jargon that they do not understand; lazy use of terms like "PTSD," "reinforcement," "basic reflective listening," and "Axis II diagnosis" can have a distancing or irritating effect. However, clarity about expectations and aims can help, as can trainers and trainees understanding the genuinely transferable skills held by acute medical colleagues.

Structure and Content of Training

Reviews of the evidence on staff training indicate that "one shot" training events are unlikely to achieve genuine skills transfer (Fixsen, Naoom, Blasé, Friedman, & Wallace, 2005). Evidence supports training that involves practical skills teaching followed by ongoing supervision and supported learning. From an ACT perspective, skills training can be seen as functioning either as an effective exposure and willingness exercise or as a more superficial exercise leaving fundamental behavioral processes untouched. The dismal literature on dissemination of evidence-based therapies shows how easy it is to conduct training that has no real effect. However, brief ACT interventions have been shown to be effective, and ACT training can produce effective therapists over a relatively short time (Bond & Bunce, 2000; Lappal ainen et al., 2007). Skills training can function as exposure in training physicians. Medical communication training has been shown to alter staff "defense mechanisms"; this psychodynamic research shows how skills practice can alter how professionals approach or avoid stress and difficulty (Bernard, de Roten, Despland, & Stiefel, 2009).

Successful training relies on selecting the appropriate level of input for the audience. Mental health professionals can forget that they have a high level of training and prior experience in communication skills, role-playing, and exerting conscious control over their communication style. There is a genuine danger of trying to build ACT skills on a foundation that does not exist. Training is made easier when one is clear about the level of talk therapy skill that is presumed, and also the level of ACT competence that trainees are expected to achieve.

It is unfair to expect a psychologist to walk onto a medical ward and insert a cannula. Similarly, it can be unrealistic to expect physical health colleagues to immediately engage fluently in advanced role-play practice. Professionals have had variable amounts of training in using psychological techniques in their clinical interactions. For example, core training in the physical health professions usually encourages repertoires of skilled questioning, information giving, and explanation of treatment rationale. Psychological techniques can be built into this repertoire, where a professional does motivational interviewing or carries out a CBT technique. However, this is still quite distant from a professional genuinely realizing the extent to which his or her own demeanor and style partly determines the patient's response. This awareness is usually only developed with role-play and feedback. Personal styles such as pace, tone, and level of directiveness can be brought under conscious control (and should be, in any psychotherapeutic training), but this is a high-level skill. ACT training can rapidly plunge trainees into grappling with these issues. This can be appropriate, so long as trainers are fully aware of the demands they are creating and of the trainees' history with this type of work.

Trainers can also usefully ask themselves "What level of ACT competence am I expecting my trainees to achieve?" It is unproductive to expect to turn all colleagues into psychotherapists, and this agenda also disrespects their core skills as physical health professionals. A health care team usually benefits far more from having an ACT-consistent nurse who functions as a nurse than it would from a nurse who is being expected to turn into an ACT psychotherapist. Thus, when planning training it is useful to reflect on the different types of understanding below.

- **Correct intellectual understanding:** The professional may not be able to use ACT, but he or she understands it well enough to collaborate with ACT-trained colleagues and to discuss ACT accurately with patients who may be receiving the therapy from someone else.

- **Use of metaphor and technique:** The professional can use ACT metaphors and techniques in a "book-consistent" fashion. However, application of the full ACT therapeutic stance is variable or not under full conscious control.

- **Use of the therapeutic agenda in clinical work:** The professional can pursue ACT therapeutic goals in his or her own professional work, with or without the use of formal ACT techniques. For example, a physiotherapist might aim to foster valued living, awareness of struggle, and present-moment focus quite accurately, with or without using formal ACT techniques or metaphors.

- **Full use of ACT as a skilled psychological professional:** At this idealized level, an individual should be able to flexibly apply the ACT stance and technique to a high level of skill, even when treating the most intense distress or inflexible behavior. The therapist would model high levels of personal acceptance and awareness. This level is probably built on years of practice in psychological therapy.

The purpose of the scheme above is not to create a false hierarchy for ACT training, but rather to allow trainers flexibility in determining the goals of their interventions. Both trainers and trainees benefit from apt, realistic interventions that take into account individuals' pre-existing knowledge and skill.

Mental health professionals can also forget their level of experience and fluency in dealing with psychosocial "danger areas" such as suicidality, domestic abuse, and child abuse. These areas all involve genuine risk and become more distressing to the listener as a greater degree of emotional expression and contact is permitted. Physical health professionals can have a genuine, and warranted, fear of "opening Pandora's box" in straying from their usual remit. Trainers need to acknowledge this openly as legitimate, while helping trainees to identify that difficulties are usually being uncovered, rather than created, and that these difficulties are usually profoundly important to treatment even if they are not acknowledged.

Trainees may also be unfamiliar with the overall approach of formulation, case conceptualization, or functional analysis. It is hard to discuss clinical thinking in an ACT model without such a shared framework. Physical health staff can often generate astute intuitive hypotheses about patient behavior. However, these ideas can sometimes be unfalsifiable or include factors that cannot be influenced, for example hypothesizing that "the problem is his difficult wife," or "he is a typical only child." It is hard to discuss precise ACT clinical thinking without trainees knowing that in individual psychological therapy these difficulties would be conceptualized as "why he cannot deal effectively with his wife" and "what it is about being an only child that affects his life now." Training that helps colleagues locate problems within individual behavior and its barriers in the present moment, as well as avoiding unfalsifiable hypotheses, is essential before one attempts more-advanced ACT case discussion. It is also helpful to point out that ACT thinking and formulation does not take the place of effective, broad psychosocial assessment, or psychiatric evaluation.

Despite the added complexities of training this group of professionals, there are several generally workable topics for initial training. The concept of workability is easily explained and a good root idea for many ACT interventions. Physical health professionals are often aware of the difficulty of changing human behavior, for example in the area of medication adherence, diet, exercise, or sexual behavior. They have abundant evidence of the need to go beyond information giving and skills training. Also, as in the general ACT approach, it is helpful to analyze the workability of behavior patterns that are always present. Professionals already have many examples of situations where (for example) information, reassurance, diagnostic testing, advice, and attempts at expert-led symptom control are not working; a gentle analysis of the long-term workability of some clinical impulses can be a useful prelude to discussing change.

Conceptualizing Staff Behavior: The Hexaflex

Although skills training can be psychologically potent, it is evident to most professionals that clinical behavior is affected by personal psychological factors. A range of recent review papers in medical and psychological journals acknowledge this, with Meier, Back, and Morrison's paper (2001) being an excellent reflection on the effect of doctors' emotions on medical practice. Personal factors can influence health care by affecting (1) the clinician's practice, (2) his or her physical and emotional health, and (3) the health and functioning of the broader team. Although some literature addresses this, the best papers are high-quality anecdotal analyses. There have been no attempts to apply a clear theoretical framework to this issue. Meier and colleagues (2001) adopt a broadly psychodynamic view of doctors' emotions that is, in application, ACT consistent. Other studies on the failure of cognitive behavioral therapy (CBT) dissemination have mentioned clinician thoughts and beliefs in explaining the difficulty (Shafran et al., 2009; Waller, 2009). Thus, there is an opportunity to bring conceptual clarity to the issue of clinician behavior and health.

Important behavioral processes within the clinician can be conceptualized within the "hexaflex" model of ACT processes (see chapter 1). Below, ACT-relevant clinical behavior is conceptualized within the hexaflex, in the service of guiding intervention. ACT training usually includes experiential exercises that address the trainee's private content. The examples in table 13.1 may help trainers to target exercises at specific processes, choosing emotionally laden aspects of clinical life rather than trainees' more personal

359

content. This is a useful level for training, as it addresses emotionally relevant aspects of clinical behavior that might be improved to the patient's (and therapist's) benefit, while avoiding potentially more intimate or threatening personal material. Using the "hexaflex" also emphasizes that the goal of training is psychological flexibility. In this context, this means clinical behavior that is skillfully matched to the current context and demands, with minimal inflexibility induced by private events. Specifically, the goal is not purely to produce clinicians who can recall ACT metaphors or deliver ACT exercises aptly.

This hexaflex analysis (table 13.1) is based on anecdotal observation rather than evidence. However, a handful of studies show the influence of ACT-relevant processes on clinical behavior and clinician well-being. A review of the reasons why physicians order diagnostic tests showed that lower test-ordering was associated with doctors who had more experience, more confidence in their own judgment, more pride, and a low fear of risk taking or uncertainty. Time pressure and fear of litigation were associated with ordering more tests (Whiting et al., 2007). McCracken and Yang (2008) have studied ACT processes in relation to well-being in rehabilitation workers. Acceptance, mindfulness, and values-based action were all independently important predictors of well-being and reduced burnout, accounting jointly for appreciable proportions of the variance. There are also a number of studies on mindfulness with regard to well-being and clinical practice, summarized in chapter 12. As there is so little evidence, it is important to remain flexible and and not presume that evidence derived from populations of people with psychiatric disorders will always apply to functioning clinicians under regular external stress. For example, a study by Mitmansgruber, Beck, and Schüßler (2008) suggested that paramedics benefit from being stern with themselves and unsympathetic toward their own emotional reactions. This would not usually be regarded as consistent with an ACT approach, and it argues for continuing openness and more research.

TABLE 13.1

Hexaflex Analysis of Clinical Behavior, Clinician Health, and Team Working

ACT-Relevant Clinical Behavior:
Flexible/Workable Behavior

Acceptance

- Ability to accept clinical uncertainty, nonresponse, and failure

- Willingness to "do nothing" where this is workable

- Ability to encounter patient distress openly without this rigidly driving clinical decisions

- Ability to work smoothly with colleagues who are following a different clinical model

Defusion

- Ability to acknowledge own strong views and biases about clinical situation

- Ability to step back from own professional background

- Avoiding dichotomies such as "the condition is either mental or physical"

- Flexibility about the use of medical and psychological techniques; willing to *not use* ACT techniques

- Amusement at own tendency to make excuses and be defensive about own clinical work

Present-moment focus

- Contact with the patient as a person, even if patients present themselves as a medical problem

- Ability to focus on the present moment, even when the mind is fixed on plans, diagnoses, and actions

- Dealing with colleagues as people, as well as "roles" in a team

Self-as-context

- Awareness of self as a present human, as well as a professional, expert, caregiver, or other role

- Concerns about success, role, or expertise are recognized but not seen as going to the core of "self"

Committed action

- Ability to take clinical actions without watering them down or equivocating

- Ability to communicate with patient freely without skirting around topics or avoiding difficulty

- Ability to commit to genuine clinical inaction, where workable

- With colleagues who have a different view, willingness to either collaborate without grumbling or discuss differences openly and immediately

Values

- In contact with deeply held values about clinical work

- Values about clinical work have some breadth (for example, including education and growth as well as "caring" or "helping")

- Expressing thoughts and feelings about team and team working within a values context

ACT-Relevant Clinical Behavior: Inflexible/Potentially Unworkable Behavior

Experiential avoidance

- Reactivity to own distress or sense of pressure from patient

- Proneness to activist attempts to gain clarity or a clear course of therapeutic action ("therapeutic mania"; Main, 1957)

- Attempting to be "positive" and "professional" leading to thought/emotional rebound and bursts of irritation

- Critical of colleagues working in a different style

Cognitive fusion

- Blaming patient or other professionals

- Application of rigid dichotomies (for example, physical/psychological, safe/unsafe, functional/organic, on/off protocol, medical/nursing, CBT/ACT)

- Inflexible application of pseudo-ACT perspectives (for example, "Never reassure patients" or "Nothing will change while he's so fused")

- Belief that ACT holds the answer to all clinical problems

- Giving reasons for clinical judgments and defending them unreflectively

Preoccupation with the past or future

- Mind preoccupied with fear of future failure, or past struggles with this patient

- No awareness of emotional or physical state as preoccupied with clinical tasks

- Mind dwelling on team politics and historical resentments when dealing with colleagues

Inaction or impulsive persistence

- Diluting therapeutic actions (for example, refusing requests for an MRI but acceding to a specialist referral "just to be sure")

- Encouraging self-management but retaining an expert role or emphasizing a patient safety net (for example, "See how you do managing on your own, but if you have the slightest difficulty, call the ward")

- Within teams, covert grumbling about decisions rather than open discussion

Self-as-content

- Self seen as doctor, psychologist, professional, expert

- Challenge to expert role or profession experienced as deeply unsettling

Lack of values clarity

- "Negatively reinforced clinician" motivated by getting to the end of shift or clinic, or motivated by avoidance of complaint or litigation

- Values for clinical work experienced with distance and absence of freshness

- Engaging in training as a mandatory chore rather than linking it to values for clinical work

Training and Implementation: Summary

In training and working with physical health colleagues, it is useful to bear in mind their fundamental level of "talking skill" and fears about taking on a psychological role. Sometimes the trainer will need to state clearly what would be self-evident to a talk therapy professional. A key goal is to allow trainees to experience the workability of ACT principles in relation to their own emotional experiences, thoughts, bodily sensations, and urges, which is a countercultural approach to training in this context. However, physical health professionals often engage well and can readily discuss their own private content with regard to challenging patients or work stress.

Summary and Conclusions

Introducing ACT into physical health settings can be rewarding, and its benefits for certain clinical conditions are self-evident. Staff in these settings can be trained at a number of levels, from practicing their core work in an ACT-consistent fashion, to becoming fully trained ACT therapists. However, it is seldom straightforward to introduce new psychosocial perspectives into physical health teams, and ACT can appear particularly counterintuitive. Dissemination is helped by welcoming trainee fears and anxieties, meeting resistance without defense, and working consciously within trainee willingness and consent. It is important to clearly state the intent of training, and to pitch training at the right level. Understanding systemic pressures on staff and the effect of patient expectations is essential. However, experiential learning can be as effective in training as it is in therapy, and it can work well in physical health teams, particularly when facilitated by a senior member of the team who supports ACT outcomes and models ACT stances such as emotional openness. Trainers can gain theoretical clarity and target interventions effectively by applying the standard ACT hexaflex model to clinical behavior patterns. The most effective trainers understand and respect physical health "cultures" and realize that their own talk therapy background has its own peculiarities and biases.

References

Andrews, G., & Titov, N. (2009). Hit and miss: innovation and dissemination of evidence-based psychological treatments. *Behaviour Research and Therapy*, DOI:10.1016/j.brat.2009.07.007.

Bernard, M., de Roten, Y., Despland, J-N., & Stiefel, F. (2009). Communication skills training and clinicians' defences in oncology: An exploratory, controlled study. *Psycho-Oncology*, DOI: 10.1002/pon.1558.

Bond, F. W., & Bunce, D. (2000). Mediators of change in emotion-focused and problem-focused worksite stress management interventions. *Journal of Occupational Health Psychology*, 5, 156–163.

Deshpande, A., Furlan, A. D., Mailis-Gagnon, A., Atlas, S., & Turk, D. (2007). Opioids for chronic low-back pain. *Cochrane Database of Systematic Reviews*, 3. Art. No.: CD004959. DOI: 10.1002/14651858. CD004959.pub3.

Dworkin, R. H., Turk, D. C., Farrar, J. T., Haythornthwaite, J. A., Jensen, M. P., Katz, N. P., et al. (2005). Core outcome measures for chronic pain clinical trials: IMMPACT recommendations. *Pain, 113*, 9–19.

Engel, G. L. (1989). The need for a new medical model: A challenge for biomedicine. *Journal of Interprofessional Care, 4*(1), 37–53.

Fixsen, D. L., Naoom, S. F., Blasé, K. A., Friedman, R. M., & Wallace, F. (2005). *Implementation Resesarch: A synthesis of the literature.* Tampa, FL: University of South Florida, Louis de la Parte Florida Mental Health Institute, The National Implementation Research Network.

Gallagher, T. H., Lo, B., Chesney, M., & Christensen, K. (1997). How do physicians respond to patients' requests for costly, unindicated services? *Journal of General Internal Medicine, 12*, 663–668.

Gawande, A. (2007). *Better: A surgeon's notes on performance.* New York: Picador.

Kravitz, R. L. (2001). Measuring patients' expectations and requests. *Annals of Internal Medicine, 134*, 881–888.

Kravitz, R. L., & Callahan, E. J. (2000). Patients' perceptions of omitted examinations and tests: A qualitative analysis. *Journal of General Internal Medicine, 15*, 38–45.

Lappalainen, R., Lehtonen, T., Skarp, E., Taubert, E., Ojanen, M., & Hayes, S. C. (2007). The impact of CBT and ACT models using psychology trainee therapists: A preliminary controlled effectiveness trial. *Behavior Modification, 31*(4), 488–511.

Main, T. F. (1957). The ailment. *British Journal of Medical Psychology, 30,* 129–145.

McCracken, L. M., & Yang, S-Y. (2008). A contextual cognitive-behavioral analysis of rehabilitation workers' health and well-being: Influences of acceptance, mindfulness, and values-based action. *Rehabilitation Psychology, 53*(4), 479–485.

Meier, D. E., Back, A. L., & Morrison, R. S. (2001). The inner life of physicians and the care of the seriously ill. *Journal of the American Medical Association, 286*(23), 3007–3014.

Menzies-Lyth, I. (1960). Social systems as a defence against anxiety: an empirical study of the nursing service of a general hospital. *Human Relations, 13,* 95–121.

Mitmansgruber, H., Beck, T. N., & Schüßler, G. (2008). "Mindful helpers": Experiential avoidance, meta-emotions and emotional regulation in paramedics. *Journal of Research in Personality, 42,* 1358–1363.

National Institute for Health and Clinical Excellence. (2008). *Spinal cord stimulation for chronic pain of neuropathic or ischaemic origin (TA159).* London: National Institute for Health and Clinical Excellence.

Shafran, R., Clark, D. M., Fairburn, C. G., Arntz, A., Barlow, D. H., Ehlers, A., et al. (2009). Mind the gap: Improving the dissemination of CBT. *Behaviour Research and Therapy,* doi:10.1016/j.brat.2009.07.003.

Strauman, E., & Goodier, B. C. (2008). Not your grandmother's doctor show: A review of *Grey's Anatomy, House* and *Nip/Tuck. Journal of Medical Humanities, 29,* 127–131.

Turk, D. C., & Burwinkle, T. M. (2005). Clinical outcomes, cost-effectiveness, and the role of psychology in treatments for chronic pain sufferers. *Professional Psychology: Research and Practice, 36*(6), 602–610.

Wade, D. T., & Halligan, P. W. (2007). Social roles and long-term illness: Is it time to rehabilitate convalescence? *Clinical Rehabilitation, 21,* 291–298.

Waller, G. (2009). Evidence-based treatment and therapist drift. *Behaviour Research and Therapy, 47,* 119–127. .

Waring, J. J. (2005). Beyond blame: Cultural barriers to medical incident reporting. *Social Science and Medicine, 60,* 1927–1935.

Whiting, P., Toerien, M., de Salis, I., Sterne, J. A. C., Dieppe, P., Egger, M., el al. (2007). A review identifies and classifies reasons for ordering diagnostic tests. *Journal of Clinical Epidemiology, 60,* 981–989.

World Health Organization. (2006). Constitution of the World Health Organization. Retrieved October 27, 2009, from http://www.who.int/governance/eb/who_constitution_en.pdf

Editor **Lance M. McCracken, Ph.D.,** is a consultant clinical psychologist and clinical director of the Centre for Pain Services at the Royal National Hospital for Rheumatic Diseases in Bath, UK. He is also a senior lecturer in the department for health and a senior visiting fellow in the department of psychology at the University of Bath. He has more than twenty years of clinical and research experience in chronic pain management and behavioral medicine.

INDEX

A

acceptance, 17–18; chronic pain and, 39, 41, 201; clinical behavior and, 361; definitions of, 189, 249; diabetes and, 91, 94; epilepsy and, 67, 69–70; insomnia and, 147; instruments for measuring, 198–207; mindfulness related to, 190, 322–323; smoking cessation and, 111, 113, 122; of therapist distress, 262–263

Acceptance and Action Diabetes Questionnaire (AADQ), 202

Acceptance and Action Epilepsy Questionnaire (AAEpQ), 72, 202–203

Acceptance and Action Questionnaire (AAQ/AAQ-II), 86, 199–201, 288

Acceptance and Action Questionnaire for Weight (AAQW), 86, 204

acceptance and commitment therapy (ACT): assessment measures for, 198–207; avoidance behaviors in, 244–245; behavioral medicine and, 4, 24–25, 187–188; case conceptualization in, 247; chronic pain and, 38–52, 53, 350; cognitive behavioral therapy vs., 111–112, 244–248; core therapeutic processes of, 16–19; diabetes and, 92, 93–94; education used in, 256; epilepsy and, 67–76; exposure used in, 251; focus on behavior change in, 222–223; goals and values in, 257–258; hexaflex model of, 359–364; imagery techniques and, 255; insomnia and, 147–148, 152; integrating with CBT, 248–262, 263–264; maintenance of behavior change in, 236–238; medical settings for, 341–343, 346–348; medication use and, 261–262; meta-analyses of, 23–24; mindfulness related to, 24–25, 33, 252, 327, 328; model and process of, 13–21; Motivational Interviewing compared to, 220–228, 238; obesity/weight problems and, 85, 86–87; philosophical roots of, 13, 223–225, 245; physical exercise and, 258; prejudice and, 285–290; psychological inflexibility and, 15–16; relational frame theory and, 13–15, 227, 246; relaxation training and, 253; resistance to change in, 229–230; self-efficacy in, 233–234; skills training in, 259–260; smoking cessation and, 110–124; therapeutic stance in, 19–21, 49–51, 221–222; as "third wave" approach, 33, 244; training health professionals in, 354–365;

C

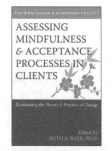